Real Options Analysis

*Tools and Techniques
for Valuing Strategic
Investments and Decisions*

John Wiley & Sons

Founded in 1807, John Wiley & Sons is the oldest independent publishing company in the United States. With offices in North America, Europe, Australia, and Asia, Wiley is globally committed to developing and marketing print and electronic products and services for our customers' professional and personal knowledge and understanding.

The Wiley Finance series contains books written specifically for finance and investment professionals as well as sophisticated individual investors and their financial advisors. Book topics range from portfolio management to e-commerce, risk management, financial engineering, valuation and financial instrument analysis, as well as much more.

For a list of available titles, please visit our Web site at *www.WileyFinance.com*.

Additional Praise for Real Options Analysis

"*Real Options Analysis* is the clearest book on real options that we have read to date. It does an excellent job of demystifying a difficult and complex subject. It provides a solid basis for conceiving, assessing, and evaluating real option investments, which will make it useful to practitioners and students alike."

—*Ian C. MacMillan, Ph.D.,*
The Fred Sullivan Professor of Entrepreneurship
and Department Chair,
Wharton School, University of Pennsylvania (USA)

"Mun demystifies real options analysis and delivers a powerful, pragmatic guide for decision-makers and practitioners alike. Finally, there is a book that equips professionals to easily recognize, value, and seize real options in the world around them."

—*Jim Schreckengast, Sr. Vice President,*
R&D Strategy – Gemplus International SA (France)

"Written from the viewpoint of an educator and a practitioner, Mun's book offers a readable reference full of insightful decision-making tools to satisfy both the novice and the experienced veteran."

—*Richard Kish, Ph.D., Associate Professor of Finance,*
Lehigh University (USA)

"Mun has converted his tacit financial knowledge into a digestible user-friendly book. He effectively leads the reader on a solid path starting from *discounted cash flow*, progressing through *Monte Carlo analysis* and evolving to *real options* to get even closer to the target of achieving confident corporate decisions. His ability to clearly explain the relationships of popular competing analysis methods will make this a must-have reference book for today's decision-makers."

—Kenneth English, Director of R&D,
The Timken Company (USA)

"The book leads the field in real options analytics and is a must-read for anyone interested in performing such analyses. Mun has made a formidable subject crystal clear and exponentially easy for senior management to understand. *Monte Carlo simulation* and *real options* software alone is worth the book price many times over."

—Morton Glantz, Renowned educator in finance, author
of several books, financial advisor to government (USA)

"The book is far and away the clearest, most comprehensive guide to real options analysis to date, and is destined to be a classic—it is a complete guide to the practical application of real options analysis. It strikes a superb balance between solid intuition, rigorous analysis, and numerous practical examples."

—John Hogan, Ph.D.,
Boston College (USA)

Real Options
Analysis

Tools and Techniques
for Valuing Strategic
Investments and Decisions

JOHNATHAN MUN

John Wiley & Sons, Inc.

Library of Congress Cataloging-in-Publication Data:

Mun, Johnathan.
   Real options analysis : tools and techniques for valuing strategic
investments and decisions / Johnathan Mun.
    p. cm. (Wiley finance series)
   ISBN 0-471-25696-X (CLOTH/CD-ROM : alk. paper)
   1. Real options (Finance)   I. Title.   II. Series
HG6042 .M86 2002
332.63—dc21   2002008978

Printed in the United States of America

10 9 8 7 6 5 4 3 2 1

about the cd-rom

INTRODUCTION

The enclosed CD-ROM contains the Real Options Analysis Toolkit software demo, a trial version of Crystal Ball® 2000 Monte Carlo Simulation software, sample Excel worksheets on real options, and sample problems from the book.

CD-ROM TABLE OF CONTENTS

Directory Name	File Name	Description
Real Options Analysis Toolkit (Demo)	setup.exe	Installs the Real Options Analysis Toolkit software
Microsoft® .Net Framework	dotnetfx.exe	Installs Microsoft® .Net Framework
Crystal Ball® Simulation (Trial)	setup.exe	Installs the Crystal Ball® software
Book Examples	*.xls	Sample Excel real options spreadsheets
Problems	*.doc	Chapter problems

MINIMUM SYSTEM REQUIREMENTS

- IBM PC or compatible computer with Pentium II or higher processor
- 64 MB RAM
- 75 MB hard-disk space
- CD-ROM drive
- SVGA monitor with 256 colors
- Excel 98, 2000, XP, or later
- Windows 98, 2000, NT, ME, XP, or higher

HOW TO INSTALL THE SOFTWARE ONTO YOUR COMPUTER

There are three separate programs available on the CD-ROM. They are Real Options Analysis Toolkit software, Microsoft® .Net Framework, and finally, Crystal Ball® 2000 Monte Carlo Simulation software. You will need to run a different setup program for each. To run the setup programs, do the following:

1. Insert the enclosed Real Options CD-ROM into the CD-ROM drive of your computer.

2. Open Windows Explorer, and locate the folders on the CD-ROM drive.

3. Open the *Real Options folder,* and double-click on the *SETUP.EXE* file to install the Real Options software. Read and follow the online instructions. .Net Framework will automatically install at the same time.

4. Open the *Crystal Ball® Simulation folder,* and double-click on the *SETUP.EXE* file to install the Crystal Ball® Monte Carlo software. Read and follow the online instructions to continue. Leave the registration number empty for a 30-day trial period.

USING THE SOFTWARE

Refer to Chapter 9 in the book *Real Options Analysis* for using the Real Options Analysis Toolkit software and to Appendix 9A for information on getting started with Crystal Ball® 2000.

USER ASSISTANCE

If you have questions about obtaining the fully functional software, please contact Dr. Johnathan Mun at *JohnathanMun@cs.com.*

If you need assistance or have a damaged disk, please contact Wiley Technical Support at:

Phone: (201) 748-6753
Fax: (201) 748-6450 (Attention: Wiley Technical Support)
E-mail: *techhelp@wiley.com*

To place additional orders or to request information about Wiley products, call (800) 225-5945.

Specially dedicated to my wife Penny, the love and sunshine of my life, without whose encouragement, advice, support, and phenomenal editorial talents, this book would never have been completed. I would also like to dedicate this book to my parents, for all their love and support for these many years.

"If you will walk in my ways and keep my requirements, then you will govern my house and have charge of my courts, and I will give you a place among these standing here."

Zechariah 3:7 (NIV)

D r. Johnathan C. Mun is currently the Vice President of Analytical Services at Decisioneering, Inc., the makers of Crystal Ball® Real Options and the Crystal Ball® suite of products, including applications of Monte Carlo simulation, optimization, and forecasting. He heads up the development of real options and financial analytics software products, consulting, and training. He is also a Visiting and Adjunct Professor and has taught courses in financial management, investments, real options, economics, and statistics at the undergraduate and the graduate M.B.A. levels. He has taught at universities all over the world, from the University of Applied Sciences (Chur, Switzerland) to Golden Gate University (California) and St. Mary's College (California). Prior to joining Decisioneering, he was a Consulting Manager and Financial Economist in the Valuation Services and Global Financial Services practice of KPMG Consulting and a Manager with the Economic Consulting Services practice at KPMG LLP. He has extensive experience in econometric modeling, financial analysis, real options, economic analysis, and statistics. During his tenure both at Decisioneering and at KPMG Consulting, he consulted on real options and financial valuation for many Fortune 100 firms. His experience prior to joining KPMG included being Department Head of financial planning and analysis at Viking Inc. of FedEx, performing financial forecasting, economic analysis, and market research. Prior to that, he had also performed some financial planning and freelance financial consulting work.

Dr. Mun received his Ph.D. in Finance and Economics from Lehigh University, where his research and academic interests were in the areas of Investment Finance, Econometric Modeling, Financial Options, Corporate Finance, and Microeconomic Theory. He also has an M.B.A. from Nova Southeastern University and a B.S. in Biology and Physics from the University of Miami. He is Certified in Financial Risk Management (FRM), is Certified in Financial Consulting (CFC), and is currently a Level III candidate for the Chartered Financial Analysts (CFA). He is a member of the American Mensa, Phi Beta Kappa Honor Society, and Golden Key Honor Society as well as several other professional organizations, including the Eastern and Southern Finance Associations, American Economic Association, and Global Association of Risk Professionals. Finally, he has written many academic articles published in the *Journal of the Advances in Quantitative Accounting and Finance, The Global Finance Journal, The International Financial Review,* and *The Journal of Financial Analysis.*

Johnathan Mun, Ph.D.
JohnathanMun@cs.com

table of contents

CHAPTER 4   The Real Options Process

CHAPTER 5   Real Options, Financial Options, Monte Carlo Simulation, and Optimization

PART TWO

Application   133

CHAPTER SUMMARIES   135

CHAPTER 6   Behind the Scenes   139

CHAPTER 9 Real Options Analysis Toolkit Software (CD-ROM) 277

CHAPTER 10 Results Interpretation and Presentation 317

list of figures

acknowledgments

I want to offer a word of thanks to the development crew at Decisioneering, Inc. A special thanks to Cameron Harris and Eric Wainwright. They were also particularly helpful in consistently providing insights into the nature of software development and application, particularly in the area of Monte Carlo simulation. In addition, a special word of thanks and gratitude to Robert Barnett, from PricewaterhouseCoopers, for his comments and thoughts.

A special thank you to the business case contributors including Kenneth English, William Bailey, Tracy Gomes, Jim Schreckengast, Marty Nevshemal, and Mark Akason.

Finally, a word of special thanks to Vladimir Dobric, Ph.D., Professor of Mathematics at Lehigh University, Visiting Professor at Yale University, and a good friend. Vladimir provided significant insights into the nature of real options, especially in the areas of technical financial mathematics, and I am greatly indebted to him.

Real Options Analysis provides a novel view of evaluating capital investment strategies by taking into consideration the strategic decision-making
process. The book provides a qualitative and quantitative description
of real options, the methods used in solving real options, why and when
they are used, and the applicability of these methods in decision-making. In
addition, multiple business cases and real-life scenarios are discussed. This
includes presenting and framing the problems, as well as introducing a stepwise quantitative process developed by the author for solving these problems
using the different methodologies inherent in real options. Included are technical presentations of models and approaches used as well as their theoretical and mathematical justifications.

The book is divided into two parts. The first part looks at the qualitative
nature of real options, providing actual business cases and applications of real
options in the industry, as well as high-level explanations of how real options
provide much-needed insights in decision-making. The second part of the
book looks at the quantitative analysis, complete with worked-out examples
and mathematical formulae.

This book is targeted at both the uninitiated professional as well as those
verbose in real options applications. It is also applicable for use as a second-
year M.B.A.-level or introductory Ph.D.-level textbook. A comprehensive
CD-ROM is included in the book. The CD-ROM consists of Real Options
Analysis Toolkit software with 69 real options models, Crystal Ball® Monte
Carlo Simulation software, and a series of example options analysis spreadsheets.

For those who are interested in further expanding their knowledge of
real options analysis and applying it to real-life corporate situations, a com-
panion book of business cases and supporting software by the same author
will be available by Wiley in early 2003. Please visit *www.wileyfinance.com*
for more information. The upcoming book focuses purely on real options
business problems and their step-by-step resolution. The problems are
solved both analytically and using the accompanying real options software.
The methodolgies employed include stochastic forecasting, discounted cash
flow analysis, Monte Carlo simulation, stochastic optimization, and real
options analysis (using binomial lattices, risk-neutral probability, market-
replicating approach, state-pricing, trinomials, and closed-form models).

one

Theory

chapter summaries

CHAPTER 1: A NEW PARADIGM?

Introduction

This chapter looks at the issues of new decision-making challenges and provides an introduction to real options analysis as the solution to these new challenges. The chapter briefly defines real options analysis and its many forms, when it is used, who has used it in the past, and why it is used. Examples provided come from multiple industries, including oil and gas exploration and production, pharmaceutical research and development, e-commerce valuation, IT infrastructure investment justification, prioritization of venture capital investments, mergers and acquisitions, research and development, Internet start-up valuation, structuring of venture capital contracts, timing of investments, parallel portfolio development, profitability profiling, and so forth. The chapter also profiles the types of options, defines real options analysis, and introduces several sample business cases of how real options are used as well as quotations of what the experts are saying. Finally, actual business cases from industry are provided in the appendixes. These appendixes are contributed by major corporations detailing the applications of real options in their respective companies.

A Paradigm Shift

The new economy provides a challenge for the corporate decision-maker. Corporate valuation may no longer depend on traditional fundamentals but rather on future expectations. Investment strategies with high risks and uncertainty or irreversible corporate decisions coupled with managerial flexibility provide the best candidates for real options. In this chapter, the reader will find that real options analysis is indeed a new way of thinking rather than simply the application of advanced analytical procedures.

Sample Business Cases Where Traditional Approaches Break Down

These sections introduce the issues, concerns, and problems of traditional methods, issues that are addressed using a real options framework. The sections also introduce several business cases requiring the use of real options analysis. These cases include IT investments in a new operating system, prioritizing e-commerce strategies, pharmaceutical research and development, oil and gas exploration, manufacturing contractual decisions, valuation of different venture capital opportunities, capital structuring and valuation of an Internet start-up firm, and selecting capital investment projects within the context of a portfolio. In each of these cases, the reader delves into the minds of people closest to the analysis and decision-making process, and examines their thinking and analytical approach.

The Real Options Solution and Issues to Consider

These two sections detail the use of real options in terms of thinking strategically, identifying strategic optionalities, valuing and prioritizing strategies, optimizing and timing strategies, as well as the overall management of strategies. In addition, they describe where real options value comes from and why in certain cases the true value of a project may be less than its option value.

Industry Leaders Embracing Real Options

This section details actual corporate cases and Fortune 500 firms embracing this new valuation concept. Firms highlighted include General Motors, HP-Compaq, Boeing, and AT&T. Included are consulting success stories of how these firms have looked at business decisions through the lens of real options. More industry cases are provided in the appendixes.

What the Experts Are Saying

This section details what the experts are saying in terms of the uses of real options, including quotations from the *Wall Street Journal, Business Week, Harvard Business Review, CFO,* and others. The upshot is that firms are fast embracing this new hot valuation approach, which has the potential of being the next new business breakthrough. It would seem apparent from the brief excerpts that real options analysis is not simply a financial fad but the methodology is here to stay for the long-term. A more detailed listing and summary of research articles, journal publications, and professional articles are provided at the end of the book, in Appendix 10A.

CHAPTER 2: TRADITIONAL VALUATION APPROACHES

Introduction

This chapter introduces the pitfalls of using only traditional discounted cash flow analysis and how a real options process framework captures the strategic valuation a traditional approach cannot. A brief overview of traditional analyses includes the income approach, the market approach, and the cost approach. In addition, the chapter focuses on the issues and concerns regarding the discounted cash flow analysis. The chapter concludes with two appendixes discussing the details of financial statement analysis and the calculation of an appropriate discount rate.

The Traditional Views

Traditional analysis includes the income, cost, and market approaches, which involve using forecast profit and loss statements, comparable multiples, ratio analysis, common sizing, and so forth. The traditional approaches view risk and return on investment in a very static view. However, not all uncertainty is risk, and not all risk is bad. Real options view capital investments in terms of a dynamic approach and view upside risk as an ally that can be capitalized on.

Practical Issues Using Traditional Valuation Methodologies

This section highlights the pitfalls of the three fundamental approaches: income approach, cost approach, and market approach. These pitfalls include the incorrect use of discount rates, risk-free rates, terminal value calculations, and others.

CHAPTER 3: REAL OPTIONS ANALYSIS

Introduction

This chapter introduces the fundamental concepts of real options through several simple examples showing why an options framework provides much better insights than traditional valuation approaches do. In order to compare the results from different approaches, a simplified example is presented, starting with traditional analyses. The example continues with the application of Monte Carlo simulation and ends with the use of real options analysis.

The Fundamental Essence of Real Options

This section starts with the example of how an analyst would perform a financial analysis for the purpose of project selection. It then shows the virtues of using simulation to capture uncertainties rather than using simple single-point estimates. The analysis is complicated further by using active and passive waiting strategies. Finally, this section demonstrates how real options can be applied to more accurately assess a project's value by better defining the variables underlying a project and its potential value creation.

The Basics of Real Options, and a Simplified Example of Real Options in Action

A simple example illustrates the power of real options through the execution of an option to wait. The option to defer the execution of a second-phase clinical trial until receiving updated news of market demand adds value to a pharmaceutical research and development division's project in general. The example uses a simple discounted cash flow model to make the case.

Advanced Approaches to Real Options, and Why Are Real Options Important?

These two sections show the importance of looking at decision-making processes as a series of dynamic options and describe the types of generic options that exist in corporate investment strategies. In addition, several advanced real options techniques are discussed briefly. Some of these techniques— for example, the use of binomial lattices, Monte Carlo simulation, partial-differential equations, and closed-form exotic options analysis—are also discussed.

Comparing Traditional Approaches with Real Options

A protracted example is provided on a sample business case. The example starts from a simple static discounted cash flow analysis and proceeds with sensitivity analysis. Then an additional layer of sophistication is introduced, with the application of Monte Carlo simulation. Finally, real options analysis is applied to the problem. The results are then compared, starting with a static discounted cash flow approach, to the simulation results, as well as to the real options results.

CHAPTER 4: THE REAL OPTIONS PROCESS

Introduction, and Critical Steps in Performing Real Options Analysis

This chapter introduces the eight phases in a real options process framework as developed by the author and used by Crystal Ball® Real Options software—a new software product currently in development by Decisioneering, Inc. The first phase starts with the qualification of projects through management screening, which weeds out the projects that management wishes to evaluate. The second phase starts with the construction of a traditional discounted cash flow model under the base case condition. Next, Monte Carlo simulation is applied, and the results are in turn inserted directly into the real options analysis. This phase covers the identification of strategic options that exist for a particular project under review. Based on the type of problem framed, the relevant real options models are chosen and executed.

Depending on the number of projects as well as management-set constraints, portfolio optimization is performed. The efficient allocation of resources is the outcome of this analysis. The next phase involves creating reports and explaining to management the analytical results. This is a critical step in that an analytical process is only as good as its expositional ease. Finally, the last phase involves updating the analysis over time. Real options analysis adds tremendous value to projects with uncertainty, but when uncertainty becomes resolved through the passage of time, old assumptions and forecasts have now become historical facts. Therefore, existing models must be updated to reflect new facts and data. This continual improvement and monitoring is vital in making clear, precise, and definitive decisions over time.

CHAPTER 5: REAL OPTIONS, FINANCIAL OPTIONS, MONTE CARLO SIMULATION, AND OPTIMIZATION

Introduction

This chapter explains the differences between financial options and real options by first describing the fundamentals of financial options theory. The chapter then goes into the importance of Monte Carlo simulation for financial analysis and ends with the application of portfolio optimization and the efficient allocation of resources. The chapter's technical appendixes discuss the specifics of financial options, Monte Carlo simulation, financial forecasting, and portfolio optimization.

Real Options versus Financial Options

This section details the basics of financial options and how they relate to real options. For instance, the underlying asset in most real options analysis is non-tradable—that is, there usually exists no liquid market for the asset or project in question. Nonetheless, there exist many similarities between the two, and the underlying analytics of financial options may be applicable, with a few exceptions and modifications.

Monte Carlo Simulation

How are simulation techniques important in real options analysis? This discussion explains how certain key variables are obtained through the use of Monte Carlo simulation. An example depicts the error of means and why simulation should be used when uncertainty abounds. Further examples show the different strategies that would have been executed otherwise without the use of real options.

A New Paradigm?

INTRODUCTION

This chapter attempts to demystify the concepts of real options. Specifically, it attempts to answer several basic questions: what are real options, how are companies using real options, what types of options exist, why are real options important, who uses real options, where are real options most appropriately used, and what are the experts saying about real options? The chapter starts by reviewing the basic concepts of real options as a new paradigm shift in the way of thinking about and evaluating projects. The chapter reviews several business cases in different industries and situations involving pharmaceutical, oil and gas, manufacturing, IT infrastructure, venture capital, Internet start-ups, and e-business initiatives. The chapter then concludes with some industry "war stories" on using real options as well as a summary of what the experts are saying in journal publications and the popular press.

A PARADIGM SHIFT

In the past, corporate investment decisions were cut-and-dried. Buy a new machine that is more efficient, make more products costing a certain amount, and if the benefits outweigh the costs, execute the investment. Hire a larger pool of sales associates, expand the current geographical area, and if the marginal increase in forecast sales revenues exceeds the additional salary and implementation costs, start hiring. Need a new manufacturing plant? Show that the construction costs can be recouped quickly and easily by the increase in revenues it will generate through new and improved products, and the initiative is approved.

However, real-life business conditions are a lot more complicated. Your firm decides to go with an e-commerce strategy, but multiple strategic paths exist. Which path do you choose? What are the options that you have? If you choose the wrong path, how do you get back on the right track? How do you value and prioritize the paths that exist? You are a venture capital firm with multiple business plans to consider. How do you value a start-up firm with no proven track record? How do you structure a mutually beneficial investment deal? What is the optimal timing to a second or third round of financing?

Real options are useful not only in valuing a firm through its strategic business options but also as a strategic business tool in capital investment decisions. For instance, should a firm invest millions in a new e-commerce initiative? How does a firm choose among several seemingly cashless, costly, and unprofitable information technology infrastructure projects? Should a firm indulge its billions in a risky research and development initiative? The consequences of a wrong decision can be disastrous or even terminal for certain firms. In a traditional discounted cash flow model, these questions cannot be answered with any certainty. In fact, some of the answers generated through the use of the traditional discounted cash flow model are flawed because the model assumes a static, one-time decision-making process while the real options approach takes into consideration the strategic managerial options certain projects create under uncertainty and management's flexibility in exercising or abandoning these options at different points in time, when the level of uncertainty has decreased or has become known over time.

The real options approach incorporates a learning model such that management makes better and more informed strategic decisions when some levels of uncertainty are resolved through the passage of time. The discounted cash flow analysis assumes a static investment decision, and assumes that strategic decisions are made initially with no recourse to choose other pathways or options in the future. To create a good analogy of real options, visualize it as a strategic road map of long and winding roads with multiple perilous turns and forks along the way. Imagine the intrinsic and extrinsic value of having such a strategic road map when navigating through unfamiliar territory, as well as having road signs at every turn to guide you in making the best and most informed driving decisions. This is the essence of real options.

> *Business conditions are fraught with uncertainty and risks. These uncertainties hold with them valuable information. When uncertainty becomes resolved through the passage of time, managers can make the appropriate mid-course corrections through a change in business decisions and strategies. Real options incorporate this learning model, akin to having a strategic road map, while traditional analyses that neglect this managerial flexibility will grossly undervalue certain projects and strategies.*

The answer to evaluating such projects lies in real options analysis, which can be used in a variety of settings, including pharmaceutical drug development, oil and gas exploration and production, manufacturing, e-business, start-up valuation, venture capital investment, IT infrastructure, research and development, mergers and acquisitions, e-commerce and e-business, intellectual capital development, technology development, facility expansion, business project prioritization, enterprise-wide risk management, business unit capital budgeting, licenses, contracts, intangible asset valuation, and the like. The following section illustrates some business cases and how real options can assist in identifying and capturing additional strategic value for a firm.

EXPANSION AND COMPOUND OPTIONS: THE CASE OF THE OPERATING SYSTEM

You are the Chief Technology Officer of a large multinational corporation, and you know that your firm's operating systems are antiquated and require an upgrade, say to the new Microsoft Windows XP series. You arrange a meeting with the CEO, letting him in on the situation. The CEO quips back immediately, saying that he'll support your initiative if you can prove to him that the monetary benefits outweigh the costs of implementation—a simple and logical request. You immediately arrange for a demonstration of the new operating system, and the highly technical experts from Microsoft provide you and your boss a marvelous presentation of the system's capabilities and value-added enhancements that took in excess of a few billion dollars and several years to develop. The system even fixes itself in times of dire circumstances and is overall more reliable and stable than its predecessors. You get more excited by the minute and have made up your mind to get the much-needed product upgrade. There is still one hurdle, the financial hurdle, to prove not only that the new system provides a better operating environment but also that the plan of action is financially sound. Granted, the more efficient and sophisticated system will make your boss's secretary a much happier person and hence more productive. Then again, so will an extra week's worth of vacation and a bigger bonus check, both of which are a lot cheaper and easier to implement. The new system will not help your sales force sell more products and generate higher revenues because the firm looks state-of-the-art only if a customer questions what version of Windows operating system you are using—hardly an issue that will arise during a sales call. Then again, when has using the latest software ever assisted in closing a deal, especially when you are a contract global-freight and logistics solutions provider?

You lose sleep over the next few days pondering the issue, and you finally decide to assemble a task force made up of some of your top IT personnel. The six of you sit in a room considering the same issues and trying to brainstorm a few really good arguments. You link up the value-added propositions provided in the Microsoft technician's presentation and come up with a series of potential cost reduction drivers. Principally, the self-preservation and self-fixing functionality will mean less technical assistance and help-desk calls, freeing up resources and perhaps leading to the need for fewer IT people on staff. Your mind races through some quick figures, you feel your heart pounding faster, and you see a light at the end of the tunnel. Finally you will have your long-awaited operating system, and all your headaches will go away. Wait—not only does it reduce the help-desk time, but also it increases efficiency because employees will no longer have to call or hold for technical assistance.

Your team spends the next few days scouring through mountains of data on help-desk calls and issues—thank God for good record-keeping and relational databases. Looking for issues that could potentially become obsolete with the new system, you find that at least 20 percent of your help-desk calls could be eliminated by having the new system in place because it is more stable, is capable of self-fixing these critical issues, can troubleshoot internal hardware conflicts, and so forth. Besides, doesn't employee morale count? Satisfied with your analysis, you approach the CEO and show him your findings.

Impressed with your charts and analytical rigor in such a short time frame, he asks several quick questions and points out several key issues. The cost reduction in technical assistance is irrelevant because you need these people to install and configure the new system. The start-up cost and learning curve might be steep, and employees may initially have a tough time adjusting to the new operating environment—help-desk calls may actually increase in the near future, albeit slowing down in time. But the firm's mission has always been to cultivate its employees and not to fire them needlessly. Besides, there are five people on staff at the help desk, and a 20 percent reduction means one less full-time employee out of 5,000 in the entire firm—hardly a cost reduction strategy! As for the boss's secretary's productivity, you noticed two first-class air tickets to Maui on his desk, and you're pretty sure one of them is for her. Your mind races with alternate possibilities—including taking a trip to Hawaii with a high-powered digital-zoom camera but deciding against it on your way out. He notices your wandering eyes and tries to change the subject. You still have not sufficiently persuaded your boss on getting the new operating system, and you are up a tree and out on a limb. Thoughts of going shopping for a camera haunt you for the rest of the day.

Sound familiar? Firms wrestle with similar decisions daily, and vendors wrestling with how to make their products more marketable have to first address this financial and strategic issue. Imagine you're the sales director for Microsoft, or any software and hardware vendor for that matter. How do you close a sale like this?

Performing a series of simple traditional analyses using a discounted cash flow methodology or economic justification based on traditional analyses will fail miserably, as we have seen above. The quantifiable financial benefits do not exceed the high implementation costs. How do you justify and correctly value such seemingly cashless and cash-flow draining projects? The answer lies in real options. Instead of being myopic and focusing on current savings, the implementation of large-scale servers or operating systems will generate future strategic options for the firm. That is, having the servers and system in place provides you a springboard to a second-, third-, or fourth-phase IT implementation. That is, having a powerful connected system gives you the technical feasibility to pursue online collaboration, global data access, video-conferencing, digital signatures, encryption security, remote installations, document recovery, and the like, which would be impossible to do without it.

> *An expansion option provides management the right and ability to expand into different markets, products and strategies or to expand its current operations under the right conditions. A chooser option implies that management has the flexibility to choose among several strategies, including the option to expand, abandon, switch, contract, and so forth. A sequential compound option means that the execution and value of future strategic options depend on previous options in sequence of execution.*

Hence, the value of upgrading to a new system provides the firm an *expansion option,* which is the right and ability, but not the obligation, to invest and pursue some of these value-added technologies. Some of these technologies such as security enhancements and global data access can be highly valuable to your global freight company's supply chain management. You may further delineate certain features into groups of options to execute at the same time—that is, create a series of *compound options* where the success of one group of initiatives depends on the success of another in sequence.

> *A compound option means that the execution and value of a strategic option depend on another strategic option.*

Notice that using an extrapolation of the traditional analytic approaches would be inappropriate here because all these implementation possibilities are simply options that a senior manager has, and not guaranteed execution by any means. When you view the whole strategic picture, value is created and identified where there wasn't any before, thereby making you able to clearly justify financially your plans for the upgrade. You would be well on your way to getting your new operating system installed.

EXPANSION OPTIONS:
THE CASE OF THE E-BUSINESS INITIATIVE

The e-business boom has been upon us for a few years now, and finally the investment bank you work for has decided to join the Internet age. You get a decree from the powers that be to come up with a solid e-commerce initiative. The CEO calls you into his office and spends an hour expounding on the wisdom of bringing the firm closer to the electronic Web. After hours of meetings, you are tasked with performing a feasibility analysis, choosing the right strategy, and valuing the wisdom of going e-commerce. Well, it sounds simple enough, or so you think.

The next two weeks are spent with boardroom meetings, conference calls with e-commerce consulting firms, and bottles of Alka Seltzer. Being a newly endowed expert on the e-business strategies after spending two weeks in Tahiti on a supposedly world-renowned e-commerce crash course, you realize you really still know nothing. One thing is for certain: the Internet has revolutionized the way businesses are run. The traditional Sun Tzu business environment of "know thy enemy and know thyself and in a hundred battles you will be victorious" hadn't met the Internet. The competitive playing field has been leveled, and your immediate competitors are no longer the biggest threat. The biggest threat is globalization, when new competitors halfway around the world crawl out of the woodwork and take half of your market-share just because they have a fancy Web site capable of attracting, diverting, and retaining Web traffic, and capable of taking orders around the world, and you don't. Perhaps the CEO's right; it's a do-or-die scenario. When a 12-year-old girl can transform her parents' fledgling trinket store into an overnight success by going to the Internet, technology seems to be the biggest foe of all. You either ride the technological wave or are swept under.

Convinced of the necessity of e-commerce and the strong desire to keep your job, you come up with a strategic game plan. You look at the e-commerce options you have and try to ascertain the correct path to traverse, knowing very well that if you pick the wrong one, it may be ultimately disastrous, for you and your firm, in that particular order. In between updating your curriculum vitae, you decide to spend some time pondering the issues. You realize that there are a large number of options in going e-commerce, and you have decided on several potential pathways to consider as they are most appropriate to the firm's core business.

Do we simply create a static Web site with nice graphics, text explaining what we do, and perhaps a nice little map showing where we are located and the hours of availability, and get fired? Do we perhaps go a little further and provide traditional banking services on the Web? Perhaps a way for our customers to access their accounts, pay bills, trade stocks, apply for loans, and perhaps get some free stock advice or free giveaways and pop-up ads to divert traffic on the Web? Perhaps we can take it to the extreme and use state-of-the-art technology to enable items like digital television access, live continuous streaming technology, equity trading on personal digital assistants and cellular phones, interaction with and direct access to floor specialists and traders on the New York Stock Exchange for the larger clients, and all the while using servers in Enron-like offshore tax havens. The potentials are endless.

You suddenly feel queasy, and the inkling of impending doom. What about competition? Ameritrade and a dozen other online trading firms currently exist. Most major banks are already on the Web, and they provide the same services. What makes us so special? Then again, if we do not follow the other players, we may be left out in the cold. Perhaps there are some ways to differentiate our services. Perhaps some sort of geographical expansion; after all, the Internet is global, so why shouldn't we be? What about market penetration effects and strategies, country risk analysis, legislative and regulatory risks? What if the strategy is unsuccessful? What will happen then? Competitive effects are unpredictable. The threats of new entrants and low barriers to entry may elicit even more competitors than you currently have. Is the firm ready to play in the big leagues and fight with the virtual offshore banking services? Globalization—what an ugly word it is right about now. What about new technology: Do we keep spending every time something new comes out? What about market share, market penetration, positioning, and being first to market with a new and exciting product? What about future growth opportunities, e-traffic management, and portal security? The lists go on and on. Perhaps you should take a middle ground, striking an alliance with established investment banking firms with the applicable IT infrastructure already in place. Why build when you can buy? You reach for your Alka-Seltzer and realize you need something a lot stronger.

How do you prioritize these potential strategies, perform a financial and strategic feasibility analysis, and make the right decision? Will the firm survive if we go down the wrong path? If we find out we are on the wrong path, can we navigate our way back to the right one? What options can we create to enable this? Which of these strategies is optimal? Upon identifying what these strategies are, including all their downstream *expansion options,* you can then value each of these strategic pathways. The identification, valuation, prioritization, and selection of strategic projects are where real options analysis can provide great insights and value. Each project initiative should not be viewed in its current state. Instead, all downstream opportunities should be viewed and considered as well. Otherwise, wrong decisions may be made because only projects with immediate value will be chosen, while projects that carry with them great future potential are abandoned simply because management is setting its sights on the short term.

EXPANSION AND SEQUENTIAL OPTIONS: THE CASE OF THE PHARMACEUTICAL R&D

Being the chief chemist of a small pharmaceutical firm that is thinking of developing a certain drug useful in gene therapy, you have the responsibility to determine the right biochemical compounds to create. Understanding very well that the future of the firm rests on pursuing and developing the right portfolio of drugs, you take your evaluation task rather seriously. Currently, the firm's management is uncertain whether to proceed with developing a group of compounds and is also uncertain regarding the drug development's financial feasibility. From historical data and personal experience, you understand that development "home runs" are few and far between. As a matter of fact, you realize that less than 5 percent of all compounds developed are superstars. However, if the right compounds are chosen, the firm will own several valuable patents and bolster its chances of receiving future rounds of funding. Armed with that future expectation, you evaluate each potential compound with care and patience.

For example, one of the compounds you are currently evaluating is called Creatosine. Management knows that Creatosine, when fully developed, can be taken orally, but has the potential to be directly injected into the bloodstream, which increases its effectiveness. As there is great uncertainty in the development of Creatosine, management decides to develop the oral version for now and wait for a period of several years before deciding on investing additional funds to develop the injectable version. Thus, management has created an *expansion option*—that is, the option but not the obligation to expand Creatosine into an injectable version at any time between now and several years. The firm thus creates no value in developing the injection version after that time period. By incorporating real options strategy, your firm has mitigated its risks in developing the drug into both an oral and injectable form at initiation. By waiting, scientific and market risks become resolved through the passage of time, and your firm can then decide whether to pursue the second injectable phase. This risk-hedging phenomenon is common in financial options and is applicable here for real options.

However, there are other drug compounds to analyze as well. You go through the list with a fine-tooth comb and realize that you must evaluate each drug by not only its biochemical efficacies, but also by its financial feasibility. Given the firm's current capital structure, you would need to not only value, prioritize, and select the right compounds, but also find the optimal portfolio mix of compounds, subject to budget, timing, and risk constraints. On top of that, you would have to value your firm as a whole in terms of a portfolio of strategic options. The firm's value lies not only in its forecast revenues less its costs subject to time valuation of money but also in all the current research and development initiatives under way, where a single home run will double or triple the firm's valuation. These so-called future *growth options,* which are essentially growth opportunities that the firm has, are highly valuable. These *growth options* are simply *expansion options* because your firm owns the right infrastructure, resources, and technology to pursue these future opportunities but not the obligation to do so unless both internal research and external market conditions are amenable.

Another approach you decide to use is to create a strategic development road map, knowing that every drug under development has to go through multiple phases. At each phase, depending on the research results, management can decide to continue its development to the next phase or abandon it assuming it doesn't meet certain pre-specified criteria. That is, management has the *option to choose* whether a certain compound will continue to the next stage. Certain drugs in the initial phases go through a *sequential compound option,* where the success of the third phase, for example, depends on the success of the second phase, which in turn depends on the success of the first phase in the drug development cycle. Valuing such sequences of options using a traditional approach of taking expected values with respect to the probabilities of success is highly dubious and incorrect. The valuation will be incorrect at best and highly misleading at worst, driving management to select the wrong mix of compounds at the wrong time.

EXPANSION AND SWITCHING OPTIONS: THE CASE OF THE OIL AND GAS EXPLORATION AND PRODUCTION

The oil and gas industry is fraught with strategic options problems. This is because oil and gas exploration and production involves significant amounts of risk and uncertainty. For example, when drilling for oil, the reservoir properties, fluidic properties, trap size and geometry, porosity, seal containment, oil and gas in place, expulsion force, losses due to migration, development costs, and so forth are all unknowns. How then is a reservoir engineer going to recommend to management the value of a particular drill site? Let's explore some of the more frequent real options problems encountered in this industry.

Being a fresh M.B.A. graduate from a top finance program, you are hired by a second-tier independent oil and gas firm, and your first task is to value several primary and secondary reservoir recovery wells. You are called into your boss's office, and she requests you to do an independent financial analysis on a few production wells. You were given a stack of technical engineering documents to review. After spending a fortnight scouring through several books on the fundamentals of the oil and gas industry, you finally have some basic understanding of the intricacies of what a secondary recovery well is. Needing desperately to impress your superiors, you decide to investigate a little further into some new analytics for solving these types of recovery-well problems.

Based on your incomplete understanding of the problem, you begin to explore all the possibilities and come to the conclusion that the best analytics to use may be the application of a Monte Carlo simulation and real options analysis. Instead of simply coming up with the value of the project, you decide to also identify where value can be added to the projects by incorporating strategic real optionality.

Suppose that the problem you are analyzing is a primary drilling site that has its own natural energy source, complete with its gas cap on one side and a water drive on the other. These energy sources maintain a high upward pressure on the oil reservoir to increase the ease of drilling and, therefore, the site's productivity. However, knowing that the level of energy may not be sustainable for a long time and its efficacy is unknown currently, you recognize that one of the strategies is to create an *expansion option* to drill a secondary recovery well near the primary site. Instead of drilling, you can use this well to inject water or gas into the ground, thereby increasing the upward pressure and keeping the reservoir productive. Building this secondary well is an option and not an obligation for the next few years.

The first recommendation seems to make sense given that the geological structure and reservoir size are difficult to estimate. Yet these are not the only important considerations. The price of oil in the market is also something that fluctuates dramatically and should be considered. Assuming that the price of oil is a major factor in management's decisions, your second recommendation includes separating the project into two stages. The first stage is to drill multiple wells in the primary reservoir, which will eventually maximize on its productivity. At that time a second phase can be implemented through smaller satellite reservoirs in the surrounding areas that are available for drilling but are separated from the primary reservoir by geological faults. This second stage is also an *expansion option* on the first; when the price of oil increases, the firm is then able to set up new rigs over the satellite reservoirs, drill, and complete these wells. Then, using the latest technology in subsurface robotics, the secondary wells can be tied back into the primary platform, thereby increasing and expanding the productivity of the primary well by some expansion factor. Obviously, although this is a strategic option that the firm has, the firm does not have the obligation to drill secondary wells unless the market price of oil is favorable enough. Using some basic intuition, you plug some numbers into your models and create the optimal oil price levels such that secondary drillings are profitable. However, given your brief conversation with your boss and your highly uncertain career future, you decide to dig into the strategy a little more.

Perhaps the company already has several producing wells at the reservoir. If that is so, the analysis should be tweaked such that instead of being an *expansion option* by drilling more wells, the firm can retrofit these existing wells in strategic locations from producers into injectors, creating a *switching option*. Instead of drilling more wells, the company can use the existing wells to inject gas or water into the surrounding geological areas in the hopes that this will increase the energy source, forcing the oil to surface at a higher rate. Obviously, these secondary production wells should be

> *A switching option provides the right and ability but not the obligation to switch among different sets of business operating conditions, including different technologies, markets, or products.*

switched into injectors when the recovery rate of the secondary wells is relatively low and the marginal benefits of the added productivity on primary wells far outstrip the retrofit costs. In addition, some of the deep-sea drilling platforms that are to be built in the near future can be made into *expansion options,* where slightly larger platforms are built at some additional cost (premium paid to create this option), such that if oil prices are optimally high, the flexible capacity inherent in this larger platform can be executed to boost production.

Finally, depending on the situation involved, you can also create a *sequential compound option* for the reservoir. That is, the firm can segregate its activities into different phases. Specifically, we can delineate the strategic option into four phases. Phases I to III are exploration wells, and Phase IV is a development well.

> Phase I: Start by performing seismic surveys to get information on the structures of subsurface reservoirs (the costs incurred include shooting the survey, processing data, mapping, etc.).

> Phase II: If auto-clines and large structures are found, drill an exploration well; if not, then abandon now.

> Phase III: If the exploration well succeeds industrially or commercially (evaluated on factors such as cost, water depth, oil price, rock, reservoir, and fluid properties), drill more delineation or "step out" wells to define the reservoir.

> Phase IV: If the reservoir is productive enough, commit more money for full development (platform building, setting platform, drilling development wells).

ABANDONMENT OPTIONS: THE CASE OF THE MANUFACTURER

You work for a mid-sized hardware manufacturing firm located in the heartland of America. Having recently attended a corporate finance seminar on real options, you set out to determine whether you can put some of your new-found knowledge to good use within the company. Currently, your firm purchases powerful laser-guided robotic fabrication tools that run into tens and even hundreds of millions of dollars each. These tools have to be specially ordered more than a year in advance, due to their unique and advanced specifications. They break down easily, and if any one of the three machines that your firm owns breaks down, it may be disastrous because part of the manufacturing division may have to be shut down temporarily for a period exceeding a year. So, is it always desirable to have at least one fabrication tool under order at all times, just as a precaution? A major problem arises when the newly ordered tool arrives, but the three remaining ones are fully functional and require no replacement. The firm has simply lost millions of dollars. In retrospect, certainly having a backup machine sitting idle that costs millions of dollars is not optimal. On the other hand, millions can also be lost if indeed a tool breaks down and a replacement is a year away. The question is, what do you do, and how can real options be used in this case, both as a strategic decision-making tool and as a valuation model?

Using traditional analysis, you come to a dead end, as the tool's breakdown has never been consistent and the ordered parts never arrive on schedule. Turning to real options, you decide to create a strategic option with the vendor. Instead of having to wait more than a year before a new machine arrives, while during that time not knowing when your existing machines will break down, you decide to create a mutually agreeable contract. Your firm decides to put up a certain amount of money and to enter into a contractual agreement whereby the vendor will put you on its preferred list. This cuts down delivery time from one year to two months. If your firm does not require the equipment, you will have to pay a penalty exit fee equivalent to a certain percentage of the machine's dollar value amount, within a specified period, on a ratcheted scale, with different exit penalties at different exit periods. In essence, you have created an *abandonment option* whereby your firm has the right not to purchase the equipment should circumstances force your hand, but hedging yourself to obtain the machine at a moment's notice should there be a need. The price of the option's premium is the contractual price paid for such an arrangement. The savings come in the form of not having to close down part of your plant and losing revenues. By incorporating real options insights into the problem, the firm saves millions and ends up with the optimal decision.

EXPANSION AND BARRIER OPTIONS: THE CASE OF THE LOST VENTURE CAPITALIST

You work in a venture capital firm and are in charge of the selection of strategic business plans and performing financial analysis on their respective feasibility and operational viability. The firm gets more than a thousand business plans a year, and your boss does not have the time to go through each of them in detail and relies on you to sniff out the ones with the maximum potential in the least amount of time. Besides, the winning plans do not wait for money. They often have money chasing after them. Having been in the field of venture capital funding for 10 years and having survived the bursting of the dot-com bubble, your judgment is highly valued in the firm, and you are more often than not comfortable with the decisions made. However, with the changing economic and competitive landscape, even seemingly bad ideas may turn into the next IPO success story. Given the opportunity of significant investment returns, the money lost on bad ideas is a necessary evil in not losing out on the next eBay® or Yahoo®! just because the CEO is not a brilliant business plan author. Your qualitative judgment may still be valid, but the question is what next? What do you do after you've selected your top 100 candidates? How do you efficiently allocate the firm's capital to minimize risk and maximize return? Picking the right firms the wrong way only gets you so far, especially when banking on start-ups hoping for new technological breakthroughs. A diversified portfolio of firms is always prudent, but a diversified portfolio of the right firms is much better. Prioritizing, ranking, and coming up with a solid financing structure for funding start-ups is tricky business, especially when traditional valuation methodologies do not work.

The new economy provides many challenges for the corporate decision-maker. Market equity value of a firm now depends on expectations and anticipation of future opportunities in novel technologies rather than on a traditional bricks-and-mortar environment. This shift in underlying fundamentals from tangible goods to technological innovation has created an issue in valuing the firm. Even the face of the intangibles created by technological innovation has changed. In most cases, a significant portion of a firm's value or its strategic investment options is derived from the firm's intangibles. Intangibles generally refer to elements in a business that augment the revenue-generating process but do not themselves have a physical or monetary appearance while still holding significant value to the firm. Intangibles may range from more traditional items like intellectual property, property rights, patents, branding, and trademarks to a new generation of so-called e-intangibles created in the new economy.

Examples of this new generation of e-intangibles include items like marketing intangibles, process and product technologies, trade dress, customer loyalty, branding, proprietary software, speed, search engine efficiency, online data catalogs, server efficiency, traffic control and diversion, streaming technology, content, experience, collaborative filtering, universal-resource-locator-naming conventions, hubs, Web page hits, imprints, and community relationships. New entries in the e-commerce economy over the past few years include the financial sector (bank wires, online bill payments, online investing), health care sector (cross-border medical teaching), publication and retail auctions (e-pocket books, Web magazines, Web papers, eBay, Web-Van, Auto-Web). The new trend seems to continue, and new start-ups emerge in scores by the minute to include sophisticated and complex structures like online cross-border banking services, virtual offshore banks, cross-border medical diagnostic imaging, and online-server game-playing. However, other less sophisticated e-business strategies have also been booming of late, including service-based Web sites, which provide a supposedly value-added service at no charge to consumers, such as online greeting cards and online e-invitations. Lower barriers to entry and significant threat of new entrants and substitution effects characterize these strategies.

Even using fairly well-known models like the discounted cash flow analysis is insufficient to value these types of firms. For instance, as a potential venture capitalist, how do you go about identifying the intangibles and intellectual property created when traditional financial theory is insufficient to justify or warrant such outrageous price-to-earnings multiples? Trying to get on the bandwagon in initial public offerings with large capital gains is always a good investment strategy, but randomly investing in start-ups with little to no fundamental justification of potential future profitability is a whole other issue. Perhaps there is a fundamental shift in the way the economy works today or is expected to work in the future as compared to the last decade. Whether there is indeed an irrational exuberance in the economy, or whether there is perhaps a shift in the fundamentals, we need a newer, more accurate, and sophisticated method of quantifying the value of such intangibles.

How do you identify, value, select, prioritize, justify, optimize, time, and manage large corporate investment decisions with high levels of uncertainty such that when a decision is made, the investment becomes irreversible? How do you value and select among several start-up firms to determine whether they are ideal venture candidates, and how do you create an optimal financing structure? These types of cashless return investments provide no immediate increase in revenues, and the savings are only marginal compared to their costs. How do you justify such outrageous market equity prices?

There must be a better way to value these investment opportunities. Having read press releases by Motley Fool on Credit Suisse First Boston, and how the firm used real options to value stocks of different companies, you begin looking into the possibilities of applying real options yourself. The start-up firm has significant value even when its cash flow situation is hardly something to be desired because the firm has strategic *growth options*. That is, a particular start-up may have some technology that may seem untested today, but it has the *option to expand* into the marketplace quickly and effortlessly should the technology prove to be highly desirable in the near future. Obviously the firm has the right to also pursue other ancillary technologies but only if the market conditions are conducive. The venture firm can capitalize on this *option to expand* by hedging itself with multiple investments within a venture portfolio. The firm can also create strategic

---

A barrier option means that the execution and value of a strategic option depend on breaching an artificial barrier.

---

value through setting up contractual agreements with a *barrier option* where for the promise of seed financing, the venture firm has the right of first refusal, but not the obligation, to invest in a second or third round should the start-up achieve certain management-set goals or barriers. The cost of this *barrier option* is seed financing, which is akin to the premium paid on a stock option. Should the option be in-the-money, the option will be executed through second- and third-round financing. By obtaining this strategic option, the venture firm has locked itself into a guaranteed favorable position should the start-up be highly successful, similar to the characteristics of a financial call option of unlimited upside potential. At the same time, the venture firm has hedged itself against missing the opportunity with limited downside proportional to the expenditure of a minimal amount of seed financing.

When venture capital firms value a group of companies, they should consider all the potential upsides available to these companies. These strategic options may very well prove valuable. A venture firm can also hedge itself through the use of barrier-type options. The venture firm should then go through a process of portfolio optimization analysis, to decide what proportion of its funds should be disseminated to each of the chosen firms. This portfolio optimization analysis will maximize returns and minimize the risks borne by the venture firm on a portfolio level subject to budget or other constraints.

COMPOUND EXPANSION OPTIONS: THE CASE OF THE INTERNET START-UP

In contrast, one can look at the start-up entrepreneur. How do you obtain venture funding, and how do you position the firm such that it is more attractive to the potential investor? Your core competency is in developing software or Web-enabled vehicles on the Internet, not financial valuation. How do you then structure the financing agreements such that your firm will be more attractive yet at the same time the agreements are not detrimental to your operations, strategic plans, or worse, your personal equity stake? What are your projected revenues and costs? How do you project these values when you haven't even started your business yet? Are you undervaluing your firm and its potential such that an unscrupulous venture firm will capitalize on your lack of sophistication and take a larger piece of the pie for itself? What are your strategic alternatives when you are up and running, and how do you know it's optimal for you to proceed with the next phase of your business plan?

All these questions can be answered and valued through a real options framework. Knowing what strategic options your firm has is significant because this value-added insight not only provides the firm an overall strategic road map but also increases its value. The real option that may exist in this case is something akin to a *compound expansion option*. For example, the firm can expand its product and service offerings by branching out into ancillary technologies or different applications, or expanding into different vertical markets. However, these expansions will most certainly occur in stages, and the progression from one stage to another depends heavily on the success of the previous stages.

THE REAL OPTIONS SOLUTION

Simply defined, real options is a systematic approach and integrated solution using financial theory, economic analysis, management science, decision sciences, statistics, and econometric modeling in applying options theory in valuing real physical assets, as opposed to financial assets, in a dynamic and uncertain business environment where business decisions are flexible in the context of strategic capital investment decision-making, valuing investment opportunities, and project capital expenditures.

Real options are crucial in:

- Identifying different corporate investment decision pathways or projects that management can navigate given the highly uncertain business conditions;

- Valuing each strategic decision pathway and what it represents in terms of financial viability and feasibility;

- Prioritizing these pathways or projects based on a series of qualitative and quantitative metrics;

- Optimizing the value of your strategic investment decisions by evaluating different decision paths under certain conditions or using a different sequence of pathways to lead to the optimal strategy;

- Timing the effective execution of your investments and finding the optimal trigger values and cost or revenue drivers; and

- Managing existing or developing new optionalities and strategic decision pathways for future opportunities.

> *Real options are useful for identifying, understanding, valuing, prioritizing, selecting, timing, optimizing, and managing strategic business and capital allocation decisions.*

ISSUES TO CONSIDER

Strategic options do have significant intrinsic value, but this value is only realized when management decides to execute the strategies. Real options theory assumes that management is logical and competent and that it acts in the best interests of the company and its shareholders through the maximization of wealth and minimization of risk of losses. For example, suppose a firm owns the rights to a piece of land that fluctuates dramatically in price. An analyst calculates the volatility of prices and recommends that management retain ownership for a specified time period, where within this period there is a good chance that the price of real estate will triple.

Therefore, management owns a call option, an *option to wait* and defer sale for a particular time period. The value of the real estate is therefore higher than the value that is based on today's sale price. The difference is simply this option to wait. However, the value of the real estate will not command the higher value if prices do triple but management decides not to execute the option to sell. In that case, the price of real estate goes back to its original levels after the specified period and then management finally relinquishes its rights.

> *Strategic optionality value can only be obtained if the option is executed; otherwise, all the options in the world are worthless.*

Was the analyst right or wrong? What was the true value of the piece of land? Should it have been valued at its explicit value on a deterministic basis where you know what the price of land is right now and, therefore, this is its value; or should it include some type of optionality where there is a good probability that the price of land could triple in value and, hence, the piece of land is truly worth more than it is now and should therefore be valued accordingly? The latter is the real options view. The additional strategic optionality value can only be obtained if the option is executed; otherwise, all the options in the world are worthless. This idea of explicit versus implicit value becomes highly significant when management's compensation is tied directly to the actual performance of particular projects or strategies.

To further illustrate this point, suppose the price of the land in the market is currently $10 million. Further, suppose that the market is highly liquid and volatile, and that the firm can easily sell it off at a moment's notice within the next five years, the same amount of time the firm owns the rights to the land. If there is a 50 percent chance the price will increase to $15 million and a 50 percent chance it will decrease to $5 million within this time period, is the property worth an expected value of $10 million? If prices rise to $15 million, management should be competent and rational enough to execute the option and sell that piece of land immediately to capture the additional $5 million premium. However, if management acts inappropriately or decides to hold off selling in the hopes that prices will rise even further, the property value may eventually drop back down to $5 million. Now, how much is this property really worth? What if there happens to be an *abandonment option?* Suppose there is a perfect counterparty to this transaction who decides to enter into a contractual agreement whereby for a contractual fee, the counterparty agrees to purchase the property for $10 million within the next five years, regardless of the market price and executable at the whim of the firm that owns the property. Effectively, a safety net has been created whereby the minimum floor value of the property has been set at $10 million (less the fee paid). That is, there is a limited downside but an unlimited upside, as the firm can always sell the property at market price if it exceeds the floor value. Hence, this strategic abandonment option has increased the value of the property significantly. Logically, with this abandonment option in place, the value of the land with the option is definitely worth more than $10 million.

INDUSTRY LEADERS EMBRACING REAL OPTIONS

Industries using real options as a tool for strategic decision-making started with oil and gas as well as mining companies, and later expanded into utilities, biotechnology, pharmaceuticals, and now into telecommunications, high-tech, and across all industries. Below are some examples of how real options have been or should be used in different industries.

Automobile and Manufacturing Industry. In automobile manufacturing, General Motors (GM) applies real options to create *switching options* in producing its new series of autos. This is essentially the option to use a cheaper resource over a given period of time. GM holds excess raw materials and has multiple global vendors for similar materials with excess contractual obligations above what it projects as necessary. The excess contractual cost is outweighed by the significant savings of switching vendors when a certain raw material becomes too expensive in a particular region of the world. By spending the additional money in contracting with vendors as well as meeting their minimum purchase requirements, GM has essentially paid the premium on purchasing a *switching option*. This is important especially when the price of raw materials fluctuates significantly in different regions around the world. Having an option here provides the holder a hedging vehicle against pricing risks.

Computer Industry. In the computer industry, HP-Compaq used to forecast sales of printers in foreign countries months in advance. It then configured, assembled, and shipped the highly specific printers to these countries. However, given that demand changes rapidly and forecast figures are seldom correct, the preconfigured printers usually suffer a higher inventory holding cost or the cost of technological obsolescence. HP-Compaq can create a *delay option* through building assembly plants in these foreign countries. Parts can then be shipped and assembled in specific configurations when demand is known, possibly weeks in advance rather than months in advance. These parts can be shipped anywhere in the world and assembled in any configuration necessary, while excess parts are interchangeable across different countries. The premium paid on this option is building the assembly plants, and the upside potential is the savings from not making wrong demand forecasts.

Airline Industry.   In the airline industry, Boeing spends billions of dollars and several years to decide if a certain aircraft model should even be built. Should the wrong model be tested in this elaborate strategy, Boeing's competitors may gain a competitive advantage relatively quickly. Because so many technical, engineering, market, and financial uncertainties are involved in the decision-making process, Boeing can conceivably create an *option to choose* through parallel development of multiple plane designs simultaneously, knowing very well the increased cost of developing multiple designs simultaneously with the sole purpose of eliminating all but one in the near future. The added cost is the premium paid on the option. However, Boeing will be able to decide which models to abandon or continue when these uncertainties and risks become known over time. Eventually, all the models will be eliminated save one. This way, the company can hedge itself against making the wrong initial decision, as well as benefit from the knowledge gained through multiple parallel development initiatives.

Oil and Gas Industry.   In the oil and gas industry, companies spend millions of dollars to refurbish their refineries and add new technology to create an *option to switch* their mix of outputs among heating oil, diesel, and other petrochemicals as a final product, using real options as a means of making capital and investment decisions. This option allows the refinery to switch its final output to one that is more profitable based on prevailing market prices, to capture the demand and price cyclicality in the market.

Telecommunications Industry.   In the telecommunications industry, in the past, companies like Sprint and AT&T installed more fiber-optic cable and other telecommunications infrastructure than other companies in order to create a *growth option* in the future by providing a secure and extensive network, and to create a high barrier to entry, providing a first-to-market advantage. Imagine having to justify to the Board of Directors the need to spend billions of dollars on infrastructure that will not be used for years to come. Without the use of real options, this would have been impossible to justify.

Utilities Industry.   In the utilities industry, firms have created an *option to switch* by installing cheap-to-build, inefficient energy generator peaker plants only to be used when electricity prices are high and to shut down when prices are low. The price of electricity tends to remain constant until it hits a certain capacity utilization trigger level, when prices shoot up significantly. Although this occurs infrequently, the possibility still exists, and by having a cheap standby plant, the firm has created the option to turn on the switch whenever it becomes necessary, to capture this upside price premium.

Real Estate Industry.   In the real estate arena, leaving land undeveloped creates an option to develop at a later date at a more lucrative profit level. However, what is the optimal wait time? In theory, one can wait for an infinite amount of time, and real options provide the solution for the optimal *timing option.*

Pharmaceutical Research and Development Industry.   In pharmaceutical research and development initiatives, real options can be used to justify the large investments in what seems to be cashless and unprofitable under the discounted cash flow method but actually creates *compounded expansion options* in the future. Under the myopic lenses of a traditional discounted cash flow analysis, the high initial investment of, say, a billion dollars in research and development may return a highly uncertain projected few million dollars over the next few years. Management will conclude under a net-present-value analysis that the project is not financially feasible. However, a cursory look at the industry indicates that research and development is performed everywhere. Hence, management must see an intrinsic strategic value in research and development. How is this intrinsic strategic value quantified? A real options approach would optimally time and spread the billion-dollar initial investment into a multiple-stage investment structure. At each stage, management has an *option to wait* and see what happens as well as the *option to abandon* or the *option to expand* into the subsequent stages. The ability to defer cost and proceed only if situations are permissible creates value for the investment.

High-Tech and e-Business Industry.   In e-business strategies, real options can be used to prioritize different e-commerce initiatives and to justify those large initial investments that have an uncertain future. Real options can be used in e-commerce to create incremental investment stages, *options to abandon,* and other future growth options, compared to a large one-time investment (invest a little now, wait and see before investing more).

All these cases where the high cost of implementation with no apparent payback in the near future seems foolish and incomprehensible in the traditional discounted cash flow sense are fully justified in the real options sense when taking into account the strategic options the practice creates for the future, the uncertainty of the future operating environment, and management's flexibility in making the right choices at the appropriate time.

WHAT THE EXPERTS ARE SAYING

The trend in the market is quickly approaching the acceptance of real options, as can be seen from the following sample publication excerpts.[1]

According to an article in *Bloomberg Wealth Manager* (November 2001):

> *Real options provide a powerful way of thinking and I can't think of any analytical framework that has been of more use to me in the past 15 years that I've been in this business.*

According to a *Wall Street Journal* article (February 2000):

> *Investors who, after its IPO in 1997, valued only Amazon.com's prospects as a book business would have concluded that the stock was significantly overpriced and missed the subsequent extraordinary price appreciation. Though assessing the value of real options is challenging, without doing it an investor has no basis for deciding whether the current stock price incorporates a reasonable premium for real options or whether the shares are simply overvalued.*

CFO Europe (July/August 1999) cites the importance of real options in that:

> *[A] lot of companies have been brainwashed into doing their valuations on a one-scenario discounted cash flow basis . . . and sometimes our recommendations are not what intuition would suggest, and that's where the real surprises come from—and with real options, you can tell exactly where they came from.*

According to a *Business Week* article (June 1999):

> *The real options revolution in decision-making is the next big thing to sell to clients and has the potential to be the next major business breakthrough. Doing this analysis has provided a lot of intuition you didn't have in the past . . . and as it takes hold, it's clear that a new generation of business analysts will be schooled in options thinking. Silicon Valley is fast embracing the concepts of real options analytics, in its tradition of fail fast so that other options may be sought after.*

In *Products Financiers* (April 1999):

> *Real options are a new and advanced technique that handles uncertainty much better than traditional evaluation methods. Since many managers feel that uncertainty is the most serious issue they have to face, there is no doubt that this method will have a bright future as any industry faces uncertainty in its investment strategies.*

A *Harvard Business Review* article (September/October 1998) hits home:

> *Unfortunately, the financial tool most widely relied on to estimate the value of a strategy is the discounted cash flow which assumes*

*that we will follow a predetermined plan regardless of how events
unfold. A better approach to valuation would incorporate both
the uncertainty inherent in business and the active decision-making
required for a strategy to succeed. It would help executives to think
strategically on their feet by capturing the value of doing just that —
of managing actively rather than passively and real options can
deliver that extra insight.*

This book provides a novel approach in applying real options to
answering these issues and more. In particular, a real options framework is
presented. It takes into account managerial flexibility in adapting to ever-
changing strategic, corporate, economic, and financial environments over
time as well as the fact that in the real business world, opportunities and
uncertainty exist and are dynamic in nature. This book provides a real options
process framework to identify, justify, time, prioritize, value, and manage
corporate investment strategies under uncertainty in the context of applying
real options.

The recommendations, strategies, and methodologies outlined in this
book are not meant to replace traditional discounted cash flow analysis but
to complement it when the situation and the need arise. The entire analysis could be done, or parts of it could be adapted to a more traditional
approach. In essence, the process methodology outlined starts with traditional analyses and continues with value- and insight-adding analytics,
including Monte Carlo simulation, real option analysis, and portfolio optimization. The real options approach outlined is not the only viable alternative nor will it provide a set of infallible results. However, if utilized
correctly with the traditional approaches, it may lead to a set of more
robust, accurate, insightful, and plausible results. The insights generated
through real options analytics provide significant value in understanding a
project's true strategic value.

SUMMARY

Real options analysis simply defined is the application of financial options,
decision sciences, corporate finance, and statistics to evaluating real or physical assets as opposed to financial assets. Industry analysts, experts, and aca-
demics all agree that real options provide significant insights to project
evaluation that traditional types of analysis like the discounted cash flow
approach cannot provide. Sometimes the simple task of thinking and framing the problem within a real options context is highly valuable. The simple
types of real options discussed include expansion, abandonment, contraction, chooser, compound, barrier, growth, switching, and sequential compound options.

CHAPTER 1 QUESTIONS

1. What are some of the characteristics of a project or a firm that is best suited for a real options analysis?

2. Define the following:

   a. Compound option

   b. Barrier option

   c. Expansion option

3. If management is not credible in acting appropriately through profit-maximizing behavior, are strategic real options still worth anything?

The Timken Company on Real Options in R&D and Manufacturing

The following is contributed by Kenneth P. English, Director of R&D Emerging Technology, The Timken Company, Canton, Ohio. The Timken Company is a public company traded on the NYSE, and is a leading international manufacturer of highly engineered bearings, alloy and specialty steels and components, as well as related products and services. With operations in 24 countries, the company employs about 18,700 associates worldwide and recorded 2001 sales of U.S. $2.4 billion.

The Timken Company's journey toward real options analysis began approximately six years ago in 1996 when the corporation made the decision to focus on profitably growing the business by 10 percent per year. We started with the creation of a gate-type process to identify and evaluate project opportunities that would generate the necessary profits for our growth requirements. During the numerous gate meetings, the process actually highlighted gaps in our process more than the anticipated growth project opportunities we had expected. The first group of gaps identified during the process was the lack of expertise in project management and market research; the second was poorly defined and documented product and corporate strategies; and, finally, financial evaluation capabilities. The gaps identified in project management, market research, and strategy were addressed over the following years by recruiting various consulting firms to assist with those disciplines. The financial evaluation gap was initially addressed with the assistance of our internal financial department by applying the same financial modeling tools used when the corporation built new physical plants. These models focused on NPV, payback, and project terminal value. Project terminal value caused considerable controversy with the reviewers.

As these parallel consulting efforts continued for months/years, the corporation became more adroit at the terminology of product development. As the refinements and understanding of these other areas evolved, it was realized that the financial model used on the gate templates was not adequate for the dynamic uncertain environment of product development. At this time, Monte Carlo simulation was being used in benchmarked growth industries to determine the range of risk for projects. Our first response was to acquire books on the subject of Monte Carlo simulation.

The financial department was familiar with the model but was not prepared to assist with implementation of it in the product development environment. After some time and frustration, the Crystal Ball® software product for Monte Carlo simulation at a company named Decisioneering, Inc. was discovered. The timing was excellent, since the corporation was reviewing a high-profile project that contained hidden ranges of risk. The Crystal Ball® product was immediately purchased and inserted into our gate templates to address the issue of risk. Within weeks, some of our corporate leadership was looking at risk with a much different perspective. Previously, we identified risk and noted it, then proceeded on a product development path without sensitivity to the dynamic ramifications of the risk. The Monte Carlo simulation put focus on the importance of the corporation's gaps in detailed market research and the absence of aligned product and corporate strategy for Horizon II projects. The software made the complex and time-consuming financial formulas into a quick, user-friendly tool to assist with the difficult task of defining the range of risk and promoting timely decision-making. It was painfully obvious that the real object of successful product development was to enable speedy decisions to either fund or kill projects and not the joy of being comfortable with seeing the old favorite projects and connected potential acquisitions lingering on with several lives.

Two and a half years into the quest for profitable growth, we identified the next barrier to our success. That barrier was the absence of a project portfolio process. The major issue with any initially installed gate-oriented process in a previous incremental corporate culture structure is that the gatekeepers only have the opportunity to evaluate the presented projects against other projects presented during that particular gate meeting. This situation exerts pressure to find a tool/process that will allow the gatekeepers to prioritize all the product and project efforts of the corporation to give maximum return on investment. The concept of projects in a portfolio becomes very important to the corporate allocation of funds. Portfolio management was a very foreign concept to us since our corporate orientation to projects was based on NPV and payback and not mitigation of risk, maximizing efforts, and cost of capital. We responded to the corporate learning piece of the puzzle by creating a manual portfolio simulation exercise to sensitize our executives and gatekeepers to how they looked at projects and their synergies. It also broadened their view of the significant impact that strategic fit, selection, and timing has with respect to financial success.

With the success of the portfolio simulation, we were then sensitized to the issue of the corporate benefit of cultivating a mindset of timing projects *(timing options)* in a way that could maximize the impact to our growth requirements. The writings regarding real options began appearing in the business literature, magazines, and seminars, but the application was initially geared toward the practice of financial options. Again, we were put in a position of educating ourselves (the change agents) and subsequently the corporate culture to a different way of thinking. We searched the available real options course selection taught at the university level. The universities were interested in real options but did not have coursework in place to conduct educational sessions.

The Timken Company established the R&D Emerging Technology Department in June of 2002. The focus of the department is to scan the world for dispersed technologies that are not part of the present corporate portfolio. These technologies contain varying degrees of risk, which require an even higher level of evaluation techniques to take advantage of numerous options.

Publicity from Decisioneering, Inc. about the upcoming real options software and the one-day lecture and workshop on real options appeared to be the best vehicle to take us to the next level of portfolio decision-making. We contacted Dr. Mun to give a real options lecture and workshop to bring our financial department and executives up to speed. The time spent was very useful, and the culture is starting to communicate in real option terms. We at The Timken Company are anticipating that the new software for real options from Decisioneering, Inc. will get us closer to the target of achieving more confident corporate project decisions, resulting in assisting us in our goal of sustained profitability and growth.

Schlumberger on Real Options in Oil and Gas

The following is contributed by William Bailey, Ph.D., Senior Research Engineer at Schlumberger—Doll Research, Ridgefield, Connecticut. The company is involved in global technology services, with corporate offices in New York, Paris, and The Hague. Schlumberger has more than 80,000 employees, representing 140 nationalities, working in nearly 100 countries. The company consists of two business segments: Schlumberger Oilfield Services, which includes Schlumberger Network Solutions, and Schlumberger-Sema. Schlumberger Oilfield Services supplies products, services, and technical solutions to the oil and gas exploration and production (E&P) industry, with Schlumberger Network Solutions providing information technology (IT) connectivity and security solutions to both the E&P industry and a range of other markets. Schlumberger-Sema provides IT consulting, systems integration, managed services, and related products to the oil and gas, telecommunications, energy and utilities, finance, transport, and public-sector markets.

Long gone are those heady days in the petroleum industry when a pith-helmeted geologist could point to an uninspiring rock outcrop, declare confidently "drill here," and then find an oil field the size of a small country. Over the past 30 years, however, the situation for the oil industry has become very different indeed. As we search to replenish our ever-decreasing hydrocarbon supplies, oil explorationists now find themselves looking in some of the most inaccessible parts of the globe and in some of the deepest and most inhospitable seas. What could have been achieved in the past with a relatively small investment is now only attainable at a considerably greater cost. In other words, developing an oil and/or gas field nowadays is subject to considerably larger investments in time, money, and technology. Furthermore, such large investments are almost always based on imperfect, scant, and uncertain information. It is no accident, therefore, that when teaching the concepts of risk analysis, many authors cite the oil industry as a classic case in point. This is not by accident for few other industries exhibit such a range of uncertainty and possible downside exposure (in technical, financial, environmental, and human terms). Indeed this industry is almost ubiquitous when demonstrating risk analysis concepts.

Consequently real options have a natural place in the oil industry management decision-making process. The process and discipline in such an analysis captures the presence of uncertainty, limited information, and the existence of different—but valid—development scenarios. The fact that petroleum industry management are faced with multi-million (sometimes billion) dollar decisions is nothing new. Such people are used to making critical decisions on a mixture of limited information, experience, and best judgment. What is new is that we now have a coherent tool and framework that explicitly considers uncertainty and available choices in a timely and effective manner.

This short appendix is intended to provide just a brief glimpse into the types of applications real options have been used for in the petroleum industry. To guide the reader unfamiliar with the finer points of the oil and gas industry, it may be prudent to outline the basic process in an "average" petroleum development. In so doing, the reasons why the oil industry is deemed such a prime example for use of real options (and risk analysis in general) will become clear.

In the 1959 film of Jules Verne's 1864 novel *Journey to the Center of the Earth,* James Mason and others found themselves sailing on a dark sea in a mighty cavern many miles down in the earth's crust. This was, of course, just science fiction, not science fact. Unfortunately it is still a common misconception that oil is found in such "caverns" forming black lakes deep beneath our feet. While such images may be romantic and wishful, reality is far more intricate. For the most part oil (and gas) is found in the microscopic pore spaces present between individual grains making up the rock. For example, hydrocarbon-bearing sandstone may have porosity levels (the percentage of pore space in the rock) of about 15 percent. This means that if all the pore space in the rock is full of oil, then 15 percent of the total rock volume contains oil. Of course, things are not as simple as that because water and other minerals serve to reduce the available pore volume.[1] As oil and gas are liquid, they will flow. Unless the rock itself provides some form of seal (or trap) to contain these fluids, over time they will simply seep to the surface and be lost. (Azerbaijan has some good examples of such seepage with whole hillsides being awash with flame from seeping gas for as long as recorded history.) So not only do we need a rock that contains oil (or gas) but also the oil (or gas) must be trapped somehow, ready for exploitation. For a readable and well-informed summary of petroleum geology, refer to Selley (1998).[2]

Extraction of oil (and/or gas) from a virgin field is undertaken in typically four stages: exploration and appraisal; development; production; and abandonment. This is a gross simplification, of course, for within each phase there are a multitude of technical, commercial, and operational considerations. Keeping one eye on real options, in their crudest form these phases can be briefly described as follows:

■ **Exploration and Appraisal.** Seismic data is obtained and a picture of the subsurface is then revealed. Coupled with geological knowledge, experience, and observations, it is then possible to generate a more detailed depiction of a possible hydrocarbon-bearing zone. Seismic data cannot tell what fluids are present in the rock, so an exploratory well needs to be drilled, and from this one is then able to better establish the nature, size, and type of an oil and gas field.

Exploration and Appraisal Phase—Where Real Options Come In. The decision-maker has numerous options available to him/her, which may include:

□ Extent of investment needed in acquiring seismic data. For example should one invest in 3D seismic studies that provide greater resolution but are significantly more expensive? Should 4D (time-dependent) seismic data be considered? While advanced seismic data (and interpretation) certainly provides improved representation of the subsurface environment, one needs to assess whether it is worthwhile investing in this information. Will it reduce uncertainty concerning the size and nature of the reservoir sufficiently to pay off the investment?

□ Given inherent uncertainty about the reserves, if possible, how much should the company share in the risk (extent of contract partnership)?

□ How many exploration wells are appropriate to properly delineate the field? One, two, five, or more?

■ **Development.** Once sufficient data has been obtained (from seismic or exploratory wells) to make an educated judgment on the size of the prize, we enter into the development phase. Here we decide upon the most commercially viable way for exploiting this new resource by engineering the number (and type) of producing wells, process facilities, and transportation. We must also establish if, at all, any pressure support is necessary.[3]

Development Phase—Where Real Options Come In. This is where decision-makers face possibly the greatest number of valid alternatives. Valid development options include:

□ How many wells should be drilled? Where should they be located? In what order should they be drilled?

□ Should producers be complex (deviated/horizontal) wells located at the platform, or should they be simple but tied-back to a sub-sea manifold?

□ How many platforms or rigs will be needed? If offshore, should they be floating or permanent?

□ What potential future intervention should be accommodated? Intervention refers to an ability to re-enter a well to perform either routine maintenance or perform major changes—referred to as a work-over.

□ How many injectors (if any at all) should be drilled? Where should they be located?

□ How large should the processing facility[4] be? If small, then capital expenditure will be reduced but may ultimately limit throughput (the amount of hydrocarbons sent to market thereby restricting cash flow). If the process facility is made too large, then it may be costly and also operationally inefficient.

□ Are there adjacent fields waiting to be developed? If so, should the process facility be shared? Is this a valid and reasonable future possibility in anticipation of uncertain future throughput?

□ Should a new pipeline be laid? If so, where would it be best to land it, or is it possible to tie it into an existing pipeline elsewhere with available capacity? Should other transportation methods be considered (e.g., FPSO[5])?

The number of different engineering permutations available at this stage means that management may be faced with several viable alternatives—which are contingent upon the assumptions on which they were developed. Real options enable uncertainty to be explicitly quantified at this stage.

■ **Production.** Depending on the size of the reserve (and how prolific the wells are) the engineer must manage this resource as carefully as any other valuable asset. Reservoir management (the manner and strategy in which we produce from a field) has become increasingly important over the past few years. Older, less technically advanced, production methods were inefficient, often leaving 75 percent or more of the oil in the ground— oil that cannot be easily extracted afterward, if at all. Increasing the efficiency of our production from our reservoirs is now a crucial part of any engineering effort (unfortunately, nature prevents us from extracting 100 percent of the oil; there will always be some left behind).

Production Phase—Where Real Options Come In. Valid production options include:

□ Are there any areas of the field that are un-swept[6] and can be exploited by drilling more wells?

□ Should we farm-out (divest) some, or all, of the asset to other companies?

□ Should we consider further seismic data acquisition?

- ☐ Should we consider taking existing production wells and converting them into injection wells to improve the overall field performance?
- ☐ What options does one have to extend the life of the field?
- ☐ Should we consider reentering certain wells and performing various actions to improve their performance (e.g., re-perforating some or all of the well, shutting off poorly producing zones, drilling a smaller branch-well [known as a sidetrack] to access un-swept reserves, etc.)? What information needs to be collected to be able to make these operational decisions? How is such information best obtained? At what cost and at what operational risk? (Reentering a well may be a hazardous and potentially damaging act.)

Once again, there are many opportunities during the production phase to make decisions that are still subject to considerable uncertainty. Even though the field may be mature and much experience has been accumulated, the operator is still faced with many management options that can impact ultimate reservoir performance and economic viability.

- ■ **Decommissioning (also known as Abandonment).** Once reserves have been depleted, the infrastructure can either be left to decay or—increasingly—it must be dismantled in an environmentally and economically efficient manner. This is especially true for the North Sea and offshore USA.

  Decommissioning Phase—Where Real Options Come In. Valid production options include:
  - ☐ What will the ultimate abandonment cost be, and what is the likelihood that this will remain true at the end of the life of the field?
  - ☐ Should the full cost of abandonment be included in the initial development strategy, or is there a way to hedge some or all of this cost?
  - ☐ What contingency should be built in to account for changes in legislation?
  - ☐ At what threshold does abandonment cost make the project unprofitable, and how would this impact our initial development strategy?

This brief (and admittedly incomplete) list of bullet points at least demonstrates why the oil industry is ideally suited for a real options-type analysis because they exhibit all the necessary ingredients:

- ■ Large capital investments.
- ■ Uncertain revenue streams.
- ■ Often long lead times to achieve these uncertain cash flows.
- ■ Uncertainty in the amount of potential production (reservoir size and quality).
- ■ Numerous technical alternatives at all stages of development.

- Political risk and market exposure (external influences outside the control of the operating company).

FINAL WORD

Early examples of options-based analysis are found in the oil and gas industry.[7] The impact and wholesale adoption so far has been limited. Why this is the case in the oil industry raises important issues that should be kept in mind when considering adopting real options as a practice in any company.

Real options are technically demanding, with a definite learning curve in the oil industry, and have three main hurdle classifications:[8]

- **Marketing Problem.** Selling real options to management, appreciating the utility and benefit, understanding their capabilities and strengths (as well as weaknesses), and ultimately communicating these ideas (companies usually have a few volunteer champions/early adopters, but they often remain isolated unless there is suitable communication of these concepts, particularly in a non-technical capacity, which may be easier said than done).

- **Analysis Problem.** Problem framing and correct technical analysis (not too difficult to resolve if suitably trained technical people are available—and have read this book).

- **Impact Problem.** Not really the interpretation of results but rather acting on them, implementing them, monitoring and benchmarking them, then communicating them (a recurring theme), and finally managing the whole process.

These issues should be kept in mind when communicating the concepts and results of a real options analysis.

Intellectual Property Economics on Real Options in Patent and Intangible Valuation

The following is contributed by A. Tracy Gomes, President and CEO of Intellectual Property Economics, LLC, located in Dallas, Texas. Gomes's firm specializes in the valuation of intellectual property and intangibles, for the purposes of corporate financial planning and tax transactions.

Real options analysis is designed to explicitly incorporate and analyze risk and uncertainty associated with real assets. Intellectual property (IP), whether defined in its strictest, most narrow legal sense—patents, trademarks, trade secrets, and copyrights—or more broadly to encompass all intellectual/ intangible assets created from human conceptual endeavor, is the poster child of uncertainty, and exemplifies the great challenge and promise that is real options analysis.

In this information- and knowledge-based age that is the post-modern economy, IP is the most fundamental and valuable asset in business today. From 1978 to 1998, the composition of market value of the S&P 500 has been transformed from 80 percent physical assets, 20 percent intangible assets, to 20 percent physical assets, 80 percent intangible assets.[1] Since 1990, the annual revenue realized from just the licensing of patented technology has grown from less than $10 billion to nearly $120 billion (not counting the direct administrative and maintenance costs, which are likely less than one-half of one percent; that is $120 billion in net, bottom-line profit).

But this is just the IP that is visible, that the marketplace can actually see and has already put a value on. The goal and application for real options analysis lies in the vast uncovered trove of IP that is unseen and hidden, and like a giant iceberg lies just below the surface. For younger, emerging companies, this is likely to be IP that is in process—research and development projects in varying stages of development. For older companies, IP value is likely to be found not only in those efforts still in the pipeline but perhaps even more so in those efforts long ago completed and placed on the shelf.

Kevin Rivette, in his seminal book, *Rembrandts in the Attic,* recounts the embarrassing legacy of Xerox, which discarded such "worthless" ideas as the PC, laser printing, the Ethernet, and graphical user interface (GUI), only to see them transformed from trash to cash by someone else. Leading industry companies have gotten religious and are fast about combing through their patent portfolios. Procter & Gamble, after a three-year internal audit, estimates that it is utilizing only about 10 percent of its 25,000-patent port-folio. Dupont has allocated each of its 29,000 patents to one of 15 business units. And IBM has literally thrown open its vaults, declaring each and every patent, each technology and process, even trade secrets as potentially "up for sale."

Recognizing that something is of potential value, and knowing what the value of that something is, are two different things. Information and knowl-edge are the guideposts of strategic business decision-making and the glue of economic transactions. When information is incomplete or unknown, busi-ness decisions tend to be delayed and markets fail to clear. Stereotypical examples in the case of IP are the individual sole inventors who think their ideas are worth millions and the giant multinational corporations who are only willing to pay pennies. Unfortunately, the reality of today's IP business transactions is all too often characterized by divergent bid/offer sheets, lengthy negotiations, and tortured contractual terms,[2] leading to excessively high and wasteful transaction costs. Perhaps even more disheartening are the thousands of IP deals in which buyer and seller don't even get a chance to meet—IP left orphaned on countless Internet exchanges, or projects aban-doned or put back on the shelf because they are thought to be too costly or their markets too remote or too shallow.

It is here that real options analysis holds so much promise, to be applied to those IP assets and projects that were thought to be too vague, too unknown, and too iffy. Not that it can predict the future success or failure of IP devel-opment or the creation of some still hypothetical market, or that it can turn perennial duds into potential deals. Real options analysis is not magic, nor does it make risk or uncertainty vanish and go away. What it does do is attempt to make risk and uncertainty explicit through rational statistical means. In this way, uncertainty is bounded and risk quantified such that information becomes more clear and tangible, and the knowledge base expanded, thereby aiding decision-making.

Unlike financial assets, there are no existing liquid markets for intangi-ble "real" assets. Real options analysis seeks to change that by providing a means to demystify the risk and uncertainty surrounding IP and supply poten-tial buyers and sellers with objective, quantifiable information to shortcut uncertainty, clarify risk, and clear the path to shorter, smoother, and less costly IP deal-making. Two examples provide a case in point.

A small automotive engineering start-up identifies a cutting-edge technology being developed by a private research institute. They approach the institute, seeking the acquisition or license of the technology. Given that the technology is a couple years from commercialization, and the expectant market, which is being driven by governmental regulation (and resisted by manufacturers), is several more years into the future, instead of jumping into negotiations, the two sides agree to an outside independent economic analysis.

Due to cost considerations, simplified real options analysis was performed modeling future auto demand and holding government regulation constant. The real options valuation, though nearly twice as high as the conventional DCF analysis, gave both parties a clearer view of uncertainty and amount of risk facing the technology. After the two-month analysis, the parties entered into negotiations and within two months completed discussions, and drafted and signed an agreement.

A second case involves a medium-sized contract research organization with a proprietary portfolio of nearly 400 patents, processes, trade secrets, and disclosures spread over an area of half a dozen different fields of technology. Seeking to extract value from its IP assets, and develop an additional revenue stream, the firm selected a sampling of assets (in varying stages of development) from several of its portfolio segments and contracted for a risk assessment—the beginning stages of an options analysis prior to modeling. The assessment identified several key parameters, including various risks (technical, competition, and regulatory) as well as timing issues, both technical and market. And, while not a complete options analysis, the assessment did provide management with valuable, tangible information with which to assess and prioritize the sampling of assets, and develop a template to evaluate all its IP on a go-forward basis.

Uncertainty and risk are nowhere more real and tangible than in the case of intellectual property. Understandably, this uncertainty makes firms hesitant in decision-making regarding IP, and virtually hamstrung in IP deal-making. The role of real options analysis in IP is to identify (and quantify) uncertainty, to illuminate risk, and thereby to increase confidence and realize the full value of the IP.

Gemplus on Real Options in High-Tech R&D

The following is contributed by Jim Schreckengast, Sr. Vice President of Gemplus International SA, the world's leading provider of smart cards and solutions for the telecommunications, financial, government, and IT industries. Gemplus is one of the most innovative companies of its kind, carrying a significant investment in research and development (R&D) aimed at driving forward the state-of-the-art in secure, ultra-thin computing platforms, wireless security, identity, privacy, content protection, and trusted architectures.

Gemplus is a high-tech company. Such companies assign great importance to R&D, because high-tech companies often derive their primary competitive advantage through technology, and R&D plays a pivotal role in determining the technology position of these companies. Effective management of R&D is difficult and involves significant uncertainty. Moreover, company resources are limited, so it is critical for management to invest R&D resources wisely, considering the many types of value that can be produced by these resources. Gemplus recognizes the complexity of managing R&D efforts in rapidly changing and competitive environments and has used real options analysis to improve the effectiveness of R&D investment decisions.

One of the most significant challenges in R&D is the management of innovation. Management of this process is difficult, because successful innovation usually involves the discovery and generation of knowledge, while exploiting existing knowledge and capabilities in an attempt to generate value through new products and services, to differentiate existing offerings, to lower costs, and to disrupt the competitive landscape. Each successful innovation may be used as a building block for further R&D efforts, enabling the firm to create a sustainable competitive advantage through a cohesive R&D program that blends and builds upon previous results. For example, a firm pursuing low-power, wireless communications technologies for tiny wearable computers might discover that their latest approach to reducing power requirements has the capability to generate fine-grained location and speed information as a side effect of communication. This location information could enable the firm to begin generating a new family of location-based services, while enhancing routing and switching in dynamic wireless networks. Further, the company might recognize that expansion of investment in fine-grained location technologies could position the firm favorably to compete in context-rich service delivery, if the market for these services materializes in two years. In addition, the R&D director might conclude that investment in this technology will improve the firm's ability to manage bandwidth and resource utilization, if the results of current research in peer-to-peer network architectures prove promising.

The chain of loosely connected innovations in the previous example is surprisingly representative of the events that unfold in practice within a "high-tech" industry. While prediction of a specific sequence of innovations is usually infeasible, successful companies often develop innovation systems that recognize the potential for these chains and develop R&D systems that can stimulate their creation while retaining the flexibility to capitalize on the most promising among them over time.

The complexities of analyzing technical uncertainty, market uncertainty, and competitive movements in a rapidly changing industry often drive management to either shorten the time horizon of R&D projects to the extent that each project has a very predictable (and often unremarkable) outcome, or to assemble R&D projects as a collection of desperate "bets" in the hopes of finding one that "wins" for the company. The former approach tends to restrict flexibility, since project managers will focus energy and resources on short-term tasks that are directly linked to the limited scope of each project. The latter approach dilutes R&D resources across many unrelated projects and overlooks potential synergies between the outcomes of these efforts. Furthermore, by viewing the R&D portfolio as a collection of "bets," management may fail to recognize the many opportunities that usually exist to control, refine, and combine the intermediate results of these projects in a way that enhances the total value of R&D.

Traditional valuation techniques for R&D (e.g., decision trees and NPV) may exacerbate the fundamental problems associated with investment analysis and portfolio management, because these techniques rely solely on information that is available at the time of the analysis and cannot accurately value flexibility over time. The limitations of these techniques often go unrecognized by decision-makers, resulting in suboptimal R&D investment decisions.

Gemplus uses an R&D management approach that recognizes three key realities for its industry:

1. Uncertainties are resolved on a continuous basis as R&D is conducted, competitive conditions change, and market expectations evolve.

2. There is a significant lag that exists between the time a company begins to invest in a technology and the time when the company can wield that technology effectively to generate new products and services.

3. The most valuable R&D investments are those that simultaneously build on existing, distinctive competencies while generating capabilities that enhance the firm's flexibility in light of existing uncertainties.

These realities compel Gemplus to manage R&D on a continuous basis, and to invest while significant uncertainties exist, valuing the flexibility that is created by R&D investments. Each R&D project carries a primary purpose but may also carry a number of secondary objectives that relate to the value of real options associated with expected capabilities delivered by the project. Gemplus manages a portfolio of R&D innovation efforts in the context of a technology road map that makes the most significant real options apparent, and relates the strategic direction of the company to the flexibility and competitive advantage sought by its R&D efforts.

Once the most significant real options have been identified, each R&D project is valued in the context of this road map. Research proposals are evaluated based on the value of the information generated by the work, together with the relevant capabilities that may be generated and the flexibility this affords the company. Gemplus has seen up to 70 percent of the value of a research proposal arise from the real options generated by the research. Development projects are typically valued for their primary purpose and for real options arising from R&D management flexibility (i.e., expansion and contraction in the course of portfolio management), technology switching capabilities (e.g., when it is unclear which technology will emerge as a dominant design), and real options created in the context of the technology road map (e.g., multipurpose technologies). Although a development project usually has a much smaller percentage of its value attributed to real options, the difference can be significant enough to alter R&D investment decisions that would have otherwise favored a less flexible or less synergistic effort.

R&D efforts also result in the generation of intellectual property. Patents are of particular interest, because they can affect the firm's ability to protect products and services derived from the patented technology. Further, patents may be licensed, sold, or used to erect barriers (i.e., entry, switching, substitution, and forward or backward integration), as well as to counter infringement claims by third parties. Thus, patents may carry significant value for the firm, and this value reflects the real options associated with the invention now and in the future. Gemplus believes that correct valuation of intellectual property, and patents in particular, leads to improved intellectual property strategies and more effective research prioritization. Thus, Gemplus has changed its intellectual property strategy and valuation process to explicitly incorporate the value of real options created by R&D patents.

Acquiring technology from outside the firm is often an integral element of a good technology strategy. Thus, R&D managers must determine how to value technologies accurately. Like direct R&D investments, technology acquisitions may carry a significant value associated with real options. Acquisition valuation should include comparables, the value for direct exploitation of the technology, and the value of real options associated with the technology. Such valuation should also consider real options forgone by the current technology owner and the game theoretic aspects of bidding competitively for the technology with others. Gemplus considers real options analysis to be a critical ingredient to accurate valuation of technology acquisitions and has augmented its process to include this analysis.

It should be noted that recognition of the value associated with real options in R&D must be combined with a process for acting on the decisions associated with these real options. If real options are not effectively linked with the ongoing R&D management process, it may be difficult to realize the values projected by the real options analysis. For instance, Gemplus found that the value of R&D management options was highly dependent upon the life cycle and review that was applied to projects and programs. For example, a hardware development project often follows a traditional "waterfall" life cycle with natural checkpoints at the conclusion of investigation, specification, design, and implementation. These checkpoints present an opportunity to take advantage of what has been learned over time, and to alter the course of the project. The project could be expanded or reduced, changed to incorporate a new capability from a recently completed research project, or perhaps altered in a more fundamental way. Software development projects, on the other hand, may follow a more iterative life cycle, with less time between cycles and fewer natural checkpoints. These differences should be considered carefully when identifying management options associated with a project.

Of course, all of the activity associated with real options analysis in R&D is aimed at more accurately valuing technological choices, so that the best decisions are made for the firm. The experience at Gemplus thus far suggests that these efforts are worthwhile. Real options analysis is a powerful financial tool that meshes nicely with the complexities of managing a collection of projects and research activities that inherently carry significant uncertainty, but also represent great potential value for the firm.

Sprint on Real Options in Telecommunications

The following is contributed by Marty Nevshemal (FMDP, Global Markets Division) and Mark Akason (FMDP, Local Telecommunications Division) of Sprint. Sprint is a global communications company serving 23 million business and residential customers in more than 70 countries. With more than 80,000 employees worldwide and $23 billion in annual revenues, the West-wood, KS-based company is represented on the New York Stock Exchange by the FON group and the PCS group. On the wireline side, the Sprint FON Group (NYSE: FON) comprises Sprint's Global Markets Group and the Local Telecommunications Division, as well as product distribution and directory publishing businesses. On the wireless side, the Sprint PCS Group (NYSE: PCS) consists of Sprint's wireless PCS operations. Sprint is widely recognized for developing, engineering, and deploying state-of-the-art technologies in the telecommunications industry, including the nation's first nationwide all-digital, fiber-optic network. The Global Markets Group provides a broad suite of communications services to business and residential customers. These services include domestic long-distance and international voice service; data service like Internet, frame relay access and transport, Web hosting, and managed security; and broadband.

In the twentieth century, telecommunications has become ubiquitous in developed countries. In 1999, total telecommunications revenues in the United States were in excess of $260 billion and had grown in excess of 10 percent per year for the prior four years.[1] By December 2000, there were more than 100 million mobile wireless subscribers in the United States.[2] Even more staggering is the capital intensity necessary to drive this revenue and provide this service. In 2000, the largest telecom company, AT&T, required assets of $234 billion to drive revenue of $56 billion, a ratio of greater than

4:1.[3] Not only is simple growth in population and locations driving the industry, but also new technologies and applications such as wireless and the Internet are fueling that growth. Given the capital intensity and sheer size of the investments, to be successful in the telecom industry it is critical that companies make decisions that properly value and assess the new technologies and applications. This is where real options can play a role.

The goal of any company is to make the right decision regarding its investments. One of the goals of any investment decision is to optimize value while preserving flexibility. Often though, optimum value and flexibility are at odds. An example of this dichotomy is that one can choose a strategy of leading the industry by investing in and implementing new, unproven technologies that will hopefully become the platform(s) for future profitable products and services. Or one can choose a wait-and-see strategy, holding back on investments until the technology standard is recognized industry-wide. Both strategies have obvious advantages and disadvantages. The first strategy opens a telecom company up to the risk of investing in a technology that may not become the industry standard, may be a dead end (remember BETA tapes?), or may not meet all the desired specifications. Furthermore, the magnitude of the "cutting edge" technology bet, if it does not work, could adversely impact the financial viability of the firm.

Therefore, it is critically important for a telecommunications company such as Sprint to ensure that their decision-making process includes a structured method that recognizes both the benefits and pitfalls of a particular technology investment as soon as information about that technology becomes available. This method should quickly get information in usable form to decision-makers so that they can take appropriate action. Finally, this structured method must ensure that timely decision points be identified, where actions can be taken to either improve the development results or give the option to re-deploy resources to better opportunities.

One of the ways that Sprint believes that this strategic flexibility for technology investments can be systematically implemented throughout the organization is through the adoption of real options analysis. The very nature of the analysis forces managers to think about the growth and flexibility options that may be available in any technology investment decision. Real options analysis has a process for valuing these options, and it identifies decision points along the way.

Systemic to the telecom industry is the requirement of management to make critically important strategic decisions regarding the implementation and adaptation of various telecom technologies that will have significant impact on the value of their firm over the long term. Overall, these technologies are extremely capital intensive, especially in the start-up phase, and take an extended period to develop and implement, and have an extended payoff period.

Here are a couple of examples of capital-intensive telecom technology bets that a telecom company has to make:

■ Selection of wireless technology (e.g., TDMA—Time Division Multiple Access, CDMA—Code Division Multiple Access, or GSM—Global System for Mobile Communications).

■ Third Generation (3G) build-out and timing of a commercial rollout.

■ 3G wireless technology applications.

■ Location and construction of Metropolitan Area Networks (MANs), Central Offices (COs), and Points-of-Presence (POPs).

■ Capacity of its backbone fiber network.

■ Technology of the backbone network (ATM—Asynchronous Transfer Mode versus IP—Internet Protocol).

Generally speaking, there are three basic outcomes to any technology decision using a strategy to lead. Each outcome has distinct effects on the company, both operationally and financially:

■ The right technology choice generally leads to success in its many forms: sustainable competitive advantage in pricing/cost structure, first-to-market benefits, greater market share, recognition as a superior brand, operational efficiencies, superior financial results, and industry recognition.

■ The wrong technology choice without strategic options to redirect the assets or re-deploy resources could lead to a sustained competitive disadvantage and/or a technology dead end from which it takes considerable financial and operational resources to recover.

■ However, the wrong initial choice can also lead to success eventually— if viable strategic and tactical options are acted upon in a timely manner. At a minimum, these options can help avoid financial distress and/or reduce its duration and/or the extent of a competitive disadvantage.

It is important to implement valuation techniques that improve the analysis of business opportunities, but perhaps more important, telecom managers should strive to implement a structured thought/analysis process that builds operational flexibility into every business case.

This is where real options analysis has shown to have definite benefits. More specifically, the thought process that forces management to look for and demand strategic flexibility is critical. Furthermore, similar to the value of Monte Carlo simulations that educate management to better understand the input variables as opposed to concentrating on a final output NPV (net present value), real options analysis also forces management to better understand these input variables. However, it goes a couple of steps further by valuing strategic flexibility and identifying trigger points where the direction of the business plan may be amended. The challenge is how to implement the mechanics of real options analysis.

In the telecom industry there are typically no natural trigger points where hard-stop reviews are required as there are in the pharmaceutical industry or in the oil and gas industry. Within the pharmaceutical industry, for example, there are natural gates/decision points, such as FDA reviews, that act as trigger points where the strategic direction of the product/project can be and typically must be revisited.

For technology companies like Sprint, these trigger points are not implicit. Instead, they need to be actively defined by management and built into a structured analysis. These trigger points can be based on fixed time line reviews (monthly/quarterly/yearly) or can occur when a technology reaches a natural review stage such as the completion of product design, product development, market analysis, or pricing. Other milestones include when financial and operational thresholds are realized (project overspent/competing technology introduced/growth targets exceeded).

When implementing new technology, historical benchmark data regarding the chance that a particular event will occur is not available. For example, there is no historical precedent to show the percentage chance that CDMA rather than GSM technology will be the preferred wireless technology in the United States over the long run. Yet, the adoption of one technology over the other may have serious financial ramifications for the various wireless carriers. Therefore, management, in many cases, will base the value of the option on their subjective analysis of the situation. With real options, the final outcome of management's analysis is determined through thorough analysis and critical thinking, and the result has considerable value.

Similar cases are present throughout the telecom industry and may result in considerable subjective leeway that allows for wide swings in the value of any particular option. This is not to say that this dilutes the value of real options analysis. On the contrary, just having the structured thought process that recognizes that there is value in strategic flexibility and in trying to put a value on this flexibility is important unto itself.

In summary, applying the key principles of real options analysis is important and valuable; and overall, real options analysis complements traditional analysis tools and in many cases is an improvement over them.

The following examples are telecom-specific areas where various types of real options can be used to determine the financial viability of the project.

- **Wireless Minutes of Use (MOU) and Replacement of Wireline MOU.** In today's competitive wireless landscape, most, if not all, of the nationwide wireless carriers are offering long-distance plans as part of their wireless package. As wireless penetration increases, this drives MOU to the long-distance carriers and may change the economics of the wireline build-out for some carriers. Furthermore, because wireless subscribers have long distance bundled into their monthly recurring charge (MRC), many are replacing their wireline phones with wireless phones for long distance. Therefore, real options analysis can be done to place a value on both wireless and wireline carriers.

- **Valuing New Technologies Using Sequential Compound and Re-Deploy Resources Options.** 3G can be seen as both a sequential compound and re-deploy resources option. Some wireless carriers in the United States, such as Sprint, will be able to implement 3G by deploying software upgrades throughout the existing network, while others will need to build-out new networks. Companies that find 3G a *sequential compound option* can upgrade their network to 3G capable with very little (if any) incremental investment over what the wireless company would normally invest to build-out capacity. In addition, the subscribers of these companies will be able to utilize existing phones that are not 3G capable for voice services.

  □ Wireless companies that cannot upgrade sequentially to 3G must re-deploy resources from the existing wireless network. These companies must spend billions of dollars acquiring the spectrum to enable the build-out of 3G networks. In Europe alone, an estimated $100 billion was spent acquiring the spectrum to allow 3G. These companies must re-deploy these significant resources to build-out their 3G-capable network, while maintaining their existing networks. In addition, the customers of these companies must purchase new handsets because their existing phones will not function on the new 3G-capable networks.

  □ The options that wireless carriers face today can be traced back to an option that faced the companies years ago. As stated earlier, a real option existed between CDMA, TDMA, and GSM for wireless technologies that the industry is just now getting better visibility on. The decisions made then have consequences today and in the future for the viability of these companies' 3G offerings.

- **Leveraging Local Assets Using New Market Penetration and Change Technology Options.** Incumbent local exchange carriers (ILEC) are in a unique competitive position and therefore can use a new market penetration option analysis when valuing expenditures on their existing local infrastructure. This can be used to offer long-distance service with minimal infrastructure upgrade to allow the ILECs to enter new markets as well as to offer new technologies like high speed data, video, and the Internet to existing local customers.

  □ The change of technology option is one that is facing or will be facing all major ILECs. The existing circuit-switched network is not efficient enough to handle the increasing amount of traffic from both data and voice. Carriers built their networks to handle peak voice traffic during the business day, but in actuality the peak times of the network now occur during the evening because of Internet and data use. The change to a packet-based data network is an option that local carriers are facing today. The change to packet technology will create a much more efficient network that will handle both the increasing voice and data traffic. This change technology option to a packet-based network also enables more options in the future by opening the possibility of creating new markets and products that cannot exist on the old circuit-based network.

- **Infrastructure Build-Out (Expand versus Contract Options).** The expand/contract option is gaining more and more validity in the current telecom environment. Network build-out is a capital-intensive requirement that has forced many carriers to leverage their balance sheets with a large amount of debt. However, demand for telecommunications services has not kept up with supply, resulting in excess fiber capacity. Depending on the location and availability of excess capacity, it may be cheaper for a telco to lease existing capacity from another telco than to build out its own network. In addition, due to the strained finances of some carriers, this capacity may be acquired at prices that offer a considerable discount to any unilateral build-out scenario.

Traditional Valuation Approaches

INTRODUCTION

This chapter begins with an introduction to traditional analysis, namely, the discounted cash flow model. It showcases some of the limitations and shortcomings through several examples. Specifically, traditional approaches underestimate the value of a project by ignoring the value of its flexibility. Some of these limitations are addressed in greater detail, and potential approaches to correct these shortcomings are also addressed. Further improvements in the areas of more advanced analytics are discussed, including the potential use of Monte Carlo simulation, real options analysis, and portfolio resource optimization.

THE TRADITIONAL VIEWS

Value is defined as the single time-value discounted number that is representative of all future net profitability. In retrospect, the market price of an asset may or may not be identical to its value. (Assets, projects, and strategies are used interchangeably.) For instance, when an asset is sold at a significant bargain, its price may be somewhat lower than its value, and one would surmise that the purchaser has obtained a significant amount of value. The idea of valuation in creating a fair market value is to determine the price that closely resembles the true value of an asset. This true value comes from the physical aspects of the asset as well as the non-physical, intrinsic, or intangible aspect of the asset. Both aspects have the capabilities of generating extrinsic monetary or intrinsic strategic value. Traditionally, there are three mainstream approaches to valuation, namely, the market approach, the income approach, and the cost approach.

Market Approach. The market approach looks at comparable assets in the marketplace and their corresponding prices and assumes that market forces will tend to move the market price to an equilibrium level. It is further assumed that the market price is also the fair market value, after adjusting for transaction costs and risk differentials. Sometimes a market-, industry-, or firm-specific adjustment is warranted, to bring the comparables closer to the operating structure of the firm whose asset is being valued. These approaches could include common-sizing the comparable firms, performing quantitative screening using criteria that closely resemble the firm's industry, operations, size, revenues, functions, profitability levels, operational efficiency, competition, market, and risks.

Income Approach.   The income approach looks at the future potential profit or free-cash-flow-generating potential of the asset and attempts to quantify, forecast, and discount these net free cash flows to a present value. The cost of implementation, acquisition, and development of the asset is then deducted from this present value of cash flows to generate a net present value. Often, the cash flow stream is discounted at a firm-specified hurdle rate, at the weighted average cost of capital, or at a risk-adjusted discount rate based on the perceived project-specific risk, historical firm risk, or overall business risk.

> *The three approaches to valuation include the market approach, income approach, and cost approach.*

Cost Approach.   The cost approach looks at the cost a firm would incur if it were to replace or reproduce the asset's future profitability potential, including the cost of its strategic intangibles if the asset were to be created from the ground up. Although the financial theories underlying this approach are sound in the more traditional deterministic view, they cannot reasonably be used in isolation when analyzing the true strategic flexibility value of a firm, project, or asset.

Other Approaches.   Other approaches used in valuation, more appropriately applied to the valuation of intangibles, rely on quantifying the economic viability and economic gains the asset brings to the firm. There are several well-known methodologies to intangible-asset valuation, particularly in valuing trademarks and brand names. These methodologies apply the combination of the market, income, and cost approaches described above.

The first method compares pricing strategies and assumes that by having some dominant market position by virtue of a strong trademark or brand recognition—for instance, Coca-Cola—the firm can charge a premium price for its product. Hence, if we can find market comparables producing similar products, in similar markets, performing similar functions, facing similar market uncertainties and risks, the price differential would then pertain exclusively to the brand name. These comparables are generally adjusted to account for the different conditions under which the firms operate. This price premium per unit is then multiplied by the projected quantity of sales, and the outcome after performing a discounted cash flow analysis will be the residual profits allocated to the intangible. A similar argument can be set forth in using operating profit margin in lieu of price per unit. Operating profit before taxes is used instead of net profit after taxes because it avoids the problems of comparables having different capital structure policies or carry-forward net operating losses and other tax-shield implications.

Another method uses a common-size analysis of the profit and loss statements between the firm holding the asset and market comparables. This takes into account any advantage from economies of scale and economies of scope. The idea here is to convert the income statement items as a percentage of sales, and balance sheet items as a percentage of total assets. In addition, in order to increase comparability, the ratio of operating profit to sales of the comparable firm is then multiplied by the asset-holding firm's projected revenue structure, thereby eliminating the potential problem of having to account for differences in economies of scale and scope. This approach uses a percentage of sales, return on investment, or return on asset ratio as the common-size variable.

PRACTICAL ISSUES USING TRADITIONAL VALUATION METHODOLOGIES

The traditional valuation methodology relying on a discounted cash flow series does not get at some of the intrinsic attributes of the asset or investment opportunity. Traditional methods assume that the investment is an all-or-nothing strategy and do not account for managerial flexibility that exists such that management can alter the course of an investment over time when certain aspects of the project's uncertainty become known. One of the value-added components of using real options is that it takes into account management's ability to create, execute, and abandon strategic and flexible options.

There are several potential problem areas in using a traditional discounted cash flow calculation on strategic optionalities. These problems include undervaluing an asset that currently produces little or no cash flow, the nonconstant nature of the weighted average cost of capital discount rate through time, the estimation of an asset's economic life, forecast errors in creating the future cash flows, and insufficient tests for plausibility of the final results. Real options when applied using an options theoretical framework can mitigate some of these problematic areas. Otherwise, financial profit level metrics like net present value (NPV), or internal rate of return (IRR), will be skewed and not provide a comprehensive view of the entire investment value. However, the discounted cash flow model does have its merits:

Discounted Cash Flow Advantages

- Clear, consistent decision criteria for all projects.
- Same results regardless of risk preferences of investors.
- Quantitative, decent level of precision, and economically rational.
- Not as vulnerable to accounting conventions (depreciation, inventory valuation, etc.).
- Factors in the time value of money and risk structures.
- Relatively simple, widely taught, widely accepted.
- Simple to explain to management: "If benefits outweigh the costs, do it!"

In reality, there are several issues that an analyst should be aware of prior to using discounted cash flow models, as shown in Table 2.1. The most important aspects include the business reality that risks and uncertainty abound when decisions have to be made and that management has the strategic flexibility to make and change decisions as these uncertainties become known over time. In such a stochastic world, using deterministic models like the discounted cash flow may potentially grossly underestimate the value of a particular project. A deterministic discounted cash flow model assumes at the outset that all future outcomes are fixed. If this is the case, then the discounted cash flow model is correctly specified as there would be no fluctuations in business conditions that would change the value of a particular project. In essence, there would be no value in flexibility. However, the actual business environment is highly fluid, and if management has the flexibility to make appropriate changes when conditions differ, then there is indeed value in flexibility, a value that will be grossly underestimated using a discounted cash flow model.

Figure 2.1 shows a simple example of applying discounted cash flow analysis. Assume that there is a project that costs $1,000 to implement at Year 0 that will bring in the following projected positive cash flows in the subsequent five years: $500, $600, $700, $800, and $900. These projected values are simply subjective best-guess forecasts on the part of the analyst. As can be seen in Figure 2.1, the timeline shows all the pertinent cash flows and their respective discounted present values. Assuming that the analyst decides that the project should be discounted at a 20 percent risk-adjusted discount rate using a weighted average cost of capital (WACC), we calculate the NPV to be $985.92 and a corresponding IRR of 54.97 percent.[1] Furthermore, the analyst assumes that the project will have an infinite economic

TABLE 2.1 Disadvantages of DCF: Assumptions versus Realities

DCF Assumptions	Realities
Decisions are made now, and cash flow streams are fixed for the future.	Uncertainty and variability in future outcomes. Not all decisions are made today, as some may be deferred to the future, when uncertainty becomes resolved.
Projects are "mini firms," and they are interchangeable with whole firms.	With the inclusion of network effects, diversification, interdependencies, and synergy, firms are portfolios of projects and their resulting cash flows. Sometimes projects cannot be evaluated as stand-alone cash flows.
Once launched, all projects are passively managed.	Projects are usually actively managed through project life cycle, including checkpoints, decision options, budget constraints, and so forth.
Future free cash flow streams are all highly predictable and deterministic.	It may be difficult to estimate future cash flows as they are usually stochastic and risky in nature.
Project discount rate used is the opportunity cost of capital, which is proportional to non-diversifiable risk.	There are multiple sources of business risks with different characteristics, and some are diversifiable across projects or time.
All risks are completely accounted for by the discount rate.	Firm and project risk can change during the course of a project.
All factors that could affect the outcome of the project and value to the investors are reflected in the DCF model through the NPV or IRR.	Because of project complexity and so-called externalities, it may be difficult or impossible to quantify all factors in terms of incremental cash flows. Distributed, unplanned outcomes (e.g., strategic vision and entrepreneurial activity) can be significant and strategically important.
Unknown, intangible, or immeasurable factors are valued at zero.	Many of the important benefits are intangible assets or qualitative strategic positions.

life and assumes a long-term growth rate of cash flows of 5 percent. Using the Gordon constant growth model, the analyst calculates the terminal value of the project's cash flow at Year 5 to be $6,300. Discounting this figure for five years at the risk-adjusted discount rate and adding it to the original NPV yields a total NPV with terminal value of $3,517.75.

The calculations can all be seen in Figure 2.1, where we further define *w* as the weights, *d* for debt, *ce* for common equity, and *ps* for preferred stocks, FCF as the free cash flows, *tax* as the corporate tax rate, *g* as the long-term growth rate of cash flows, and *rf* as the risk-free rate.

Even with a simplistic discounted cash flow model like this, we can see the many shortcomings of using a discounted cash flow model that are worthy of mention. Figure 2.2 lists some of the more noteworthy issues. For instance, the NPV is calculated as the present value of future net free cash flows (benefits) less the present value of implementation costs (investment costs). However, in many instances, analysts tend to discount both benefits and investment costs at a single identical market risk-adjusted discount rate, usually the WACC. This, of course, is flawed.

The benefits should be discounted at a market risk-adjusted discount rate like the WACC, but the investment cost should be discounted at a reinvestment rate similar to the risk-free rate. Cash flows that have market risks should be discounted at the market risk-adjusted rate, while cash flows that have private risks should be discounted at the risk-free rate. This is because the market will only compensate the firm for taking on the market risks but not private risks. It is usually assumed that the benefits are subject to market risks (because benefit free cash flows depend on market demand, market prices, and other exogenous market factors), while investment costs depend on internal private risks (such as the firm's ability to complete building a project in a timely fashion or the costs and inefficiencies incurred beyond what is projected). On occasion, these implementation costs may

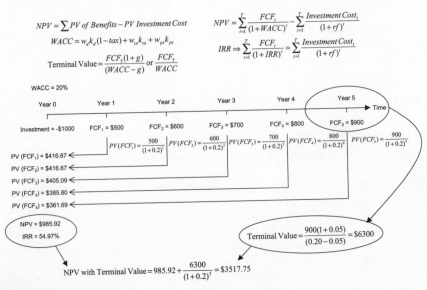

$$NPV = \sum PV \text{ of Benefits} - PV \text{ Investment Cost}$$

$$WACC = w_d k_d (1 - tax) + w_{ce} k_{ce} + w_{ps} k_{ps}$$

$$\text{Terminal Value} = \frac{FCF_5(1+g)}{(WACC-g)} \text{ or } \frac{FCF_5}{WACC}$$

$$NPV = \sum_{t=1}^{T} \frac{FCF_t}{(1+WACC)^t} - \sum_{t=1}^{T} \frac{Investment\,Cost_t}{(1+rf)^t}$$

$$IRR \Rightarrow \sum_{t=1}^{T} \frac{FCF_t}{(1+IRR)^t} = \sum_{t=1}^{T} \frac{Investment\,Cost_t}{(1+rf)^t}$$

WACC = 20%

Investment = -$1000

FCF$_1$ = $500 FCF$_2$ = $600 FCF$_3$ = $700 FCF$_4$ = $800 FCF$_5$ = $900

$$PV(FCF_1) = \frac{500}{(1+0.2)^1}$$ $$PV(FCF_2) = \frac{600}{(1+0.2)^2}$$ $$PV(FCF_3) = \frac{700}{(1+0.2)^3}$$ $$PV(FCF_4) = \frac{800}{(1+0.2)^4}$$ $$PV(FCF_5) = \frac{900}{(1+0.2)^5}$$

PV (FCF$_1$) = $416.67
PV (FCF$_2$) = $416.67
PV (FCF$_3$) = $405.09
PV (FCF$_4$) = $385.80
PV (FCF$_5$) = $361.69

NPV = $985.92
IRR = 54.97%

$$\text{Terminal Value} = \frac{900(1+0.05)}{(0.20-0.05)} = \$6300$$

$$NPV \text{ with Terminal Value} = 985.92 + \frac{6300}{(1+0.2)^5} = \$3517.75$$

FIGURE 2.1 Applying Discounted Cash Flow Analysis

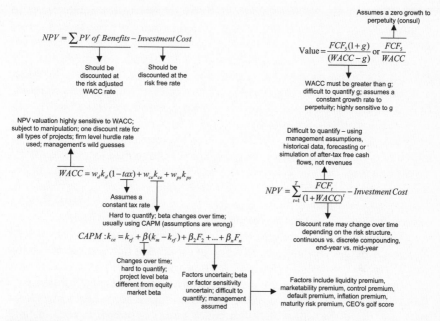

FIGURE 2.2 Shortcomings of Discounted Cash Flow Analysis

also be discounted at a rate slightly higher than a risk-free rate, such as a money-market rate or at the opportunity cost of being able to invest the sum in another project yielding a particular interest rate. Suffice it to say that benefits and investment costs should be discounted at different rates if they are subject to different risks. Otherwise, discounting the costs at a much higher market risk-adjusted rate will reduce the costs significantly, making the project look as though it were more valuable than it actually is.

> *Variables with market risks should be discounted at a market risk-adjusted rate, which is higher than the risk-free rate, which is used to discount variables with private risks.*

The discount rate that is used is usually calculated from a WACC, capital asset-pricing model (CAPM), multifactor asset-pricing model (MAPT), or arbitrage pricing theory (APT), set by management as a requirement for the firm, or as a hurdle rate for specific projects.[2] In most circumstances, if we were to perform a simple discounted cash flow model, the most sensitive variable is usually the discount rate. The discount rate is also the most difficult variable to correctly quantify. Hence, this leaves the discount rate open to potential abuse and subjective manipulation. A target NPV value can be obtained by simply massaging the discount rate to a suitable level. In addition, certain input assumptions required to calculate the discount rate are also subject to question. For instance, in the WACC, the input for cost of common equity is usually derived using some form of the CAPM. In the CAPM, the infamous beta (β) is extremely difficult to calculate. In financial assets, we can obtain beta through a calculation of the covariance between a firm's stock prices and the market portfolio, divided by the variance of the market portfolio. Beta is then a sensitivity factor measuring the co-movements of a firm's equity prices with respect to the market. The problem is that equity prices change every few minutes! Depending on the time frame used for the calculation, beta may fluctuate wildly. In addition, for non-traded physical assets, we cannot reasonably calculate beta this way. Using a firm's tradable financial assets' beta as a proxy for the beta on a project within a firm that has many other projects is ill-advised.

There are risk and return diversification effects among projects as well as investor psychology and overreaction in the market that are not accounted for. There are also other more robust asset-pricing models that can be used to estimate a project's discount rate, but they require great care. For instance, the APT models are built upon the CAPM and have additional risk factors that may drive the value of the discount rate. These risk factors include maturity risk, default risk, inflation risk, country risk, size risk, nonmarketable risk, control risk, minority shareholder risk, and others. Even the firm's CEO's golf score can be a risk hazard (e.g., rash decisions may be made after a bad game or bad projects may be approved after a hole-in-one, believing in a lucky streak.) The issue arises when one has to decide which risks to include and which not to include. This is definitely a difficult task, to say the least.[3]

One other method that is widely used is that of comparability analysis. By gathering publicly available data on the trading of financial assets by stripped-down entities with similar functions, markets, risks and geographical location, analysts can then estimate the beta (a measure of systematic risk) or even a relevant discount rate from these comparable firms.

> *The methods to find a relevant discount rate include using a WACC, CAPM, APT, MAPT, comparability analysis, management assumptions, and a firm- or project-specific hurdle rate.*

For instance, an analyst who is trying to gather information on a research and development effort for a particular type of drug can conceivably gather market data on pharmaceutical firms performing only research and development on similar drugs, existing in the same market, and having the same risks. The median or average beta value can then be used as a market proxy for the project currently under evaluation. Obviously, there is no silver bullet, but if an analyst were diligent enough, he or she could obtain estimates from these different sources and create a better estimate. Monte Carlo simulation is most preferred in situations like these.[4] The analyst can define the relevant simulation inputs using the range obtained from the comparable firms and simulate the discounted cash flow model to obtain the range of relevant variables (typically the NPV or IRR).

Now that you have the relevant discount rate, the free cash flow stream should then be discounted appropriately. Herein lies another problem: forecasting the relevant free cash flows and deciding if they should be discounted on a continuous basis or a discrete basis, versus using end-of-year or mid-year conventions. Free cash flows should be net of taxes, with the relevant noncash expenses added back.[5] Because free cash flows are generally calculated starting with revenues and proceeding through direct cost of goods sold, operating expenses, depreciation expenses, interest payments, taxes, and so forth, there is certainly room for mistakes to compound over time.

Forecasting cash flows several years into the future is oftentimes very difficult and may require the use of fancy econometric regression modeling techniques, time-series analysis, management hunches, and experience. A recommended method is not to create single-point estimates of cash flows at certain time periods but to use Monte Carlo simulation and assess the relevant probabilities of cash flow events. In addition, because cash flows in the distant future are certainly riskier than in the near future, the relevant discount rate should also change to reflect this. Instead of using a single discount rate for all future cash flow events, the discount rate should incorporate the changing risk structure of cash flows over time. This can be done by either weighing the cash flow streams' probabilistic risks (standard deviations of forecast distributions) or using a stepwise technique of adding the maturity risk premium inherent in U.S. Treasury securities at different maturity periods. This bootstrapping approach allows the analyst to incorporate what the market experts predict the future market risk structure looks like.

Finally, the issue of terminal value is of major concern for anyone using a discounted cash flow model. Several methods of calculating terminal values exist, such as the Gordon constant growth model (GGM), zero growth perpetuity consul, and the supernormal growth models. The GGM is the most widely used, where at the end of a series of forecast cash flows, the GGM assumes that cash flow growth will be constant through perpetuity. The GGM is calculated as the free cash flow at the end of the forecast period multiplied by a relative growth rate, divided by the discount rate less the long-term growth rate. Shown in Figure 2.2, we see that the GGM breaks down when the long-term growth rate exceeds the discount rate. This growth rate is also assumed to be fixed, and the entire terminal value is highly sensitive to this growth rate assumption. In the end, the value calculated is highly suspect because a small difference in growth rates will mean a significant fluctuation in value. Perhaps a better method is to assume some type of growth curve in the free cash flow series. These growth curves can be obtained through some basic time-series analysis as well as using more advanced assumptions in stochastic modeling. Nonetheless, we see that even a well-known, generally accepted and applied discounted cash flow model has significant analytical restrictions and problems. These problems are rather significant and can compound over time, creating misleading results. Great care should be given in performing such analyses. Later chapters introduce the concepts of Monte Carlo simulation, real options, and portfolio optimization. These new analytical methods address some of the issues discussed above. However, it should be stressed that these new analytics do not provide the silver bullet for valuation and decision-making. They provide value-added insights, and the magnitude of insights and value obtained from these new methods depend solely on the type and characteristic of the project under evaluation.

The applicability of traditional analysis versus the new analytics across a time horizon is depicted in Figure 2.3. During the shorter time period,

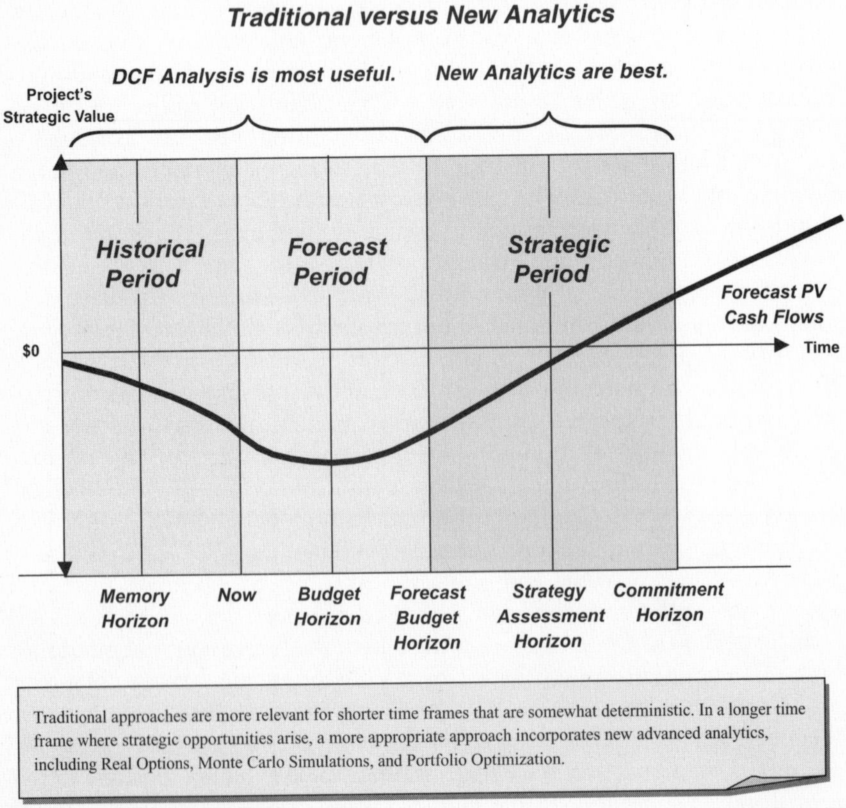

Traditional versus New Analytics

Traditional approaches are more relevant for shorter time frames that are somewhat deterministic. In a longer time frame where strategic opportunities arise, a more appropriate approach incorporates new advanced analytics, including Real Options, Monte Carlo Simulations, and Portfolio Optimization.

FIGURE 2.3 Using the Appropriate Analysis

holding everything else constant, the ability for the analyst to predict the near future is greater than when the period extends beyond the historical and forecast periods. This is because the longer the horizon, the harder it is to fully predict all the unknowns, and hence, management can create value by being able to successfully initiate and execute strategic options.

The traditional and new analytics can also be viewed as a matrix of approaches as seen in Figure 2.4, where the analytics are segregated by its analytical perspective and type. With regard to perspective, the analytical approach can be either a top-down or a bottom-up approach. A top-down approach implies a higher focus on macro variables than on micro variables. The level of granularity from the macro to micro levels include starting from the global perspective, and working through market or economic conditions, impact on a specific industry, and more specifically, the firm's competitive options. At the firm level, the analyst may be concerned with a single project and the portfolio of projects from a risk management perspective. At the project level, detail focus will be on the variables impacting the value of the project.

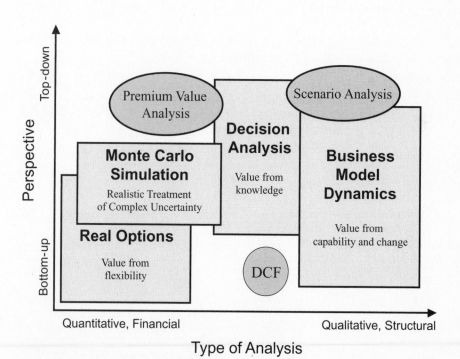

FIGURE 2.4 An Analytical Perspective

SUMMARY

Traditional analyses like the discounted cash flow are fraught with problems. They underestimate the flexibility value of a project and assume that all outcomes are static and all decisions made are irrevocable. In reality, business decisions are made in a highly fluid environment where uncertainties abound and management is always vigilant in making changes in decisions when the circumstances require a change. To value such decisions in a deterministic view may potentially grossly underestimate the true intrinsic value of a project. New sets of rules and methodology are required in light of these new managerial flexibilities. It should be emphasized that real options analysis builds upon traditional discounted cash flow analysis, providing value-added insights to decision-making. In later chapters, it will be shown that discounted cash flow analysis is a special case of real options analysis when there is no uncertainty in the project.

CHAPTER 2 QUESTIONS

1. What are the three traditional approaches to valuation?
2. Why should benefits and costs be discounted at two separate discount rates?
3. Is the following statement true? Why or why not? "The value of a firm is simply the sum of all its individual projects."
4. What are some of the assumptions in order for the CAPM to work?
5. Using the discrete and continuous discounting conventions explained in Appendix 2A, and assuming a 20 percent discount rate, calculate the net present value of the following cash flows:

Year	2002	2003	2004	2005	2006	2007
Revenues		$100	$200	$300	$400	$500
Operating Expenses		$ 10	$ 20	$ 30	$ 40	$ 50
Net Income		$ 90	$180	$270	$360	$450
Investment Costs	($450)					
Free Cash Flow	($450)	$ 90	$180	$270	$360	$450

Financial Statement Analysis

This appendix provides some basic financial statement analysis concepts used in applying real options. The focus is on calculating the free cash flows used under different scenarios, including making appropriate adjustments under levered and unlevered operating conditions. Although many versions of free cash flows exist, these calculations are examples of more generic free cash flows applicable under most circumstances. An adjustment for inflation and the calculation of terminal cash flows are also presented here. Finally, a market multiple approach that uses price-to-earnings ratios is also briefly discussed.

FREE CASH FLOW CALCULATIONS

Below is a list of some generic financial statement definitions used to generate free cash flows based on GAAP (Generally Accepted Accounting Principles):

- Gross Profits = Revenues − Cost of Goods Sold.
- Earnings Before Interest and Taxes = Gross Profits − Selling Expenses − General and Administrative Costs − Depreciation − Amortization.
- Earnings Before Taxes = Earnings Before Interest and Taxes − Interest.
- Net Income = Earnings Before Taxes − Taxes.
- Free Cash Flow = Net Income + Depreciation + Amortization − Capital Expenditures ± Change in Net Working Capital − Principal Repayments + New Debt Proceeds − Preferred Debt Dividends.

FREE CASH FLOW TO A FIRM

An alternative version of the free cash flow for an unlevered firm can be defined as:

- Free Cash Flow = Earnings Before Interest and Taxes [1 − Effective Tax Rate] + Depreciation + Amortization − Capital Expenditures ± Change in Net Working Capital.

LEVERED FREE CASH FLOW

For a levered firm, the free cash flow becomes:

- Free Cash Flow = Net Income + α [Depreciation + Amortization] $\pm \alpha$ [Change in Net Working Capital] $- \alpha$ [Capital Expenditures] $-$ Principal Repayments + New Debt Proceeds $-$ Preferred Debt Dividends

where

α is the equity-to-total-capital ratio; and

$(1 - \alpha)$ is the debt ratio.

INFLATION ADJUSTMENT

The adjustments below show an inflationary adjustment for free cash flows and discount rates from nominal to real conditions:

- $$\text{Real } CF = \frac{\text{Nominal } CF}{(1 + E[\pi])}$$

- $$\text{Real } \rho = \frac{1 + \text{Nominal } \rho}{(1 + E[\pi])} - 1$$

where

CF is the cash flow series;

π is the inflation rate;

$E[\pi]$ is the expected inflation rate; and

ρ is the discount rate.

TERMINAL VALUE

The following are commonly accepted ways of getting terminal free cash flows under zero growth, constant growth, and supernormal growth assumptions:

- Zero Growth Perpetuity:

$$\sum_{t=1}^{\infty} \frac{FCF_t}{[1 + WACC]^t} = \frac{FCF_T}{WACC}$$

- Constant Growth:

$$\sum_{t=1}^{\infty} \frac{FCF_{t-1}(1 + g_t)}{[1 + WACC]^t} = \frac{FCF_{T-1}(1 + g_T)}{WACC - g_T} = \frac{FCF_T}{WACC - g_T}$$

■ Punctuated Growth:

$$\sum_{t=1}^{N} \frac{FCF_t}{[1 + WACC]^t} + \frac{\left[\dfrac{FCF_N(1 + g_N)}{[WACC - g_N]}\right]}{[1 + WACC]^N}$$

$$WACC = \omega_e k_e + \omega_d k_d (1 - \tau) + \omega_{pe} k_{pe}$$

where

FCF	is the free cash flow series;
$WACC$	is the weighted average cost of capital;
g	is the growth rate of free cash flows;
t	is the individual time periods;
T	is the terminal time at which a forecast is available;
N	is the time when a punctuated growth rate occurs;
ω	is the respective weights on each capital component;
k_e	is the cost of common equity;
k_d	is the cost of debt;
k_{pe}	is the cost of preferred equity; and
τ	is the effective tax rate.

PRICE-TO-EARNINGS MULTIPLES APPROACH

Related concepts in valuation are the uses of market multiples. An example is using the price-to-earnings multiple, which is a simple derivation of the constant growth model shown above, breaking it down into dividends per share (*DPS*) and earnings per share (*EPS*) components.

The derivation starts with the constant growth model:

$$P_0 = \frac{DPS_0(1 + g_n)}{k_e - g_n} = \frac{DPS_1}{k_e - g_n}$$

We then use the fact that the dividend per share next period (DPS_1) is the earnings per share current period multiplied by the payout ratio (*PR*), defined as the ratio of dividends per share to earnings per share, which is assumed to be constant, multiplied by one plus the growth rate $(1 + g)$ of earnings:

$$DPS_1 = EPS_0[PR](1 + g_n)$$

Similarly, the earnings per share the following period is the same as the earnings per share this period multiplied by one plus the growth rate:

$$EPS_1 = EPS_0(1 + g_n)$$

Substituting the earnings per share model for the dividends per share in the constant growth model, we get the pricing relationship:

$$P_0 = \frac{EPS_0[PR](1 + g_n)}{k_e - g_n}$$

Because we are using price-to-earnings ratios, we can divide the pricing relationship by earnings per share to obtain an approximation of the price-to-earnings ratio (PE):

$$\frac{P_0}{EPS_1} = \frac{[PR](1 + g_n)}{k_e - g_n} \approx PE_1$$

Assuming that the PE and EPS ratios are fairly stable over time, we can estimate the current pricing structure through forecasting the next term EPS we obtain:

$$P_0 = \tilde{EPS}_1[PE_1]$$

Issues of using PE ratios include the fact that PE ratios change across different markets. If a firm serves multiple markets, it is difficult to find an adequate weighted average PE ratio. PE ratios may not be stable through time and are most certainly not stable across firms. If more efficient firms are added to less efficiently run firms, the average PE ratio may be skewed. In addition, market overreaction and speculation, particularly among high-growth firms, provide an overinflated PE ratio. Furthermore, not all firms are publicly held, some firms may not have a PE ratio and if valuation of individual projects is required, PE ratios may not be adequate because it is difficult to isolate a specific investment's profitability and its corresponding PE ratio. Similar approaches include using other proxy multiples, including Business Enterprise Value to Earnings, Price to Book, Price to Sales, and so forth, with similar methods and applications.

DISCOUNTING CONVENTIONS

In using discounted cash flow analysis, there are several conventions that require consideration: continuous versus discrete discounting, mid-year versus end-of-year convention, and beginning versus end-of-period discounting.

Continuous versus Discrete Periodic Discounting

The discounting convention is important when performing a discounted cash flow analysis. Using the same compounding period principle, future cash flows can be discounted using the effective annualized discount rate. For instance, suppose an annualized discount rate of 30 percent is used on a $100 cash flow. Depending on the compounding periodicity, the calculated present value and future value differ (see Table 2A.1).

TABLE 2A.1 Continuous versus Periodic Discrete Discounting

Periodicity	Periods/Year	Interest Factor	Future Value	Present Value
Annual	1	30.00%	$130.00	$76.92
Quarterly	4	33.55%	$133.55	$74.88
Monthly	12	34.49%	$134.49	$74.36
Daily	365	34.97%	$134.97	$74.09
Continuous	∞	34.99%	$134.99	$74.08

To illustrate this point further, a $100 deposit in a 30 percent interest-bearing account will yield $130 at the end of one year if the interest compounds once a year. However, if interest is compounded quarterly, the deposit value increases to $133.55 due to the additional interest-on-interest compounding effects. For instance,

Value at the end of the first quarter = $100.00(1 + 0.30/4)^1 = $107.50

Value at the end of the second quarter = $107.50(1 + 0.30/4)^1 = $115.56

Value at the end of the third quarter = $115.56(1 + 0.30/4)^1 = $124.23

Value at the end of the fourth quarter = $124.23(1 + 0.30/4)^1 = $133.55

That is, the annualized discount rate for different compounding periods is its effective annualized rate, calculated as

$$\left(1 + \frac{discount}{periods}\right)^{periods} - 1.$$

For the quarterly compounding interest rate, the effective annualized rate is

$$\left(1 + \frac{30.00\%}{4}\right)^4 - 1 = 33.55\%.$$

Applying this rate for the year, we have $100(1 + 0.3355) = $133.55.

This analysis can be extended for monthly, daily, or any other periodicities. In addition, if the interest rate is assumed to be continuously compounding, the continuous effective annualized rate should be used, where

$$\lim_{periods \to \infty} \left(1 + \frac{discount}{periods}\right)^{periods} - 1 = e^{discount} - 1.$$

For instance, the 30 percent interest rate compounded continuously yields $e^{0.3} - 1 = 34.99\%$. Notice that as the number of compounding periods increases, the effective interest rate increases until it approaches the limit of continuous compounding.

The annual, quarterly, monthly, and daily compounding is termed discrete periodic compounding, as compared to the continuous compounding approach using the exponential function. In summary, the higher the number of compounding periods, the higher the future value and the lower the present value of a cash flow payment. When applied to discounted cash flow analysis, if the discount rate calculated using a weighted average cost of capital is continuously compounding (e.g., interest payments and cost of capital are continuously compounding), then the net present value calculated may be overoptimistic if discounted discretely.

Full-Year versus Mid-Year Convention

In the conventional discounted cash flow approach, cash flows occurring in the future are discounted back to the present value and summed, to obtain the net present value of a project. These cash flows are usually attached to a particular period in the future, measured usually in years, quarters, or months. The time line in Figure 2A.1 illustrates a sample series of cash flows over the next five years, with an assumed 20 percent discount rate. Because the cash flows are attached to an annual time line, they are usually assumed to occur at the end of each year. That is, $500 will be recognized at the end of the first full year, $600 at the end of the second year, and so forth. This is termed the full-year discounting convention.

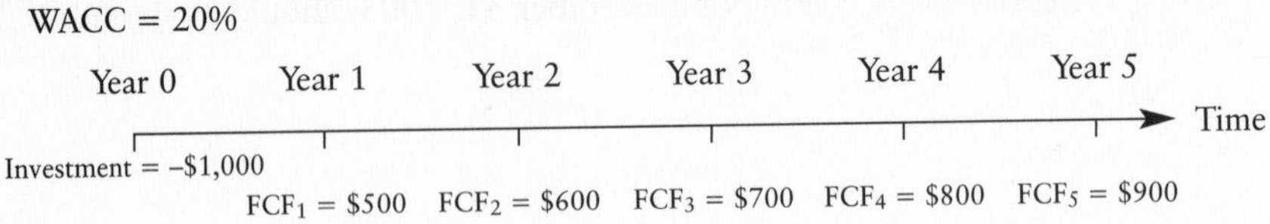

WACC = 20%

| Year 0 | Year 1 | Year 2 | Year 3 | Year 4 | Year 5 | Time |

Investment = –$1,000

$FCF_1 = \$500 \quad FCF_2 = \$600 \quad FCF_3 = \$700 \quad FCF_4 = \$800 \quad FCF_5 = \$900$

$$NPV = -\$1,000 + \frac{\$500}{(1+0.2)^1} + \frac{\$600}{(1+0.2)^2} + \frac{\$700}{(1+0.2)^3} + \frac{\$800}{(1+0.2)^4} + \frac{\$900}{(1+0.2)^5} = \$985$$

FIGURE 2A.1 Full-Year versus Mid-Year Discounting

However, under usual business conditions, cash flows tend to accrue throughout the entire year and do not arrive in a single lump sum at the end of the year. Instead, the mid-year convention may be applied. That is, the $500 cash flow gets accrued over the entire first year and should be discounted at 0.5 years, rather than 1.0 years. Using this midpoint supposes that the $500 cash flow comes in equally over the entire year.

$$NPV = -\$1,000 + \frac{\$500}{(1+0.2)^{0.5}} + \frac{\$600}{(1+0.2)^{1.5}} + \frac{\$700}{(1+0.2)^{2.5}} + \frac{\$800}{(1+0.2)^{3.5}} + \frac{\$900}{(1+0.2)^{4.5}} = \$1,175$$

End-of-Period versus Beginning-of-Period Discounting

Another key issue in discounting involves the use of end-of-period versus beginning-of-period discounting. Suppose the cash flow series are generated on a time line such as in Figure 2A.2:

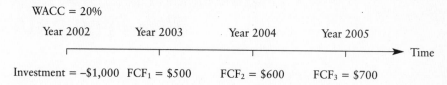

FIGURE 2A.2 End-of-Period versus Beginning-of-Period Discounting

Further suppose that the valuation date is January 1, 2002. The $500 cash flow can occur either at the beginning of the first year (January 1, 2003) or at the end of the first year (December 31, 2003). The former requires the discounting of one year and the latter, the discounting of two years. If the cash flows are assumed to roll in equally over the year—that is, from January 1, 2002, to January 1, 2003—the discounting should only be for 0.5 years.

In retrospect, suppose that the valuation date is December 31, 2002, and the cash flow series occurs at January 1, 2003, or December 31, 2003. The former requires no discounting, while the latter requires a one-year discounting using an end-of-year discounting convention. In the mid-year convention, the cash flow occurring on December 31, 2003, should be discounted at 0.5 years.

Discount Rate versus Risk-Free Rate

Generally, the weighted average cost of capital (WACC) would be used as the discount rate for the cash flow series. The only mitigating circumstance is when the firm wishes to use a hurdle rate that exceeds the WACC to compensate for the additional uncertainty, risks, and opportunity costs the firm believes it will face by investing in a particular project. As we will see, the use of a WACC is problematic, and in the real options world, the input is instead a U.S. Treasury spot rate of return with its maturity corresponding to the economic life of the project under scrutiny.

In general, the WACC is the weighted average of the cost components of issuing debt, preferred stock, and common equity: $WACC = \omega_d k_d (1 - \tau)$ $+ \omega_p k_p + \omega_e k_e$, where ω are the respective weights, τ is the corporate effective tax rate, and k are the costs corresponding to debt[1] d, preferred stocks[2] p, and common equity[3] e.

However, multiple other factors affect the cost of capital that need to be considered, including:

1. The company's capital structure used to calculate the relevant WACC discount rate may be inadequate, because project-specific risks are usually not the same as the overall company's risk structure.

2. The current and future general interest rates in the economy may be higher or lower, thus bond coupon rates may change in order to raise the capital based on fluctuations in the general interest rate. Therefore, an interest-rate-bootstrapping methodology should be applied to infer the future spot interest rates using forward interest rates.

3. Tax law changes over time may affect the tax shield enjoyed by debt repayments. Furthermore, different tax jurisdictions in different countries have different tax law applications of tax shields.

4. The firm's capital structure policy may have specific long-term targets and weights that do not agree with the current structure, and the firm may find itself moving toward that optimal structure over time.

5. Payout versus retention rate policy may change the dividend policy and thereby change the projected dividend growth rate necessary to calculate the cost of equity.

6. Investment policy of the firm, including the minimum required return and risk profile.

7. Dynamic considerations in the economy and industry both ex post and ex ante.

8. Measurement problems on specific security cost structure.

9. Small business problems making it difficult to measure costs correctly.

10. Depreciation-generated funds and off-balance sheet items are generally not included in the calculations.

11. Geometric averages and not simple arithmetic averages should be used for intra-year WACC rates.[4]

12. Market value versus book value weightings[5] in calculating the WACC.

13. The capital asset-pricing model (CAPM) is flawed.

THE CAPM VERSUS THE MULTIFACTOR ASSET-PRICING MODEL

The CAPM model states that under some simplifying assumptions, the rate of return on any asset may be expected to be equal to the rate of return on a riskless asset plus a premium that is proportional to the asset's risk relative to the market. The CAPM is developed in a theoretical and hypothetical world with multiple assumptions[6] that do not hold true in reality, and therefore it is flawed by design.[7]

The alternative is to use a multifactor model that adequately captures the systematic risks experienced by the firm. In a separate article, the author used a nonparametric multifactor asset-pricing model and showed that the results are more robust. However, the details exceed the scope of this book.

Other researchers have tested the CAPM and found that a single factor, beta, does not sufficiently explain expected returns. Their empirical research finds support for the inclusion of both size (measured using market value) and leverage variables. The two leverage variables found to be significant were the book-to-market ratio and the price-to-earnings ratio. However, when used together, the book-to-market ratio and size variable absorb the effects of the price-to-earnings ratio. With empirical support that beta alone is insufficient to capture risk, their model relies on the addition of the natural logarithm of both the book-to-market ratio and the size of the firm's market equity as

$$E[R_{i,t}] - [R_{f,t}] = \beta_{i,t}(E[R_{m,t}] - R_{f,t}) + \delta_{i,t}\ln(BME_{i,t}) + \gamma_{i,t}\ln(ME_{i,t})$$

where $R_{i,t}$, $R_{m,t}$, and $R_{f,t}$ are the individual expected return for firm i, the expected market return, and the risk-free rate of return at time t, respectively. $BME_{i,t}$ and $ME_{i,t}$ are the book-to-market ratio and the size of the total market equity value for firm i at time t, respectively.

Other researchers have confirmed these findings, that a three-factor model better predicts expected returns than the single-factor CAPM. Their main conjecture is that asset-pricing is rational and conforms to a three-factor model that does not reduce to the standard single-factor CAPM. One of the major problems with the single-factor CAPM is that of determining a good proxy for the market, which should truly represent all traded securities. In addition, the expected return on the market proxy typically relies on ex-post returns and does not truly capture expectations. Therefore, the multifactor model is an attempt to recover the expected CAPM results without all the single-factor model shortcomings. A variation of the three-factor model is shown as

$$E[R_{i,t}] - [R_{f,t}] = \beta_{i,t}(E[R_{m,t}] - R_{f,t}) + \xi_{i,t}\ln(SMB_{i,t}) + \psi_{i,t}\ln(HML_{i,t})$$

where $SMB_{i,t}$ is the time-series of differences in average returns from the smallest and largest capitalization stocks. $HML_{i,t}$ is the time-series of differences in average returns from the highest to the lowest book-to-market ratios, after ranking the market portfolios into differing quartiles.

We can adapt this multifactor model to accommodate any market and any industry. The factors in the model above can be sector- or industry-specific. The macroeconomic variables used will have to be highly correlated to historical returns of the firm. If sufficient data are available, a multifactor regression model can be generated, and variables found to be statistically significant can then be used. Obviously, there is potential for abuse and misuse of the model.[8] If used correctly, the model will provide a wealth of information on the potential risks that the project or asset holds. However, in the end, the jury is still out on what constitutes a good discount rate model.

Real Options Analysis

INTRODUCTION

This chapter introduces the fundamental essence of real options, providing the reader several simplified but convincing examples of why a real options approach provides more insights than traditional valuation methodologies do. A lengthy but simplified example details the steps an analyst might go through in evaluating a project. The example expounds on the different decisions that will be made depending on which methodology is employed, and introduces the user to the idea of adding significant value to a project by looking at the different optionalities that exist, sometimes by even creating strategic optionalities within a project, thereby enhancing its overall value to the firm.

THE FUNDAMENTAL ESSENCE OF REAL OPTIONS

The use of traditional discounted cash flow alone is inappropriate in valuing certain strategic projects involving managerial flexibility. Two finance professors, Michael Brennan and Eduardo Schwartz, provided an example on valuing the rights to a gold mine. In their example, a mining company owns the rights to a local gold mine. The rights provide the firm the option, and not the legal obligation, to mine the gold reserves supposedly abundant in said mine. Therefore, if the price of gold in the market is high, the firm might wish to start mining and, in contrast, stop and wait for a later time to begin mining should the price of gold drop significantly in the market. Suppose we set the cost of mining as X and the payoff on the mined gold as S, taking into consideration the time value of money. We then have the following payoff schedule:

$$S - X \quad \text{if and only if} \quad S > X$$
$$0 \quad \text{if and only if} \quad S \leq X$$

This payoff is identical to the payoff on a call option on the underlying asset, the value of the mined gold. If the cost exceeds the value of the underlying asset, the option is left to expire worthless, without execution; otherwise, the option will be exercised. That is, mine if and only if S exceeds X; otherwise, do not mine.

As an extension of the gold mine scenario, say we have a proprietary technology in development or a patent that currently and in the near future carries little or no cash flow but nonetheless is highly valuable due to the potential strategic positioning it holds for the firm that owns it. A traditional discounted cash flow method will grossly underestimate the value of this asset. A real options approach is more suitable and provides better insights into the actual value of the asset. The firm has the option to either develop the technology if the potential payoff exceeds the cost or abandon its development should the opposite be true.

For instance, assume a firm owns a patent on some technology with a 10-year economic life. To develop the project, the present value of the total research and development costs is $250 million, but the present value of the projected sum of all future net cash flows is only $200 million. In a traditional discounted cash flow sense, the net present value will be −$50 million, and the project should be abandoned. However, the proprietary technology is still valuable to the firm given that there's a probability it will become more valuable in the future than projected or that future projects can benefit from the technology developed. If we apply real options to valuing this simplified technology example, the results will be significantly different. By assuming the nominal rate on a 10-year risk-free U.S. Treasury note is 6 percent and simulating the standard deviation of the projected cash flow, we calculate the value of the research and development initiative to be $2 million. This implies that the value of flexibility is $52 million or 26 percent of its static NPV value.[1] By definition, a research and development initiative involves creating something new and unique or developing a more enhanced product. The nature of most research and development initiatives is that they are highly risky and involve a significant investment up-front, with highly variable potential cash flows in the future that are generally skewed toward the low end. In other words, most research and development projects fail to meet expectations and generally produce lower incremental revenues than deemed profitable. Hence, in a traditional discounted cash flow sense, research and development initiatives are usually unattractive and provide little to no incentives. However, a cursory look at the current industry would imply otherwise. Research and development initiatives abound, implying that senior management sees significant intrinsic value in such initiatives. So there arises a need to quantify such strategic values.

THE BASICS OF REAL OPTIONS

Real options, as its name implies, use options theory to evaluate physical or real assets, as opposed to financial assets or stocks and bonds. In reality, real options have been in the past very useful in analyzing distressed firms and firms engaged in research and development with significant amounts of managerial flexibility under significant amounts of uncertainty. Only in the past decade has real options started to receive corporate attention in general.

A SIMPLIFIED EXAMPLE OF REAL OPTIONS IN ACTION

Suppose a client is currently researching and developing new pharmaceutical products, and the initial outlay required for initiating this endeavor is $100 million. The projected net revenues, using free cash flow as a proxy, resulting from this research and development effort brings about positive cash flows of $8 million, $12 million, $15 million, $12 million, $11 million, and $10 million for the first six years, starting next year. Furthermore, assume that there is a salvage value of $155 million in year six.[2] These cash flows result from routine business functions associated with the firm's research and development efforts (assuming the firm is a specialized firm engaged strictly in research and development). Panel A in Table 3.1 shows a simple discounted cash flow series resulting in a discounted net present value of $24.85 million using a given 12 percent market risk-adjusted weighted average cost of capital (WACC).

Assume that the research and development efforts are successful and that in three years, there is a potential to invest more funds to take the product to market. For instance, in the case of the pharmaceutical firm, suppose the first two to three years of research have paid off, and the firm is now ready to produce and mass-market the newly discovered drug. Panel B shows the series of cash flows relevant to this event, starting with an initial outlay of another $382 million in year three, which will in turn provide the positive free cash flows of $30 million, $43 million, and $53 million in years four through six. In addition, a terminal value of $454 is calculated using the Gordon constant growth model for the remaining cash flows based on economic life considerations. The net present value is calculated as –$24.99 million for this second phase. The total net present value for Panels A and B is therefore –$0.14 million, indicating that the project is not viable. Using this traditional net present value calculation underestimates the value of the research and development effort significantly.

There are a few issues that need to be considered. The first is the discount rate used on the second initial outlay of $382 million. The second is the optionality of the second series of cash flow projections.

TABLE 3.1 Comparing Real Options and Discounted Cash Flow

Panel A

($ millions)							
Time	0	1	2	3	4	5	6
Initial Outlay	$(100.00)						
Cash Flow		$8.00	$12.00	$15.00	$12.00	$11.00	$ 10.00
Terminal Value							$155.00
Net Cash Flow	$(100.00)	$8.00	$12.00	$15.00	$12.00	$11.00	$165.00
Discount Rate	0%	12%	12%	12%	12%	12%	12%
Present Value	$(100.00)	$7.14	$ 9.57	$10.68	$ 7.63	$ 6.24	$ 83.59
Net Present Value	$ 24.85						

Panel B

($ millions)							
Time	0	1	2	3	4	5	6
Initial Outlay				$(382.00)			
Cash Flow					$30.00	$43.00	$ 53.00
Terminal Value							$454.00
Net Cash Flow				$(382.00)	$30.00	$43.00	$507.00
Discount Rate				5.50%	12%	12%	12%
Present Value				$(325.32)	$19.07	$24.40	$256.86
Net Present Value	$(24.99)						
Total NPV	$ (0.14)						
Calculated Call Value	$ 73.27						
Value of the Investment	$ 98.12						

All positive cash flow projections are discounted at a constant 12 percent WACC, but the second initial outlay is discounted at 5.5 percent, as seen in Panel B in Table 3.1. In reality, the discount rate over time should theoretically change slightly due to different interest rate expectations as risks change over time. An approach is to use a recursive interest rate bootstrap based on market-forward rates adjusted for risk; but in our simple analysis, we assume that the 12 percent does not change much over time. The three-year spot Treasury risk-free rate of 5.5 percent is used on the second investment outlay because this cash outflow is projected at present and is assumed to be susceptible only to private risks and not market risks;

hence, the outlay should be discounted at the risk-free rate. If the cost outlay is discounted at the 12 percent WACC, the true value of the investment will be overinflated. To prepare for this payment in the future, the firm can set aside the funds equal to $382 million for use in three years. The firm's expected rate of return is set at the corresponding maturity spot Treasury risk-free rate, and any additional interest income is considered income from investing activities. The 12 percent market risk-adjusted weighted average cost of capital should not be used because the firm wants a 12 percent rate of return on its research and development initiatives by taking on risk of failure where the future cash flows are highly susceptible to market risks; but the $382 million is not under similar risks at present. In financial theory, we tend to separate market risks (unknown future revenues and free cash flow streams that are susceptible to market fluctuations) at a market risk-adjusted discount rate—in this case, the 12 percent WACC—and private risks (the second investment outlay that may change due to internal firm cost structures and not due to the market, meaning that the market will not compensate the firm for its cost inefficiencies in taking the drug to market) at a risk-free rate of 5 percent.

Next, the optionality of the second cash flow series can be seen as a call option. The firm has the option to invest and pursue the product to market phase but not the obligation to do so. If the projected net present value in three years indicates a negative amount, the firm may abandon this second phase; or the firm may decide to initiate the second phase should the net present value prove to be positive and adequately compensate the risks borne. So, if we value the second phase as a call option, the total net present value of the entire undertaking, phase one and two combined, would be a positive $98.12 million (calculated by adding the call value of $73.27 million and the phase one net present value of $24.85 million). This is the true intrinsic strategic value of the project, because if things do not look as rosy in the future, the firm does not have the obligation to take the drug to market but can always shelf the product for later release, sell its patent rights, or use the knowledge gained for creating other drugs in the future. If the firm neglects this ability to not execute the second phase, it underestimates the true value of the project.

ADVANCED APPROACHES TO REAL OPTIONS

Clearly, the example above is a simple single-option condition. In more protracted and sophisticated situations, more sophisticated models have to be used. These include closed-form exotic options solutions, partial-differential equations through the optimization of objective functions subject to constraints through dynamic programming, trinomial and multinomial branch models, binomial lattices, and stochastic simulations. This book goes into some of these more advanced applications in later chapters, along with their corresponding technical appendixes, and shows how they can be applied in actual business cases. However, for now, we are interested only in the high-level understanding of what real options are and how even thinking in terms of strategic optionality helps management make better decisions and obtain insights that would be unavailable otherwise.

WHY ARE REAL OPTIONS IMPORTANT?

An important point is that the traditional discounted cash flow approach assumes a single decision pathway with fixed outcomes, and all decisions are made in the beginning without the ability to change and develop over time. The real options approach considers multiple decision pathways as a consequence of high uncertainty coupled with management's flexibility in choosing the optimal strategies or options along the way when new information becomes available. That is, management has the flexibility to make midcourse strategy corrections when there is uncertainty involved in the future. As information becomes available and uncertainty becomes resolved, management can choose the best strategies to implement. Traditional discounted cash flow assumes a single static decision, while real options assume a multidimensional dynamic series of decisions, where management has the flexibility to adapt given a change in the business environment.

> *Traditional approaches assume a static decision-making ability, while real options assume a dynamic series of future decisions where management has the flexibility to adapt given changes in the business environment.*

Another way to view the problem is that there are two points to consider, one, the initial investment starting point where strategic investment decisions have to be made; and two, the ultimate goal, the optimal decision that can ever be made to maximize the firm's return on investment and shareholder's wealth. In the traditional discounted cash flow approach, joining these two points is a straight line, whereas the real options approach looks like a map with multiple routes to get to the ultimate goal, where each route is conjoint with others. The former implies a one-time decision-making process, while the latter implies a dynamic decision-making process wherein the investor learns over time and makes different updated decisions as time passes and events unfold.

As outlined above, traditional approaches coupled with discounted cash flow analysis have their pitfalls. Real options provide additional insights beyond the traditional analyses. At its least, real options provide a sobriety test of the results obtained using discounted cash flow and, at its best, provide a robust approach to valuation when coupled with the discounted cash flow methodology. The theory behind options is sound and reasonably applicable.

Some examples of real options using day-to-day terminology include:

- Option for future growth.
- Option to wait and see.
- Option to delay.
- Option to expand.
- Option to contract.
- Option to choose.
- Option to switch resources.
- Option for phased and sequential investments.

Notice that the names used to describe the more common real options are rather self-explanatory, unlike the actual model names such as a "Barone-Adesi-Whaley approximation model for an American option to expand." This is important because when it comes to explaining the process and results to management, the easier it is for them to understand, the higher the chances of acceptance of the methodology and results. We will, with greater detail, revisit this idea of making a series of black-box analytics transparent and expositionally easy in Chapter 10.

Traditional approaches to valuing projects associated with the value of a firm, including any strategic options the firm possesses, or flexible management decisions that are dynamic and have the capacity to change over time, are flawed in several respects. Projects valued using the traditional discounted cash flow model often provide a value that grossly understates the true fair market value of the asset. This is because projects may provide a low or zero cash flow in the near future but nonetheless be valuable to the firm. In addition, projects can be viewed in terms of owning the option to execute the rights, not owning the rights per se, because the owner can execute the option or allow it to expire should the opportunity cost outweigh the benefits of execution. The recommended options approach takes into consideration this option to exercise and prices it accordingly. Compared to traditional approaches, real options provide added elements of robustness to the analysis. Its inputs in the option-pricing model can be constructed via multiple alternatives, thus providing a method of stress testing or sensitivity testing of the final results. The corollary analysis resulting from real options also provides a ready means of sobriety checks without having to perform the entire analysis again from scratch using different assumptions.

The following example provides a simplified analogy to why optionality is important and should be considered in corporate capital investment strategies. Suppose you have an investment strategy that costs $100 to initiate and you anticipate that on average, the payoff will yield $120 in exactly one year. Assume a 15 percent weighted average cost of capital and a 5 percent risk-free rate, both of which are annualized rates. As Figure 3.1 illustrates, the net present value of the strategy is $4.3, indicating a good investment potential because the benefits outweigh the costs.

However, if we wait and see before investing, when uncertainty becomes resolved, we get the profile shown in Figure 3.2, where the initial investment outlay occurs at time one and positive cash inflows are going to occur only at time two. Let's say that your initial expectations were correct and that the average or expected value came to be $120 with good market demand providing a $140 cash flow and in the case of bad demand, only $100. If we had the option to wait a year, then we could better estimate the trends in demand and we would have seen the payoff profile bifurcating into two scenarios. Should the scenario prove unfavorable, we would have the option to abandon the investment because the costs are identical to the cash inflow (−$100 versus +$100), and we would rationally not pursue this avenue. Hence, we would pursue this investment only if a good market demand is observed for the product, and our net present value for waiting an extra year will be $10.6. This analysis indicates a truncated downside where there is a limited liability because a rational investor would never knowingly enter a sure-loss investment strategy. Therefore, the value of flexibility is $6.3.

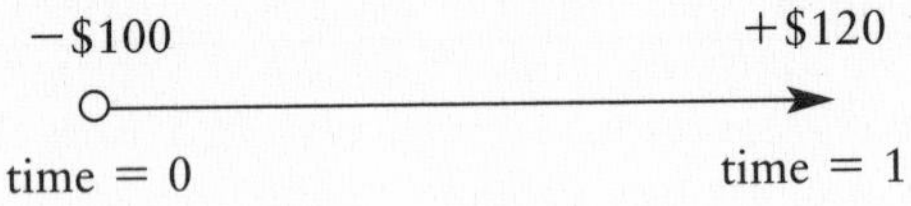

$$-\$100 \qquad\qquad\qquad +\$120$$

time = 0 $\qquad\qquad\qquad$ time = 1

$$\text{Net Present Value} = \frac{120}{(1.15)^1} - 100 = \$4.3$$

FIGURE 3.1 Why Optionality Is Important

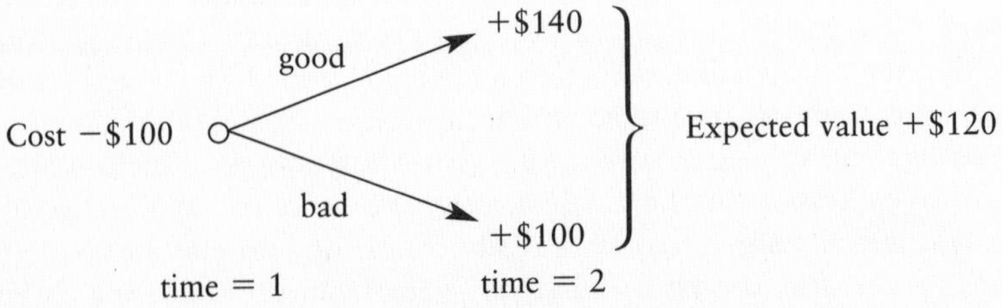

good $\qquad$ +$140

Cost −$100 $\qquad$ Expected value +$120

bad $\qquad$ +$100

time = 1 $\qquad$ time = 2

$$\text{Net Present Value} = \frac{140}{(1.15)^2} - \frac{100}{(1.05)^1} = \$10.6$$

FIGURE 3.2 If We Wait until Uncertainty Becomes Resolved

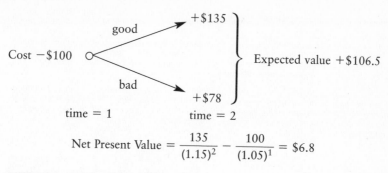

$$\text{Net Present Value} = \frac{135}{(1.15)^2} - \frac{100}{(1.05)^1} = \$6.8$$

FIGURE 3.3   Realistic Payoff Schedule

However, a more realistic payoff schedule should look like Figure 3.3. By waiting a year and putting off the investment until year two, you are giving up the potential for a cash inflow now, and the leakage or opportunity cost by not investing now is the $5 less you could receive ($140 – $135). However, by putting off the investment, you are also defraying the cost of investing in that the cost outlay will only occur a year later. The calculated net present value in this case is $6.8.

COMPARING TRADITIONAL APPROACHES WITH REAL OPTIONS

Figures 3.4 through 3.9 show a step-by-step analysis comparing a traditional analysis with that of real options, from the analyst's viewpoint. The analysis starts off with a discounted cash flow model in analyzing future cash flows. The analyst then applies sensitivity and scenario analysis. This is usually the extent of traditional approaches. As the results are relatively negative, the analyst then decides to add some new analytics. Monte Carlo simulation is then used, as well as real options analysis. The results from all these analytical steps are then compared and conclusions are drawn. This is a good comparative analysis of the results and insights obtained by using the new analytics. In this example, the analyst has actually added significant value to the overall project by creating optionalities within the project by virtue of actively pursuing and passively waiting for more information to become available prior to making any decisions.

Of course, several simplifying assumptions have to be made here, including the ability for the firm to simply wait and execute a year from now without any market or competitive repercussions. That is, the one-year delay will not allow a competitor to gain a first-to-market advantage or capture additional market share, where the firm's competitor may be willing to take the risk and invest in a similar project and gain the advantage while the firm

Comparing Traditional Approaches and Real Options with Simulation

A. Discounted Cash Flow
The extended example below shows the importance of waiting. That is, suppose a firm needs to make a rather large capital investment decision but at the same time has the Option to Wait and Defer on making the decision until later. The firm may be involved in pharmaceutical research and development activities, IT investment activities, or simply in marketing a new product that is yet untested in the market.

Suppose the analyst charged with performing a financial analysis on the project estimates that the most probable level of net revenues generated through the implementation of the project with an economic life of 5 years is presented in the time line below. Further, s/he assumes that the implementation cost is $200 million and the project's risk-adjusted discount rate is 20%, which also happens to be the firm's weighted average cost of capital. The calculated net present value (NPV) is found to be at a loss of -$26.70M.

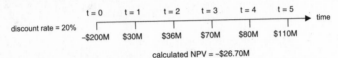

calculated NPV = -$26.70M

B. Sensitivity Analysis on Discounted Cash Flow
Even though the NPV shows a significant negative amount, the analyst feels that the investment decision can be better improved through more rigor. Hence, s/he decides to perform a sensitivity analysis. Since in this simplified example, we only have three variables (discount rate, cost, and future net revenue cash flows), the analyst increases each of these variables by 10% to note the sensitivity of calculated NPV to these changes.

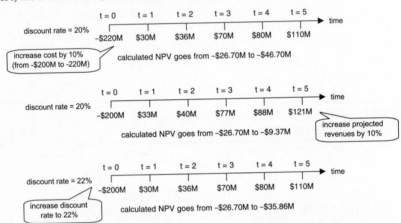

The entire set of possible sensitivities are presented in the table below, arranged in descending order based on the range of potential outcomes (indication of the variable's sensitivity). A Tornado Diagram is also created based on this sensitivity table.

| | Expected NPV | | | Input | | |
Variable	Downside	Upside	Range	Downside	Upside	Base Case
Cost	($46.70)	($6.70)	$40.00	($220)	($180)	($200)
Discount Rate	($16.77)	($35.86)	$19.09	18%	22%	20%
Cash Flow 5	($31.12)	($22.28)	$8.84	$99	$121	$110
Cash Flow 3	($30.75)	($22.65)	$8.10	$63	$77	$70
Cash Flow 4	($30.56)	($22.85)	$7.72	$72	$88	$80
Cash Flow 1	($29.20)	($24.20)	$5.00	$27	$33	$30
Cash Flow 2	($29.20)	($24.20)	$5.00	$32	$40	$36

FIGURE 3.4 Discounted Cash Flow Model

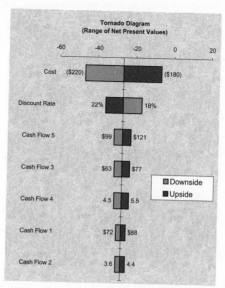

C. Scenario Analysis

Next, scenarios were generated. The analyst creates three possible scenarios and provides a subjective estimate of the probabilities each scenario will occur. For instance, the worst case scenario is 50% of the nominal scenario's projected revenues, while the best case scenario is 150% of the nominal scenario's projected revenues.

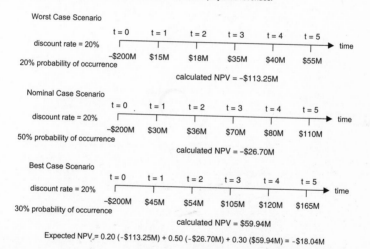

NPVs for each of the scenarios are calculated, and an Expected NPV is calculated to be -$18.04M based on the probability assumptions. The problem here is obvious. The range of possibilities is too large to make any inferences. That is, which figure should be believed? The -$18.04 or perhaps the nominal case of -$26.70? In addition, the upside potential and downside risks are fairly significantly different from the nominal or expected cases. What are the chances that any of these will actually come true? What odds or bets or faith can one place in the results? The analyst then decides to perform some Monte Carlo simulations to answer these questions.

FIGURE 3.5 Tornado Diagram and Scenario Analysis

D. Simulation

There are two ways to perform a Monte Carlo simulation in this example. The first is to take the scenario analysis above and simulate around the calculated NPVs. This assumes that the analyst is highly confident of his/her future cash flow projections and that the worst-case scenario is indeed the absolute minimum the firm can attain and the best-case scenario is exactly at the top of the range of possibilities. The second approach is to use the most likely or nominal scenario and simulate its inputs based on some management-defined ranges of possible cost and revenue structures.

(i) Simulating around scenarios

The analyst simulates around the three scenarios using a Triangular Distribution with the worst-case, nominal-case and best-case scenarios as input parameters into the simulation model. The example below uses Decisioneering, Inc.'s Crystal Ball simulation package. The results are shown below.

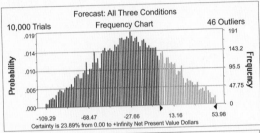

Mean	-27.06
Standard Deviation	35.31
Range Minimum	-112.21
Range Maximum	57.43
Range Width	169.64

We see that the range is fairly large since the scenarios were rather extreme. In addition, there is only a 23.89% chance that the project will break even or have an NPV > 0.

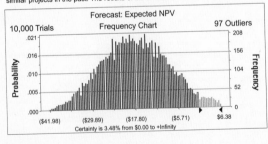

The 90% statistical confidence interval is between -$85.15M and $33.22M, which is also rather wide. Given such a huge swing in possibilities, we are much better off with performing a simulation using the second method, that is, to look at the nominal case and simulate around that case's input parameters.

(ii) Simulating around the nominal scenario

Since in the scenario analysis, the analyst created two different scenarios (worst case and best case) based on a 50% fluctuation in projected revenues from the base case, here we simply look at the base case and by simulation, generate 10,000 scenarios. Looking back at the Tornado diagram, we noticed that discount rate and cost were the two key determining factors in the analysis; the second approach can take the form of simulating these two key factors. The analyst simulates around the nominal scenario assuming a normal distribution for the discount rate with a mean of 20% and a standard deviation of 2% based on historical data on discount rates used in the firm. The cost structure is simulated assuming a uniform distribution with a minimum of -$180M and a maximum of -$220M based on input by management. This cost range is based on management intuition and substantiated by similar projects in the past. The results of the simulation are shown below.

Forecast: Expected NPV

10,000 Trials	Frequency Chart	97 Outliers

Mean	-25.06
Standard Deviation	14.3
Range Minimum	-69.54
Range Maximum	38.52
Range Width	108.06

Here we see that the range is somewhat more manageable and we can make more meaningful inferences. Based on the simulation results, there is only a 3.48% chance that the project will break even.

FIGURE 3.6   Simulation

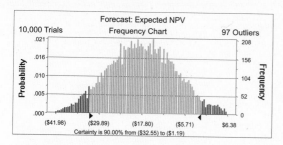

The 90% statistical confidence interval is between –$32.55M and –$1.19M.

Most of the time, the project is in negative NPV territory, suggesting a rather grim outlook for the project. However, the project is rather important to senior management and they wish to know if there is some way to add value to this project or make it financially justifiable to invest in. The answer lies in using Real Options.

E. Real Options

We have the option to wait or defer investing until a later date. That is, wait until uncertainty becomes resolved and then decide on the next course of action afterwards. Invest in the project only if market conditions indicate a good scenario and decide to abandon the project if the market condition is akin to the nominal or worst-case scenarios as they both bear negative NPVs.

(i) Option to Wait I (Passive Wait and See Strategy)

Say we decide to wait one year and assuming that we will gather more valuable information within this time frame, we can then decide whether to execute the project or not at that time. Below is a decision tree indicating our decision path.

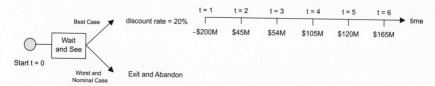

Calculated NPV after waiting for one year on new information = $49.95M

We see here that the NPV is positive since if after waiting for a year, the market demand is nominal or sluggish, then management has the right to pull the plug on the project. Otherwise, if it is a great market which meets or exceeds the best-case scenario, management has the option to execute the project, thereby guaranteeing a positive NPV. The calculated NPV is based on the forecast revenue stream and is valued at $49.95M.

(ii) Option to Wait II (Active Market Research Strategy)

Instead of waiting passively for the market to reveal itself over the one-year period as expected previously, management can decide on an active strategy of pursuing a market research strategy. If the market research costs $5M to initiate and takes 6 months to obtain reliable information, the firm saves additional time without waiting for the market to reveal itself. Here, if the market research indicates a highly favorable condition where the best-case scenario revenue stream is to be expected, then the project will be executed after 6 months. The strategy path and time lines are shown below.

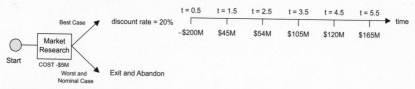

Calculated NPV after active market research = $49.72M
(after accounting for the -$5M in market research costs)

The calculated NPV here is $49.72M, relatively close to the passive waiting strategy. However, the downside is the $5M which also represents the greatest possible loss, which is also the premium paid to obtain the option to execute given the right market conditions.

FIGURE 3.7   Real Options Analysis (Active versus Passive Strategies)

In retrospect, management could find out the maximum it is willing to pay for the market research in order to cut down the time it has to wait before making an informed decision. That is, at what market research price would the first option to wait be the same as the second option to wait? Setting the difference between $49.95M and $49.72M as the reduction in market research cost brings down the initial $5M to $4.77M. In other words, the maximum amount the firm should pay for the market research should be no more than $4.77M; otherwise, it is simply wise to follow the passive strategy and wait for a year.

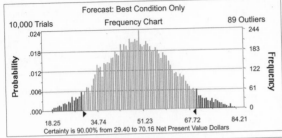

Mean	
Standard Deviation	49.73
Range Minimum	12.43
Range Maximum	-0.25
Range Width	94.57
	94.82

The resulting distribution range is less wide, providing a more meaningful inference. Based on the simulation results, the 90% confidence interval has the NPV between $29.40M and $70.16M. The range, which means almost 100% of the time, the NPV takes on a positive value.

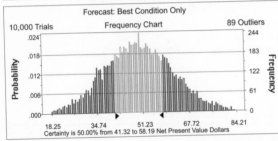

The 50% confidence interval has the NPV between $41.32M and $58.19M. We can interpret this range as the expected value range since 50% of the time, the real NPV will fall within this range, with a mean of $49.73M.

F. Observations

We clearly see that by using the three Scenarios versus an Expected Value approach, we obtain rather similar results in terms of NPV but through simulation, the Expected Value approach provides a much tighter distribution and the results are more robust as well as easier to interpret. Once we added in the Real Options approach, the risk has been significantly reduced and the return dramatically increased. The overlay chart below compares the simulated distributions of the three approaches. The blue series is the Scenario approach incorporating all three scenarios and simulating around them. The green series is the Expected Value approach, simulating around the nominal revenue projections, and the red series is the Real Options approach where we only execute if the best condition is obtained.

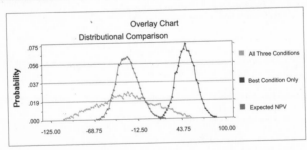

FIGURE 3.8   Analysis Observations

The example here holds true in most cases when we compare the approach used in a traditional Discounted Cash Flow (DCF) method to Real Options. Since we can define risk as uncertain fluctuations in revenues and the NPV level, all downside risks are mitigated in Real Options because you do not execute the project if the nominal or worst-case scenario occurs in time. In retrospect, the upside risks are maximized such that the returns are increased because the project will only be executed when the best-case scenario occurs. This creates a win-win situation where risks are mitigated and returns are enhanced, simply by having the right strategic optionalities available, acting appropriately, and valuing the project in terms of its "real" or intrinsic value, which includes this opportunity to make midcourse corrections when new information becomes available.

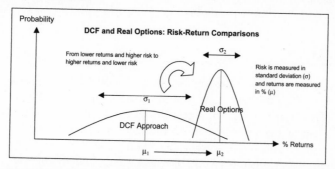

In addition, what seems on the outset as an unprofitable project yielding an NPV of -$26.70M can be justified and made profitable because the project has in reality an Option to Wait or Defer until a later date. Once uncertainty becomes resolved and we have more available information, management can then decide whether to go forward based on market conditions. This call option could be bought through the use of active market research. By having this delay tactic, the firm has indeed truncated any downside risks but still protected its upside potential.

Next, if we look at the Minimax Approach, where we attempt to Minimize the Maximum regret of making a decision, the maximum level of regret for pursuing the project blindly using a DCF approach may yield the worst-case scenario of -$113.25M while using an Option to Wait but simultaneously pursuing an active marketing research strategy will yield a maximum regret of -$4.77M. This is because the levels of maximum regret occur under the worst possible scenario. If this occurs, investing in the project blindly will yield the worst case of -$113.25, but the maximum loss in the real options world is the limited liability of the premium paid to run the market research, adding up to only -$4.77M because the firm would never execute the project when the market is highly unfavorable.

In addition, the Value of Perfect Information can be calculated as the increase in value created through the Option to Wait as compared to the naïve Expected NPV approach. That is, the Value of having Perfect Information is $68M. We obtain this level of perfect information through the initiation of a marketing research strategy which costs an additional $4.77M. This means that the strategic Real Options thinking and decision-making process has created a leverage of 14.25 times. This view is analogous to a financial option where we can purchase a call option for, say, $5 with a specified exercise price for a specified time of an underlying common equity with a current market price of $100. With $5, the call purchaser has leveraged his purchasing power into $100, or 20 times. In addition, if the equity price rises to $150 (50% increase akin to our example above), the call holder will execute the option, purchase the stock at $100, turn around and sell it for $150, less the $5 cost and yield a net $45. The option holder has, under this execution condition, leveraged the initial $5 into a $45 profit, or 9 times the original investment.

Finally and more importantly is that we see by adding in a strategic option, we have increased the value of the project immensely. It is therefore wise for management to consider an optionality framework in the decision-making process. That is, to find the strategic options that exist in different projects or to create strategic options in order to increase the project's value.

FIGURE 3.9 Analysis Conclusions

is not willing to do so. In addition, the cost and cash flows are assumed to be the same whether the project is initiated immediately or in the future. Obviously, these more complex assumptions can be added into the analysis, but for illustration purposes, we assume the basic assumptions hold, where costs and cash flows remain the same no matter the execution date, and that competition is negligible.

SUMMARY

Having real options in a project can be highly valuable, both in recognizing where these optionalities exist and in introducing and strategically setting up options in the project. Strategic options can provide decision-makers the opportunity to hedge their bets in the face of uncertainty. By having the ability to make midcourse corrections downstream when these uncertainties become known, decision-makers have essentially hedged themselves against any downside risks. As seen in this chapter, a real options approach provides the decision-maker not only a hedging vehicle but also significant leverage. In comparing approaches, real options analysis shows that not only can a project's risk be reduced but also returns can be enhanced by strategically creating options in projects.

CHAPTER 3 QUESTIONS

1. Can an option take on a negative value?
2. Why are real options sometimes viewed as strategic maps of convoluted pathways?
3. Why are real options seen as risk-reduction and revenue-enhancement strategies?
4. Why are the real options names usually self-explanatory and not based on names of mathematical models?
5. What is a Tornado diagram as presented in Figure 3.5's example?

The Real Options Process

INTRODUCTION

This chapter introduces the reader to the real options process framework. This framework comprises eight distinct phases of a successful real options implementation, going from a qualitative management screening process to creating clear and concise reports for management. The process was developed by the author based on previous successful implementations of real options both in the consulting arena and in industry-specific problems. These phases can be performed either in isolation or together in sequence for a more robust real options analysis.

CRITICAL STEPS IN PERFORMING REAL OPTIONS ANALYSIS

Figure 4.1 at the end of the chapter shows the real options process up close. We can segregate the real options process into the following eight simple steps. These steps include:

- Qualitative management screening.
- Base case net present value analysis.
- Monte Carlo simulation.
- Real options problem framing.
- Real options modeling and analysis.
- Portfolio and resource optimization.
- Reporting.
- Update analysis.

Qualitative Management Screening

Qualitative management screening is the first step in any real options analysis (Section A of Figure 4.1). Management has to decide which projects, assets, initiatives, or strategies are viable for further analysis, in accordance with the firm's mission, vision, goal, or overall business strategy. The firm's mission, vision, goal, or overall business strategy may include market penetration strategies, competitive advantage, technical, acquisition, growth, synergistic, or globalization issues. That is, the initial list of projects should be qualified in terms of meeting management's agenda. Often this is where the most valuable insight is created as management frames the complete problem to be resolved.

Base Case Net Present Value Analysis

For each project that passes the initial qualitative screens, a discounted cash flow model is created (Section B of Figure 4.1). This serves as the base case analysis, where a net present value is calculated for each project. This also applies if only a single project is under evaluation. This net present value is calculated using the traditional approach of forecasting revenues and costs, and discounting the net of these revenues and costs at an appropriate risk-adjusted rate.

The use of time-series forecasting may be appropriate here if historical data exist and the future is assumed to be somewhat predictable using past experiences. Otherwise, management assumptions may have to be used.[1]

Monte Carlo Simulation

Because the static discounted cash flow produces only a single-point estimate result, there is oftentimes little confidence in its accuracy given that future events that affect forecast cash flows are highly uncertain. To better estimate the actual value of a particular project, Monte Carlo simulation may be employed (Section C of Figure 4.1).

Usually, a sensitivity analysis is first performed on the discounted cash flow model. That is, setting the net present value as the resulting variable, we can change each of its precedent variables and note the change in the resulting variable. Precedent variables include revenues, costs, tax rates, discount rates, capital expenditures, depreciation, and so forth, which ultimately flow through the model to affect the net present value figure. By tracing back all these precedent variables, we can change each one by a preset amount and see the effect on the resulting net present value. A graphical representation can then be created, which is often called a Tornado Diagram, because of its shape, where the most sensitive precedent variables are listed first, in descending order of magnitude. Armed with this information, the analyst can then decide which key variables are highly uncertain in the future and which are deterministic. The uncertain key variables that drive the net present value and hence the decision are called critical success drivers. These critical success drivers are prime candidates for Monte Carlo simulation.[2] Because some of these critical success drivers may be correlated—for example, operating costs may increase in proportion to quantity sold of a particular product, or prices may be inversely correlated to quantity sold—a correlated Monte Carlo simulation may be required. Typically these correlations can be obtained through historical data. Running correlated simulations provides a much closer approximation to the variables' real-life behaviors.

Real Options Problem Framing

Framing the problem within the context of a real options paradigm is the next critical step (Section D of Figure 4.1). Based on the overall problem identification occurring during the initial qualitative management screening process, certain strategic optionalities would have become apparent for each particular project. The strategic optionalities may include, among other things, the option to expand, contract, abandon, switch, choose, and so forth. Based on the identification of strategic optionalities that exist for each project or at each stage of the project, the analyst can then choose from a list of options to analyze in more detail.[3]

Real Options Modeling and Analysis

Through the use of Monte Carlo simulation, the resulting stochastic discounted cash flow model will have a distribution of values. In real options, we assume that the underlying variable is the future profitability of the project, which is the future cash flow series. An implied volatility of the future free cash flow or underlying variable can be calculated through the results of a Monte Carlo simulation previously performed. Usually, the volatility is measured as the standard deviation of the logarithmic returns on the free cash flows stream. In addition, the present value of future cash flows for the base case discounted cash flow model is used as the initial underlying asset value in real options modeling (Section E of Figure 4.1).

Portfolio and Resource Optimization

Portfolio optimization is an optional step in the analysis (Section F of Figure 4.1). If the analysis is done on multiple projects, management should view the results as a portfolio of rolled-up projects. This is because the projects are in most cases correlated with one another and viewing them individually will not present the true picture. As firms do not only have single projects, portfolio optimization is crucial. Given that certain projects are related to others, there are opportunities for hedging and diversifying risks through a portfolio. Because firms have limited budgets, have time and resource constraints, while at the same time have requirements for certain overall levels of returns, risk tolerances, and so forth, portfolio optimization takes into account all these to create an optimal portfolio mix. The analysis will provide the optimal allocation of investments across multiple projects.[4]

Reporting

The analysis is not complete until reports can be generated (Section G of Figure 4.1).[5] Not only are results presented but also the process should be shown. Clear, concise, and precise explanations transform a difficult black-box set of analytics into transparent steps. Management will never accept results coming from black boxes if they do not understand where the assumptions or data originate and what types of mathematical or financial massaging takes place.

Update Analysis

Real options analysis assumes that the future is uncertain and that management has the right to make midcourse corrections when these uncertainties become resolved or risks become known; the analysis is usually done ahead of time and thus, ahead of such uncertainty and risks. Therefore, when these risks become known, the analysis should be revisited to incorporate the decisions made or revising any input assumptions. Sometimes, for long-horizon projects, several iterations of the real options analysis should be performed, where future iterations are updated with the latest data and assumptions.

SUMMARY

Understanding the steps required to undertake real options analyses is important because it provides insight not only into the methodology itself but also into how it evolves from traditional analyses, showing where the traditional approach ends and where the new analytics start. The eight phases discussed include performing a qualitative management screening process, base case net present value or discounted cash flow analysis, Monte Carlo simulation, real options analysis, real options modeling, portfolio optimization, reporting, and update analysis.

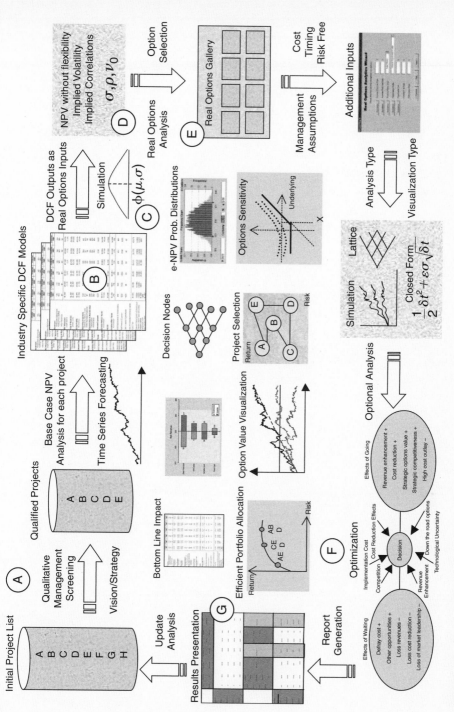

FIGURE 4.1 Real Options Process

CHAPTER 4 QUESTIONS

1. What is Monte Carlo simulation?
2. What is portfolio optimization?
3. Why is update analysis required in a real options analysis framework?
4. What is problem framing?
5. Why are reports important?

Real Options, Financial Options, Monte Carlo Simulation, and Optimization

INTRODUCTION

This chapter discusses the differences between real options and financial options, understanding that real options theory stems from financial options but that there are key differences. These differences are important to note because they will inevitably change the mathematical structure of real options models. The chapter then continues with an introduction to Monte Carlo simulation and portfolio optimization, discussing how these two concepts relate to the overall real options analysis process. Example applications are included, as are more detailed technical appendixes on financial options, simulation, and portfolio optimization.

REAL OPTIONS VERSUS FINANCIAL OPTIONS

Real options apply financial options theory in analyzing real or physical assets. Therefore, there are certainly many similarities between financial and real options. However, there are key differences, as listed in Figure 5.1. For example, financial options have short maturities, usually expiring in several months. Real options have longer maturities, usually expiring in several years, with some exotic-type options having an infinite expiration date. The underlying asset in financial options is the stock price, as compared to a multitude of other business variables in real options. These variables may include free cash flows, market demand, commodity prices, and so forth. Thus, when applying real options analysis to analyzing physical assets, we have to be careful in discerning what the underlying variable is. This is because the volatility measures used in options modeling pertain to the underlying variable. In

FINANCIAL OPTIONS	**REAL OPTIONS**
• Short maturity, usually in months.	• Longer maturity, usually in years.
• Underlying variable driving its value is equity price or price of a financial asset.	• Underlying variables are free cash flows, which in turn are driven by competition, demand, management.
• Cannot control option value by manipulating stock prices.	• Can increase strategic option value by management decisions and flexibility.
• Values are usually small.	• Major million and billion dollar decisions.
• Competitive or market effects are irrelevant to its value and pricing.	• Competition and market drive the value of a strategic option.
• Have been around and traded for more than three decades.	• A recent development in corporate finance within the last decade.
• Usually solved using closed-form partial differential equations and simulation/variance reduction techniques for exotic options.	• Usually solved using closed-form equations and binomial lattices with simulation of the underlying variables, not on the option analysis.
• Marketable and traded security with comparables and pricing info.	• Not traded and proprietary in nature, with no market comparables.
• Management assumptions and actions have no bearing on valuation.	• Management assumptions and actions drive the value of a real option.

FIGURE 5.1   Financial Options versus Real Options

financial options, due to insider trading regulations, options holders cannot, at least in theory, manipulate stock prices to their advantage. However, in real options, because certain strategic options can be created by management, their decisions can increase the value of the project's real options. Financial options have relatively less value (measured in tens or hundreds of dollars per option) than real options (thousands, millions, or even billions of dollars per strategic option).

Financial options have been traded for several decades, but the real options phenomenon is only a recent development, especially in the industry at large. Both types of options can be solved using similar approaches, including closed-form solutions, partial-differential equations, finite-differences, binomial lattices, and simulation; but industry acceptance for real options has been in the use of binomial lattices. This is because binomial lattices are much more easily explained to and accepted by management because the methodology is much simpler to understand. Finally, financial options models are based on market-traded securities and visible asset prices making their construction easier and more objective. Real options tend to be based on non-market-traded assets, and financially traded proxies are seldom available. Hence management assumptions are key in valuing real options and relatively less important in valuing financial options. Given a particular project, management can create strategies that will provide itself options in the future. The value of these options can change depending on how they are constructed.

In several basic cases, real options are similar to financial options. Figure 5.2 shows the payoff charts of a call option and a put option. On all four charts, the vertical axes represent the value of the strategic option and the

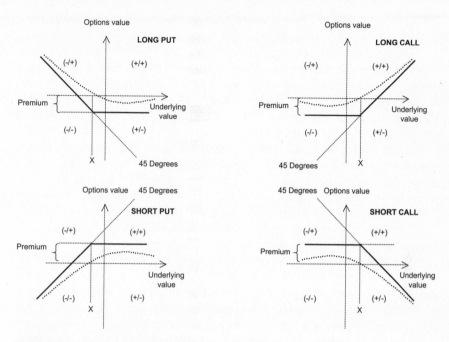

FIGURE 5.2 Option Payoff Charts

horizontal axes represent the value of the underlying asset. The kinked bold line represents the payoff function of the option at termination, effectively the project's net present value, because at termination, maturity effectively becomes zero and the option value reverts to the net present value (underlying asset less implementation costs). The dotted curved line represents the payoff function of the option prior to termination, where there is still time before maturity and hence uncertainty still exists and option value is positive. The curved line is the net present value, including the strategic option value. Both lines effectively have a horizontal floor value, which is effectively the premium on the option, where the maximum value at risk is the premium or cost of obtaining the option, indicating the option's maximum loss as the price paid to obtain it.

The position of a long call or the buyer and holder of a call option is akin to an *expansion option*. This is because an expansion option usually costs something to create or set up, which is akin to the option's premium or purchase price. If the underlying asset does not increase in value over time, the maximum losses incurred by the holder of this expansion option will be the cost of setting up this option (e.g., market research cost). When the value of the underlying asset increases sufficiently above the strike price (denoted X in the charts), the value of this expansion option increases. There is unlimited upside to this option, but the downside is limited to the premium paid for the option. The break-even point is where the bold line crosses the horizontal axis, which is equivalent to the strike price plus the premium paid.

The long put option position or the buyer and holder of a put option is akin to an *abandonment option*. This is because an abandonment option usually costs something to create or set up, which is akin to the option's premium or purchase price. If the value of the underlying asset does not decrease over time, the maximum losses incurred by the holder of this abandonment option will be the cost of setting up this option (seen as the horizontal bold line equivalent to the premium). When the value of the underlying asset decreases sufficiently below the strike price (denoted X in the charts), the value of this abandonment option increases. The option holder will find it more profitable to abandon the project currently in existence. There is unlimited upside to this option but the downside is limited to the premium paid for the option. The break-even point is where the bold line crosses the horizontal axis, which is equivalent to the strike price less the premium paid.[1]

The short positions or the writer and seller on both calls and puts have payoff profiles that are horizontal reflections of the long positions. That is, if you overlay both a long and short position of a call or a put, it becomes a zero-sum game. These short positions reflect the side of the issuer of the option. For instance, if the expansion and contraction options are based on some legally binding contract, the counterparty issuer of the contract would hold these short positions.

MONTE CARLO SIMULATION

Simulation is any analytical method that is meant to imitate a real-life system, especially when other analyses are too mathematically complex or too difficult to reproduce. Spreadsheet risk analysis uses both a spreadsheet model and simulation to analyze the effect of varying inputs based on outputs of the modeled system. One type of spreadsheet simulation is Monte Carlo simulation, which randomly generates values for uncertain variables over and over to simulate a real-life model.

History. Monte Carlo simulation was named after Monte Carlo, Monaco, where the primary attractions are casinos containing games of chance. Games of chance such as roulette wheels, dice, and slot machines exhibit random behavior. The random behavior in games of chance is similar to how Monte Carlo simulation selects variable values at random to simulate a model. When you roll a die, you know that a 1, 2, 3, 4, 5, or 6 will come up, but you don't know which for any particular trial. It is the same with the variables that have a known or estimated range of values but an uncertain value for any particular time or event (e.g., interest rates, staffing needs, revenues, stock prices, inventory, discount rates).

For each variable, you define the possible values with a probability distribution. The type of distribution you select depends on the conditions surrounding the variable. For example, some common distribution types are those shown in Figure 5.3.

During a simulation, the value to use for each variable is selected randomly from the defined possibilities.

Why Are Simulations Important?   A simulation calculates numerous scenarios of a model by repeatedly picking values from the probability distribution for the uncertain variables and using those values for the event. As all those scenarios produce associated results, each scenario can have a forecast. Forecasts are events (usually with formulas or functions) that you define as important outputs of the model. These usually are events such as totals, net profit, or gross expenses.

An example of why simulation is important can be seen in the case illustration in Figures 5.4 and 5.5, termed the Flaw of Averages. It shows how an analyst may be misled into making the wrong decisions without the use of simulation. As the example shows, the obvious reason why this error occurs is that the distribution of historical demand is highly skewed while the cost structure is asymmetrical. For example, suppose you are in a meeting room, and your boss asks what everyone made last year. You take a quick poll and realize that the salary ranges from $60,000 to $150,000. You perform a quick calculation and find the average to be $100,000. Then, your boss tells you that he made $20 million last year! Suddenly, the average for the group becomes $1.5 million. This value of $1.5 million clearly in no way represents how much each of your peers made last year. In this case, the median may be more appropriate. Here you see that simply using the average will provide highly misleading results.[2]

Continuing with the example, Figure 5.5 shows how the right inventory level is calculated using simulation. The approach used here is called *nonparametric simulation*. It is nonparametric because in the simulation approach, no distributional parameters are assigned. Instead of assuming some preset distribution (normal, triangular, lognormal, or the like) and assumed parameters (mean, standard deviation, and so forth) as required in a Monte Carlo parametric simulation, nonparametric simulation uses the data themselves to tell the story.

Imagine you collect a year's worth of historical demand levels and write down the demand quantity on a golf ball for each day. Throw all 365 balls

Normal   Triangular   Uniform   Lognormal

FIGURE 5.3   The Few Most Basic Distributions

The Flaw of Averages

Actual	**5**	Average	5.00
Inventory Held	**6**		

Historical Data (5 Yr)

		Month	Actual
Perishable Cost	$100	1	12
Fed Ex Cost	$175	2	11
		3	7
Total Cost	$100	4	0
		5	0
		6	2
		7	7
		8	0
		9	11
		10	12
		11	0
		12	9
		13	3
		14	5
		15	0
		16	2
		17	1
		18	10
		58	3
		59	2
		60	17

Your company is a retailer in perishable goods and you were tasked with finding the optimal level of inventory to have on hand. If your inventory exceeds actual demand, there is a $100 perishable cost while a $175 Fed Ex cost is incurred if your inventory is insufficient to cover the actual level of demand. These costs are on a per unit basis. Your first inclination is to collect historical demand data as seen on the right, for the past 60 months. You then take a simple average, which was found to be 5 units. Hence, you select 5 units as the optimal inventory level. You have just committed a major mistake called the Flaw of Averages!

The actual demand data are shown here on the right. Rows 19 through 57 are hidden to conserve space. Being the analyst, what must you then do?

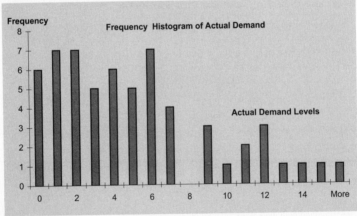

FIGURE 5.4 The Flaw of Averages

into a large basket and mix it. Pick a golf ball out at random and write down its value on a piece of paper, then place the ball back into the basket and mix the basket again. Do this 365 times, and calculate the average. This is a single grouped trial. Perform this entire process several thousand times, with replacement. The distribution of these averages represents the outcome of the simulation. The expected value of the simulation is simply the average value of these thousands of averages. Figure 5.5 shows an example of the distribution stemming from a nonparametric simulation. As you can see, the optimal inventory rate that minimizes carrying costs is nine units, far from the average value of five units previously calculated in Figure 5.4. Nonparametric simulation can be performed fairly easily using Crystal Ball's® simulation software's *Bootstrap* function.

Figure 5.6 shows a simple example of performing a nonparametric simulation using Excel. There are limitations on what can be performed using Excel's functionalities. The example shown in Figure 5.6 assumes nine simple cases with varying probabilities of occurrence. The simulation can be set up in three simple steps. However, the number of columns and rows may be unmanageable because a large number of simulations are needed to obtain a good sampling distribution. The analysis can be modified easily for the flaw of averages example by simply listing out all the cases (the actual demand levels) with equal probabilities on each case. Obviously, performing large-scale simulations with Excel is not recommended. The optimal solution is to use a software like Crystal Ball® to run simulations, as shown in Figure 5.7.

Figure 5.7 shows an example of using Crystal Ball® in conjunction with an Excel spreadsheet. The highlighted cells are simulation assumption cells, forecast result cells, and decision variable cells. For more details, consult Appendix 9B on getting started with and using Monte Carlo simulation

Fixing the Flaw of Averages with Simulation

Simulated Average Actual Demand	8.53	Simulated Demand Range	From 7.21 and 9.85
Inventory Held	9.00	Simulated Cost Range	From 178.91 to 149

Perishable Cost	$100
Fed Ex Cost	$175
Total Cost	$46.88

The best method is to perform a nonparametric simulation where we use the actual historical demand levels as inputs to simulate the most probable level of demand going forward, which we found as 8.53 units. Given this demand, the lowest cost is obtained through a trial inventory of 9 units, a far cry from the original Flaw of Averages estimate of 5 units.

Trial Inventory	Total Cost
1.00	$1,318
2.00	$1,143
3.00	$968
4.00	$793
5.00	$618
6.00	$443
7.00	$268
8.00	$93
9.00	$47
10.00	$147
11.00	$247
12.00	$347
13.00	$447
14.00	$547
15.00	$647
16.00	$747

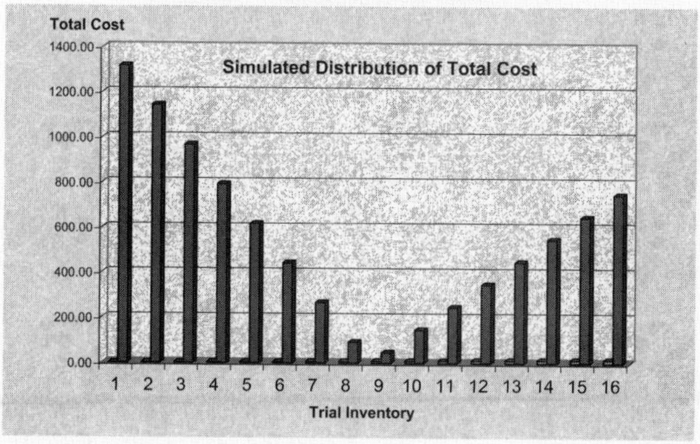

FIGURE 5.5 The Need for Simulation

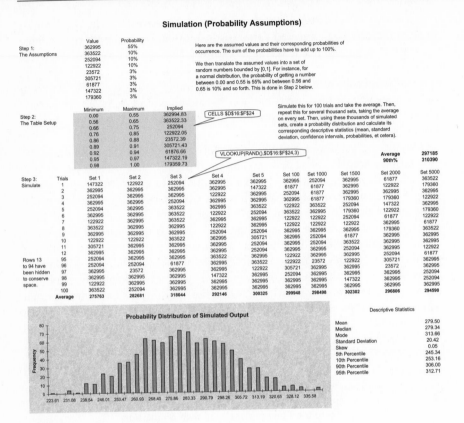

FIGURE 5.6   Simulation in Excel

software. Remember that there is also a complimentary trial version of Crystal Ball's® simulation software on CD-ROM included at the back of this book, complete with example spreadsheets and Real Options Analysis Toolkit demo software.

Obviously there are many uses of simulation, and we are barely scratching the surface with these examples. One additional use of simulation deserves mention: simulation can be used in forecasting. Specifically, an analyst can forecast future cash flows, cost, revenues, prices, and so forth using simulation. Figure 5.8 shows an example of how stock prices can be forecasted using simulation. This example is built upon a stochastic process called the Geometric Brownian Motion.[3] Using this assumption, we can simulate the price path of a particular stock. Three stock price paths are shown here, but in reality, thousands of paths are generated, and a probability distribution of the outcomes can then be created. That is, for a particular time period in the future—say, on day 100—we can determine the probability distribution of prices on that day. We can apply similar concepts to forecasting demand,

Monte Carlo Simulation on Financial Analysis

Project A

		2001	2002	2003	2004	2005
Revenues		$1,010	$1,111	$1,233	$1,384	$1,573
Opex/Revenue Multiple		0.09	0.10	0.11	0.12	0.13
Operating Expenses		$91	$109	$133	$165	$210
EBITDA		$919	$1,002	$1,100	$1,219	$1,363
FCF/EBITDA Multiple		0.20	0.25	0.31	0.40	0.56
Free Cash Flows	($1,200)	$187	$246	$336	$486	$760
Initial Investment	($1,200)					
Revenue Growth Rates		10.00%	11.00%	12.21%	13.70%	15.58%

NPV	$126
IRR	15.68%
Risk Adjusted Discount Rate	12.00%
Growth Rate	3.00%
Terminal Value	$8,692
Terminal Risk Adjustment	30.00%
Discounted Terminal Value	$2,341
Terminal to NPV Ratio	18.52
Payback Period	3.89
Simulated Risk Value	$390

Project B

		2001	2002	2003	2004	2005
Revenues		$1,200	$1,404	$1,683	$2,085	$2,700
Opex/Revenue Multiple		0.09	0.10	0.11	0.12	0.13
Operating Expenses		$108	$138	$181	$249	$361
EBITDA		$1,092	$1,266	$1,502	$1,836	$2,340
FCF/EBITDA Multiple		0.10	0.11	0.12	0.14	0.16
Free Cash Flows	($400)	$109	$139	$183	$252	$364
Initial Investment	($400)					
Revenue Growth Rates		17.00%	19.89%	23.85%	29.53%	38.25%

NPV	$149
IRR	33.74%
Risk Adjusted Discount Rate	19.00%
Growth Rate	3.75%
Terminal Value	$2,480
Terminal Risk Adjustment	30.00%
Discounted Terminal Value	$668
Terminal to NPV Ratio	4.49
Payback Period	2.83
Simulated Risk Value	$122

Project C

		2001	2002	2003	2004	2005
Revenues		$950	$1,069	$1,219	$1,415	$1,678
Opex/Revenue Multiple		0.13	0.15	0.17	0.20	0.24
Operating Expenses		$124	$157	$205	$278	$395
EBITDA		$827	$912	$1,014	$1,136	$1,283
FCF/EBITDA Multiple		0.20	0.25	0.31	0.40	0.56
Free Cash Flows	($1,100)	$168	$224	$309	$453	$715
Initial Investment	($1,100)					
Revenue Growth Rates		12.50%	14.06%	16.04%	18.61%	22.08%

NPV	$29
IRR	15.99%
Risk Adjusted Discount Rate	15.00%
Growth Rate	5.50%
Terminal Value	$7,935
Terminal Risk Adjustment	30.00%
Discounted Terminal Value	$2,137
Terminal to NPV Ratio	74.73
Payback Period	3.88
Simulated Risk Value	$53

Project D

		2001	2002	2003	2004	2005
Revenues		$1,200	$1,328	$1,485	$1,681	$1,932
Opex/Revenue Multiple		0.08	0.08	0.09	0.09	0.10
Operating Expenses		$90	$107	$129	$159	$200
EBITDA		$1,110	$1,221	$1,355	$1,522	$1,732
FCF/EBITDA Multiple		0.14	0.16	0.19	0.23	0.28
Free Cash Flows	($750)	$159	$200	$259	$346	$483
Initial Investment	($750)					
Revenue Growth Rates		10.67%	11.80%	13.20%	14.94%	17.17%

NPV	$26
IRR	21.57%
Risk Adjusted Discount Rate	20.00%
Growth Rate	1.50%
Terminal Value	$2,648
Terminal Risk Adjustment	30.00%
Discounted Terminal Value	$713
Terminal to NPV Ratio	26.98
Payback Period	3.38
Simulated Risk Value	$56

	Implementation Cost	Sharpe Ratio	Weight	Project Cost	Project NPV	Risk Parameter	Payback Period	Technology Level	Tech Mix
Project A	$1,200	0.02	5.14%	$62	$6	29%	3.89	5	0.26
Project B	$400	0.31	25.27%	$101	$38	15%	2.83	3	0.76
Project C	$1,100	0.19	34.59%	$380	$10	21%	3.88	2	0.69
Project D	$750	0.17	35.00%	$263	$9	17%	3.38	4	1.40
Total	$3,450	0.17	100.00%	$806	$63	28%	3.49	3.5	3.11

Constraints:

	Lower Barrier	Upper Barrier	
Budget	$0	$900	(10 percentile at top 900)
Payback Mix	0.10	1.00	
Technology Mix	0.40	4.00	
Per Project Mix	5%	35%	

FIGURE 5.7 Monte Carlo Simulation

cost, and any other variables of interest. The enclosed CD-ROM has an example spreadsheet on simulating price paths.

SUMMARY

This chapter reviews the similarities between financial options and real options. The most important difference is that the latter revolves around physical assets that are usually not traded in the market, as compared to highly volatile financial assets that are actively traded in the market with shorter maturities for financial options. Monte Carlo simulation is also introduced as an important and integral approach when performing real options. The example on the flaw of using simple averages shows that without the added insights of probabilities and simulation, wrong decisions will be made. The chapter concludes with more detailed appendixes on financial options, simulation, and optimization, for the analyst requiring more in-depth understanding of the topics.

Conceptualizing the Lognormal Distribution
A Simple Simulation Example
We need to perform many simulations to obtain a valid distribution

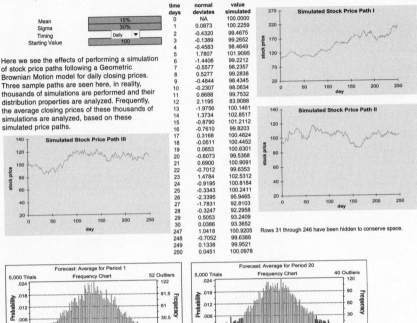

Here we see the effects of performing a simulation of stock price paths following a Geometric Brownian Motion model for daily closing prices. Three sample paths are seen here, in reality, thousands of simulations are performed and their distribution properties are analyzed. Frequently, the average closing prices of these thousands of simulations are analyzed, based on these simulated price paths.

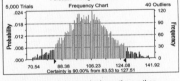

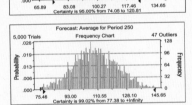

The thousands of simulated price paths are then tabulated into probability distributions. Here are three sample price paths at three different points in time, for periods 1, 20, and 250. There will be a total of 250 distributions for each time period, which corresponds to the number of trading days a year.

We can also analyze each of these time-specific probability distributions and calculate relevant statistically valid confidence intervals for decision-making purposes.

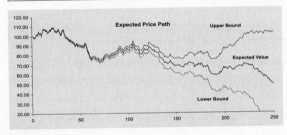

We can then graph out the confidence intervals together with the expected values of each forecasted time period.

Notice that as time increases, the confidence interval widens because there will be more risk and uncertainty as more time passes.

FIGURE 5.8 Lognormal Simulation

CHAPTER 5 QUESTIONS

1. What do you believe are the three most important differences between financial options and real options?

2. In the Flaw of Averages example, a nonparametric simulation approach is used. What does nonparametric simulation mean?

3. In simulating a sample stock price path, a stochastic process called Geometric Brownian Motion is used. What does a stochastic process mean?

4. What are some of the restrictive assumptions used in the Black-Scholes equation?

5. Using the example in Figure 5.8, simulate a sample revenue path in Excel, based on a Geometric Brownian Motion process, where $\delta S_t = S_{t-1}\left[\mu\delta t + \sigma\varepsilon\sqrt{\delta t}\right]$. Assume a 50 percent annualized volatility (σ), mean drift rate (μ) of 2 percent, and a starting value (S_0) of \$100 on January 2002. Create a monthly price path simulation for the period January 2002 to December 2004. Use the function: "=NORMSINV(RAND( ))" in Excel to re-create the simulated standard normal random distribution value ε.

Financial Options

Below are several key points to note in financial options, which are fairly similar to real options, because the underlying theoretical justifications are identical in nature.

Definitions

- An *option* is a contract that gives the owner/holder the right but not the legal obligation to conduct a transaction involving an underlying asset—for example, the purchase or sale of the asset—at a predetermined future date or within a specified period of time and at a predetermined price (the exercise or strike price); but the option only provides the long position the right to decide whether or not to trade and the seller the obligation to perform.

- A *call option* is an option to buy a specified number of shares of a security within some future period at pre-specified prices.

- A *put option* is an option to sell a specified number of shares of a security within some future period at pre-specified prices.

- The *exercise price* is the strike price or the price stated in the option contract at which the security can be bought or sold.

- The *option price* is the market price of the option contract.

- The *expiration date* is the date the option expires or matures.

- The *formula value* is the extrinsic value of an option or value of a call option if it were exercised today, which is equal to the current stock price minus the strike price.

- A *naked option* is an option sold without the stock to back it up.

- A *derivative* is a security whose value is derived from the values of other assets.

Black-Scholes Model. Basic options pricing models like the Black-Scholes make the following assumptions:

- That the stocks underlying the call options provide no dividends during the life of the options.
- That there are no transaction costs involved with the sale or purchase of either the stock or the option.
- That the short-term risk-free interest rate is known and is constant during the life of the option.
- That the security buyers may borrow any fraction of the purchase price at the short-term risk-free rate.
- That short-term selling is permitted without penalty and sellers receive immediately the full cash proceeds at today's price for securities sold short.
- That a call or put option can be exercised only on its expiration date.
- That security trading takes place in continuous time and stock prices move in continuous time.

Using the Black-Scholes paradigm:

- The value of a call option increases (decreases) as the current stock price increases (decreases).
- As the call option's exercise price increases (decreases), the option's value decreases (increases).
- As the term to maturity lengthens, the option's value increases.
- As the risk-free rate increases, the option's value tends to increase.
- The greater the variance of the underlying stock price, the greater the possibility the stock's price will exceed the call option's exercise price—thus, the more valuable the option will be.

Other Key Points

- The owner of a *call option* has the right to purchase the underlying good at a specific price for a specific time period, while the owner of a *put option* has the right to sell the underlying stock within a specified time period. To acquire these rights, owners of options must buy them by paying a price called the *premium* to the seller of the option.
- For every owner of an option, there must be a seller, called the *option writer.*
- Notice there are four possible positions: buyer of the call option, the seller or writer of the call option, the buyer of a put option, and the seller or writer of a put option.

- At termination, if the stock price S is above the strike price X, a call option has value and is said to be in-the-money—that is, when $S - X > 0$, a call option is in-the-money.

- At termination, if the stock price S is at the strike price X, a call option has no value and is said to be at-the-money—that is, when $S - X = 0$, a call option is at-the-money.

- At termination, if the stock price S is below the strike price X, a call option has no value and is said to be out-of-the-money—that is, when $S - X < 0$, a call option is out-of-the-money.

- At termination, if the stock price S is above the strike price X, a put option has no value and is said to be out-of-the-money—that is, when $S - X > 0$, a put option is out-of-the-money.

- At termination, if the stock price S is at the strike price X, a put option has no value and is said to be at-the-money—that is, when $S - X = 0$, a put option is at-the-money.

- At termination, if the stock price S is below the strike price X, a put option has value and is said to be in-the-money—that is, when $S - X < 0$, a put option is in-the-money.

- American options allow the owner to exercise the option at any time before or at expiration.

- European options can only be exercised at expiration.

- If both options have the same characteristics, an American option is worth more or at least the same as a European option if there are dividend outflows. Otherwise, it is never optimal to exercise an American option early and therefore the American option value reverts to the European option value when dividend outflows are negligible.

Simulation

UNDERSTANDING PROBABILITY DISTRIBUTIONS

To begin to understand probability, consider this example: You want to look at the distribution of nonexempt wages within one department of a large company. First, you gather raw data—in this case, the wages of each nonexempt employee in the department. Second, you organize the data into a meaningful format and plot the data as a frequency distribution on a chart. To create a frequency distribution, you divide the wages into group intervals and list these intervals on the chart's horizontal axis. Then you list the number or frequency of employees in each interval on the chart's vertical axis. Now you can easily see the distribution of nonexempt wages within the department.

A glance at Figure 5B.1 reveals that most of the employees (approximately 60 out of a total of 180) earn from $7.00 to $9.00 per hour.

You can chart this data as a probability distribution. A probability distribution shows the number of employees in each interval as a fraction of the

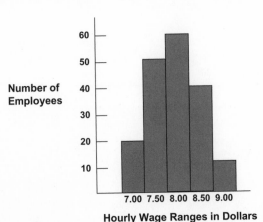

FIGURE 5B.1 Number of Employees and Hourly Wages

total number of employees. To create a probability distribution, you divide the number of employees in each interval by the total number of employees and list the results on the chart's vertical axis.

Figure 5B.2 shows you the number of employees in each wage group as a fraction of all employees; you can estimate the likelihood or probability that an employee drawn at random from the whole group earns a wage within a given interval. For example, assuming the same conditions exist at the time the sample was taken, the probability is 0.33 (a one in three chance) that an employee drawn at random from the whole group earns between $8.00 and $8.50 an hour.

Probability distributions are either discrete or continuous. *Discrete probability distributions* describe distinct values, usually integers, with no intermediate values, and are shown as a series of vertical bars, such as in the binomial distribution in the example above. A discrete distribution, for example, might describe the number of heads in four flips of a coin as 0, 1, 2, 3, or 4. *Continuous distributions* are actually mathematical abstractions because they assume the existence of every possible intermediate value between two numbers. That is, a continuous distribution assumes there is an infinite number of values between any two points in the distribution. However, in many situations, you can effectively use a continuous distribution to approximate a discrete distribution even though the continuous model does not necessarily describe the situation exactly.

SELECTING A PROBABILITY DISTRIBUTION

Plotting data is one guide to selecting a probability distribution. The following steps provide another process for selecting probability distributions that best describe the uncertain variables in your spreadsheets.

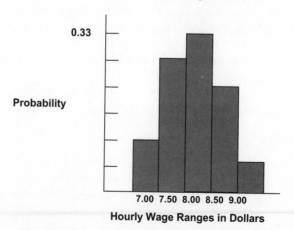

FIGURE 5B.2   Probability and Hourly Wages

To select the correct probability distribution, use the following steps:

- Look at the variable in question. List everything you know about the conditions surrounding this variable. You might be able to gather valuable information about the uncertain variable from historical data. If historical data are not available, use your own judgment, based on experience, listing everything you know about the uncertain variable.
- Review the descriptions of the probability distributions.
- Select the distribution that characterizes this variable. A distribution characterizes a variable when the conditions of the distribution match those of the variable.

SAMPLING METHODS

During each trial of a simulation, Crystal Ball® selects a random value for each assumption in your model. Crystal Ball® selects these values based on the sampling options. The two sampling methods are

Monte Carlo

> Randomly selects any valid value from each assumption's defined distribution.

Latin Hypercube

> Randomly selects values but spreads the random values evenly over each assumption's defined distribution.

Monte Carlo

With Monte Carlo, Crystal Ball® generates random values for each assumption's probability distribution that are totally independent. In other words, the random value selected for one trial has no effect on the next random value generated.

Using Monte Carlo sampling to approximate the true shape of the distribution requires a larger number of trials than Latin Hypercube does.

Use Monte Carlo sampling when you want to simulate "real world" what-if scenarios for your spreadsheet model.

Latin Hypercube

With Latin Hypercube sampling, Crystal Ball® divides each assumption's probability distribution into non-overlapping segments, each having equal probability. Crystal Ball® then selects a random assumption value for each segment according to the segment's probability distribution. The collection of values forms the Latin Hypercube sample. After Crystal Ball® uses all the values from the sample, it generates a new batch of values. Latin Hypercube sampling is generally more precise than conventional Monte Carlo sampling when calculating simulation statistics, because the entire range of the distribution is sampled more evenly and consistently. Thus, with Latin Hypercube sampling, you do not need as many trials to achieve the same statistical accuracy as with Monte Carlo sampling. The added expense of this method is the extra memory required to hold the full sample for each assumption while the simulation runs. Use Latin Hypercube sampling when you are concerned primarily with the accuracy of the simulation statistics.

Confidence Intervals

Monte Carlo simulation is a technique that uses random sampling to estimate model results. Statistics computed on these results, such as mean, standard deviation, and percentiles, will always contain some kind of measurement error. A confidence interval (CI) is a bound calculated around a statistic that attempts to measure this error with a given level of probability. For example, a 95 percent confidence interval around the mean statistic is defined as a 95 percent chance that the mean will be contained within the specified interval. Conversely, there is a 5 percent chance that the mean will lie outside the interval.

For most statistics, the confidence interval is symmetric around the statistic so that $X = (CI_{max} - Mean) = (Mean - CI_{min})$. This lets you make statements of confidence such as "the mean will equal the estimated mean plus or minus X with 95 percent probability."

Confidence intervals are important for determining the accuracy of statistics and, hence, the accuracy of the simulation. Generally speaking, as more trials are calculated, the confidence interval narrows and the statistics become more accurate.

MOST COMMONLY USED DISTRIBUTIONS

Below is a detailed listing of the different types of probability distributions that can be used in Monte Carlo simulation. This listing is included in the Appendix simply for the reader's reference.

Uniform Distribution

All values between the minimum and maximum occur with equal likelihood.

Conditions.   The three conditions underlying uniform distribution are:

- The minimum value is fixed.
- The maximum value is fixed.
- All values between the minimum and maximum occur with equal likelihood.

Normal Distribution

The normal distribution is the most important distribution in probability theory because it describes many natural phenomena, such as people's IQs or heights. Decision-makers can use the normal distribution to describe uncertain variables such as the inflation rate or the future price of gasoline.

Conditions.   The three conditions underlying the normal distribution are:

- Some value of the uncertain variable is the most likely (the mean of the distribution).
- The uncertain variable could as likely be above the mean as it could be below the mean (symmetrical about the mean).
- The uncertain variable is more likely to be in the vicinity of the mean than far away.

Triangular Distribution

The triangular distribution describes a situation where you know the minimum, maximum, and most likely values to occur. For example, you could describe the number of cars sold per week when past sales show the minimum, maximum, and usual number of cars sold.

Conditions.   The three conditions underlying the triangular distribution are:

- The minimum number of items is fixed.
- The maximum number of items is fixed.
- The most likely number of items falls between the minimum and maximum values, forming a triangular-shaped distribution, which shows that values near the minimum and maximum are less likely to occur than those near the most likely value.

Binomial Distribution

The binomial distribution describes the number of times a particular event occurs in a fixed number of trials, such as the number of heads in 10 flips of a coin or the number of defective items in 50 items.

Conditions.   The parameters for this distribution are the number of trials (n) and the probability (p). The three conditions underlying the binomial distribution are:

- For each trial, only two outcomes are possible.
- The trials are independent. What happens in the first trial does not affect the second trial, and so on.

- The probability of an event occurring remains the same from trial to trial.

Poisson Distribution

The Poisson distribution describes the number of times an event occurs in a given interval, such as the number of telephone calls per minute or the number of errors per page in a document.

Conditions.   The three conditions underlying the Poisson distribution are:

- The number of possible occurrences in any interval is unlimited.
- The occurrences are independent. The number of occurrences in one interval does not affect the number of occurrences in other intervals.
- The average number of occurrences must remain the same from interval to interval.

Geometric Distribution

The geometric distribution describes the number of trials until the first successful occurrence, such as the number of times you need to spin a roulette wheel before you win.

Conditions.   The three conditions underlying the geometric distribution are:

- The number of trials is not fixed.
- The trials continue until the first success.
- The probability of success is the same from trial to trial.

Hypergeometric Distribution

The hypergeometric distribution is similar to the binomial distribution in that both describe the number of times a particular event occurs in a fixed number of trials. The difference is that binomial distribution trials are independent, while hypergeometric distribution trials change the probability for each subsequent trial and are called "trials without replacement." For example, suppose a box of manufactured parts is known to contain some defective parts. You choose a part from the box, find it is defective, and remove the part from the box. If you choose another part from the box, the probability that it is defective is somewhat lower than for the first part because you have removed a defective part. If you had replaced the defective part, the probabilities would have remained the same, and the process would have satisfied the conditions for a binomial distribution.

Conditions. The conditions underlying the hypergeometric distribution are:

- The total number of items or elements (the population size) is a fixed number, a finite population. The population size must be less than or equal to 1,750.
- The sample size (the number of trials) represents a portion of the population.
- The known initial probability of success in the population changes slightly after each trial.

Lognormal Distribution

The lognormal distribution is widely used in situations where values are positively skewed, for example in financial analysis for security valuation or in real estate for property valuation.

Stock prices are usually positively skewed rather than normally (symmetrically) distributed. Stock prices exhibit this trend because they cannot fall below the lower limit of zero but might increase to any price without limit. Similarly, real estate prices illustrate positive skewness as property values cannot become negative.

Conditions. The three conditions underlying the lognormal distribution are:

- The uncertain variable can increase without limits but cannot fall below zero.
- The uncertain variable is positively skewed, with most of the values near the lower limit.
- The natural logarithm of the uncertain variable yields a normal distribution.

Generally, if the coefficient of variability is greater than 30 percent, use a lognormal distribution. Otherwise, use the normal distribution.

Lognormal Parameter Sets

By default, the lognormal distribution uses the arithmetic mean and standard deviation. For applications for which historical data are available, it is more appropriate to use either the logarithmic mean and standard deviation, or the geometric mean and standard deviation.

Exponential Distribution

The exponential distribution is widely used to describe events recurring at random points in time, such as the time between failures of electronic equipment or the time between arrivals at a service booth. It is related to the Poisson distribution, which describes the number of occurrences of an event in a given interval of time. An important characteristic of the exponential distribution is the "memoryless" property, which means that the future lifetime of a given object has the same distribution, regardless of the time it existed. In other words, time has no effect on future outcomes.

Conditions. The condition underlying the exponential distribution is:

- The exponential distribution describes the amount of time between occurrences.

LESS COMMONLY USED DISTRIBUTIONS

Weibull Distribution (Rayleigh Distribution)

The Weibull distribution describes data resulting from life and fatigue tests. It is commonly used to describe failure time in reliability studies as well as the breaking strengths of materials in reliability and quality control tests. Weibull distributions are also used to represent various physical quantities, such as wind speed.

The Weibull distribution is a family of distributions that can assume the properties of several other distributions. For example, depending on the shape parameter you define, the Weibull distribution can be used to model the exponential and Rayleigh distributions, among others. The Weibull distribution is very flexible. When the Weibull shape parameter is equal to 1.0, the Weibull distribution is identical to the exponential distribution. The Weibull location parameter lets you set up an exponential distribution to start at a location other than 0.0. When the shape parameter is less than 1.0, the Weibull distribution becomes a steeply declining curve. A manufacturer might find this effect useful in describing part failures during a burn-in period.

Beta Distribution

The beta distribution is a very flexible distribution commonly used to represent variability over a fixed range. One of the more important applications of the beta distribution is its use as a conjugate distribution for the parameter of a Bernoulli distribution. In this application, the beta distribution is used to represent the uncertainty in the probability of occurrence of an event. It is also used to describe empirical data and predict the random behavior of percentages and fractions.

The value of the beta distribution lies in the wide variety of shapes it can assume when you vary the two parameters, alpha and beta. If the parameters are equal, the distribution is symmetrical. If either parameter is 1 and the other parameter is greater than 1, the distribution is J-shaped. If alpha is less than beta, the distribution is said to be positively skewed (most of the values are near the minimum value). If alpha is greater than beta, the distribution is negatively skewed (most of the values are near the maximum value). Because the beta distribution is very complex, the methods for determining the parameters of the distribution are beyond the scope of this appendix.

Conditions. The two conditions underlying the beta distribution are:

- The uncertain variable is a random value between 0 and a positive value.
- The shape of the distribution can be specified using two positive values.

Gamma Distribution (Erlang and Chi-Square)

The gamma distribution applies to a wide range of physical quantities and is related to other distributions: lognormal, exponential, Pascal, Erlang, Poisson, and chi-square. It is used in meteorological processes to represent pollutant concentrations and precipitation quantities. The gamma distribution is also used to measure the time between the occurrence of events when the event process is not completely random. Other applications of the gamma distribution include inventory control, economics theory, and insurance risk theory.

Conditions. The gamma distribution is most often used as the distribution of the amount of time until the rth occurrence of an event in a Poisson process. When used in this fashion, the conditions underlying the gamma distribution are:

- The number of possible occurrences in any unit of measurement is not limited to a fixed number.
- The occurrences are independent. The number of occurrences in one unit of measurement does not affect the number of occurrences in other units.
- The average number of occurrences must remain the same from unit to unit.

Logistic Distribution

The logistic distribution is commonly used to describe growth (i.e., the size of a population expressed as a function of a time variable). It can also be used to describe chemical reactions and the course of growth for a population or individual.

Calculating Parameters. There are two standard parameters for the logistic distribution: mean and scale. The mean parameter is the average value, which for this distribution is the same as the mode, because this is a symmetrical distribution.

After you select the mean parameter, you can estimate the scale parameter. The scale parameter is a number greater than 0. The larger the scale parameter, the greater the variance.

Pareto Distribution

The Pareto distribution is widely used for the investigation of distributions associated with such empirical phenomena as city population sizes, the occurrence of natural resources, the size of companies, personal incomes, stock price fluctuations, and error clustering in communication circuits.

Calculating Parameters. There are two standard parameters for the Pareto distribution: location and shape. The location parameter is the lower bound for the variable.

After you select the location parameter, you can estimate the shape parameter. The shape parameter is a number greater than 0, usually greater than 1. The larger the shape parameter, the smaller the variance and the thicker the right-tail of the distribution appears.

Extreme Value Distribution

The extreme value distribution (Type 1) is commonly used to describe the largest value of a response over a period of time: for example, in flood flows, rainfall, and earthquakes. Other applications include the breaking strengths of materials, construction design, and aircraft loads and tolerances. The extreme value distribution is also known as the Gumbel distribution.

Calculating Parameters. There are two standard parameters for the extreme value distribution: mode and scale. The mode parameter is the most likely value for the variable (the highest point on the probability distribution). After you select the mode parameter, you can estimate the scale parameter. The scale parameter is a number greater than 0. The larger the scale parameter, the greater the variance.

Negative Binomial Distribution

The negative binomial distribution is useful for modeling the distribution of the number of trials until the rth successful occurrence, such as the number of sales calls you need to make to close a total of 10 orders. It is essentially a *super*-distribution of the geometric distribution.

Conditions. The three conditions underlying the negative binomial distribution are:

- The number of trials is not fixed.
- The trials continue until the rth success.
- The probability of success is the same from trial to trial.

Forecasting

In the broadest sense, forecasting refers to the act of predicting the future, usually for purposes of planning and managing resources. There are many scientific approaches to forecasting. You can perform "what-if" forecasting by creating and simulating a model, such as with Crystal Ball®, or by collecting data over a period of time and analyzing the trends and patterns. Forecasting uses this latter concept, that is, the patterns of a time-series, to forecast future data.

These scientific approaches usually fall into one of several categories of forecasting:

Time-series   Performs time-series analysis on past patterns of data to forecast results. This works best for stable situations where conditions are expected to remain the same.

Regression   Forecasts results using past relationships between a variable of interest and several other variables that might influence it. This works best for situations where you need to identify the different effects of different variables. This category includes multiple linear regression.

Simulation   Randomly generates many different scenarios for a model to forecast the possible outcomes. This method works best where you might not have historical data but you can build the model of your situation to analyze its behavior.

Qualitative   Uses subjective judgment and expert opinion to forecast results. These methods work best for situations for which there are no historical data or models available.

TIME-SERIES FORECASTING

Time-series forecasting is a category of forecasting that assumes that the historical data is a combination of a pattern and some random error. Its goal is to isolate the pattern from the error by understanding the pattern's level, trend, and seasonality. You can then measure the error using a statistical measurement both to describe how well a pattern reproduces historical data and to estimate how accurately it forecasts the data into the future.

MULTIPLE LINEAR REGRESSION

Multiple linear regression is used for data where one data series (the dependent variable) is a function of, or depends on, other data series (the independent variables). For example, the yield of a lettuce crop depends on the amount of water provided, the hours of sunlight each day, and the amount of fertilizer used.

The goal of multiple linear regression is to find an equation that most closely matches the historical data. The word "multiple" indicates that you can use more than one independent variable to define your dependent variable in the regression equation. The word "linear" indicates that the regression equation is a linear equation. The linear equation describes how the independent variables (x_1, x_2, x_3, . . .) combine to define the single dependent variable (y). Multiple linear regression finds the coefficients for the equation:

$$y = b_0 + b_1x_1 + b_2x_2 + b_3x_3 + \ldots + e$$

where b_1, b_2, *and* b_3, are the coefficients of the independent variables, b_0 is the y-intercept, and e is the error.

If there is only one independent variable, the equation defines a straight line. This uses a special case of multiple linear regression called simple linear regression, with the equation:

$$y = b_0 + b_1x + e$$

where b_0 is the place on the graph where the line crosses the y axis, x is the independent variable, and e is the error. When the regression equation has only two independent variables, it defines a plane. When the regression equation has more than two independent variables, it defines a hyperplane. To find the coefficients of these equations, you can use singular value decomposition.[1]

Optimization

In most simulation models, there are variables over which you have control, such as how much to charge for a product or how much to invest in a project. These controlled variables are called decision variables. Finding the optimal values for decision variables can make the difference between reaching an important goal and missing that goal. This section details the optimization process at a high level, while Appendix 9C provides a step-by-step example on resource optimization solved using Crystal Ball's® OptQuest software.

Obtaining optimal values generally requires that you search in an iterative or ad-hoc fashion. This involves running a simulation for an initial set of values, analyzing the results, changing one or more values, rerunning the simulation, and repeating the process until you find a satisfactory solution. This process can be very tedious and time consuming even for small models, and it is often not clear how to adjust the values from one simulation to the next.

A more rigorous method systematically enumerates all possible alternatives. This approach guarantees optimal solutions. Suppose that a simulation model depends on only two decision variables. If each variable has 10 possible values, trying each combination requires 100 simulations (10^2 alternatives). If each simulation is very short (e.g., two seconds), then the entire process could be done in approximately three minutes of computer time.

However, instead of two decision variables, consider six, then consider that trying all combinations requires 1,000,000 simulations (10^6 alternatives). It is easily possible for complete enumeration to take weeks, months, or even years to carry out.

WHAT IS AN OPTIMIZATION MODEL?

In today's competitive global economy, companies are faced with many difficult decisions. These decisions include allocating financial resources, building or expanding facilities, managing inventories, and determining product-mix strategies. Such decisions might involve thousands or millions of potential alternatives. Considering and evaluating each of them would be impractical or even impossible. A model can provide valuable assistance in incorporating relevant variables when analyzing decisions, and finding the best solutions for making decisions. Models capture the most important features of a problem and present them in a form that is easy to interpret. Models often provide insights that intuition alone cannot. An optimization model has three major elements: decision variables, constraints, and an objective.

- **Decision variables** are quantities over which you have control; for example, the amount of a product to make, the number of dollars to allocate among different investments, or which projects to select from among a limited set. In real options, portfolio optimization analysis includes a go or no-go decision on particular projects. In addition, the dollar or percentage budget allocation across multiple projects can also be structured as decision variables.

- **Constraints** describe relationships among decision variables that restrict the values of the decision variables. For example, a constraint might ensure that the total amount of money allocated among various investments cannot exceed a specified amount, or at most one project from a certain group can be selected. In real options analysis, this could include budget constraints, timing restrictions, minimum returns, or risk tolerance levels.

- **Objective** gives a mathematical representation of the model's objective, such as maximizing profit or minimizing cost, in terms of the decision variables. In real options, the objective may be to maximize returns while minimizing risks (maximizing the returns-to-risk ratio).

Conceptually, an optimization model might look like Figure 5D.1:

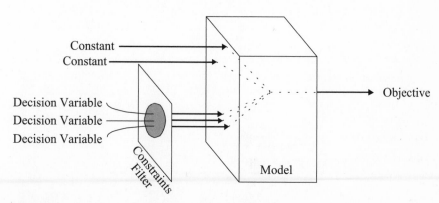

FIGURE 5D.1 Deterministic Optimization Model

The solution to an optimization model provides a set of values for the decision variables that optimizes (maximizes or minimizes) the associated objective. If the world were simple and the future were predictable, all data in an optimization model would be constant, making the model deterministic.

In many cases, however, a deterministic optimization model cannot capture all the relevant intricacies of a practical decision environment. When model data are uncertain and can only be described probabilistically, the objective will have some probability distribution for any chosen set of decision variables. You can find this probability distribution by simulating the model using Crystal Ball®.

An optimization model with uncertainty has several additional elements:

- **Assumptions** capture the uncertainty of model data using probability distributions.

- **Forecasts** are frequency distributions of possible results for the model.

- **Forecast statistics** are summary values of a forecast distribution, such as the mean, standard deviation, and variance. You control the optimization by maximizing, minimizing, or restricting forecast statistics.

- **Requirements** are additional restrictions on forecast statistics. You can set upper and lower limits for any statistic of a forecast distribution. You can also define a range of requirement values by defining a variable requirement (*see* Figure 5D.2).

DECISION VARIABLES

Decision variables are variables in your model which you have control over, such as how much to charge for a product or how much money to invest in a project. In real options, decision variables are the dollar or percentage budget allocation across multiple projects that make up the portfolio.

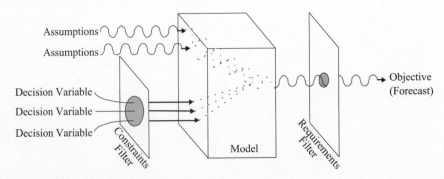

FIGURE 5D.2 Optimization with Uncertainty Model

When you define a decision variable, you define its:

- **Bounds,** which define the upper and lower limits for the variable.

- **Type,** which defines whether the variable is discrete or continuous. A discrete variable can assume integer or non-integer values and must have a defined step size that is greater than 0 (integer or non-integer). A continuous variable requires no step size, and any given range contains an infinite number of possible values. In real options, a discrete variable includes a go or no-go decision on each project. A continuous variable implies the dollar or percentage allocation in each project can take on any continuous value.

- **Step size,** which defines the difference between successive values of a discrete decision variable in the defined range. For example, a discrete decision variable with a range of 1 to 5 and a step size of 1 can only take on the values 1, 2, 3, 4, or 5; a discrete decision variable with a range of 0 to 2 with a step size of 0.25 can only take on the values 0, 0.25, 0.5, 0.75, 1.0, 1.25, 1.5, 1.75, and 2.0.

In an optimization model, you select which decision variables to optimize from a list of all the defined decision variables. The values of the decision variables you select will change with each simulation until the best value for each decision variable is found within the available time limit.

CONSTRAINTS

Constraints restrict the decision variables by defining relationships among them. For example, if the total amount of money invested in two projects must be $50,000, you can define this as

$$\text{Project } X + \text{Project } Y = \$50,000$$

Or if your budget restricts your spending on both projects to $2,500, you can define this as

$$\text{Project } X + \text{Project } Y \le \$2,500$$

FEASIBILITY

A feasible solution is one that satisfies all constraints. Infeasibility occurs when no combination of values of the decision variables can satisfy a set of constraints. Note that a solution (i.e., a single set of values for the decision variables) can be infeasible, by failing to satisfy the problem constraints, and this doesn't imply that the problem or model itself is infeasible.

For example, suppose that an investor insists on finding an optimal investment portfolio with the following constraints:

$$\text{Project } X + \text{Project } Y \leq \$10{,}000$$

$$\text{Project } X + \text{Project } Y \geq \$12{,}000$$

Clearly, there is no combination of investments that will make the sum of the projects no more than \$10,000 and at the same time greater than or equal to \$12,000.

Or, for this same example, suppose the bounds for a decision variable were

$$\$15{,}000 \leq \text{portfolio expenses} \leq \$25{,}000$$

And a constraint was

$$\text{portfolio expenses} \leq \$5{,}000$$

This also results in an infeasible problem.

You can make infeasible problems feasible by fixing the inconsistencies of the relationships modeled by the constraints.

OBJECTIVE

Each optimization model has one objective, a forecast variable, that mathematically represents the model's objective in terms of the assumption and decision variables. Optimization's job is to find the optimal value of the objective by selecting and improving different values for the decision variables.

When model data are uncertain and can only be described using probability distributions, the objective itself will have some probability distribution for any set of decision variables.

FORECAST STATISTICS

You can't use an entire forecast distribution as the objective but rather must characterize the distribution using a single summary measure for comparing and choosing one distribution over another. The statistic you choose depends on your goals for the objective. For maximizing or minimizing some quantity, the mean or median are often used as measures of central tendency, with the mean being the more common of the two. For highly skewed distributions, however, the mean might become the less stable (have a higher standard error) of the two, and so the median becomes a better measure of central tendency. For minimizing overall risk, the standard deviation and the variance of the objective are the two best statistics to use. For maximizing or minimizing the extreme values of the objective, a low or high percentile might be the appropriate statistic. For controlling the shape or range of the objective, the skewness, kurtosis, or certainty statistics might be used.

MINIMIZING OR MAXIMIZING

Whether you want to maximize or minimize the objective depends on which statistic you select to optimize. For example, if your forecast is returns and you select the mean as the statistic, you would want to maximize the mean of the returns. However, if you select the standard deviation as the statistic, you might want to minimize it to limit the uncertainty of the forecast. In real options portfolio optimization, the objective to maximize is usually a returns-to-risk ratio. Maximizing this objective will automatically select the optimal allocation across projects that will maximize returns with the minimum amount of risk (obtaining an efficient frontier).

REQUIREMENTS

Requirements restrict forecast statistics. These differ from constraints, as constraints restrict decision variables (or relationships among decision variables). Requirements are sometimes called "probabilistic constraints," "chance constraints," or "goals" in other literature.

When you define a requirement, you first select a forecast (either the objective forecast or another forecast). As with the objective, you then select a statistic for that forecast, but instead of maximizing or minimizing it, you give it an upper bound, a lower bound, or both (a range). In real options, requirements may be to set the maximum and minimum allowable allocation of capital and resources on each project.

FEASIBILITY

Like constraints, requirements must be satisfied for a solution to be considered feasible. When an optimization model includes requirements, a solution that is constraint-feasible might be infeasible with respect to one or more requirements.

VARIABLE REQUIREMENTS

Variable requirements let you define a range for a requirement bound (instead of a single point) and a number of points to check within the range. When you define a variable requirement, you first select a forecast (either the objective forecast or another forecast). Like the objective or the requirement, you then select a statistic for that forecast, but instead of maximizing or minimizing it, you select to restrict the upper bound or the lower bound. You then define the upper or lower bound with a range.

TYPES OF OPTIMIZATION MODELS

Optimization models can be classified as

Model	Has:
Discrete	Only discrete decision variables
Continuous	Only continuous decision variables
Mixed	Both discrete and continuous decision variables

Linear or Nonlinear

An optimization model can be linear or nonlinear, depending on the form of the mathematical relationships used to model the objective and constraints. In a linear relationship, all terms in the formulas only contain a single variable multiplied by a constant.

For example, $3X - 1.2Y$ is a linear relationship, because the first and second terms only involve a constant multiplied by a variable. Terms such as X^2, XY, $1/X$, or 3.1^X make nonlinear relationships. Any models that contain such terms in either the objective or a constraint are classified as nonlinear.

Deterministic or Stochastic

Optimization models might also be classified as deterministic or stochastic, depending on the nature of the model data. In a deterministic model, all input data are constant or assumed to be known with certainty. In a stochastic model, some of the model data are uncertain and are described with probability distributions. Stochastic models are much more difficult to optimize because they require simulation to compute the objective.

Application

chapter summaries

CHAPTER 6: BEHIND THE SCENES

This chapter introduces the reader to some common types of real options analytics. The two main methods introduced are closed-form differential equations and binomial lattices through the use of risk-neutral probabilities. The advantages and disadvantages of each will be discussed in detail. In addition, the theoretical underpinnings surrounding the binomial equations are demystified here, leading the reader through a set of simplified discussions on how certain binomial equations are derived.

Real Options: Behind the Scenes

This section introduces the reader to the use of binomial models and closed-form solutions, which are the two mainstream approaches, used in solving real options problems. The section also discusses the advantages and disadvantages of using each approach, while demonstrating that the results from both methods approach each other at the limit.

Binomial Lattices

The binomial lattice is introduced here, complete with the application of risk-neutral probabilities, time-steps, and jump sizes.

The Look and Feel of Uncertainty, and a Firm's Real Options Provide Value in the Face of Uncertainty

The idea of uncertainty in cash flow predictions is presented in these two sections. With the use of Monte Carlo simulation, these uncertainties can be easily captured and quantified. However, if there are strategic options in these projects, there may be value in these uncertainties, which Monte Carlo simulation alone cannot capture. The upside and downside options can be better quantified using real options analysis.

Binomial Lattices as a Discrete Simulation of Uncertainty, and Granularity Leads to Precision

The cone of uncertainty is explained through the idea of increasing uncertainty over time. This cone of uncertainty can be captured using stochastic simulation methods, such as the use of Brownian Motions. The section continues with the discussion of how a binomial lattice approximates the simulation of stochastic processes. Indeed, the binomial lattice is a discrete simulation and, at the limit, approaches the results generated using continuous stochastic process simulation techniques, which can be solved using closed-form approaches.

An Intuitive Look at Binomial Equations, and Frolicking in a Risk-Neutral World

These sections look at the binomial equations and how they can be explained intuitively, without the need for difficult and high-level mathematics. The equations include the use of up and down jump-steps as well as the use of risk-neutral probabilities.

CHAPTER 7: REAL OPTIONS MODELS

This chapter looks at the different types of strategic real options, providing a step-by-step methodology in solving these options. The options covered include the options to abandon, expand, contract, and choose. In addition, compound options, changing strike options, changing volatility options, and sequential compound options are discussed. These basic option types provide the basic building blocks in analyzing more complex real options as discussed in the following chapters, including building more sophisticated real options models such as those included in the CD-ROM.

These different real options sections walk the reader through calculating by hand the various real options models. These models include using the binomial lattices and closed-form approaches. Examples of options calculated include the option to expand, contract, barrier, salvage, switch, and so on. There are also several technical appendixes on the derivation of the appropriate volatility estimate, a discussion of the Black-Scholes model, the use of path-dependent valuation using market-replicating portfolios, an example static binomial model, sensitivity models, reality checks, and trinomial trees.

CHAPTER 8: ADVANCED OPTIONS PROBLEMS

The advanced real options problems are discussed here, including exit and abandonment options, timing options, compound options, and the use of stochastic optimization. A discussion of the inappropriate use of decision trees is also included. Three technical appendixes follow the chapter, providing insights into different stochastic processes, differential equations, as well as a barrage of exotic options models.

The options models start from a simple European Black-Scholes model and extend to Black-Scholes with dividend outflows, Chooser options, Complex options, Compound options, Floating Strike options, Fixed Strike options, Forward Start options, Jump-Diffusion options, Spread options, Discrete Time Switch options, and Two Correlated Asset options. The approaches for estimating American-type options are also discussed.

CHAPTER 9: REAL OPTIONS ANALYSIS
TOOLKIT SOFTWARE (CD-ROM)

This chapter previews the Real Options Analysis Toolkit software included on the CD-ROM. A few sample applications are provided, complete with step-by-step software illustrations. In addition, three technical appendixes provide all the function calls available to the user for direct access to the Real Options Analysis Toolkit software from Microsoft Excel, as well as a getting-started guide in using Crystal Ball's® Monte Carlo simulation and stochastic optimization software package by Decisioneering, Inc.

This chapter goes into the technical details of applying real options analysis. It walks the reader through several cases using the Real Options Analysis Toolkit software. Examples of business cases are solved using the software, complete with screen shots of the software, following a step-by-step process.

A software demo of Crystal Ball® is included with this book and can be found on the back cover. The software has all the relevant documentation included on the CD-ROM. The sample case studies in this chapter can be easily replicated using the software.

CHAPTER 10: RESULTS INTERPRETATION
AND PRESENTATION

This chapter walks the reader through the results and sample reports that should be generated by a real options analyst. The chapter includes information to help the reader in interpreting the results and being able to bring the results from the analyst's desktop to the desktop of the CEO.

How do you broach the subject of real options to management? What are the links between traditional approaches versus more advanced analytical approaches? Will management "bet the farm" based on a single number generated through a fancy mathematical model the analyst can't even interpret? This chapter provides a step-by-step methodology in presenting and explaining to management a highly complicated set of analyses through the eyes of an analyst. Complete with graphical displays, charts, tables, and process flows, this chapter provides a veritable cookbook of sorts, for the exposition of the results from a real options analysis.

The results interpretation and presentation proceed through 13 steps. The steps include comparing real options analysis with traditional financial analysis, comparing their similarities, and highlighting their differences. Next, the presentation shows where traditional analyses end and where the new analytics begin, through a simple-to-understand structured evaluation process. Then the results summary is presented, where different projects with different sized investments and returns are compared. This comparison is made on the basis of returns as well as risk structures. The final prognosis is presented as an impact to the bottom line for the company as a consequence of selecting different projects. A critical success factor analysis is also presented, together with its corresponding sensitivity analyses. A Monte Carlo simulation analysis is then presented as a means of identifying and measuring risks inherent in the analysis. Finally, the assumptions and results stemming from a real options analysis are discussed, as are its corresponding risk analyses.

The chapter ends with an appendix listing some of the more relevant articles, books, and publications on the subject of real options analysis. This is done in the hopes of guiding the reader toward and providing the reader with useful resources for additional information. The articles listed are by no means complete but are simply suggested readings by the author, articles which have relevance to the topics discussed in this book.

Behind the Scenes

INTRODUCTION

This chapter and the following two chapters introduce the reader to some common types of real options and a step-by-step approach to analyzing them. The methods introduced include closed-form models, partial-differential equations, and binomial lattices through the use of risk-neutral probabilities. The advantages and disadvantages of each method are discussed in detail. In addition, the theoretical underpinnings surrounding the binomial equations are demystified here, leading the reader through a set of simplified discussions on how certain binomial equations are derived, without the use of fancy mathematics.

REAL OPTIONS: BEHIND THE SCENES

In financial options analysis, there are multiple methodologies and approaches used to calculate an option's value. These range from using closed-form equations like the Black-Scholes model and its modifications, Monte Carlo path-dependent simulation methods, lattices (for example, binomial, trinomial, quadranomial, and multinomial trees), variance reduction and other numerical techniques, to using partial-differential equations, and so forth. However, the mainstream methods that are most widely used are the closed-form solutions, partial-differential equations, and the binomial lattice trees.

Closed-form solutions are models like the Black-Scholes, where there exist equations that can be solved given a set of input assumptions. They are exact, quick, and easy to implement with the assistance of some basic programming knowledge but are difficult to explain because they tend to apply highly technical stochastic calculus mathematics. They are also very specific in nature, with limited modeling flexibility.

Binomial lattices, in contrast, are easy to implement and easy to explain. They are also highly flexible but require significant computing power and

> *Real options can be calculated in different ways, including the use of path-dependent simulation, closed-form models, partial-differential equations, and multinomial and binomial approaches.*

time-steps to obtain good approximations, as we will see later in this chapter. It is important to note, however, that in the limit, results obtained through the use of binomial lattices tend to approach those derived from closed-form solutions, and hence, it is always recommended that both approaches be used to verify the results. The results from closed-form solutions may be used in conjunction with the binomial lattice approach when presenting to management a complete real options solution. In this chapter, we explore these mainstream approaches and compare their results as well as when each approach may be best used, when analyzing the more common types of real options.

Here is an example to illustrate the point of binomial lattices approaching the results of a closed-form solution. Let us look at a European Call Option as calculated using the Generalized Black-Scholes model[1] specified below:

$$Call = Se^{-q(T)} \Phi \left[\frac{\ln(S/X) + (rf - q + \sigma^2/2)T}{\sigma\sqrt{T}} \right] - Xe^{-rf(T)} \Phi \left[\frac{\ln(S/X) + (rf - q - \sigma^2/2)T}{\sigma\sqrt{T}} \right]$$

Let us assume that both the stock price (S) and the strike price (X) are $100, the time to expiration (T) is one year, with a 5 percent risk-free rate (rf) for the same duration, while the volatility (σ) of the underlying asset is 25 percent with no dividends (q). The Generalized Black-Scholes calculation yields $12.3360, while using a binomial lattice we obtain the following results:

N = 10 steps	$12.0923
N = 20 steps	$12.2132
N = 50 steps	$12.2867
N = 100 steps	$12.3113
N = 1,000 steps	$12.3335
N = 10,000 steps	$12.3358
N = 50,000 steps	$12.3360

Notice that even in this oversimplified example, as the number of time-steps (N) gets larger, the value calculated using the binomial lattice approaches the closed-form solution. Do not worry about the computation at this point as we will detail the stepwise calculations in a moment. Suffice it to say, many steps are required for a good estimate using binomial lattices. It has been shown in past research that 1,000 time-steps are usually sufficient for a good approximation.

We can define time-steps as the number of branching events in a lattice. For instance, the binomial lattice shown in Figure 6.1 has three time-steps, starting from time 0. The first time-step has two nodes (S_0u and S_0d), while the second time-step has three nodes (S_0u^2, S_0ud, and S_0d^2), and so on. Therefore, as we have seen previously, to obtain 1,000 time-steps, we need to calculate 1, 2, 3 . . . 1,001 nodes, which is equivalent to calculating 501,501 nodes. If we intend to perform 10,000 simulation trials on the options calculation, we will need approximately 5×10^9 nodal calculations, equivalent to 299 Excel spreadsheets or 4.6 GB of memory space. Definitely a daunting task, to say the least, and we clearly see here the need for using software to facilitate such calculations.[2] One noteworthy item is that the tree below is something called a recombining tree, where at time-step 2, the middle node (S_0ud) is the same as time-step 1's lower bifurcation of S_0u and upper bifurcation of S_0d.

Figure 6.2 is an example of a two time-step binomial lattice that is non-recombining. That is, the center nodes in time-step 2 are different (S_0ud' is not the same as S_0du'). In this case, the computational time and resources are even higher due to the exponential growth of the number of nodes— specifically, 2^0 nodes at time-step 0, 2^1 nodes at time-step 1, 2^2 nodes at time-step 2, and so forth, until $2^{1,000}$ nodes at time-step 1,000 or approximately 2×10^{301} nodes, taking your computer potentially weeks or months to calculate the entire binomial tree! Recombining and non-recombining binomial lattices yield the same results at the limit, so it is definitely easier to

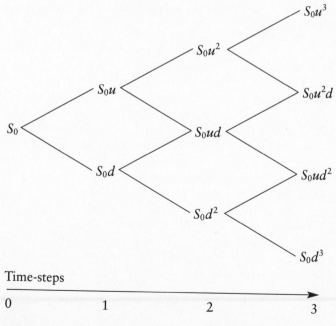

FIGURE 6.1 Three Time-Steps (Recombining Lattice)

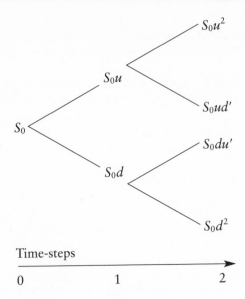

FIGURE 6.2   Two Time-Steps
                (Non-Recombining Lattice)

use recombining lattices for most of our analysis. However, there are exceptions where non-recombining lattices are required, especially when there are two or more stochastic underlying variables or when volatility of the single underlying variable changes over time. Appendix 7I details the use of non-recombining lattices with multiple volatilities, and the use of multiple recombining lattices to recreate a non-recombining lattice.

As you can see, closed-form solutions certainly have computational ease compared to binomial lattices. However, it is more difficult to explain the exact nature of a fancy stochastic calculus equation than it would be to explain a binomial lattice tree that branches up and down. Because both methods tend to provide the same results in the limit anyway, for ease of exposition, the binomial lattice should be presented for management discussions. There are also other issues to contend with in terms of advantages and disadvantages of each technique. For instance, closed-form solutions are mathematically elegant but very difficult to derive and are highly specific in nature. Tweaking a closed-form equation requires facility with sophisticated stochastic mathematics. Binomial lattices, however, although sometimes computationally stressful, are easy to build and require no more than simple algebra, as we will see later. Binomial lattices are also very flexible in that they can be tweaked easily to accommodate most types of real options problems. Nevertheless, there are more advanced options problems for which binomial trees are less useful—for instance, the option types discussed in Chapter 8 and its technical appendixes, where closed-form equations do rather nicely.

We continue the rest of the book with introductions to various types of common real options problems and their associated solutions, using closed-form models, partial-differential equations, and binomial lattices, wherever appropriate. We further use, for simplicity, recombining lattices with only five time-steps in most cases. The reader can very easily extend these five time-step examples into thousands of time-steps using the same algorithms.

BINOMIAL LATTICES

In the binomial world, several basic similarities are worth mentioning. No matter the types of real options problems you are trying to solve, if the binomial lattice approach is used, the solution can be obtained in one of two ways. The first is the use of risk-neutral probabilities, and the second is the use of market-replicating portfolios. Throughout this book, the former approach is used. An example of the market-replicating portfolio approach is shown in Appendix 6B for the sake of completeness. The use of a replicating portfolio is more difficult to understand and apply, but the results obtained from replicating portfolios are identical to those obtained through risk-neutral probabilities. So it does not matter which method is used; nevertheless, application and expositional ease should be emphasized.

Market-replicating portfolios' predominant assumptions are that there are no arbitrage opportunities and that there exist a number of traded assets in the market that can be obtained to replicate the existing asset's payout profile. A simple illustration is in order here. Suppose you own a portfolio of publicly traded stocks that pay a set percentage *dividend* per period. You can, in theory, assuming no trading restrictions, taxes, or transaction costs, purchase a second portfolio of several *non-dividend-paying* stocks and replicate the payout of the first portfolio of *dividend-paying* stocks. You can, for instance, sell a particular number of shares per period to replicate the first portfolio's dividend payout amount at every time period. Hence, if both payouts are identical although their stock compositions are different, the value of both portfolios should then be identical. Otherwise, there will be arbitrage opportunities, and market forces will tend to make them equilibrate in value. This makes perfect sense in a financial securities world where stocks are freely traded and highly liquid. However, in a real options world where physical assets and firm-specific projects are being valued, financial purists would argue that this assumption is hard to accept, not to mention the mathematics behind replicating portfolios are also more difficult to apply.

Compare that to using something called a risk-neutral probability approach. Simply stated, instead of using a risky set of cash flows and discounting them at a risk-adjusted discount rate akin to the discounted cash flow models, one can instead easily risk-adjust the probabilities of specific cash flows occurring at specific times. Thus, using these risk-adjusted probabilities on the cash flows allows the analyst to discount these cash flows (whose risks have now been accounted for) at the risk-free rate. This is the essence of binomial lattices as applied in valuing options. The results obtained are identical.

Let's now see how easy it is to apply risk-neutral valuation. In any options model, there is a minimum requirement of at least two lattices. The first lattice is always the lattice of the underlying asset, while the second lattice is the option valuation lattice. No matter what real options model is of interest, the basic structure almost always exists, taking the form:

$$\text{Inputs: } S, X, \sigma, T, rf, b$$

$$u = e^{\sigma\sqrt{\delta t}} \text{ and } d = e^{-\sigma\sqrt{\delta t}} = \frac{1}{u}$$

$$p = \frac{e^{(rf - b)(\delta t)} - d}{u - d}$$

The basic inputs are the present value of the underlying asset (S), present value of implementation cost of the option (X), volatility of the natural logarithm of the underlying free cash flow returns in percent (σ), time to expiration in years (T), risk-free rate or the rate of return on a riskless asset (rf), and continuous dividend outflows in percent (b). In addition, the binomial lattice approach requires two additional sets of calculations, the up and down factors (u and d) as well as a risk-neutral probability measure (p). We see from the equations above that the up factor is simply the exponential function of the cash flow volatility multiplied by the square root of time-steps or stepping time (δt). Time-steps or stepping time is simply the time scale between steps. That is, if an option has a one-year maturity and the binomial lattice that is constructed has 10 steps, each time-step has a stepping time of 0.1 years. The volatility measure is an annualized value; multiplying it by the square root of time-steps breaks it down into the time-step's equivalent volatility. The down factor is simply the reciprocal of the up factor. In addition, the higher the volatility measure, the higher the up and down factors. This reciprocal magnitude ensures that the lattices are recombining because the up and down steps have the same magnitude but different signs; at places along the future path these binomial bifurcations must meet.

The second required calculation is that of the risk-neutral probability, defined simply as the ratio of the exponential function of the difference between risk-free rate and dividend, multiplied by the stepping time less the down factor, to the difference between the up and down factors. This risk-neutral probability value is a mathematical intermediate and by itself has no particular meaning. One major error real options users commit is to extrapolate these probabilities as some kind of subjective or objective probabilities that a certain event will occur. Nothing is further from the truth. There is no economic or financial meaning attached to these risk-neutralized probabilities save that it is an intermediate step in a series of calculations. Armed with these values, you are now on your way to creating a binomial lattice of the underlying asset value, shown in Figure 6.3.

> *Binomial lattices can be solved through the use of risk-neutral probabilities and market-replicating portfolios. In using binomial and multinomial lattices, the higher the number of time-steps, the higher the level of granularity, and hence, the higher the level of accuracy.*

Starting with the present value of the underlying asset at time zero (S_0), multiply it with the up (u) and down (d) factors as shown below, to create a binomial lattice. Remember that there is one bifurcation at each node, creating an up and a down branch. The intermediate branches are all recombining. This evolution of the underlying asset shows that if the volatility is zero, in a deterministic world where there are no uncertainties, the lattice would be a straight line, and a discounted cash flow model will be adequate because the value of the option or flexibility is also zero. In other words, if volatility (σ) is zero, then the up ($u = e^{\sigma\sqrt{\delta t}}$) and down ($d = e^{-\sigma\sqrt{\delta t}}$) jump sizes are equal to one. It is because there are uncertainties and risks, as captured by the volatility measure, that the lattice is not a

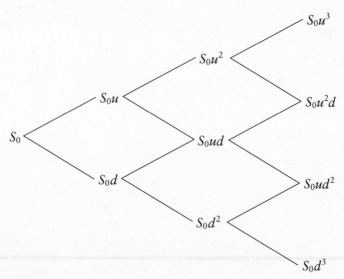

FIGURE 6.3 Binomial Lattice of the Underlying Asset Value

straight horizontal line but comprises up and down movements. It is this up and down uncertainty that generates the value in an option. The higher the volatility measure, the higher the up and down factors as previously defined, the higher the potential value of an option as higher uncertainties exist and the potential upside for the option increases.

Chapter 7 goes into more detail on how certain real options problems can be solved. Each type of problem is introduced with a short business case. Then a closed-form equation is used to value the strategic option. A binomial lattice is then used to confirm the results. In the binomial approach, each problem starts with the lattice evolution of the underlying value, similar to what we have seen thus far. The cases conclude with a summary of the results and relevant interpretations. In each case, a limited number of time-steps are used to facilitate the exposition of the stepwise methodology. The reader can very easily extend the analysis to incorporate more time-steps as necessary.

THE LOOK AND FEEL OF UNCERTAINTY

In most financial analyses, the first step is to create a series of free cash flows, which can take the shape of an income statement or statement of cash flows. The resulting free cash flows are depicted on a time line, akin to that shown in Figure 6.4. These cash flow figures are in most cases forecasts of the

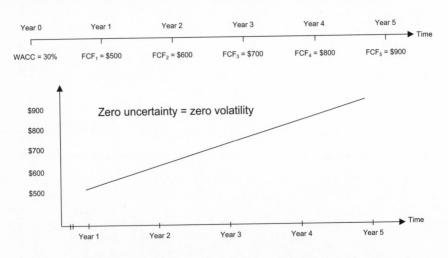

This straight-line cash flow projection is the basics of DCF analysis. This assumes a static and known set of future cash flows.

FIGURE 6.4   Straight-Line Discounted Cash Flow

unknown future. In this simple example, the cash flows are assumed to follow a straight-line growth curve. Similar forecasts can be constructed using historical data and fitting these data to a time-series model or a regression analysis. Whatever the method of obtaining said forecasts or the shape of the growth curve, these are point estimates of the unknown future. Performing a discounted cash flow analysis on these static cash flows provides an accurate value of the project assuming all the future cash flows are known with certainty—that is, no uncertainty exists, and hence, there exists zero volatility around the forecast values.

However, in reality, business conditions are hard to forecast. Uncertainty exists, and the actual levels of future cash flows may look more like those in Figure 6.5. That is, at certain time periods, actual cash flows may be above, below, or at the forecast levels. For instance, at any time period, the actual cash flow may fall within a range of figures with a certain percent probability. As an example, the first year's cash flow may fall anywhere between $480 and $520. The actual values are shown to fluctuate around the forecast values at an average volatility of 20 percent.[3] Certainly this example provides a much more accurate view of the true nature of business conditions, which are fairly difficult to predict with any amount of certainty.

Figure 6.6 shows two sample actual cash flows around the straight-line forecast value. The higher the uncertainty around the actual cash flow levels,

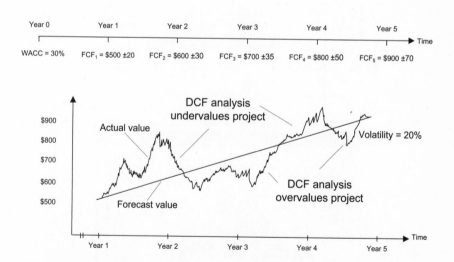

This shows that in reality, at different times, actual cash flows may be above, below, or at the forecast value line due to uncertainty and risk.

FIGURE 6.5 Discounted Cash Flow with Simulation

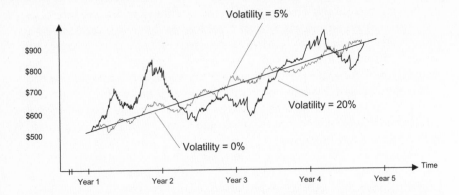

The higher the risk, the higher the volatility and the higher the fluctuation of actual cash flows around the forecast value. When volatility is zero, the values collapse to the forecast straight-line static value.

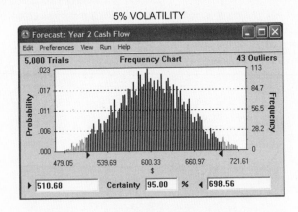

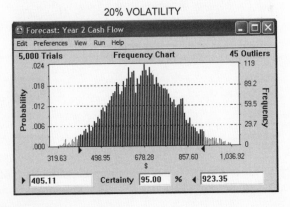

FIGURE 6.6   The Face of Uncertainty

the higher the volatility. The darker line with 20 percent volatility fluctuates more wildly around the forecast values. These values can be quantified using Monte Carlo simulation. For instance, Figure 6.6 also shows the Monte Carlo simulated probability distribution output for the 5 percent volatility line, where 95 percent of the time, the actual values will fall between $510 and $698. Contrast this to a 95 percent confidence range of between $405 and $923 for the 20 percent volatility case. This implies that the actual cash flows can fluctuate anywhere in these ranges, where the higher the volatility, the higher the range of uncertainty.

A FIRM'S REAL OPTIONS PROVIDE VALUE IN THE FACE OF UNCERTAINTY

As seen previously, Monte Carlo simulation can be applied to quantify the levels of uncertainty in cash flows. However, simulation does not consider the strategic alternatives that management may have. For instance, simulation accounts for the range and probability that actual cash flows can be above or below predicted levels but does not consider what management can do if such conditions occur.

Consider Figure 6.7 for a moment. The area above the mean predicted levels, assuming that management has a strategic option to expand into

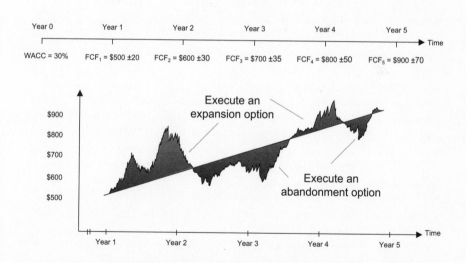

If a firm is strategically positioned to take advantage of these fluctuations, there is value in uncertainty.

FIGURE 6.7 The Real Options Intuition

different markets or products, or develop a new technology, means that executing such an option will yield considerable value. Conversely, if management has the option to abandon a particular technology, market, or development initiative when operating conditions deteriorate, possessing and executing such an abandonment or switching strategy may be valuable. This assumes that management not only has the flexibility to execute these options but also has the willingness to follow through with these strategies when the appropriate time comes. Often, when faced with an abandonment decision, even when it is clearly optimal to abandon a particular project, management may still be inclined to keep the project alive in the hopes that conditions would revert and make the project profitable once again. In addition, management psychology and project attachment may come into play. When the successful execution of a project is tied to some financial remuneration, reputation, or personal strive for merit and achievement, abandoning a project may be hard to do even when it is clearly the optimal decision.

The value of a project's real options requires several assumptions. First, operating, technological, market, and other factors are subject to uncertainty and change. These uncertainties have to drive a project or initiative's value.

Real options have strategic value only when
  (i)   *There is uncertainty.*
  (ii)   *Uncertainty drives project value.*
  (iii) *Management has flexibility.*
  (iv)   *Flexibility strategies are credible and executable.*
  (v)   *Management is rational in executing strategies.*

Furthermore, there exists managerial flexibility or strategic options that management can execute along the way as these uncertainties become resolved over time. Finally, management must not only be able but also willing to execute these options when it becomes optimal to do so. That is, we have to assume that management is rational and execute strategies where the additional value generated is at least commensurate with the risks undertaken. Ignoring such strategic value will grossly underestimate the value of a project. Real options not only provide an accurate accounting of this flexibility value but also indicate the conditions under which executing certain strategies becomes optimal.

Projects that are at-the-money or out-of-the-money—that is, projects with static net present values that are negative or close to breaking even—are most valuable in terms of applying real options. Because real options analysis captures strategic value that is otherwise overlooked in traditional analyses, the additional value obtained may be sufficient to justify projects that are barely profitable.

BINOMIAL LATTICES AS A DISCRETE SIMULATION OF UNCERTAINTY

As uncertainty drives the value of projects, we need to further the discussion on the nature of uncertainty. Figure 6.8 shows a "cone of uncertainty," where we can depict uncertainty as increasing over time. Notice that risk may or may not increase over time, but uncertainty does increase over time. For instance, it is usually much easier to predict business conditions a few months in advance, but it becomes more and more difficult the further one goes into the future, even when business risks remain unchanged. This is the nature of the cone of uncertainty. If we were to attempt to forecast future cash flows while attempting to quantify uncertainty using simulation, a well-prescribed method is to simulate thousands of cash flow paths over time, as shown in Figure 6.8. Based on all the simulated paths, a probability distribution can be constructed at each time period. The simulated pathways were generated using a Geometric Brownian Motion with a fixed volatility. A Geometric Brownian Motion can be depicted as

$$\frac{\delta S}{S} = \mu(\delta t) + \sigma\varepsilon\sqrt{\delta t},$$

where a percent change in the variable S (denoted $\frac{\delta S}{S}$)

is simply a combination of a deterministic part ($\mu(\delta t)$) and a stochastic part ($\sigma\varepsilon\sqrt{\delta t}$). Here, μ is a drift term or growth parameter that increases at a factor of time-steps δt, while σ is the volatility parameter, growing at a

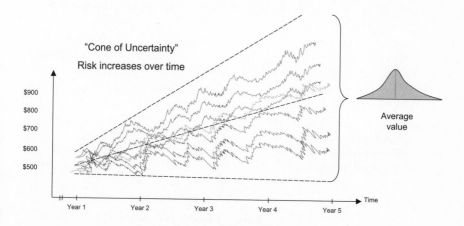

To quantify the risk and forecast the actual cash
flows, multiple simulations are run.

FIGURE 6.8 The Cone of Uncertainty

rate of the square root of time, and ε is a simulated variable, usually following a normal distribution with a mean of zero and a variance of one. Note that the different types of Brownian Motions are widely regarded and accepted as standard assumptions necessary for pricing options. Brownian Motions are also widely used in predicting stock prices.

Notice that the volatility (σ) remains constant throughout several thousand simulations. Only the simulated variable (ε) changes every time.[4] This is an important aspect that will become clear when we discuss the intuitive nature of the binomial equations required to solve a binomial lattice, because one of the required assumptions in options modeling is the reliance on Brownian Motion. Although the risk or volatility measure (σ) in this example remains constant over time, the level of uncertainty increases over time at a factor of ($\sigma\sqrt{\delta t}$). That is, the level of uncertainty grows at the square root of time and the more time passes, the harder it is to predict the future. This is seen in the cone of uncertainty, where the width of the cone increases over time.

Based on the cone of uncertainty, which depicts uncertainty as increasing over time, we can clearly see the similarities in triangular shape between a cone of uncertainty and a binomial lattice as shown in Figure 6.9. In essence, a binomial lattice is simply a discrete simulation of the cone of uncertainty. Whereas a Brownian Motion is a continuous stochastic simulation process, a binomial lattice is a discrete simulation process.

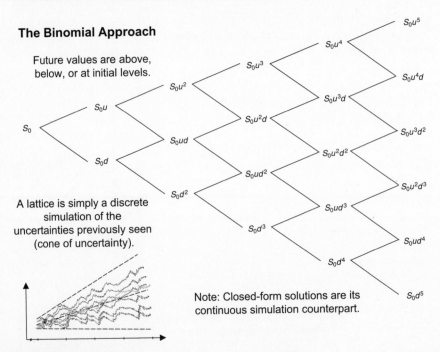

The Binomial Approach

Future values are above, below, or at initial levels.

A lattice is simply a discrete simulation of the uncertainties previously seen (cone of uncertainty).

Note: Closed-form solutions are its continuous simulation counterpart.

FIGURE 6.9   Discrete Simulation Using Binomial Lattices

At the limit, where the time-steps approach zero and the number of steps approach infinity, the results stemming from a binomial lattice approach those obtained from a Brownian Motion process. Solving a Brownian Motion in a discrete sense yields the binomial equations, while solving it in a continuous sense yields closed-form equations like the Black-Scholes and its ancillary models. The following few sections show the simple intuitive discrete derivation of the Brownian Motion process to obtain the binomial equations.

> *A binomial lattice is a type of discrete simulation, whereas a Brownian Motion stochastic process is a continuous simulation.*

As a side note, multinomial models that involve more than two bifurcations at each node, such as the trinomial (three-branch) models or quadranomial (four-branch) models, require a similar Brownian Motion assumption but are mathematically more difficult to solve. No matter how many branches are at each node, these models provide exactly the same results in the limit, the difference being that the more branches at each node, the faster the results are reached. For instance, a binomial model may require a hundred steps to solve a particular real options problem, while a trinomial model probably only requires half the number of steps. However, due to the complexity involved in solving trinomial trees as compared to the easier mathematics required for binomial trees, most real options problems are more readily solved using binomials. For the sake of completeness, Appendix 7H provides an example of how to solve a trinomial tree.

To continue the exploration into the nature of binomial lattices, Figure 6.10 shows the different binomial lattices with different volatilities. This means that the higher the volatility, the wider the range and spread of values between the upper and lower branches of each node in the lattice. Because binomial lattices are discrete simulations, the higher the volatility, the wider the spread of the distribution. This can be seen on the terminal nodes, where the range between the highest and lowest values at the terminal nodes is higher for higher volatilities than the range of a lattice with a lower volatility.

At the extreme, where volatility equals zero, the lattice collapses into a straight line. This straight line is akin to the straight-line cash flow model shown in Figure 6.4. We will further show through an example that for a binomial lattice calculation involving cash flows with zero volatility, the results approach those calculated using a discounted cash flow model's net present value approach. This is important because if there is zero uncertainty and risk, meaning that all future cash flows are known with absolute certainty, then there is no strategic real options value. The discounted cash flow model will suffice. It is because business conditions are fraught with uncertainty, and hence volatility exists and can be captured using a binomial lattice. Therefore,

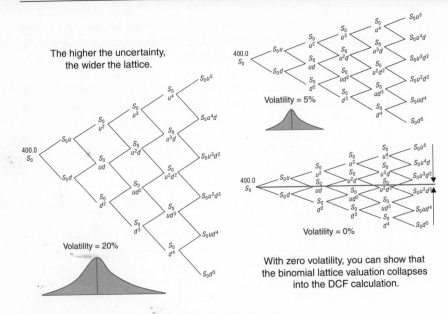

FIGURE 6.10   Volatility and Binomial Lattices

the discounted cash flow model can be seen as a special case of a real options model, when uncertainty is negligible and volatility approaches zero. Hence, discounted cash flow is not necessarily wrong at all; it only implies zero uncertainty in the future forecast of cash flows.

GRANULARITY LEADS TO PRECISION

Another key concept in the use of binomial lattices is the idea of steps and precision. For instance, if a five-year real options project is valued using five steps, each time-step size (δt) is equivalent to one year. Conversely, if 50 steps are used, then δt is equivalent to 0.1 years per step. Recall that the up and down step sizes were $e^{\sigma\sqrt{\delta t}}$ and $e^{-\sigma\sqrt{\delta t}}$, respectively. The smaller δt is, the smaller the up and down steps, and the more granular the lattice values will be.

An example is in order. Figure 6.11 shows the example of a simple European *financial* call option. Suppose the call option has an asset value of $100 and a strike price of $100 expiring in one year. Further, suppose that the corresponding risk-free rate is 5 percent and the calculated volatility of historical logarithmic returns is 25 percent. Because the option pays no dividends and is only exercisable at termination, a Black-Scholes equation will suffice.

- Example of a European *financial call* option with an asset value *(S)* of $100, a strike price *(X)* of $100, a 1-year expiration *(T)*, 5% risk free rate *(r)*, and 25% volatility *(σ)* with no dividend payments
- Using the Black-Scholes equation, we obtain $12.3360

$$Call = S\Phi\left[\frac{\ln(S/X)+(r+\sigma^2/2)T}{\sigma\sqrt{T}}\right] - Xe^{-rT}\Phi\left[\frac{\ln(S/X)+(r-\sigma^2/2)T}{\sigma\sqrt{T}}\right]$$

- Using a 5 step Binomial approach, we obtain $12.79
  - Step I in the Binomial approach:

  $$\text{Given } S = 100, X = 100, \sigma = 0.25, T = 1, rf = 0.05$$

  $$u = e^{\sigma\sqrt{\delta t}} = 1.1183 \text{ and } d = e^{-\sigma\sqrt{\delta t}} = 0.8942$$

  $$p = \frac{e^{rf(\delta t)} - d}{u - d} = 0.5169$$

FIGURE 6.11 European Option Example

The call option value calculated using the Black-Scholes equation is $12.3360, which is obtained by

$$Call = S\Phi\left[\frac{\ln(S/X)+(rf+\sigma^2/2)T}{\sigma\sqrt{T}}\right] - Xe^{-rf(T)}\Phi\left[\frac{\ln(S/X)+(rf-\sigma^2/2)T}{\sigma\sqrt{T}}\right]$$

$$Call = 100\Phi\left[\frac{\ln(100/100)+(0.05+0.25^2/2)1}{0.25\sqrt{1}}\right]$$

$$-100e^{-0.05(1)}\Phi\left[\frac{\ln(100/100)+(0.05-0.25^2/2)1}{0.25\sqrt{1}}\right]$$

$$Call = 100\Phi[0.325] - 95.13\Phi[0.075] = 100(0.6274) - 95.13(0.5298) = 12.3360$$

A binomial lattice can also be applied to solve this problem, as seen in the example in Figures 6.12 and 6.13.

The first step is to solve the binomial lattice equations, that is, to calculate the up step size, down step size, and risk-neutral probability. This assumes that the step size (δt) is 0.2 years (one-year expiration divided by five steps). The calculations proceed as follows:

$$u = e^{\sigma\sqrt{\delta t}} = e^{0.25\sqrt{0.2}} = 1.1183$$

$$d = e^{-\sigma\sqrt{\delta t}} = e^{-0.25\sqrt{0.2}} = 0.8942$$

$$p = \frac{e^{rf(\delta t)} - d}{u - d} = \frac{e^{0.05(0.2)} - 0.8942}{1.1183 - 0.8942} = 0.5169$$

Figure 6.12 illustrates the first lattice in the binomial approach. In a real options world, this lattice is created based on the evolution of the underlying asset's present value of future cash flows. However, in a financial option analysis, this is the $100 initial stock price level. This $100 value evolves over time due to the uncertainty and volatility that exist. For instance, the $100 value becomes $111.8 ($100 × 1.118) on the upper bifurcation at the first time period and $89.4 ($100 × 0.894) on the lower bifurcation. This up and down compounding effect continues until the end terminal, where given a 25 percent annualized volatility, stock prices can, after a period of five years, be anywhere between $57.2 or $174.9. Recall that if volatility is zero, then the lattice collapses into a straight line, where at every time-step interval, the value of the stock will be $100. It is when uncertainty exists that stock prices can vary within this $57.2 to $174.9 interval.

Notice on the lattice in Figure 6.12 that the values are path-independent. That is, the value on node H can be attained through the multiplication of S_0u^2d, which can be arrived at by going through paths ABEH, ABDH, or ACEH. The value of path ABEH is $S \times u \times d \times u$, the value of path ABDH is $S \times u \times u \times d$, and the value of path ACEH is $S \times d \times u \times u$, all of which yields S_0u^2d.

Figure 6.13 shows the calculation of the European option's valuation lattice. The valuation lattice is calculated in two steps, starting with the terminal node and then the intermediate nodes, through a process called

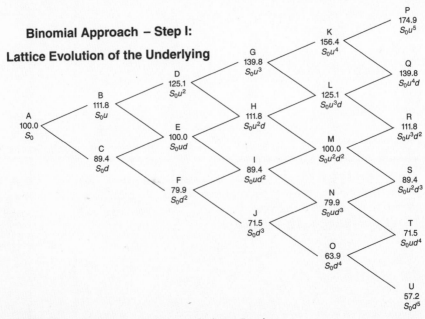

FIGURE 6.12 European Option Underlying Lattice

backward induction. For instance, the circled terminal node shows a value of $74.9, which is calculated through the maximization between executing the option and letting the option expire worthless if the cost exceeds the benefits of execution. The value of executing the option is calculated as $174.9 − $100, which yields $74.9. The value $174.9 comes from Figure 6.12's (node P) lattice of the underlying, and $100 is the cost of executing the option, leaving a value of $74.9.

The second step is the calculation of intermediate nodes. The circled intermediate node illustrated in Figure 6.13 is calculated using a risk-neutral probability analysis. Using the previously calculated risk-neutral probability of 0.5169, a backward induction analysis is obtained through

$$[(p)up + (1 − p)down]\exp[(−riskfree)(\delta t)]$$

$$[(0.5169)41.8 + (1 − 0.5169)16.2]\exp[(−0.05)(0.2)] = 29.2$$

Using this backward induction calculation all the way back to the starting period, the option value at time zero is calculated as $12.79.

Figure 6.14 shows a series of calculations using a Black-Scholes closed-form solution, binomial lattices with different time-steps, and Monte Carlo simulation. Notice that for the binomial lattice, the higher the number of

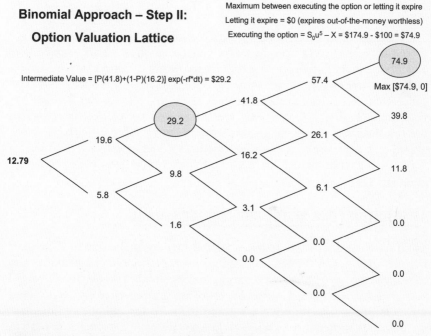

FIGURE 6.13 European Option Valuation Lattice

- Comparison of approaches
  - Black-Scholes: $12.3360
  - Binomial:
    - N = 5 steps $12.7946 ⸺ OVERESTIMATES
    - N = 10 steps $12.0932 ⎤
    - N = 20 steps $12.2132 ⎥
    - N = 50 steps $12.2867 ⎬ UNDERESTIMATES
    - N = 100 steps $12.3113 ⎥
    - N = 1,000 steps $12.3335 ⎥
    - N = 10,000 steps $12.3358 ⎦
    - N = 50,000 steps $12.3360 ⸺ EXACT VALUE
  - Simulation: (10,000 simulations: $12.3360)

FIGURE 6.14   More Time-Steps, Higher Accuracy

time-steps, the more accurate the results become. At the limit, when the number of steps approaches infinity—that is, the time between steps (δt) approaches zero—the discrete simulation in a binomial lattice approaches that of a continuous simulation model, which is the closed-form solution. The Black-Scholes model is applicable here because there are no dividend payments and the option is only executable at termination. When the number of steps approaches 50,000, the results converge. However, in most cases, the level of accuracy becomes sufficient when the number of steps reaches 1,000. Notice that the third method, using Monte Carlo simulation, also converges at 10,000 simulations.

Figure 6.15 shows another concept of binomial lattices. When there are more time-steps in a lattice, the underlying lattice shows more granularities and, hence, higher accuracy. The first lattice shows five steps and the second 20 steps (truncated at 10 steps due to space limitations). Notice the similar values that occur over time. For instance, the value 111.83 in the first lattice occurs at step 1 versus step 2 in the second lattice. All the values in the first lattice recur in the second lattice, but the second lattice is more granular in the sense that more intermediate values exist. As seen in Figure 6.14, the higher number of steps means a higher precision due to the higher granularity.

AN INTUITIVE LOOK AT THE BINOMIAL EQUATIONS

The following discussion provides an intuitive look into the binomial lattice methodology. Although knowledge of some stochastic mathematics and Martingale processes is required to fully understand the complexities involved even in a simple binomial lattice, the more important aspect is to understand how a lattice works, intuitively, without the need for complicated math.

Recall that there are two sets of key equations to consider when calculating a binomial lattice. These equations, shown in Figure 6.16, consist of

5 TIME-STEPS

100.00	111.83	125.06	139.85	156.39	174.90
	89.42	100.00	111.83	125.06	139.85
		79.96	89.42	100.00	111.83
			71.50	79.96	89.42
				63.94	71.50
					57.18

20 TIME-STEPS

100.00	105.75	111.83	118.26	125.06	132.25	139.85	147.89	156.39	165.39	174.90
	94.56	100.00	105.75	111.83	118.26	125.06	132.25	139.85	147.89	156.39
		89.42	94.56	100.00	105.75	111.83	118.26	125.06	132.25	139.85
			84.56	89.42	94.56	100.00	105.75	111.83	118.26	125.06
				79.96	84.56	89.42	94.56	100.00	105.75	111.83
					75.62	79.96	84.56	89.42	94.56	100.00
						71.50	75.62	79.96	84.56	89.42
							67.62	71.50	75.62	79.96
								63.94	67.62	71.50
									60.46	63.94
										57.18

FIGURE 6.15   More Steps, More Granularity, More Accuracy

$$u = e^{\sigma\sqrt{\delta t}} \text{ and } d = e^{-\sigma\sqrt{\delta t}} = \frac{1}{u}$$

$$p = \frac{e^{(rf-b)(\delta t)} - d}{u - d}$$

- The first equation is simply a discrete simulation step size used in the first lattice of the underlying.

- The second equation is a risk-neutral probability calculation.

FIGURE 6.16   The Lattice Equations

an *up/down* equation (which are simply the discrete simulation's step size in a binomial lattice used in creating a lattice of the underlying asset) and a *risk-neutral probability* equation (used in valuing a lattice through backward induction). These two sets of equations are consistently applied to all real options binomial modeling regardless of its complexity.[5] In Figure 6.16, we see that the up step size (u) is shown as $u = e^{\sigma\sqrt{\delta t}}$, and the down step size (d) is shown as $d = e^{-\sigma\sqrt{\delta t}}$, where σ is the volatility of logarithmic cash flow returns and δt is the time-step in a lattice. The risk-neutral probability (p) is shown as

$$p = \frac{e^{(rf-b)\delta t} - d}{u - d},$$

where *rf* is the risk-free rate in percent, and *b* is the continuous dividend payout in percent.

The intuition behind the lattice equations is somewhat more cumbersome but is nonetheless important. An analyst must not only have the mathematical aptitude but also the ability to explain what goes on behind the scenes when calculating a real options model. Figures 6.17 and 6.18 provide an intuitive look and feel of the derivation of the binomial lattice equations in a very simplified and intuitive format, as opposed to using cumbersome financial mathematics.

As Figure 6.17 shows, in the deterministic case where uncertainty is not built into a financial valuation model, future cash flows can be forecast using regression analysis on historical data, using time-series analysis, or using management assumptions. However, in a stochastic case when uncertainty exists and is built into the model, several methods can be applied, including simulating a Brownian Motion. As seen earlier, Brownian Motion processes are used in financial forecasting and option pricing models.

Starting with an Exponential Brownian Motion, where

$$\frac{\delta S}{S} = e^{\mu(\delta t) \, + \, \sigma \varepsilon \sqrt{\delta t}},$$

we can segregate the process into a deterministic and a stochastic part, where we have

$$\frac{\delta S}{S} = e^{\mu(\delta t)} e^{\sigma \varepsilon \sqrt{\delta t}}.$$

The deterministic part of the model ($e^{\mu(\delta t)}$) accounts for the slope or growth rate of the Brownian process. If you recall, in real options analysis, the underlying asset variable (usually denoted S in options modeling) is the present value of future free cash flows, which means that the growth rates in cash flows from one period to the next have already been intuitively accounted for in the discounted cash flow analysis.[6] Hence, we only have to account for the stochastic term ($e^{\sigma \varepsilon \sqrt{\delta t}}$), which has a highly variable simulated term (ε).

The stochastic term ($e^{\sigma \varepsilon \sqrt{\delta t}}$) has a volatility component (σ), a time component (δt), and a simulated component (ε). Again, recall that the binomial lattice approach is a discrete simulation model; we no longer need to re-simulate at every time period, and the simulated variable (ε) drops out. The remaining stochastic term is simply $e^{\sigma \sqrt{\delta t}}$.

Finally, in order to obtain a recombining binomial lattice, the up and down step sizes have to be symmetrical in magnitude. Hence, if we set the up step size as $e^{\sigma \sqrt{\delta t}}$, we can set the down step size as its reciprocal, or $e^{-\sigma \sqrt{\delta t}}$.

These up and down step sizes are used in the creation of a lattice evolution of the underlying asset, the first step in a real options binomial modeling approach. Notice that the values on the lattice evolution of the underlying depend on nothing more than the volatility and time-steps between nodes. Each up and down jump size is identical no matter how far out on the lattice you go, but the cumulative effects of these jumps increase over time. That is, the up (u) value in Figure 6.16 is the same no matter which node you are on. However, the further out one goes, the cumulative effects (u^3 or u^2d, etc.) increase at the rate of $e^{\sigma\sqrt{\delta t}}$ or $e^{-\sigma\sqrt{\delta t}}$. This means that the higher the volatility, the wider the range of observed values on the lattice. In addition,

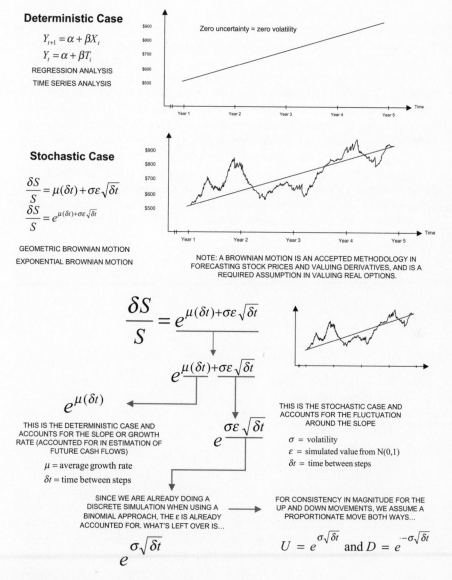

FIGURE 6.17 Up and Down Lattice Equations

the lower the value of the time-steps, the more granular and detailed the lattice becomes, as shown in Figure 6.15.

The second equation for the binomial model is that of a risk-neutral probability. The risk-neutral probability is defined in Figure 6.18 as

$$p = \frac{e^{(rf-b)\delta t} - d}{u - d}.$$

Figure 6.18 shows an intuitive derivation of the risk-neutral probability, and Figure 6.19 explains what a risk-neutral probability is and what it does. Start with a simple example of a coin toss, where heads would yield a $1 payoff and tails would yield a $0 payoff. Assuming you start with a fair coin, the expected payoff for this game would be *$0.50 = 50%($1) + 50%($0)*. That is, the game has a value of $0.50, where if you were risk-neutral, you would be indifferent between betting $0.50 on the game and walking away. If you are risk-taker, you would be willing to bet more than $0.50 on the game, and a risk-adverse person would probably only enter into the game if the cost of entry is less than the $0.50 expected payoff.

Figure 6.18 shows a similar problem using a decision node with two bifurcations and their associated probabilities of occurrence. The expected value of the binomial tree is calculated the same way as the coin toss game described above, where the expected value of the starting point is simply

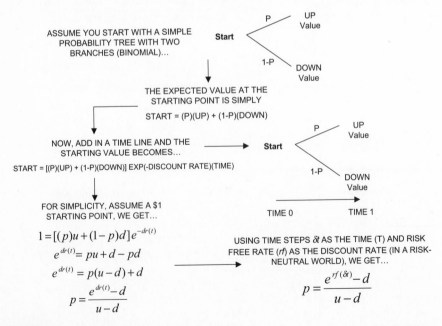

FIGURE 6.18   Risk-Neutral Probability Equation

(p) *up* + (1 − p) *down*. Now, if a time line is added to the analysis—that is, if the game takes time *t* (e.g., a whole year) to complete—the game payoffs should be discounted for the time value of money. If the payouts are not guaranteed values but have some risk associated with their levels, then they should be discounted at a market risk-adjusted discount rate. That is, the expected starting present value of the payoffs should be [(p) *up* + (1 − p) *down*]*exp*(−*discount rate*)(*time*).[7] If we define *dr* as discount rate, *t* as time, *u* as the payoff in the event of an up condition, and *d* for the payoff in the event of a down condition on the binomial branch, the starting present value of this problem can be shown as $Start = [(p)u + (1 − p)d]e^{-dr(t)}$.

For simplicity, if we assume that the starting value is unity, a basic and well-accepted assumption that is used in option pricing models, then we can rewrite the starting value as $1 = [(p)u + (1 − p)d]e^{-dr(t)}$. Multiplying both sides with the reciprocal of $e^{-dr(t)}$ yields $(p)u + (1 − p)d = e^{dr(t)}$. Expanding and regrouping the terms yield $p(u − d) + d = e^{dr(t)}$, and solving for *p* yields

$$p = \frac{e^{dr(t)} − d}{u − d}.$$

This risk-neutral probability is simply the solution for the probabilities on a binomial lattice. As in the binomial lattice paradigm, the time is simply the time-steps between nodes; we can denote *t* as δ*t*. In addition, as will be explained later, this probability *p* is used in a risk-neutral world, a world where risks have already been accounted for; hence, the discount rate *dr* is simply the risk-free rate *rf*. Replacing these values, we get the binomial equation

$$p = \frac{e^{rf(\delta t)} − d}{u − d}.$$

However, when there are continuous streams of dividend present, this risk-free rate is modified to risk-free rate less the dividend yield (*rf* − *b*).

FROLICKING IN A RISK-NEUTRAL WORLD

A risk-neutral world simply means that a certain variable is stripped of its risks. In our example, the certain variable is the cash flow payouts. These cash flow payouts can be stripped off their risks or, in common finance language, discounted of risks by risk-adjusting in two ways. The first method is simply to risk-adjust the cash flow payouts themselves. This implies the use of a discounted cash flow method, applying the appropriate market risk-adjusted discount rate, which is typically higher than the risk-free rate. The second method is to adjust the probabilities that lead to the payouts, then, using the original cash flows, discount them by the risk-free rate, not a market risk-adjusted rate as risk has already been accounted for by the adjusted probabilities and should not be double-counted. This implies the use of risk-neutral probabilities in the binomial world. Both approaches yield the same results when applied appropriately.

Figure 6.19 illustrates both these risk-adjustment methods. For instance, if the discount rate is 22.08 percent and the payoff occurs after one year, the expected present value of the coin-toss game is $[50\%(\$1) + 50\%(\$0)]$ $exp[(-22.08\%)(1)] = \$0.40$. This $0.40 is the risk-adjusted value of the game in present dollars, as compared to the $0.50 if the payoffs are immediate. This is intuitive because a payoff that is risky and may or may not happen in a year is certainly worth less than a payoff that is certain and occurs

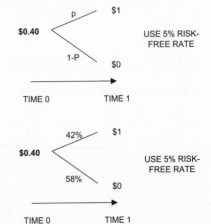

SAY YOU HAVE A GAME OF CHANCE (TOSSING A COIN), WITH A 50% CHANCE OF PAYING $1 (HEADS) AND 50% CHANCE OF PAYING $0 (TAILS). THE EXPECTED VALUE IS $0.50.

ASSUME THE PAYOUT OCCURS IN A FUTURE TIME PERIOD (TIME 1) AND THE GAME IS OBVIOUSLY RISKY. WE SHOULD THEN DISCOUNT THE PAYOUT BY A RISK-ADJUSTED DISCOUNT RATE (SAY, 22.08%) FOR THE ONE TIME PERIOD. THE VALUE OF THE GAME IS NOW...

[50% ($1) + 50% ($0)] EXP(-22.08%)(1) = $0.40

THIS IS THE RISK-ADJUSTED VALUE OF THE GAME

YOU CAN OBTAIN THE SAME $0.40 VALUE BY TWO WAYS... THE FIRST IS RISK-ADJUSTING THE CASH FLOW PAYOUTS WITH A RISK-ADJUSTED DISCOUNT RATE. THE SECOND IS USING THE SAME CASH FLOW PAYOUTS BUT RISK-ADJUSTING THE PROBABILITIES OF OCCURRENCE OF EACH CASH FLOW STREAM. IF YOU RISK ADJUST (OR RISK NEUTRALIZE) THE PROBABILITIES, THE CASH FLOW PAYOUTS SHOULD THEN BE DISCOUNTED AT A RISK-FREE RATE AND NOT A RISK-ADJUSTED DISCOUNT RATE TO AVOID DOUBLE COUNTING.

USING THE SAME GAME, WE GET...

[P($1) + (1-P) ($0)] EXP(-5%)(1) = $0.40

THE CALCULATED RISK-NEUTRAL PROBABILITY (P) IS 42%, ADJUSTED FROM THE OBJECTIVE PROBABILITY OF 50%.

CLEARLY, BOTH APPROACHES YIELD THE SAME RESULTS, FOR INSTANCE, WE SEE HERE THAT...

[42%($1) + 58%($0)] EXP(-5%)(1) = $0.40

NOTE: THE RISK-NEUTRAL PROBABILITY APPROACH IS PREFERRED IN OPTIONS ANALYSIS AS IT REDUCES THE RISK OF ESTIMATION ERRORS OF A RISK-ADJUSTED DISCOUNT RATE.

FIGURE 6.19 A Risk-Neutral World

immediately. A player should be willing to enter into a bet only if the cost of entry is lower than what the payoff is worth. This method is akin to the discounted cash flow approach where the cash flows are adjusted for risk by discounting them by the appropriate risk-adjusted discount rate.

Figure 6.19 also illustrates the second method, using risk-neutral probabilities. Using the same game parameters, the risk-neutral probabilities can be calculated. That is, as the expected value is calculated as $0.40, we can get p by imputing the expected value using $[(p)\$1 + (1 - p)\$0]exp[(-5\%)(1)]$, where the risk-neutral probability p is calculated as 42 percent, compared to the original objective probability of 50 percent. By adjusting the probabilities for risk, the cash flow payoffs should then be discounted using the risk-free rate of 5 percent. Notice that using this imputed 42 percent risk-neutral probability, we can also calculate the expected present value of the cash flows through $[42\%(\$1) + 58\%(\$0)]exp[(-5\%)(1)] = \$0.40$, the same value obtained through discounting the cash flows.

The upshot is that a risky series of cash flows should be adjusted for risk, and there exist two methods to perform the risk adjustment. The cash flow series themselves can be adjusted through a risk-adjusted discount rate; or the probabilities leading to the cash flows can be adjusted and the resulting adjusted cash flows can be discounted using a risk-free rate. The former approach is well known and widely used in discounted cash flow models and the latter for solving binomial lattices. The latter is preferred for real options analysis as it avoids having to estimate project-specific discount rates at different nodes along the binomial lattice or within the context of a decision tree analysis.

For instance, if a decision tree analysis is used (which by itself is insufficient for solving real options), then different discount rates have to be estimated at each decision node at different times because different projects at different times have different risk structures. Estimation errors will then be compounded on a large decision tree analysis. Binomial lattices using risk-neutral probabilities avoid this error.

One major conclusion that can be drawn using binomial lattices is that because risk-adjusting cash flows provides the same results as risk-adjusting the probabilities leading to those cash flows, the results stemming from a discounted cash flow analysis are identical to those generated using a binomial lattice. The only condition that is required is that the volatility of the cash flows be zero—in other words, the cash flows are assumed to be known with certainty. Because zero uncertainty exists, there is zero strategic option value, meaning that the net present value of a project is identical to its expanded net present value. Figure 6.20 illustrates this point.

Given the levels of cash flow series in Figure 6.20, the net present value is calculated to be $1,426 after being discounted using a weighted average cost of capital of 35 percent. This is essentially the first approach where cash flows are risk-adjusted by this 35 percent market risk-adjusted discount rate.

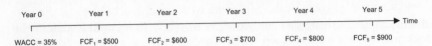

WACC = 35%   FCF$_1$ = $500   FCF$_2$ = $600   FCF$_3$ = $700   FCF$_4$ = $800   FCF$_5$ = $900

NPV = $1426

WE CAN CONSTRUCT BINOMIAL REAL OPTIONS MODEL AROUND THESE VALUES.

ASSUME THE PRESENT VALUE OF THE UNDERLYING ASSET IS $2426 AND THE IMPLEMENTATION COST IS $1000, WHICH YIELDS A NPV OF $1426. ASSUME A SIMILAR 5 YEAR PERIOD AND NO RISK-FREE RATE. SINCE WE ARE CONSTRUCTING A NPV ANALYSIS ON A BINOMIAL LATTICE, WE CAN ASSUME 0% VOLATILITY AND A RISK-NEUTRAL PROBABILITY P OF 100% (A GUARANTEED EVENT WITH NO VOLATILITY OR UNCERTAINTY).

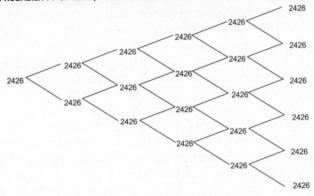

THE BINOMIAL APPROACH YIELDS THE SAME RESULT ($1426) AS THE NPV ANALYSIS WITH SIMPLE DISCOUNTING.

Maximum between executing the option or letting it expire

Letting it expire = $0 (expires out-of-the-money worthless)

Executing the option = $S_0 u^5 - X$ = $2426 - $1000 = $1426

Intermediate Value = $[P(1426)+(1-P)(1426)]\, exp(-rf*dt)$ = $1426

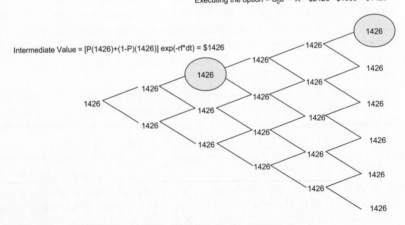

FIGURE 6.20   Solving a DCF Model with a Binomial Lattice

The second approach is the use of a binomial lattice. Notice that the starting point on a binomial lattice is the present value of future cash flows; we arbitrarily set it as $2,426, with a corresponding $1,000 implementation cost. This is acceptable as long as the net present value yields *$1,426* *($2,426 − $1,000)*. Starting with this $2,426 value, the binomial equations are calculated. First, the up and down step sizes are calculated using $u = e^{\sigma\sqrt{\delta t}} = e^{0\%\sqrt{1}} = 1$ and $d = e^{-\sigma\sqrt{\delta t}} = e^{-0\%\sqrt{1}} = 1$ since volatility is assumed to be 0 percent, and five steps are used for the five years, resulting in a time-step δt of 1. In addition, the risk-neutral probability is 100 percent: recall from Figure 6.10 that a zero volatility lattice collapses into a straight line, there is no up or down step, hence, the risk-neutral probability is 100 percent. The first binomial lattice shown in Figure 6.20 illustrates this situation, where the asset evolutions in all future states are identical to the starting value.

The second lattice shows the valuation of the binomial model. The terminal nodes are simply the maximization between executing the option or letting it expire. The value of executing the option is $2,426 − $1,000 at every terminal node, and the value of letting the option expire is $0. All intermediate nodes carry the value of the option going forward, similar to the European call option. For simplicity, assume a negligible risk-free rate. That is, the value of $[(p)\$1,426 + (1 − p)\$1,426]exp[(−0\%)(1)] = \$1,426$ at each intermediate node, going back to the starting value. In this highly simplified and special case, the calculated net present value is identical to the value calculated using a binomial lattice approach. In essence, a real options analysis is, at its most basic level, similar in nature to the net present value analysis.

Figure 6.21 illustrates this condition. In a traditional financial analysis, we usually calculate the net present value, which is nothing but benefits less cost (first equation)—that is, benefits equal the present value of future net cash flows after taxes, discounted at some market risk-adjusted cost of capital; and cost equals the present value of investment cost discounted at the risk-free rate.

Management is usually knowledgeable of net present value and the way it is calculated. Conventional wisdom is such that if benefits outweigh costs—that is, when the net present value is positive—one would be inclined to accept a particular project. This is simple and intuitive enough. However, when we turn to options theory and look at a simple call option, it is also nothing but benefits less cost (second equation), with a slight modification.

The difference is the introduction of the $\Phi(d)$ multipliers behind benefits and costs. Obviously, the multipliers are nothing but the respective probabilities of occurrence, obtained through the discrete simulation process in binomial lattices. Hence, in real options theory, one can very simply define the value of an option as nothing more than benefits less costs, taking into account the risk or probabilities of occurrence for each variable, similar to using the Black-Scholes model. Therefore, if there is no uncertainty and the

$$NPV = Benefits - Cost$$
$$Option = Benefits \; \Phi(d_1) - Cost \; \Phi(d_2)$$
$$eNPV = NPV + Options \; Value$$

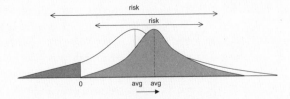

FIGURE 6.21   Real Options and Net Present Value

volatility is zero, and the probability of occurrence is 100 percent, indicating that the forecast values are guaranteed to occur, as in the special case, then the real options value collapses into the net present value when both $\Phi(d) = 100\%$. It is easy to understand that option value in this case is far superior to the net present value analysis if uncertainty exists and volatility is not equal to zero, and hence, both $\Phi(d)$ are not equal to 100 percent. Finally, we can say that the expanded net present value (*eNPV*) shown as the third equation is the sum of the deterministic base case net present value and the strategic options value. The options value takes into account the value of flexibility, that is, the ability to execute on a strategic option but not the obligation to do so; the *eNPV* accounts for both base-case analysis and the added value of flexibility.

SUMMARY

The binomial approach, partial-differential equations, and closed-form solutions are the mainstream approaches used in solving real options problems. The binomial approach is favored due to its mathematical simplicity and ease of exposition. It helps make the black box more transparent and, in turn, the results more palatable to senior management. In addition, the mathematics involved in calculating a binomial lattice—that is, the use of up/down jump sizes as well as risk-neutral probabilities—can be easily and intuitively explained without the use of often intractable stochastic mathematical techniques applied in partial-differential equations and closed-form solutions.

CHAPTER 6 QUESTIONS

1. Why does solving a real options problem using the binomial lattices approach the results generated through closed-form models?

2. Is real options analysis a special case of discounted cash flow analysis, or is discounted cash flow analysis a special case of real options analysis?

3. Explain what a risk-neutral probability means.

4. What is the difference between a recombining lattice and a non-recombining lattice?

5. Using the example in Figures 6.12 through 6.14, create and value the same European option using 10 time-steps. Verify that your answers match those given in Figure 6.14.

Real Options Models

INTRODUCTION

his chapter provides step-by-step examples of solving real options models. The common types of real options solved include abandonment, expansion, contraction, chooser, switching, compound, changing strikes, and volatility options. Chapter 8 and its accompanying appendixes discuss more advanced types of options including switching, timing, and barrier options. The examples in this chapter are useful as building blocks for solving more complicated real options models. The examples used here are intentionally kept simple, for expositional purposes. More advanced technical examples are provided in the appendixes. These examples are again revisited in Chapter 9 and solved using the enclosed Real Options Analysis Toolkit software and Crystal Ball's® Monte Carlo simulation software CD-ROM.

OPTION TO ABANDON

Suppose a pharmaceutical company is developing a particular drug. However, due to the uncertain nature of the drug's development progress, market demand, success in human and animal testing, and FDA approval, management has decided that it will create a strategic abandonment option. That is, at any time period within the next five years of development, management can review the progress of the research and development effort and decide whether to terminate the drug development program. After five years, the firm would have either succeeded or completely failed in its drug development initiative, and there exists no option value after that time period. If the program is terminated, the firm can potentially sell off its intellectual property rights of the drug in question to another pharmaceutical firm with which it has a contractual agreement. This contract with the other firm is exercisable at any time within this time period, at the whim of the firm owning the patents.

Using a traditional discounted cash flow model, the present value of the expected future cash flows discounted at an appropriate market risk-adjusted discount rate is found to be $150 million. Using Monte Carlo simulation, the implied volatility of the logarithmic returns on future cash flows is found to be 30 percent. The risk-free rate on a riskless asset for the same time frame is 5 percent, and you understand from the intellectual property officer of the firm that the drug's patent is worth $100 million if sold within the next five years. For simplicity, assume that this $100 million salvage value is fixed for the next five years. You attempt to calculate how much this abandonment option is worth and how much this drug development effort on the whole is worth to the firm. You decide to use a closed-form approximation of an American put option because the option to abandon the drug development can be exercised at any time up to the expiration date. You also decide to confirm the value of the closed-form analysis with a binomial lattice calculation. Figures 7.1 and 7.2 show the results of your analysis using a binomial approach. Using the Bjerksund closed-form American put option approximation equation (available in the Real Options Analysis Toolkit software), you calculate the value of the American option to abandon as $6.9756 million. However, using the binomial approach, you calculate the value of the abandonment option as $6.6412 million using 5 time-steps and $7.0878 million using 1,000 time-steps, thereby verifying the results obtained.[1] An example of the first lattice, the lattice of the underlying asset, is shown in Figure 7.1.

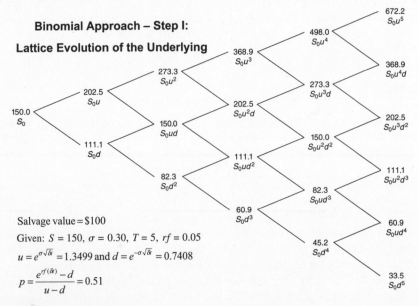

Binomial Approach – Step I:

Lattice Evolution of the Underlying

Salvage value = $100

Given: $S = 150$, $\sigma = 0.30$, $T = 5$, $rf = 0.05$

$u = e^{\sigma\sqrt{\delta t}} = 1.3499$ and $d = e^{-\sigma\sqrt{\delta t}} = 0.7408$

$p = \dfrac{e^{rf(\delta t)} - d}{u - d} = 0.51$

FIGURE 7.1 Abandonment Option (Underlying Lattice)

All the required calculations and steps in Figure 7.1 are based on the up factor, down factor, and risk-neutral probability analysis previously alluded to in Chapter 6. The up factor is calculated to be 1.3499, and the down factor is 0.7408. Hence, starting with the underlying value of $150, we multiply this value with the up and down factors to obtain $202.5 and $111.1, respectively. Readers can verify for themselves the rest of the lattice calculations in Figure 7.1. The second step is to calculate the option valuation lattice as shown in Figure 7.2, using the values calculated in Figure 7.1's lattice evolution of the underlying asset.

Creating the option valuation lattice proceeds in two steps, the valuation of the terminal nodes and the valuation of the intermediate nodes using a process called backward induction. If you recall from the first lattice, the values are created in a forward multiplication of up and down factors, from left to right. For this second lattice, the calculation proceeds in a backward manner, starting from the terminal nodes. That is, the nodes at the end of the lattice are valued first, going from right to left.

In Figure 7.2, we see that the sample circled terminal node (denoted A) reveals a value of $672.2, which can be obtained through the value maximization of abandonment versus continuation. At the end of five years, the firm has the option to both sell off and abandon its existing drug program or to continue developing. Obviously, management will choose the strategy that

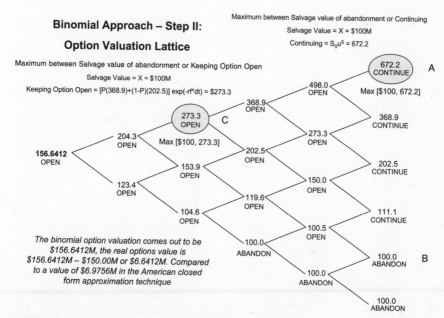

FIGURE 7.2 Abandonment Option (Valuation Lattice)

maximizes profitability. The value of abandoning the drug program is equivalent to selling the patent rights at the predetermined $100 million value. The value of continuing with development can be found in Figure 7.1's lattice evolution of the underlying at the same node (S_0u^5), which is $672.2 million. The profit-maximizing decision is to continue development; hence, we have the value $672.2 million on that node (denoted A). Similarly, for the terminal node B in Figure 7.2, we see that the value of abandoning at that time is $100 million as compared to $60.99 in Figure 7.1. Hence, the decision at that node is to abandon the project, and the profit-maximizing value of that node becomes the abandonment value of $100 million. This is very easy to understand because if the underlying asset value of pursuing the drug development is high (node A), it is wise to continue with the development. Otherwise, if circumstances force the value of the development effort down to such a low level as specified by node B, then it is more optimal to abandon the project and cut the firm's losses. This of course assumes that management will execute the optimal profit-maximizing behavior of abandoning the project when it is optimal to do so rather than hanging on to it.

Moving on to the intermediate nodes, we see that node C is calculated as $273.3 million. At this particular node, the firm again has two options, to abandon at that point or not to abandon, thereby keeping the option to abandon open and available for the future in the hopes that when things seem less rosy, the firm has the ability to execute the option and abandon the development program. The value of abandoning is again the $100 million in salvage value. The value of continuing is simply the discounted weighted average of potential future option values using the risk-neutral probability.

Because the risk adjustment is performed on the probabilities of future option cash flows, the discounting can be done using the risk-free rate. That is, for the value of keeping the option alive and open, we have $[(P)(\$368.9) + (1 - P)(\$202.5)]exp[(-rf)(\delta t)] = \$273.3$ *million*, which is higher than the abandonment value. This assumes a 5 percent risk-free rate *rf*, a time-step δt of 1 (five years divided into five time-steps means each time-step is equivalent to one year), and a risk-neutral probability P of 0.51. Using this backward induction technique, the lattice is calculated back to the starting point to obtain the value of $156.6412 million. Because the value obtained through a discounted cash flow is $150 million, we can say that the difference of $6.6412 million additional value is due to the abandonment option.

By having a safety net or way out for management given dire circumstances, the project is worth more than its static value of $150 million. The $150 million is the static NPV without flexibility, the $6.6412 million is the real options value, and the combined value of $156.6412 million is the ENPV (expanded NPV) or NPV+O (NPV with real options flexibility), the correct total value of this drug development program. Clearly, modifications to the lattice analysis can be done to further mirror actual business conditions. For instance, the abandonment salvage value can change over time, which can simply be instituted through changing the salvage amount at the appropriate times with respect to the nodes on the lattice. This could be an inflation adjustment, a growth or decline in the value of the intellectual property over time, etc.

OPTION TO EXPAND

Suppose a growth firm has a static valuation of future profitability using a discounted cash flow model (that is, the present value of the expected future cash flows discounted at an appropriate market risk-adjusted discount rate) is found to be $400 million. Using Monte Carlo simulation, you calculate the implied volatility of the logarithmic returns on the projected future cash flows to be 35 percent. The risk-free rate on a riskless asset for the next five years is found to be yielding 7 percent. Suppose that the firm has the option to expand and double its operations by acquiring its competitor for a sum of $250 million at any time over the next five years. What is the total value of this firm assuming you account for this expansion option?

You decided to use a closed-form approximation of an American call option because the option to expand the firm's operations can be exercised at any time up to the expiration date. You also decide to confirm the value of the closed-form analysis with a binomial lattice calculation. Figures 7.3 and 7.4 show the results of your analysis using a binomial approach. Using the Barone-Adesi-Whaley closed-form American call approximation equation,

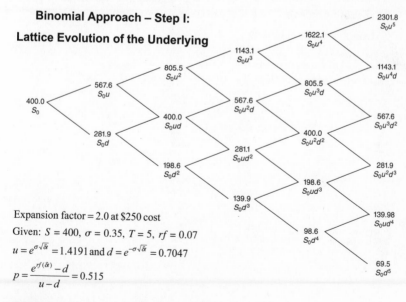

FIGURE 7.3 Expansion Option (Underlying Lattice)

you estimate the benchmark value of the American option to expand as $626.6 million.[2] However, using the binomial approach, you calculate the value of the expansion option as $638.3 million using 5 time-steps and $638.8 using 1,000 time-steps, thereby verifying the results obtained. The reader can easily verify these results using the enclosed Real Options Analysis Toolkit software CD-ROM to run the binomial analysis for 1,000 steps with the Super Lattice routine. An example of the first lattice, the lattice of the underlying asset, is shown in Figure 7.3.

All the required calculations and steps in Figure 7.3 are based on the up factor, down factor, and risk-neutral probability analysis previously alluded to in Chapter 6. The up factor is calculated to be 1.4191, and the down factor is 0.7047 as shown in Figure 7.3. Hence, starting with the underlying value of $400, we multiply this value with the up and down factors to obtain $567.6 and $281.9, respectively. Readers can verify the rest of the lattice calculations in Figure 7.3. Notice the similarities between the evolution lattice of the underlying for this expansion option and that of the abandonment option.

The second step is to calculate the option valuation lattice as shown in Figure 7.4, using the values calculated in Figure 7.3's lattice evolution of the underlying.

In Figure 7.4, we see that the sample circled terminal node (denoted D) reveals a value of $4,353.7, which can be obtained through the value

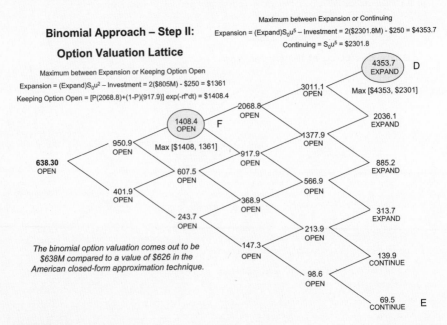

FIGURE 7.4 Expansion Option (Valuation Lattice)

maximization of expansion versus continuation. At the end of five years, the firm has the option to acquire the competition and expand its existing operations or not. Obviously, management will choose the strategy that maximizes profitability. The value of acquiring and expanding its operations is equivalent to doubling its existing capacity of $2,301.8 at the same node shown in Figure 7.3. Hence, the value of acquiring and expanding the firm's operations is double this existing capacity less any acquisition costs, or $2(\$2,301.8) - \$250 = \$4,353.7$ *million.*

The value of continuing with existing business operations can be found in Figure 7.3's lattice evolution of the underlying, at the same node (S_0u^5), which is $2,301.8 million. The profit-maximizing decision is to acquire the firm for $250 million, and hence, we have the value $4,353.7 million on that node (denoted D). Similarly, for the terminal node E in Figure 7.4, we see that the value of continuing existing operations at that time is $69.5 million as seen in Figure 7.3. In comparison, by expanding its operations through acquisition, the value is only $2(\$69.5) - \$250 = -\$111$ *million.* Hence, the decision at that node is to continue with existing operations without expanding, and the profit-maximizing value on that node is $69.5 million. This is intuitive because the underlying asset value of pursuing existing business operations is such that if it is very high based on current market conditions (node D), then it is wise to double the firm's operations through acquisition of the competitor. Otherwise, if circumstances force the value of the firm's operations down to such a low level as specified by node E, then it is more optimal to continue with the existing business and not worry about expanding because the project will be a loser at that point.

Moving on to the intermediate nodes, we see that node F is calculated as $1,408.4 million. At this particular node, the firm again has two options, to expand its operations at that point or to keep the option to expand open for the future in the hopes that when the market is up, the firm has the ability to execute the option and acquire its competitor. The value of expanding at that node is $2(\$805) - \$250 = \$1,361$ *million* (rounded). The value of continuing is simply the discounted weighted average of potential future option values using the risk-neutral probability. Because the risk adjustment is performed on the probabilities of future option cash flows, the discounting can be done using the risk-free rate. That is, for the value of keeping the option alive and open, we have $[(P)(\$2,068.8) + (1 - P)(\$917.9)]exp$ $[(-rf)(\delta t)] = \$1,408.4$ *million,* which is higher than the expansion value. This assumes a 7 percent risk-free rate *rf,* a time-step δt of 1, and a P of 0.515. Using this backward-induction technique, the lattice is calculated back to the starting point to obtain the value of $638.30 million. As the value obtained through a discounted cash flow is $400 million for current existing operations, the value of acquiring the competitor today is $2(\$400) - \$250 = \$550$ *million,* the value of twice its current operations less the acquisition costs.

By not executing the acquisition today but still having an option for management given great market and economic outlook to acquire the competitor then, the firm is worth more than its static value of $550 million. The $550 million is the static NPV without flexibility, the $88.30 million is the real options value, and the combined value of $638.30 million is the ENPV (expanded NPV) or NPV$^+$O (NPV with real options flexibility), the correct total value of this firm. The real options value is worth an additional 16 percent of existing business operations. If a real options approach is not used, the firm will be undervalued because it has a strategic option to expand its current operations but not an obligation to do so and will most likely not do so unless market conditions deem it optimal. The firm has in essence hedged itself against any potential downside if it were to acquire the competitor immediately without regard for what may potentially happen in the future. Having an option and sometimes keeping this option open are valuable given a highly uncertain business environment. Clearly, to mirror actual business conditions, the cost of acquisition can change over time, and the expansion factor (doubling its operations) can also change as business conditions change. All these variables can be accounted for in the lattice.[3]

OPTION TO CONTRACT

You work for a large aeronautical manufacturing firm that is unsure of the technological efficacy and market demand of its new fleet of long-range supersonic jets. The firm decides to hedge itself through the use of strategic options, specifically an option to contract 50 percent of its manufacturing facilities at any time within the next five years. Suppose the firm has a current operating structure whose static valuation of future profitability using a discounted cash flow model (that is, the present value of the expected future cash flows discounted at an appropriate market risk-adjusted discount rate) is found to be $1 billion. Using Monte Carlo simulation, you calculate the implied volatility of the logarithmic returns on the projected future cash flows to be 50 percent. The risk-free rate on a riskless asset for the next five years is found to be yielding 5 percent. Suppose the firm has the option to contract 50 percent of its current operations at any time over the next five years, thereby creating an additional $400 million in savings after this contraction. This is done through a legal contractual agreement with one of its vendors, who has agreed to take up the excess capacity and space of the firm, and at the same time, the firm can scale back its existing work force to obtain this level of savings.

A closed-form approximation of an American option can be used, because the option to contract the firm's operations can be exercised at any time up to the expiration date and can be confirmed with a binomial lattice calculation. Figures 7.5 and 7.6 show the results of your analysis using a binomial approach. Using the Barone-Adesi-Whaley closed-form equation, you calculate the value of the American option to contract as $102.23 million.[4] However, using the binomial approach, you calculate the value of the contraction option as $105.61 million using 5 time-steps and $102.98 million using 1,000 time-steps. An example of the first lattice, the lattice of the underlying asset, is shown in Figure 7.5.

All the required calculations and steps in Figure 7.5 are based on the up factor, down factor, and risk-neutral probability analysis previously alluded to in Chapter 6. For instance, the up factor is calculated to be 1.6487, and the down factor is 0.6065 as shown in Figure 7.5. Hence, starting with the underlying value of $1,000, we multiply this value by the up and down factors to obtain $1,649 and $607, respectively. Readers can verify for themselves the rest of the lattice calculations in Figure 7.5.

The second step is to calculate the option valuation lattice as shown in Figure 7.6, using the values calculated in Figure 7.5's lattice evolution of the underlying.

In Figure 7.6, we see that the sample terminal node (denoted G) reveals a value of $12,183, which can be obtained through the value maximization of contraction versus continuation. At the end of five years, the firm has the option to contract its existing operations or not, thereby letting the option expire. Obviously, management will choose the strategy that maximizes profitability. The value of contracting 50 percent of its operations is equivalent to half of its existing operations plus the $400 million in savings. Hence, the

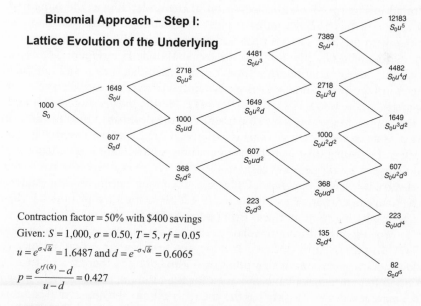

Binomial Approach – Step I:

Lattice Evolution of the Underlying

Contraction factor = 50% with $400 savings

Given: $S = 1,000$, $\sigma = 0.50$, $T = 5$, $rf = 0.05$

$u = e^{\sigma\sqrt{\delta t}} = 1.6487$ and $d = e^{-\sigma\sqrt{\delta t}} = 0.6065$

$p = \dfrac{e^{rf(\delta t)} - d}{u - d} = 0.427$

FIGURE 7.5   Contraction Option (Underlying Lattice)

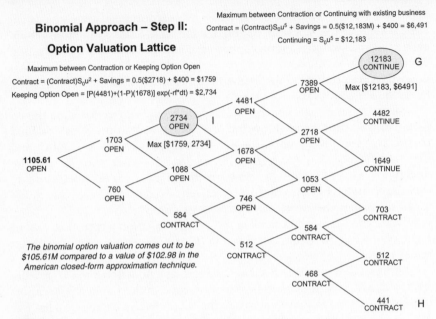

Maximum between Contraction or Continuing with existing business

Binomial Approach – Step II: Contract = (Contract)S_0u^5 + Savings = 0.5($12,183M) + $400 = 6,491

Option Valuation Lattice Continuing = S_0u^5 = $12,183

Maximum between Contraction or Keeping Option Open
Contract = (Contract)S_0u^2 + Savings = 0.5($2718) + $400 = $1759
Keeping Option Open = [P(4481)+(1-P)(1678)] exp(-rf*dt) = $2,734

12183 CONTINUE G

7389 OPEN   Max [$12183, $6491]

4481 OPEN

2734 OPEN I   4482 CONTINUE

1703 OPEN   Max [$1759, 2734]   2718 OPEN

1105.61 OPEN   1678 OPEN   1649 CONTINUE

1088 OPEN   1053 OPEN

760 OPEN

746 OPEN   703 CONTRACT

584 CONTRACT

584 CONTRACT

The binomial option valuation comes out to be   512 CONTRACT   512 CONTRACT
$105.61M compared to a value of $102.98 in the
American closed-form approximation technique.   468 CONTRACT

441 CONTRACT H

FIGURE 7.6 Contraction Option (Valuation Lattice)

value of contracting the firm's operations is $0.5(\$12,183) + \$400 = \$6,491$ *million*. The value of continuing with existing business operations can be found in Figure 7.5's lattice evolution of the underlying at the same node (S_0u^5), which is $12,183 million. The profit-maximizing decision is to continue with the firm's current level of operations at $12,183 million on that node (denoted G). Similarly, for the terminal node H in Figure 7.6, we see that the value of continuing existing operations at that time is $82 million as seen in Figure 7.5. In comparison, by contracting its operations by 50 percent, the value is $0.5(\$82) + \$400 = \$441$. Hence, the decision at that node is to contract operations by 50 percent and the profit-maximizing value on that node is $441 million. This is intuitive, because if the underlying asset value of pursuing existing business operations is such that it is very high based on current good operating conditions (node G), then it is wise to continue its current levels of operation. Otherwise, if circumstances force the value of the firm's operations down to such a low level as specified by node H, then it is optimal to contract the existing business by 50 percent.

Moving on to the intermediate nodes, we see that node I is calculated as $2,734 million. At this particular node, the firm again has two options, to contract its operations at that point or not to contract, thereby keeping the option to contract available and open for the future in the hopes that when the market is down, the firm has the ability to execute the option and contract its existing operations. The value of contracting at that node is $0.5(\$2,718) +$

$400 = $1,759 million. The value of continuing is simply the discounted weighted average of potential future option values using the risk-neutral probability. As the risk adjustment is performed on the probabilities of future option cash flows, the discounting can be done using the risk-free rate. That is, for the value of keeping the option alive and open, we have $[(P)(\$4,481) + (1 - P)(\$1,678)]exp[(-rf)(\delta t)] = \$2,734$ *million,* which is higher than the contraction value. This assumes a 5 percent risk-free rate *rf,* a time-step δt of 1, and a risk-neutral probability *P* of 0.427. Using this backward induction technique, the lattice is back-calculated to the starting point to obtain the value of $1,105.61 million. Because the value obtained through a discounted cash flow is $1,000 million for current existing operations, the option value of being able to contract 50 percent of its operations is $105.61 million. The $1,000 million is the static NPV without flexibility, the $105.61 million is the real options value, and the combined value of $1,105.61 million is the ENPV (expanded NPV) or NPV$^+$O (NPV with real options flexibility), the correct total value of this manufacturing initiative. The real options value is worth an additional 10.56 percent of existing business operations. If a real options approach is not used, the manufacturing initiative will be undervalued.

To modify the business case and make it more in line with actual business conditions, different option types can be accounted for at once (Chooser Option) or in phases (Compound Options). For instance, not only has the firm the ability to contract its operations in a down market, it also has the ability to expand its existing business in an up market, or to completely abandon its operations should the future outlook be bleak. These strategic options can exist simultaneously in time or come into being in sequence over a much longer period. With the use of binomial lattices, any and all of these conditions can be modeled and accounted for. No matter how customized the real options analysis may get, the fundamental building blocks of binomial lattice modeling hold true, and these simple cases provide the reader a set of powerful tools to start building upon, when tackling difficult real options problems.

OPTION TO CHOOSE

Suppose a large manufacturing firm decides to hedge itself through the use of strategic options. Specifically it has the option to choose among three strategies: expanding its current manufacturing operations, contracting its manufacturing operations, or completely abandoning its business unit at any time within the next five years. Suppose the firm has a current operating structure whose static valuation of future profitability using a discounted cash flow model (that is, the present value of the future cash flows discounted at an appropriate market risk-adjusted discount rate) is found to be $100 million. Using Monte Carlo simulation, you calculate the implied volatility of the logarithmic returns on the projected future cash flows to be 15 percent. The risk-free rate on a riskless asset for the next five years is found to be yielding 5 percent annualized returns. Suppose the firm has the option to contract 10 percent of its current operations at any time over the next five years, thereby creating an additional $25 million in savings after this contraction. The expansion option will increase the firm's operations by 30 percent with a $20 million implementation cost. Finally, by abandoning its operations, the firm can sell its intellectual property for $100 million.

A binomial lattice calculation can be used here. Figures 7.7 and 7.8 show the results of the analysis using a binomial approach. The real options value is calculated as $19.03 million using five time-steps. An example of the first lattice, the lattice of the underlying asset, is shown in Figure 7.7 below. Notice that for a chooser option like this example, no closed-form approximations are available. The best that an analyst can do is to use the binomial approach.

All the required calculations and steps in Figure 7.7 are based on the up factor, down factor, and risk-neutral probability analysis previously alluded to in Chapter 6. For instance, the up factor is calculated to be 1.1618, and the down factor is 0.8607 as shown in Figure 7.7. Hence, starting with the underlying value of $100.0, we multiply this value by the up and down factors to obtain $116.2 and $86.1, respectively. The reader can verify the rest of the lattice calculations in Figure 7.7.

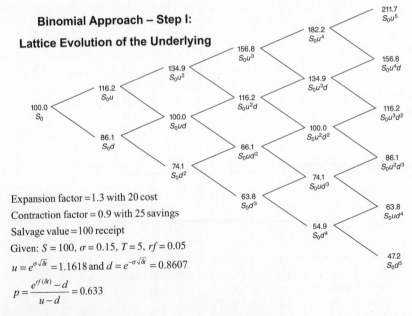

Binomial Approach – Step I:

Lattice Evolution of the Underlying

Expansion factor = 1.3 with 20 cost

Contraction factor = 0.9 with 25 savings

Salvage value = 100 receipt

Given: $S = 100$, $\sigma = 0.15$, $T = 5$, $rf = 0.05$

$u = e^{\sigma\sqrt{\delta t}} = 1.1618$ and $d = e^{-\sigma\sqrt{\delta t}} = 0.8607$

$p = \dfrac{e^{rf(\delta t)} - d}{u - d} = 0.633$

FIGURE 7.7 Option to Choose (Underlying Lattice)

The second step is to calculate the option valuation lattice as shown in Figure 7.8, using the values calculated in Figure 7.7's lattice evolution of the underlying asset.

In Figure 7.8, we see that the sample terminal node (denoted J) reveals a value of $255.2, which can be obtained through the value maximization of expansion, contraction, abandonment, and continuation. At the end of five years, the firm has the option to choose how it wishes to continue its existing operations through these options. Obviously, management will choose the strategy that maximizes profitability. The value of abandoning the firm's business unit is $100 million. The value of expansion is *1.3($211.7) − $20 = $255.2 million.* The value of contracting 10 percent of its operations is equivalent to 90 percent of its existing operations plus the $25 million in savings. Hence, the value of contracting the firm's operations is *0.9($211.7) + $25 = $215.5 million.* The value of continuing with existing business operations can be found in Figure 7.7's lattice evolution of the underlying at the same node (S_0u^5), which is $211.7 million. The profit-maximizing decision is to expand the firm's current level of operations at $255.2 million on that node (denoted J).

Similarly, for the terminal node K in Figure 7.8, we see that the value of contracting existing operations at that time is the maximum value of $102.5 million as seen in Figure 7.8; that is, by contracting the firm's operations by

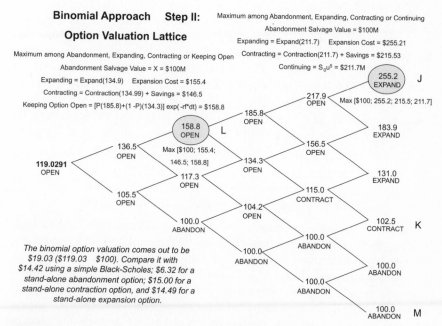

FIGURE 7.8 Option to Choose (Valuation Lattice)

10 percent, the value is *0.9($86.1) + $25 = $102.5 million*. In comparison, continuing operations is valued at $86.1 million, the abandonment strategy is valued at $100.0 million, and the expansion strategy is valued at *1.3($86.1) − $20 = 91.9 million*.

This is intuitive because if the underlying asset value of pursuing existing business operations is such that it is very high based on current market demand (node J), then it is wise to expand the firm's current levels of operation. Otherwise, if circumstances force the value of the firm's operations down to such a low level as specified by node K, then it is more optimal to contract the existing business by 10 percent. At any time below level K, for instance, at node M, it is better to abandon the business unit all together.

Moving on to the intermediate nodes, we see that node L is calculated as $158.8 million. At this particular node, the firm again has four options: to expand, contract, abandon its operations, or not execute anything, thus keeping these options open for the future. The value of contracting at that node is *0.9($134.9) + $25 = $146.5 million* (rounded). The value of abandoning the business unit is $100.0 million. The value of expanding is *1.3($134.99) − $20 = $155.4 million*. The value of continuing is simply the discounted weighted average of potential future option values using the risk-neutral probability. As the risk adjustment is performed on the probabilities of future option cash flows, the discounting can be done using the risk-free rate. That is, for the value of keeping the option alive and open, we have $[(P)(\$185.8) + (1 − P)(\$134.3)]exp[(−rf)(\delta t)] = \$158.8$ *million*, which is the maximum value. This assumes a 5 percent risk-free rate *rf*, a time-step δt of 1, and a risk-neutral probability P of 0.633. Using this backward induction technique, the lattice is calculated back to the starting point to obtain the value of $119.03 million. As the present value of the underlying is $100 million, the real options value is $19.03 million. In comparison, if we use the Black-Scholes model on the problem, we obtain an incorrect value of $14.42 million. If the project is analyzed separately, we get differing and misleading results as seen below:

Abandonment option only	$6.32 million
Contraction option only	$15.00 million
Expansion option only	$14.49 million
Sum of all individual options	$35.81 million

Clearly, valuing a combination of real options by performing them individually and then summing them yields wildly different and incorrect results. We need to account for the interaction of option types within the same project as we have done above. The reason why the sum of individual options does not equal the interaction of the same options is due to the mutually exclusive and independent nature of these specific options. That is, the firm can never both expand and contract on the same node at the same time, or to expand and abandon on the same node at the same time, and so forth.

This mutually exclusive behavior is captured using the chooser option. If performed separately on a particular node in the lattice, the expansion option analysis may indicate that it is optimal to expand, while the contraction option analysis may indicate that it is optimal to contract, and so forth, thereby creating a higher total value. However, in a chooser option, the interaction among the three options precludes this from happening, and the option is not overvalued. This is because in the example, multiple option execution cannot occupy the same state. However, in more advanced real options problems, this multiple interaction in a single state is highly desirable.

The same analysis can be further complicated by changing some parameters over time (changing the cost of implementation at some growth rate correlated to the rate of inflation, changing the salvage amount that can be obtained over time, and so forth), all of which can be easily accounted for in the binomial lattices.

COMPOUND OPTIONS

In a compound option analysis, the value of the option depends on the value of another option. For instance, a pharmaceutical company currently going through a particular FDA drug approval process has to go through human trials. The success of the FDA approval depends heavily on the success of human testing, both occurring at the same time. Suppose that the former costs $900 million and the latter $500 million. Further suppose that both phases occur simultaneously and take three years to complete. Using Monte Carlo simulation, you calculate the implied volatility of the logarithmic returns on the projected future cash flows to be 30 percent. The risk-free rate on a riskless asset for the next three years is found to be yielding 7.7 percent. The drug development effort's static valuation of future profitability using a discounted cash flow model (that is, the present value of the expected future cash flows discounted at an appropriate market risk-adjusted discount rate) is found to be $1 billion. Figures 7.9, 7.10, and 7.11 show the calculation involved in obtaining the compound option value. Figure 7.9 shows the usual first lattice of the underlying asset, Figure 7.10 shows an intermediate equity lattice of the first option, and Figure 7.11 shows the option valuation lattice of the compound option, whose valuation lattice is based on the first option as its underlying asset.

All the required calculations and steps in Figure 7.9 are based on the up factor, down factor, and risk-neutral probability analysis previously alluded to in Chapter 6. For instance, the up factor is calculated to be 1.3499, and the down factor is 0.7408 as shown in Figure 7.9. Hence, starting with the underlying value of $1,000, we multiply this value with the up and down factors to obtain $1,349.9 and $740.8, respectively. The rest of the lattice is filled in using the same approach.

Binomial Approach – Step I:

Lattice Evolution of the Underlying

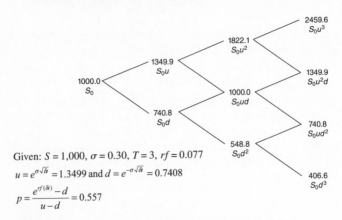

Given: $S = 1,000$, $\sigma = 0.30$, $T = 3$, $rf = 0.077$

$u = e^{\sigma\sqrt{\delta t}} = 1.3499$ and $d = e^{-\sigma\sqrt{\delta t}} = 0.7408$

$p = \dfrac{e^{rf(\delta t)} - d}{u - d} = 0.557$

FIGURE 7.9 Compound Option (Underlying Lattice)

The second step involves the calculation of the equity lattice as seen in Figure 7.10. We see that the sample terminal node (denoted N) reveals a value of $1,559.6, which can be obtained through the value maximization of executing the option or not, thereby letting the option expire worthless. The value of the option is $2,459.6 − $900 = $1,559.6 million. The profit-maximizing value is determined using $MAX[1,559.6; 0]$, which yields $1,559.6 million.

Moving on to the intermediate nodes, we see that node O is calculated as $119.6 million. At this particular node, the value of executing the option

Binomial Approach – Step II:

Equity Lattice

Maximum between Executing or 0

Execute = 2459.6 − Investment Cost 1 = $1559.6

1559.6 N

988.8

Max [$1559; 0]

605.1

361.1   449.9

231.9

119.6 O   *This is the intermediate Equity Valuation Lattice required to solve the Compound Option*

0.0

Max [$119.6; -159.2]   0.0

0.0

Maximum Executing or Keeping the Option Open

Executing = 740.8 − Investment Cost 1 = -$159.2

Keeping Option Open = [P(231.9)+(1-P)(0)] exp(-rf*dt) = $119.6

FIGURE 7.10 Compound Option (Equity Lattice)

is $740.8 − $900 = −$159.2 million$. Keep in mind that the value $740.8 comes from the lattice of the underlying at the same node as seen previously in Figure 7.9. The value of continuing is simply the discounted weighted average of potential future option values using the risk-neutral probability. As the risk adjustment is performed on the probabilities of future option cash flows, the discounting can be done using the risk-free rate. That is, for the value of keeping the option alive and open, we have $[(P)($231.9) + (1 − P)($0)]exp[(−rf)(\delta t)] = $119.6 million$, which is the maximum of the two values. This calculation assumes a 7.7 percent risk-free rate rf, a time-step δt of 1, and a risk-neutral probability P of 0.557. Using this backward induction technique, this first equity lattice is back-calculated to the starting point to obtain the value of $361.1 million.

The third step is to calculate the option valuation lattice as shown in Figure 7.11. For instance, at the terminal node P, we see the value of the option as $1,059.6, which is nothing but the maximization between zero and the option value. The option value at that node is calculated as $1,559.6 − $500 = $1,059.6 million$. Notice that the value $1,559.6 comes directly from the equity lattice in Figure 7.10 and not from the underlying asset lattice in Figure 7.9. This is because the underlying asset of a compound option is another option. At node Q, similarly, we see that the value of the option is $0, which is obtained through $MAX[−$500; 0]$. Using backward induction, the value of the compound option is calculated as $145.33 million (rounded). Notice how this compares to a static decision value of $1,000 − $900 = $100 million$ for the first investment. We obtain $165.10 by applying 1,000 steps in the software, $165.10 using a closed-form compound option model, and $165.11 using a modified American call option model, thereby verifying the results and approach.

Binomial Approach   Step III:

Option Valuation Lattice

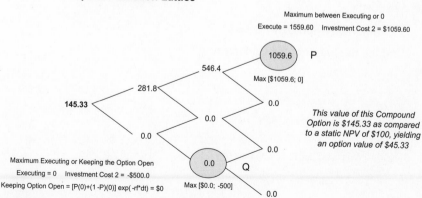

FIGURE 7.11 Compound Option (Valuation Lattice)

CHANGING STRIKES

A modification to the option types we have thus far been discussing is the idea of changing strikes—that is, implementation costs for projects may change over time. Putting off a project for a particular period may mean a higher cost. Figures 7.12 and 7.13 show the applications of this concept. Keep in mind that changing strikes can be applied to any previous option types as well; in other words, one can mix and match different option types. Suppose the implementation of a project in the first year costs $80 million but increases to $90 million in the second year due to expected increases in raw materials and input costs. Using Monte Carlo simulation, the implied volatility of the logarithmic returns on the projected future cash flows is calculated to be 50 percent. The risk-free rate on a riskless asset for the next two years is found to be yielding 7.0 percent. The static valuation of future profitability using a discounted cash flow model (that is, the present value of the expected future cash flows discounted at an appropriate market risk-adjusted discount rate) is found to be $100 million. The underlying asset lattice evolution can be seen in Figure 7.12.

Similar to the approach used for calculating an American-type call option, Figure 7.13 shows the stepwise calculations on an option with changing strike prices. Notice that the value of the call option on changing strikes is $37.53 million. Compare this to a naive static discounted cash flow net present value of $20 million for the first year and $10 million for the second year.

Obviously for simplicity in illustration, only two periods are used. In actual business conditions, multiple strike costs can be accounted for over many time periods and modeled on binomial trees with more steps. Based on the time-step size (δt), the different costs associated with different time periods can be mapped into the lattice easily. In addition, changing cost options can also be used in conjunction with all other types of real options models, such as the expansion option, compound option, volatility option, and so forth.

Binomial Approach – Step I:

Lattice Evolution of the Underlying

Cost at year 1 = \$80; cost at year 2 = \$90

Given: $S = 100$, $\sigma = 0.50$, $T = 2$, $rf = 0.07$

$u = e^{\sigma\sqrt{\delta t}} = 1.6487$ and $d = e^{-\sigma\sqrt{\delta t}} = 0.6065$

$p = \dfrac{e^{rf(\delta t)} - d}{u - d} = 0.447$

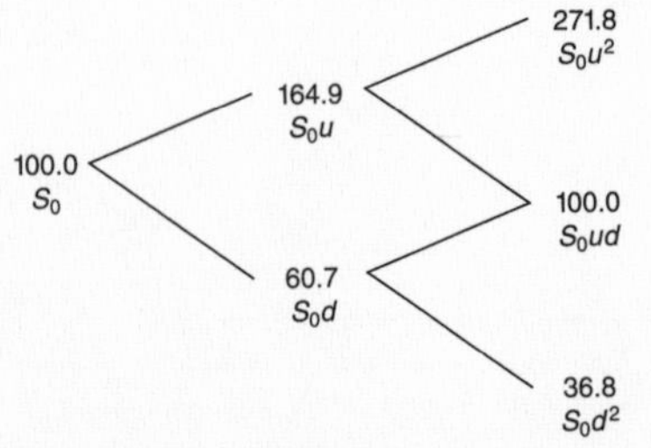

$$
\begin{array}{ccccc}
 & & & & 271.8 \\
 & & 164.9 & & S_0 u^2 \\
 & & S_0 u & & \\
100.0 & & & & 100.0 \\
S_0 & & & & S_0 ud \\
 & & 60.7 & & \\
 & & S_0 d & & \\
 & & & & 36.8 \\
 & & & & S_0 d^2 \\
\end{array}
$$

FIGURE 7.12 Changing Strike Option (Underlying Lattice)

Binomial Approach – Step II:

Option Valuation Lattice

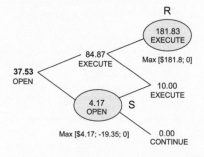

R

181.83
EXECUTE

Maximum between Executing the purchase option or 0

Executing = 271.83 – Exercise Price 2 = $181.83

84.87
EXECUTE

Max [$181.8; 0]

37.53
OPEN

10.00
EXECUTE

The binomial option valuation comes out to be $37.53. Compare this to a naïve Black-Scholes result of $36.90 or a static NPV of $20 for a 1-year exercise and $10 for a 2-year exercise.

4.17   S
OPEN

Max [$4.17; -19.35; 0]

0.00
CONTINUE

Maximum between Executing the purchase option or Keeping the Option Open

Executing = 60.65 – Exercise Price 1 = -$19.35

Keeping the Option Open = [P(10) + (1-P)(0)]exp(-riskfree*dt) = $4.17

FIGURE 7.13   Changing Strike Option (Valuation Lattice)

CHANGING VOLATILITY

Instead of changing strike costs over time, in certain cases, volatility on cash flow returns may differ over time. This can be seen in Figures 7.14 and 7.15. In Figure 7.14, we see the example for a two-year option where volatility is 20 percent in the first year and 30 percent in the second year. In this

Binomial Approach – Step I:

Lattice Evolution of the Underlying

164.87
$S_0 u_1 u_2$

122.14
$S_0 u_1$

110.52
$S_0 d_1 u_2$

100.0
S_0

81.87
$S_0 d_1$

90.48
$S_0 u_1 d_2$

60.65
$S_0 d_1 d_2$

Given: $S = 100$, $X = 110$, $T = 2$, $rf = 0.10$, $\sigma_1 = 20\%$ and $\sigma_2 = 30\%$

$$u_1 = e^{\sigma \sqrt{\delta t}} = 1.2214 \text{ and } d_1 = e^{-\sigma \sqrt{\delta t}} = 0.8187$$

$$u_2 = e^{\sigma \sqrt{\delta t}} = 1.3499 \text{ and } d_2 = e^{-\sigma \sqrt{\delta t}} = 0.7408$$

$$p_1 = \frac{e^{rf(\delta t)} - d}{u - d} = 0.7113 \text{ and } p_2 = \frac{e^{rf(\delta t)} - d}{u - d} = 0.5983$$

FIGURE 7.14   Changing Volatility Option (Underlying Lattice)

Binomial Approach   Step II:

Option Valuation Lattice

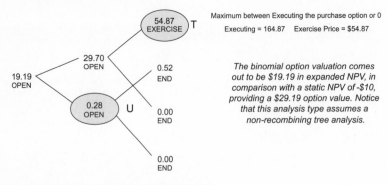

Maximum between Executing the purchase option or 0

Executing = 164.87   Exercise Price = $54.87

The binomial option valuation comes out to be $19.19 in expanded NPV, in comparison with a static NPV of -$10, providing a $29.19 option value. Notice that this analysis type assumes a non-recombining tree analysis.

Maximum between Executing the purchase option or Keeping the Option Open

Executing = 81.87   Exercise Price = -$28.13

Keeping the Option Open = [P(0.52) + (1 -P)(0.00)]exp(-riskfree*dt) = $0.28

FIGURE 7.15   Changing Volatility Option (Valuation Lattice)

circumstance, the up and down factors are different over the two time periods. Thus, the binomial lattice will no longer be recombining. As a matter of fact, the underlying asset lattice branches cross over each other as shown in Figure 7.14. The upper bifurcation of the first lower branch (from $81.87 to $110.52) crosses the lower bifurcation of the upper first branch (from $122.14 to $90.48). This complex crossover will be compounded for multiple time-steps.

Figure 7.15 shows the option valuation lattice. Similar calculations are performed for an option with changing volatilities as for other option types. For instance, node T has a value of $54.87, which is the maximum of zero and $164.87 - $110 = $54.87. For node U, the value of $0.28 million comes from the maximization of executing the option $81.87 - $110 = -$28.13 million and keeping the option open with $[(P)($0.52) + (1 - P)($0)]exp [(-rf)(\delta t)] = $0.28 million,$ which is the maximum value. This calculation assumes a 10 percent risk-free rate rf, a time-step δt of 1, and a risk-neutral probability P of 0.5983. Using this backward induction technique, this valuation lattice is back-calculated to the starting point to obtain the value of $19.19 million, as compared to the static net present value of $-$10 million (benefits of $100 million with a cost of $110 million).

More complicated analyses can be obtained through this changing volatility condition. For example, where there are multiple stochastic underlying variables driving the value of the option, each variable may have its own unique volatility, but the variables are correlated with each other. Examples include the price and quantity sold where there is a negative correlation between these two variables (the downward-sloping demand curve). The Real

Options Analysis Toolkit software CD-ROM handles some of these more difficult calculations.

SEQUENTIAL COMPOUND OPTION

A sequential compound option exists when a project has multiple phases and latter phases depend on the success of previous phases. Figures 7.16 to 7.19 show the calculation of a sequential compound option. Suppose a project has two phases, where the first phase has a one-year expiration that costs $500 million. The second phase's expiration is three years and costs $700 million. Using Monte Carlo simulation, the implied volatility of the logarithmic returns on the projected expected future cash flows is calculated to be 20 percent. The risk-free rate on a riskless asset for the next three years is found to be yielding 7.7 percent. The static valuation of future profitability using a discounted cash flow model (that is, the present value of the future cash flows discounted at an appropriate market risk-adjusted discount rate) is found to be $1,000 million. The underlying asset lattice is seen in Figure 7.16.

The calculation of this initial underlying asset lattice is similar to previous option types by first calculating the up and down factors and evolving the present value of the future cash flow for the next three years.

Figure 7.17 shows the second step in calculating the equity lattice of the second option. The analysis requires the calculation of the longer-term option first and then the shorter-term option because the value of a compound option is based on another option. At node V, the value is $1,122.1

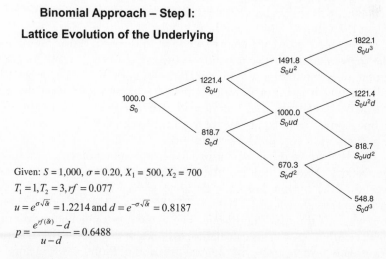

Binomial Approach – Step I:

Lattice Evolution of the Underlying

Given: $S = 1,000$, $\sigma = 0.20$, $X_1 = 500$, $X_2 = 700$

$T_1 = 1, T_2 = 3, rf = 0.077$

$u = e^{\sigma\sqrt{\delta t}} = 1.2214$ and $d = e^{-\sigma\sqrt{\delta t}} = 0.8187$

$p = \dfrac{e^{rf(\delta t)} - d}{u - d} = 0.6488$

FIGURE 7.16   Sequential Compound Option (Underlying Lattice)

Binomial Approach – Step II:

Equity Lattice

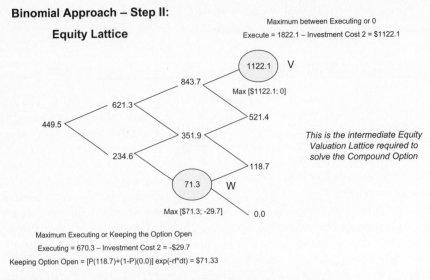

FIGURE 7.17 Sequential Compound Option (Equity Lattice)

million because it is the maximum between zero and executing the option through $1,822.1 − $700 = $1,122.1 million$. The intermediate node W is $71.3 million, its being the maximum between executing the option $670.3 − $700 = −$29.7 million$ and keeping the option open with $[(P)($118.7) + (1 − P)($0.0)]exp[(−rf)(\delta t)] = $71.3 million,$ which is the maximum value. This calculation assumes a 7.7 percent risk-free rate rf, a time-step δt of 1, and a risk-neutral probability P of 0.6488. Using this backward induction technique, this first equity lattice is back-calculated to the starting point to obtain the value of $449.5 million.

Figure 7.18 shows the equity valuation of the first, shorter-term option. The analysis on this lattice depends on the lattice of the second, longer-term option as shown in Figure 7.17. For instance, node X has a value of $121.3 million, which is the maximum between zero and executing the option $621.27 − $500 = $121.27 million$. Notice that $621.27 is the value of the second, longer-term equity lattice as shown in Figure 7.17 and $500 is the implementation cost on the first option.

Node Y on the other hand uses a backward induction calculation, where the value $72.86 million is obtained through the maximization between executing the option $449.5 − $500 = −$50.5 million$ and keeping the option open with $[(P)($121.3) + (1 − P)($0.0)]exp[(−rf)(\delta t)] = $72.86 million,$ which is the maximum value. The maximum value comes from keeping the option open. This calculation assumes a 7.7 percent risk-free rate rf, a time-step δt of 1, and a risk-neutral probability P of 0.6488. Again notice that $500 million is the implementation cost of the first option.

Binomial Approach – Step III:

Option Valuation Lattice

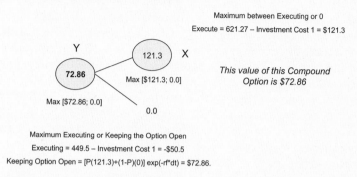

FIGURE 7.18 Sequential Compound Option (Valuation Lattice)

Figure 7.19 shows the combined option analysis from Figures 7.17 and 7.18, complete with decision points on when to invest in the first and second rounds versus keeping the option to invest open for the future.

Binomial Approach – Step IV:

Combined Option Valuation Lattice

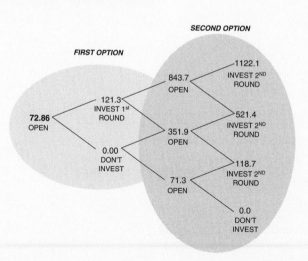

FIGURE 7.19 Sequential Compound Option (Combined Lattice)

EXTENSION TO THE BINOMIAL MODELS

As discussed in the previous examples, multiple tweaks can be performed using the binomial lattices. For instance, Figure 7.20 illustrates a simple chooser option with the same parameters as in Figure 7.7 but with a twist. For instance, the expansion factor increases at a 10 percent rate per year, while the cost of expanding decreases at a 3 percent deflation per year. Similarly, the savings projected from contracting will reduce at a 10 percent rate. However, the salvage value of abandoning increases at a 5 percent rate. Custom changes like these can be easily accommodated in a binomial lattice but are very difficult to solve in closed-form solutions, because every time a slight modification is made to a closed-form model, stochastic calculus is a necessary evil in solving the problem, as compared to a simple change in the maximization routines inherent in the binomial lattices.

Taking this approach a little further, the reader can very easily create a custom option to accommodate almost any situation, to more closely reflect actual business cases. For instance, the growth rates above can be inflation rates or changes in the cost of execution, savings, or salvage values over time. In addition, the expansion factor or contraction factor can also be changed. This is more appropriate as it is less credible to say that executing the same project at any time within a specified period will cost exactly the same no matter what the circumstances are. With these simple building blocks discussed in this chapter, readers are well on their way to developing more

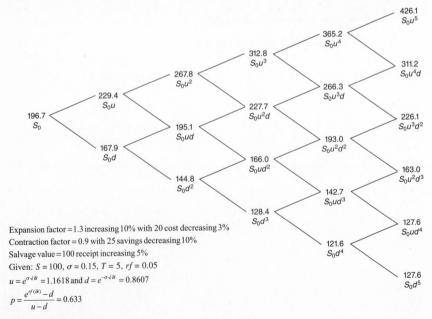

Expansion factor = 1.3 increasing 10% with 20 cost decreasing 3%
Contraction factor = 0.9 with 25 savings decreasing 10%
Salvage value = 100 receipt increasing 5%
Given: $S = 100$, $\sigma = 0.15$, $T = 5$, $rf = 0.05$
$u = e^{\sigma\sqrt{\delta t}} = 1.1618$ and $d = e^{-\sigma\sqrt{\delta t}} = 0.8607$
$p = \dfrac{e^{rf(\delta t)} - d}{u - d} = 0.633$

FIGURE 7.20   Extension to the Binomial Models

sophisticated and customized real options models. Chapter 8 briefly discusses these more advanced models and problems, while Chapter 9 illustrates how these more advanced problems can be easily tackled using the Real Options Analysis Toolkit software included in the CD-ROM.

SUMMARY

Closed-form solutions are exact, quick, and easy to implement with the assistance of some basic programming skills but are highly difficult to explain. They are also very specific in nature, with limited modeling flexibility. Binomial lattices, in contrast, are easy to implement and easy to explain. They are also highly flexible but require significant computing power and time-steps to obtain good approximations. In the limit, binomial lattices tend to approach closed-form solutions; hence, it is always recommended that both approaches be used to verify the results, whenever appropriate. The results from closed-form solutions may be used in conjunction with the binomial lattice structure when presenting to management a complete real options solution. Even a Black-Scholes model can be used as a means of credibility testing. That is, if the real options results have similar magnitude as the Black-Scholes, the analysis becomes more credible.

CHAPTER 7 QUESTIONS

1. Using the example in Figures 7.1 and 7.2 on the abandonment option, recalculate the value of the option assuming that the salvage value increases from the initial $100 (at time 0) by 10 percent at every period starting from time 1.

2. The expansion option example in Figures 7.3 and 7.4 assumes that the competitor has the same level of growth and uncertainty as the firm being valued. Describe what has to be done differently if the competitor is assumed to be growing at a different rate and facing a different set of risks and uncertainties. Rerun the analysis assuming that the competitor's volatility is 45 percent instead of 35 percent.

3. Figures 7.7 and 7.8 illustrate the chooser option, that is, the option to choose among expanding, contracting, and abandoning current operations. Rerun these three options separately using the Real Options Analysis Toolkit software in the enclosed CD-ROM and verify that the summary provided in Figure 7.8 is correct. Why is it that the sum of the individual option values does not equal the chooser option value?

4. In the compound option example illustrated in Figures 7.9 through 7.11, the first phase cost is $900 and the second phase cost is $500. However,

in a simultaneous compound option, these two phases occur concurrently. Rerun the example by changing the first phase cost to $500 and the second phase cost to $900. Should the results be comparable? Why or why not?

5. Based on the example in Appendix 7G, create a European call option model using Monte Carlo simulation in Excel. For a simulated standard-normal random distribution, use the function "=NORMSINV(RAND( ))". Assume a one-year expiration, 40 percent annualized volatility, $100 asset and strike costs, 5 percent risk-free rate, and no dividend payments. Verify your results using Black-Scholes and a binomial lattice.

6. Solve an American call option using the risk-neutral probability approach, and then solve the same option using the market-replicating portfolio approach based on the example in Appendix 7C. For the market-replicating portfolio approach, assume continuous discounting at the risk-free rate. Verify that theory holds such that both approaches obtain identical call option values. Which approach is simpler to apply? For both approaches, assume the following parameters: asset value = $100, strike cost = $100, maturity = 3 years, volatility = 10 percent, risk-free rate = 5 percent, dividends = 0 percent, and binomial lattice steps = 3.

Volatility Estimates

Probably one of the most difficult input parameters to estimate in a real options analysis is the volatility of cash flows. Below is a review of several methods used to calculate volatility, together with a discussion of their potential advantages and shortcomings.

LOGARITHMIC CASH FLOW RETURNS APPROACH

The logarithmic cash flow returns approach calculates the volatility using the individual future cash flow estimates and their corresponding logarithmic returns, as illustrated below in Table 7A.1. Starting with a series of forecast future cash flows, convert them into relative returns. Then take the natural logarithms of these relative returns. The standard deviation of these natural logarithm returns is the volatility of the cash flow series used in a real options analysis. Notice that the number of returns is one less than the total number of periods. That is, for time periods 0 to 5, we have six cash flows but only five cash flow returns.

TABLE 7A.1   Future Cash Flow Estimates and Their Corresponding Logarithmic Returns

Time Period	Cash Flows	Cash Flow Relative Returns	Natural Logarithm of Cash Flow Returns (X)
0	$100	—	—
1	$125	$125/$100 = 1.25	ln($125/$100) = 0.2231
2	$ 95	$ 95/$125 = 0.76	ln($ 95/$125) = −0.2744
3	$105	$105/$ 95 = 1.11	ln($105/$ 95) = 0.1001
4	$155	$155/$105 = 1.48	ln($155/$105) = 0.3895
5	$146	$146/$155 = 0.94	ln($146/$155) = −0.0598

The volatility estimate is then calculated as

$$volatility = \sqrt{\frac{1}{n-1}\sum_{i=1}^{n}(x_i - \bar{x})^2} = 25.58\%,$$

where n is the number of Xs, and $\bar{x}$ is the average X value. Clearly there are advantages and shortcomings to this simple approach. This method is very easy to implement, and Monte Carlo simulation is not required in order to obtain a single-point volatility estimate. This approach is mathematically valid and is widely used in estimating volatility of financial assets. However, for real options analysis, there are several caveats that deserve closer attention, including when cash flows are negative over certain time periods. That is, the relative returns will be a negative value, and the natural logarithm of a negative value does not exist. Hence, the volatility measure does not fully capture the possible cash flow downside and may produce erroneous results. In addition, autocorrelated cash flows (estimated using time-series forecasting techniques) or cash flows following a static growth rate will yield volatility estimates that are erroneous. Great care should be taken in such instances.

Monte Carlo simulation can also be used in creating the discounted cash flow model that is used to calculate the cash flows, thereby running thousands of trials and reducing the risk of obtaining a single erroneous volatility estimate. Performing a Monte Carlo simulation at the discounted cash flow level is highly appropriate because a distribution of volatilities can be obtained and used as input into a real options analysis. The results of such an analysis will then yield a forecast distribution of real options values, with its relevant probabilities of occurrence, rather than a single-point estimate.

LOGARITHMIC PRESENT VALUE APPROACH

The logarithmic present value approach collapses all future cash flow estimates into two sets of present values, one for the first time period and another for the present time. This approach was first introduced by Tom Copeland.[1] The steps are seen below. The calculations assume a constant 10 percent discount rate. The cash flows are discounted all the way to time 0 and again to time 1. Then the values are summed, and the following logarithmic ratio is calculated:

$$X = \ln\left(\frac{\sum_{i=1}^{n} PVCF_i}{\sum_{i=0}^{n} PVCF_i}\right)$$

where $PVCF_i$ is the present value of future cash flows at different time periods i.

TABLE 7A.2 Logarithmic Present Value Approach

Time Period	Cash Flows	Present Value at Time 0	Present Value at Time 1
0	$100	$\frac{\$100}{(1+0.1)^0} = \$100.00$	—
1	$125	$\frac{\$125}{(1+0.1)^1} = \$113.64$	$\frac{\$125}{(1+0.1)^0} = \$125.00$
2	$ 95	$\frac{\$95}{(1+0.1)^2} = \$ 78.51$	$\frac{\$95}{(1+0.1)^1} = \$ 86.36$
3	$105	$\frac{\$105}{(1+0.1)^3} = \$ 78.89$	$\frac{\$105}{(1+0.1)^2} = \$ 86.78$
4	$155	$\frac{\$155}{(1+0.1)^4} = \$105.87$	$\frac{\$155}{(1+0.1)^3} = \$116.45$
5	$146	$\frac{\$146}{(1+0.1)^5} = \$ 90.65$	$\frac{\$146}{(1+0.1)^4} = \$ 99.72$
SUM		$567.56	$514.31

In Table 7A.2, X is simply $ln(\$514.31/\$567.56) = -0.0985$. Using this X value, perform a Monte Carlo simulation on the discounted cash flow model and obtain the resulting forecast distribution of X. The standard deviation of the forecast distribution of X is the volatility estimate used in the real options analysis. It is important to note that only the numerator is simulated and the denominator is unchanged.

The downside to estimating volatility this way is that Monte Carlo simulation is required, but the calculated volatility measure is a single-digit estimate, as compared to the logarithmic cash flow approach, which yields a distribution of volatilities, which will in turn yield a distribution of calculated real options values. The main objection to using this method is its dependence on the variability of the discount rate used. For instance, we can expand the X equation as follows:

$$X = \ln\left(\frac{\sum_{i=1}^{n} PVCF_i}{\sum_{i=0}^{n} PVCF_i}\right)$$

$$= \ln\left(\frac{\frac{CF_1}{(1+D)^0} + \frac{CF_2}{(1+D)^1} + \frac{CF_3}{(1+D)^2} + \dots + \frac{CF_N}{(1+D)^{N-1}}}{\frac{CF_0}{(1+D)^0} + \frac{CF_1}{(1+D)^1} + \frac{CF_2}{(1+D)^2} + \dots + \frac{CF_N}{(1+D)^N}}\right)$$

D represents the constant discount rate used. Here, we see that the cash flow series CF for the numerator is offset by one period, and the discount factors are also offset by one period. Therefore, by performing a Monte Carlo simulation on the cash flows alone versus performing a Monte Carlo simulation on both cash flow variables as well as the discount rate will yield very different X values. The main critique of this approach is that in a real options analysis, the variability in the present value of cash flows is the key driver of option value and not the variability of discount rates used in the analysis. Modifications to this method include duplicating the cash flows and simulating only the numerator cash flows, thereby providing different numerator values but a static denominator value for each simulated trial, while keeping the discount rate constant. This approach reduces the measurement risks of autocorrelated cash flows and negative cash flows.

GARCH APPROACH

GARCH (generalized autoregressive conditional heteroskedasticity) models can also be utilized to estimate the cash flow volatility. GARCH models are used mainly in analyzing financial time-series data, in order to ascertain its conditional variances and volatilities. These volatilities are used to value options, but the amount of historical data necessary for a good volatility estimate remains significant. Usually, dozens—up to hundreds—of data points are required to obtain good GARCH estimates.

For instance, a GARCH (1,1) model takes the form of

$$y_t = x_t\gamma + \varepsilon_t$$
$$\sigma_t^2 = \omega + \alpha\varepsilon_{t-1}^2 + \beta\sigma_{t-1}^2$$

where the first equation's dependent variable (y_t) is a function of exogenous variables (x_t) with an error term (ε_t). The second equation estimates the variance (squared volatility σ_t^2) at time t, which depends on a historical mean (ω), news about volatility from the previous period, measured as a lag of the squared residual from the mean equation (ε_{t-1}^2), and volatility from the previous period (σ_{t-1}^2). The exact modeling specification of a GARCH model is beyond the scope of this book and will not be discussed. Suffice it to say that detailed knowledge of econometric modeling (model specification tests, structural breaks, and error estimation) is required to run a GARCH model, making it less accessible to the general analyst.

MANAGEMENT ASSUMPTION APPROACH

Another approach to estimating volatility is through management assumptions. For instance, let's say management assumes that the present value of a particular project follows a lognormal distribution with a mean of $44 million. In addition, management assumes that this expected value can fluctuate between $30 and $60 million. These values represent the worst-case 10 percent probability and 90 percent best-case probability. *See* Figure 7A.1.

Using Crystal Ball's® Monte Carlo simulation software, the percentile inputs seen in Figure 7A.2 are calculated using the software, and its corresponding standard deviation is computed to be $12.12 million. Hence, the

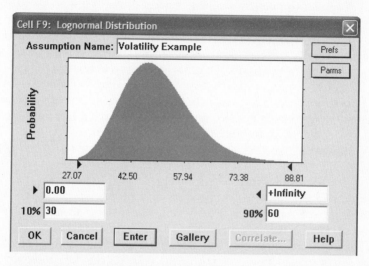

FIGURE 7A.1 Lognormal 10–90 Percentiles

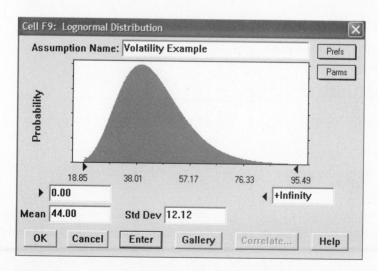

FIGURE 7A.2 Lognormal Mean and Standard Deviation

volatility estimate is \$12.12/\$44.00 or 27.55 percent. This is done in Crystal Ball's® define assumption function, choosing the alternate parameters command and entering the relevant percentiles.

MARKET PROXY APPROACH

An often used (not to mention abused and misused) method in estimating volatility applies to publicly available market data. That is, for a particular project under review, a set of market comparable firms' publicly traded stock prices are used. These firms should have functions, markets, and risks similar to those of the project under review. Then, using closing stock prices, the standard deviation of natural logarithms of relative returns is calculated. The methodology is identical to that used in the logarithm of cash flow returns approach previously alluded to. The problem with this method is the assumption that the risks inherent in comparable firms are identical to the risks inherent in the specific project under review. The issue is that a firm's equity prices are subject to investor overreaction and psychology in the stock market, as well as countless other exogenous variables that are irrelevant when estimating the risks of the project. In addition, the market valuation of a large public firm depends on multiple interacting and diversified projects. Finally, firms are levered, but specific projects are usually unlevered. Hence, the volatility used in a real options analysis (σ_{RO}) should be adjusted to discount this leverage effect by dividing the volatility in equity prices (σ_{EQUITY}) by $(1 + D/E)$, where D/E is the debt-to-equity ratio of the public firm. That is, we have

$$\sigma_{RO} = \frac{\sigma_{EQUITY}}{1 + \dfrac{D}{E}}.$$

ANNUALIZING VOLATILITY

No matter the approach, the volatility estimate used in a real options analysis has to be an annualized volatility. Depending on the periodicity of the raw cash flow or stock price data used, the volatility calculated should be converted into annualized values using $\sigma\sqrt{T}$, where T is the number of periods in a year. For instance, if the calculated volatility using monthly cash flow data is 10 percent, the annualized volatility is $10\%\sqrt{12} = 35\%$. This 35 percent figure should be used in the real options analysis. Similarly, T is 365 for daily data, 4 for quarterly data, 2 for semiannual data, and 1 for annual data.

Black-Scholes in Action

This appendix discusses the fundamentals of the Black-Scholes model, including its theoretical underpinnings and derivations. Although the Black-Scholes model is not a good approach to use in its entirety, it is often useful as a gross approximation method as well as a benchmark. Hence, understanding the fundamentals of the Black-Scholes model is important.

A REVIEW OF THE BLACK-SCHOLES MODEL

The Black-Scholes model is summarized as follows, with a detailed explanation of the procedures by which to obtain each of the variables.

$$Call = S_t\Phi(d_1) - Xe^{-rf(T)}\Phi(d_2)$$

$$\text{where } d_1 = \frac{\ln\left(\frac{S_0}{X}\right) + \left(rf + \frac{1}{2}\sigma^2\right)(T)}{\sigma\sqrt{T}}$$

$$\text{and } d_2 = d_1 - \sigma\sqrt{T}$$

Φ is the cumulative standard normal distribution function;
S is the value of the underlying asset;
X is the strike price or the cost of developing the intangible;
rf is the nominal risk-free rate;
σ is the volatility measure; and
T is the time to expiration or the economic life of the strategic option.

In order to fully understand and use the model, we need to understand the assumptions under which the model was constructed. These are essentially the caveats that go into using real options in valuing any asset. These assumptions are violated quite often, but the model should still hold up to scrutiny. The main assumption is that the underlying asset's price structure follows a Geometric Brownian Motion with static drift and volatility parameters and that this motion follows a Markov-Weiner stochastic process. The general derivation of a Markov-Weiner stochastic process takes the form of $dS = \mu S dt + \sigma S dZ$, where $dZ = \varepsilon\sqrt{dt}$ and dZ is a Weiner process, μ is the drift rate, and σ is the volatility measure. The other assumptions are fairly standard, including a fair and timely efficient market with no riskless arbitrage opportunities, no transaction costs, and no taxes. Price changes are also assumed to be continuous and instantaneous.

The variables in the Black-Scholes model have the following relationships to the resulting call value, assuming a European call:

- Underlying asset value +.
- Expiration cost −.
- Time to expiration +.
- Volatility +.
- Risk-free rate +.

Binomial Path-Dependent and Market-Replicating Portfolios

Another method for solving a real options problem includes the use of binomial lattice structures coupled with market-replicating portfolios. In order to correctly value market-replicating portfolios, we must be able to create a cash-equivalent replicating portfolio from a particular risky security and risk-free asset. This cash-equivalent replicating portfolio will have the same exact payoff series as the project in each state where the price of the cash equivalent replicating portfolio will be the value of the project itself. This is because we introduce a Martingale-based q measure, which is in essence a risk-adjusted or risk-neutral parameter. It is therefore not necessary to use probability estimates of the states of nature. The risk-adjusted discount rate is not computed, and nothing is known about the risk tolerances of the firm. All the information that is required is implicitly included in the relative prices of the risk-free asset and risky asset. The assumption is that as long as prices are in true equilibrium, the market information tells us all that we need to know. The other assumption is that the portfolio is arbitrage-free, such that the Arbitrage Pricing Theory holds true at any point in time. However, the Arbitrage Pricing Theory does not require the actual portfolio to be observable, and the portfolio set does not have to be intertemporally stationary. Compare this complicated method using market-replicating portfolio with a much simpler to use risk-neutral probability approach. In theory, both approaches obtain the same results, but the latter approach is much simpler to apply. Thus, in this book, we focus on the risk-neutral probabilities approach to solve sample real options problems. However, for completeness, the following section illustrates a simple market-replicating approach to solving a real options problem.

GENERIC BINOMIAL LATTICE STRUCTURE

Assume the terminal period as 3 and an implementation cost of $100 for the following series of free cash flows, *S* (*see* Figure 7C.1):

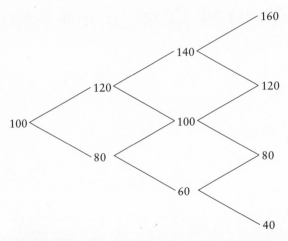

FIGURE 7C.1   Generic Binomial Lattice Structure

To simplify the example, we need an arbitrary naming convention (*see* Figure 7C.2):

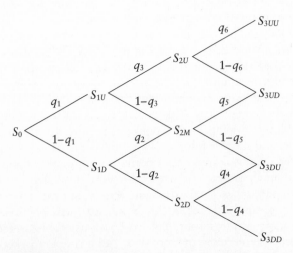

FIGURE 7C.2   Arbitrary Naming Convention

The generic formulation to use includes the following (where i is defined as the respective time-step):

- Hedge ratio (h): $h_{i-1} = \dfrac{C_{up} - C_{down}}{S_{up} - S_{down}}$

- Debt load (D): $D_{i-1} = S_i(h_{i-1}) - C_i$

- Call value (C) at node i: $C_i = S_i h_i - D_i e^{-\rho(\delta t)}$

- Risk-adjusted probability (q): $q_i = \dfrac{S_{i-1} - S_{down}}{S_{up} - S_{down}}$

  Obtained assuming $S_{i-1} = q_i S_{up} + (1 - q_i)S_{down}$

  This means that $S_{i-1} = q_i S_{up} + S_{down} - q_i S_{down}$

  and $q_i[S_{up} - S_{down}] = S_{i-1} - S_{down}$

  so we get $q_i = \dfrac{S_{i-1} - S_{down}}{S_{up} - S_{down}}$

For simplicity, assume that the discount factor is zero ($\rho = 0$) in this example, and that i ranges between 0 and 3.

1. **Step I: Get the call values at the terminal nodes.**

   As we assume the strike prices are 100 at all terminal nodes, we get (all values in $)
   $$C_{3UU} = \max[160 - 100,0] = 60$$
   $$C_{3UD} = \max[120 - 100,0] = 20$$
   $$C_{3DU} = \max[80 - 100,0] = 0$$
   $$C_{3DD} = \max[40 - 100,0] = 0$$

2. **Step II: Get the hedge ratios for the terminal branches.**

   $$h_{2U} = \frac{60 - 20}{160 - 120} = 1.0$$

   $$h_{2M} = \frac{20 - 0}{120 - 80} = 0.5$$

   $$h_{2D} = \frac{0 - 0}{80 - 40} = 0.0$$

3. **Step III: Get the debt load for the terminal branches.**

   $$D_{2U} = S_{3UU}(h_{2u}) - C_{3UU} = 160(1.0) - 60 = 100$$
   $$D_{2M} = S_{3UD}(h_{2M}) - C_{3UD} = 120(0.5) - 20 = 40$$
   $$D_{2L} = S_{3DU}(h_{2D}) - C_{3DU} = 80(0.0) - 0 = 0$$

4. Step IV: Get the call values one node back, $t = 2$.

$$C_{2U} = S_{2U}(h_{2U}) - D_{2U}e^{-\rho(\delta t)} = 140(1.0) - 100e^{-0(1)} = 40$$

$$C_{2M} = S_{2M}(h_{2M}) - D_{2M}e^{-\rho(\delta t)} = 100(0.5) - 40e^{-0(1)} = 10$$

$$C_{2D} = S_{2D}(h_{2D}) - D_{2D}e^{-\rho(\delta t)} = 60(0.0) - 0e^{-0(1)} = 0$$

5. Step V: Get the hedge ratios for the one branch back, $t = 1$.

$$h_{1U} = \frac{40 - 10}{140 - 100} = 0.75$$

$$h_{1D} = \frac{10 - 0}{100 - 60} = 0.25$$

6. Step VI: Get the debt load for one branch back, $t = 1$.

$$D_{1U} = S_{2U}(h_{1U}) - C_{2U} = 140(0.75) - 40 = 65$$

$$D_{1D} = S_{2D}(h_{1D}) - C_{2D} = 100(0.25) - 10 = 15$$

7. Step VII: Get the call values one node back.

$$C_{1U} = S_{1U}(h_{1U}) - D_{1U}e^{-\rho(\delta t)} = 120(0.75) - 65e^{-0(1)} = 25$$

$$C_{1D} = S_{1D}(h_{1D}) - D_{1D}e^{-\rho(\delta t)} = 80(0.25) - 15e^{-0(1)} = 5$$

8. Step VIII: Get the hedge ratios for two branches back, $t = 0$.

$$h_0 = \frac{25 - 5}{120 - 80} = 0.5$$

9. Step IX: Get the debt load for two branches back, $t = 0$.

$$D_0 = S_1(h_0) - C_{1U} = 120(0.5) - 25 = 35$$

10. Step X: Get the call value at $t = 0$, the option value of this analysis.

$$C_0 = S_0(h_0) - D_0e^{-\rho(\delta t)} = 100(0.5) - 35e^{-0(1)} = 15$$

11. **Step XI: Get all the risk-adjusted probabilities—for simplicity, all the probabilities have been set such that the results would be 50 percent for all instances.**

$$q_i = \frac{S_{i-1} - S_{down}}{S_{up} - S_{down}}$$

$$q_6 = \frac{140 - 120}{160 - 120} = 0.5$$

$$q_5 = \frac{100 - 80}{120 - 80} = 0.5$$

$$q_4 = \frac{60 - 40}{80 - 40} = 0.5$$

$$q_3 = \frac{120 - 100}{140 - 100} = 0.5$$

$$q_2 = \frac{80 - 60}{100 - 60} = 0.5$$

$$q_1 = \frac{100 - 80}{120 - 80} = 0.5$$

The results of the analysis are presented in Figure 7C.3, with the corresponding call values at each node and the risk-adjusted probabilities:

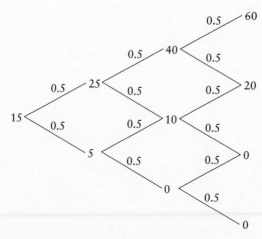

FIGURE 7C.3   Results of Analysis

Single-State Static Binomial Example

This appendix illustrates yet another approach to solving real options problems, that of basic differential equations. In this example, suppose that a certain firm has an option to change its current mummification embalming technology from the traditional Dull Old Method (D) to a new and revolutionary approach using the latest liquid nitrogen freezing equipment in Cryogenic Technology (C). Obviously, in order to do so, it would cost the firm some restructuring cost of approximately $9,000 to convert the existing lab into a freezing chamber and an additional $1,000 scrapping cost to dismantle the old equipment. Hence, the total cost of implementation is assumed to be $10,000 and, for simplicity, assumed to be fixed no matter when the implementation takes place, either at present or sometime in the future. The benefit of the new cryogenics technology is that the mummification cost will be fixed at $500 each. This incremental fixed cost is highly desirable to senior management as it assists in cost-cutting strategies and provides a really good way to forecast future profitability.

Based on the current technology using the same Dull Old Method, it costs on average $2,000 in incremental marginal cost. However, this cost fluctuates depending on market demand. For instance, if the market is good (G), where the demand for mummification increases, the firm will have to hire additional help and have employees work overtime, costing on average $3,000 marginal cost per unit. In a down or bad (B) market, when demand is significantly low, the firm can lay off individuals, put key employees on a rotating part-time schedule, and cut overhead costs significantly, resulting in only a $400 incremental marginal cost. The question is, will the new cryogenics be financially feasible assuming there is a 50 percent chance of a good upswing market for mummification and a 10 percent cost of capital (r)? If it is feasible, then should the implementation be done now or later? The cost structure is presented graphically in Figure 7D.1 (all values in $):

Restructure Cost = \$9,000 (*RC*)
Scrapping Cost = \$1,000 (*SC*)
Total Cost = *RC* + *SC* = \$10,000 (*TC*)

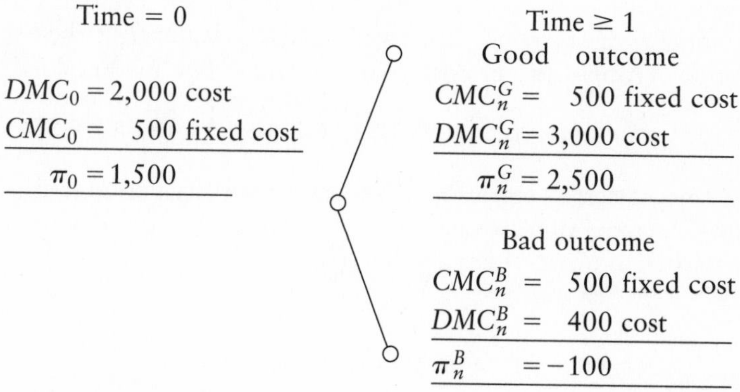

Time = 0	Time ≥ 1
	Good outcome
$DMC_0 = 2{,}000$ cost	$CMC_n^G = 500$ fixed cost
$CMC_0 = 500$ fixed cost	$DMC_n^G = 3{,}000$ cost
$\pi_0 = 1{,}500$	$\pi_n^G = 2{,}500$
	Bad outcome
	$CMC_n^B = 500$ fixed cost
	$DMC_n^B = 400$ cost
	$\pi_n^B = -100$

where we define

DMC_0	Dull Old Method's marginal cost at time 0
CMC_0	Cryogenics method's marginal cost at time 0
π_0	Profits through savings, at time 0
CMC_n^G	Cryogenics method's marginal cost at time n with good market conditions
DMC_n^G	Dull method's marginal cost at time n with good market conditions
π_n^G	Profits through savings, at time n with good market conditions
CMC_n^B	Cryogenics method's marginal cost at time n with bad market conditions
DMC_n^B	Dull method's marginal cost at time n with bad market conditions
π_n^B	Profits through savings, at time n with bad market conditions

FIGURE 7D.1 Cost Structure

If the firm moves and starts at time 0, profits or the benefits from cost savings will be

$$\pi_0 = DMC_0 - CMC_0 = \$2{,}000 - \$500 = \$1{,}500$$

This is the current period (time 0) cost savings only. Because the implementation has already begun, the future periods will also derive cost savings such that for time where $n \geq 1$, we have under the good market conditions

$$\pi_n^G = DMC_n^G - CMC_n^G = \$3{,}000 - \$500 = \$2{,}500$$

Under the bad market conditions, we have

$$\pi_n^B = DMC_n^B - CMC_n^B = \$400 - \$500 = -\$100$$

Assuming we know from historical data and experience that there is a 50 percent chance of a good versus a bad market, we can take the expected value of the profits $E(\pi)$ or cost savings of these two market conditions:

$$E(\pi_1) = p\pi_1^G + (1 - p)\pi_1^B = 0.5(\$2,500) + (0.5)(-\$100) = \$1,200$$

Because this expected value of \$1,200 occurs for every period in the future with the same fixed value with zero growth, the future cash flow stream can be summarized as perpetuities, and the present value of executing the implementation now $E(\pi_0)$ will be

$$E(\pi_0) = \sum_{n=0}^{\infty} E(\pi_n)/(1 + r)^n \cong \pi_0 + E(\pi_1)/r = \$1,500 + \frac{\$1,200}{0.1} = \$13,500$$

Hence, the net present value of the project is simply the value generated through the cost savings of the Cryogenics technology less the implementation cost:

$$NPV = \pi_0 - TC_0 = \$13,500 - \$10,000 = \$3,500$$

If the firm decides to switch at a future time when $k \geq 1$, given a good market (ω_G):

$$\Pi_k^G = \sum_{n=k}^{\infty} E(\pi_n^G/\omega_G)(1 + r)^{k-n} \cong \sum_{n=k}^{\infty} \pi_1^G(1 + r)^{k-n} \cong \pi_1^G\left[\frac{r + 1}{r}\right]$$

$$\Pi_k^G = \$2,500\left[\frac{1.1}{0.1}\right] = \$27,500$$

Similarly, given that the market is unfavorable (ω_U), at time $k \geq 1$:

$$\Pi_k^B = \sum_{n=k}^{\infty} E(\pi_n^B/\omega_u)(1 + r)^{k-n} \cong \pi_1^B\left[\frac{r + 1}{r}\right]$$

$$\Pi_k^B = -\$100\left[\frac{1.1}{0.1}\right] = -\$1,100$$

For instance, assume $k = 1$,

$$\Pi_0 = \pi_0 + [p^G(\pi_1^G) + (1 - p^G)(\pi_1^B)]/(1 + r)$$

$$\Pi_0 = \$1,500 + [0.5(\$27,500) + (1 - 0.5)(-\$1,100)]/(1 + 0.1)$$
$$= \$13,500$$

$$NPV = \Pi_0 - TC_0 = \$13,500 - \$10,000 = \$3,500$$

However, this is incorrect because we need to consider the analysis in terms of strategic optionalities. As we have the opportunity, the right to execute and not the obligation to do so, the firm would execute the option if it is financially feasible and not execute otherwise. Hence, the options are feasible only when the good market outcome occurs in the future and not executed in the bad market condition. Therefore, the actual net present value should be

$$\frac{\Pi_k^B p_B}{(1+r)} + \frac{\Pi_k^G p_G}{(1+r)} = 0 + 0.5\left[\frac{\$27,500 - \$10,000}{1.1}\right] = \$7,954$$

Hence, we can create a generic valuation structure for the option value as above. To add a level of complexity, the total cost should be discounted at a risk-free rate (r_f), as we segregate the market risk (Π_G) and private risk (TC), and the structure could be represented as

$$\Pi_{CALL} = \max\left\{[\Pi_0 - TC], \frac{p^G(\Pi_1^G)}{1+r} - \frac{TC}{1+r_f}\right\}$$

$$= \max\left\{\left[\pi_0 + \frac{E(\pi_1)}{r} - TC\right]^+, \left[\frac{p^G\pi_1^G\left(\frac{r+1}{r}\right)}{1+r} - \frac{TC}{1+r_f}\right]^+\right\}$$

This simply is to calculate the maximum value of either starting now, which is represented by $[\Pi_0 - TC]$ or starting later, which is represented as

$$\frac{p^G(\pi_1^G)}{1+r} - \frac{TC}{1+r_f}.$$

Because the future starting point has been collapsed into a single static state, any starting points in the future can be approximated by the valuation of a single period in the future.

OPTIMAL TRIGGER VALUES

A related analysis is that of optimal trigger values. Looking at the formulation for the call valuation price structure, if there is a change in total cost, that is, the initial capital outlay, something interesting occurs. The total cost in starting now is not discounted because the outlay occurs immediately. However, if the outlay occurs in the future, the total cost will have to be discounted at the risk-free rate. Therefore, the higher the initial cost outlay, the discounted effect of starting in the future decreases the effective cost in today's dollar, hence making it more efficient to wait and defer the cost until a later time. If the cost is lower and the firm becomes more operationally efficient, it is beneficial to begin now as the value of starting now is greater than waiting. The total cost break-even point can be obtained by solving the call valuation equation above for total cost and can be represented as

$$TC^* = \left[1 - \frac{1}{(1 + r_f)^n}\right]^{-1} \left[\pi_0 + \frac{E[\pi_1]}{r} - \frac{p^G \pi_1^G \left(\frac{r + 1}{r}\right)}{(1 + r)^n}\right]$$

If total cost of implementation exceeds TC^* above, it is optimal to wait, and if total cost does not exceed TC^*, it is beneficial to execute the option now. Remember that the optimal trigger value depends on the operational efficiency of the firm as well, because it is a dynamic equation given that the optimal trigger value depends on how much money can be saved with implementation of the Cryogenic modifications.

Uncertainty Effects on Profit or Cost Savings π

Suppose we keep the first moment and change the second moment, that is, change the spread and, hence, the risk or uncertainty of the profit or cost savings while leaving the expected payoffs the same. It would make sense that waiting is better. Let's see how this works. Recall that the original case had $\pi_n^G = \$2,500$, $\pi_n^B = -\$100$, with a 50 percent chance of going either way, creating an expected value of $0.5(\$2,500 - \$100) = \$1,200$. Now, suppose we change the values to $\pi_n^{G*} = \$3,000$ and $\pi_n^{B*} = -\$600$, with a 50 percent chance of going either way, creating a similar expected value of $0.5(\$3,000 - \$600) = \$1,200$ as in the original case. However, notice that the risk has increased in the second case as the variability of payoffs has increased. So, we can easily recalculate the value of

$$\Pi_k^G = \pi_1^G \left[\frac{1 + r}{r}\right] = \$3,000 \left[\frac{1.1}{0.1}\right] = \$33,000,$$

(for all $k \geqslant 1$) which is higher than the original $\$27,500$.

The conclusion is that the higher the uncertainty, the higher is the value of waiting. This is because the firm has no information on the market demand fluctuations. The higher the market volatility, the better off the firm will be by waiting until this market uncertainty has been resolved and it knows what market demand looks like before proceeding with the capital investment.

Sensitivity Analysis with Delta, Gamma, Rho, Theta, Vega, and Xi

Using the corollary outputs generated by options theory, we can use the results—namely, Delta, Gamma, Rho, Theta, Vega, and Xi—as a form of sensitivity analysis. By definition, sensitivity analysis, or stress testing, looks at the outcome of the change in the option price given a change in one unit of the underlying variables. In our case, these sensitivities reflect the instantaneous changes of the value of the option given a unit change in a particular variable, ceteris paribus. In other words, we can form a sensitivity table by simply looking at the corresponding values in Delta, Gamma, Rho, Theta, Vega, and Xi. Delta provides the change in value of the option given a unit change in the present value of the underlying asset's cash flow series. Gamma provides the rate of change in delta given a unit change in the underlying asset's cash flow series. Rho provides us with the change in the value of the option given that we change the interest rate one unit, Theta looks at the change per unit of time, Vega looks at the change per unit of volatility, and Xi looks at the change per unit of cost. In other words, one can provide a fairly comprehensive view of the way the value of the option changes given changes in these variables, thereby providing a test of the sensitivity of the option's value. A worse-case, nominal case, and best-case scenario can then be constructed. The sensitivity table not only provides a good test of the robustness of our results but also provides great insight into the value drivers in the firm, that is, which variables have the most impact on the firm's bottom line. The following provides the derivations of these sensitivity measures for a European option without dividend payments. A different approach to obtain sensitivities is through the use of Tornado diagrams.

CALL DELTA

Starting from $C = S_t N(d_1) - Xe^{-rT} N(d_2)$, where

$$d_1 = \frac{\ln\left(\frac{S_t}{X}\right) + \left(r + \frac{1}{2}\sigma^2\right)(T)}{\sigma\sqrt{T}} \quad \text{and} \quad d_2 = d_1 - \sigma\sqrt{T},$$

we can get the call Delta, defined as the change in call value for a change in the underlying asset value, that is, the partial derivative

$$\frac{\partial C_t}{\partial S_t}$$

at an instantaneous time t. Differentiating, we obtain:

$$Delta = \Delta = \frac{\partial C_t}{\partial S_t} = N(d_1) + S_t \frac{\partial N(d_1)}{\partial S_t} - Xe^{-rT} \frac{\partial N(d_2)}{\partial S_t}$$

$$\frac{\partial C_t}{\partial S_t} = N(d_1) + S_t \frac{e^{-\frac{1}{2}d_1^2}}{\sqrt{2\pi}} \frac{\partial d_1}{\partial S_t} - Xe^{-rT} \frac{e^{-\frac{1}{2}d_2^2}}{\sqrt{2\pi}} \frac{\partial d_2}{\partial S_t}$$

$$\frac{\partial C_t}{\partial S_t} = N(d_1) + S_t \frac{e^{-\frac{1}{2}d_1^2}}{\sqrt{2\pi}} \frac{1/S_t}{\sigma\sqrt{T}} - Xe^{-rT} \frac{e^{-\frac{1}{2}(d_1 - \sigma\sqrt{T})^2}}{\sqrt{2\pi}} \frac{1/S_t}{\sigma\sqrt{T}}$$

$$\frac{\partial C_t}{\partial S_t} = N(d_1) + \frac{e^{-\frac{1}{2}d_1^2}}{\sigma\sqrt{2\pi T}} \left[1 - Xe^{-rT} \frac{e^{-\frac{1}{2}\sigma^2 T + d_1\sigma\sqrt{T}}}{S_t} \right]$$

$$\frac{\partial C_t}{\partial S_t} = N(d_1) + \frac{e^{-\frac{1}{2}d_1^2}}{\sigma\sqrt{2\pi T}} \left[1 - \frac{Xe^{-rT}}{S_t} e^{-\frac{1}{2}\sigma^2 T} e^{\ln(S_t/X) + (r + \sigma^2/2)T} \right]$$

$$\frac{\partial C_t}{\partial S_t} = N(d_1) + \frac{e^{-\frac{1}{2}d_1^2}}{\sigma\sqrt{2\pi T}} \left[1 - \frac{Xe^{-rT}}{S_t} e^{-\frac{1}{2}\sigma^2 T} \frac{S_t}{X} e^{rT} e^{\frac{1}{2}\sigma^2 T} \right]$$

$$Delta = \Delta = \frac{\partial C_t}{\partial S_t} = N(d_1)$$

CALL GAMMA

$$Gamma = \Gamma = \frac{\partial \Delta}{\partial S_t}$$

$$\frac{\partial \Delta}{\partial S_t} = \frac{1}{\sqrt{2\pi}} e^{-\frac{1}{2}d_1^2} \frac{\partial d_1}{\partial S_t}$$

$$\frac{\partial \Delta}{\partial S_t} = \frac{1}{\sqrt{2\pi}} e^{-\frac{1}{2}d_1^2} \frac{1}{S_t\sigma\sqrt{T}}$$

$$Gamma = \Gamma = \frac{\partial \Delta}{\partial S_t} = \frac{e^{\frac{-d_1^2}{2}}}{S_t\sigma\sqrt{2\pi T}}$$

CALL RHO

$$Rho = P = \frac{\partial C_t}{\partial r} = S_t\frac{\partial N(d_1)}{\partial r} + XTe^{-rT}N(d_2) - Xe^{-rT}\frac{\partial N(d_2)}{\partial r}$$

$$\frac{\partial C_t}{\partial r} = S_t\frac{e^{-\frac{1}{2}d_1^2}}{\sqrt{2\pi}} \frac{\partial d_1}{\partial r} + XTe^{-rT}N(d_2) - Xe^{-rT}\frac{e^{-\frac{1}{2}d_2^2}}{\sqrt{2\pi}} \frac{\partial d_2}{\partial r}$$

$$\frac{\partial C_t}{\partial r} = \frac{e^{-\frac{1}{2}d_1^2}}{\sqrt{2\pi}}\left[S_t\frac{\partial d_1}{\partial r} - Xe^{-rT}e^{\frac{1}{2}(d_1^2 - d_2^2)}\frac{\partial d_1}{\partial r}\right] + XTe^{-rT}N(d_2)$$

$$\frac{\partial C_t}{\partial r} = \frac{e^{-\frac{1}{2}d_1^2}}{\sqrt{2\pi}}\frac{\partial d_1}{\partial r}\left[S_t - Xe^{-rT}e^{-\frac{1}{2}\sigma^2 T}e^{\ln(S/X)+(r+\sigma^2/2)T}\right] + XTe^{-rT}N(d_2)$$

$$\frac{\partial C_t}{\partial r} = \frac{e^{-\frac{1}{2}d_1^2}}{\sqrt{2\pi}}\frac{\partial d_1}{\partial r}\left[S_t - \frac{XS_t}{X}\right] + XTe^{-rT}N(d_2)$$

$$Rho = P = \frac{\partial C_t}{\partial r} = XTe^{-rT}N(d_2)$$

CALL THETA

Start with $\dfrac{\partial C_t}{\partial T} = S_t\dfrac{\partial N(d_1)}{\partial T} - X\dfrac{\partial}{\partial T}\left[e^{-rT}N(d_2)\right]$

$$\frac{\partial C_t}{\partial T} = S_t \frac{1}{\sqrt{2\pi}} e^{-\frac{1}{2}d_1^2} \frac{\partial d_1}{\partial T} + rXe^{-rT}N(d_2) - Xe^{-rT}\frac{1}{\sqrt{2\pi}} e^{-\frac{1}{2}d_2^2} \frac{\partial d_2}{\partial T}$$

As $\dfrac{\partial d_1}{\partial T} = \dfrac{-\ln\dfrac{S_t}{X}}{2\sigma T^{3/2}} + \dfrac{1}{2\sigma\sqrt{T}}\left[r + \dfrac{\sigma^2}{2}\right]$ we have $\dfrac{\partial d_2}{\partial T} = \dfrac{\partial d_1}{\partial T} - \dfrac{\sigma}{2\sqrt{T}}$ and

$$\frac{\partial C_t}{\partial T} = S_t \frac{1}{\sqrt{2\pi}} e^{-\frac{1}{2}d_1^2} \frac{\partial d_1}{\partial T} + rXe^{-rT}N(d_2) - Xe^{-rT}\frac{1}{\sqrt{2\pi}} e^{-\frac{1}{2}d_2^2}\left[\frac{\partial d_1}{\partial T} - \frac{\sigma}{2\sqrt{T}}\right]$$

$$\frac{\partial C_t}{\partial T} = \frac{e^{-\frac{1}{2}d_1^2}}{\sqrt{2\pi}}\left[S_t \frac{\partial d_1}{\partial T} - Xe^{-rT}e^{-\frac{1}{2}(d_1^2-d_2^2)}\left(\frac{\partial d_1}{\partial T} - \frac{\sigma}{2\sqrt{T}}\right)\right] + rXe^{-rT}N(d_2)$$

$$\frac{\partial C_t}{\partial T} = \frac{e^{-\frac{1}{2}d_1^2}}{\sqrt{2\pi}}\left[S_t \frac{\partial d_1}{\partial T} - Xe^{-rT}e^{-\frac{1}{2}(\sigma^2 T)}e^{\sigma d_1\sqrt{T}}\left(\frac{\partial d_1}{\partial T} - \frac{\sigma}{2\sqrt{T}}\right)\right] + rXe^{-rT}N(d_2)$$

$$\frac{\partial C_t}{\partial T} = \frac{e^{-\frac{1}{2}d_1^2}}{\sqrt{2\pi}}\left[S_t \frac{\partial d_1}{\partial T} - Xe^{-rT-\frac{1}{2}(\sigma^2 T)+\ln(S/X)+(r+\sigma^2/2)T}\left(\frac{\partial d_1}{\partial t} - \frac{\sigma}{2\sqrt{T}}\right)\right] + rXe^{-rT}N(d_2)$$

$$\frac{\partial C_t}{\partial T} = \frac{e^{-\frac{1}{2}d_1^2}}{\sqrt{2\pi}}\left[S_t \frac{\partial d_1}{\partial T} - S_t \frac{\partial d_1}{\partial T} + \frac{S_t\sigma}{2\sqrt{T}}\right] + rXe^{-rT}N(d_2)$$

$$Theta = \Theta = \frac{-\partial C_t}{\partial T} = \frac{-S\sigma e^{\frac{-d_1^2}{2}}}{2\sqrt{2\pi T}} - rXe^{-rT}N(d_2)$$

CALL VEGA

$$Vega = V = \frac{\partial C_t}{\partial \sigma} = \frac{\partial}{\partial \sigma}[S_t N(d_1) - Xe^{-rT}N(d_2)]$$

$$\frac{\partial C_t}{\partial \sigma} = \frac{S_t}{\sqrt{2\pi}} e^{-\frac{1}{2}d_1^2} \frac{\partial d_1}{\partial \sigma} - Xe^{-rT} e^{-\frac{1}{2}d_2^2} \frac{\partial d_2}{\partial \sigma}$$

$$\frac{\partial C_t}{\partial \sigma} = \frac{1}{\sqrt{2\pi}} e^{-\frac{1}{2}d_1^2}\left[S_t \frac{\partial d_1}{\partial \sigma} - Xe^{-rT} e^{-(d_1^2-d_2^2)} \frac{\partial d_2}{\partial \sigma}\right]$$

$$\frac{\partial C_t}{\partial \sigma} = \frac{1}{\sqrt{2\pi}} e^{-\frac{1}{2}d_1^2}\left[S_t \frac{\partial d_1}{\partial \sigma} - Xe^{-rT} e^{-\frac{1}{2}\sigma^2 T + d_1\sigma\sqrt{T}} \frac{\partial d_2}{\partial \sigma}\right]$$

$$\frac{\partial C_t}{\partial \sigma} = \frac{1}{\sqrt{2\pi}} e^{-\frac{1}{2}d_1^2} \left[S_t \frac{\partial d_1}{\partial \sigma} - Xe^{-rT} e^{-\frac{1}{2}\sigma^2 T} e^{\ln(S/X) + (r+\sigma^2/2)T} \frac{\partial d_2}{\partial \sigma} \right]$$

$$\frac{\partial C_t}{\partial \sigma} = \frac{1}{\sqrt{2\pi}} e^{-\frac{1}{2}d_1^2} \left[S_t \frac{\partial d_1}{\partial \sigma} - S_t \frac{\partial d_2}{\partial \sigma} \right]$$

$$\frac{\partial C_t}{\partial \sigma} = \frac{1}{\sqrt{2\pi}} e^{-\frac{1}{2}d_1^2} S_t \left[\frac{\partial d_1}{\partial \sigma} - \frac{\partial d_1}{\partial \sigma} + \sqrt{T} \right]$$

$$Vega = V = \frac{\partial C_t}{\partial \sigma} = \frac{S_t \sqrt{T} e^{\frac{-d_1^2}{2}}}{\sqrt{2\pi}}$$

CALL Xi

$$Xi = \Xi = \frac{\partial C_t}{\partial X} = -N(d_2)e^{-rT} + S_t \frac{\partial N(d_1)}{\partial X} - Xe^{-rT} \frac{\partial N(d_2)}{\partial X}$$

$$\frac{\partial C_t}{\partial X_t} = -N(d_2)e^{-rT} + S_t \frac{e^{-\frac{1}{2}d_1^2}}{\sqrt{2\pi}} \frac{\partial d_1}{\partial X} - Xe^{-rT} \frac{e^{-\frac{1}{2}d_2^2}}{\sqrt{2\pi}} \frac{\partial d_2}{\partial X}$$

$$\frac{\partial C_t}{\partial X_t} = -N(d_2)e^{-rT} + S_t \frac{e^{-\frac{1}{2}d_1^2}}{\sqrt{2\pi}} \frac{1/S_t}{\sigma\sqrt{T}} - Xe^{-rT} \frac{e^{-\frac{1}{2}(d_1 - \sigma\sqrt{T})^2}}{\sqrt{2\pi}} \frac{1/S_t}{\sigma\sqrt{T}}$$

$$\frac{\partial C_t}{\partial X_t} = -N(d_2)e^{-rT} + \frac{e^{-\frac{1}{2}d_1^2}}{\sigma\sqrt{2\pi T}} \left[1 - Xe^{-rT} \frac{e^{-\frac{1}{2}\sigma^2 T + d_1\sigma\sqrt{T}}}{S_t} \right]$$

$$\frac{\partial C_t}{\partial X_t} = -N(d_2)e^{-rT} + \frac{e^{-\frac{1}{2}d_1^2}}{\sigma\sqrt{2\pi T}} \left[1 - \frac{Xe^{-rT}}{S_t} e^{-\frac{1}{2}\sigma^2 T} e^{\ln(S_t/X) + (r+\sigma^2/2)T} \right]$$

$$\frac{\partial C_t}{\partial X_t} = -N(d_2)e^{-rT} + \frac{e^{-\frac{1}{2}d_1^2}}{\sigma\sqrt{2\pi T}} \left[1 - \frac{Xe^{-rT}}{S_t} e^{-\frac{1}{2}\sigma^2 T} \frac{S_t}{X} e^{rT} e^{\frac{1}{2}\sigma^2 T} \right]$$

$$Xi = \Xi = \frac{\partial C_t}{\partial X_t} = -N(d_2)e^{-rT}$$

Reality Checks

THEORETICAL RANGES FOR OPTIONS

One of the tests to verify whether the results calculated using the real options analytics are plausible is to revert back to financial options pricing theory. By construction, the value of a call option can be no lower than zero when the option is left to expire, that is, we have the call option value, $C \geq max [S - Xe^{-rT}, 0]$, and it can be no higher than the value of the asset, which we have defined as S, such that $C \leq S$. If the calculated results fall outside this range, we can reasonably say that the analysis is flawed, potentially due to unreasonable assumptions on creating the forecast cash flows. However, if the results fall comfortably within the range, we cannot be certain it is correct, only reasonably sure the analysis is correct assuming all the input variables are also reasonable. The main thrust of using this option range spread is to test the width of this spread, that is, the tighter the spread, the higher the confidence that the results are reasonable. Also, one could perform a sensitivity analysis by changing the input variables and assumptions to see if the spread changes, that is, if the spread widens or shifts.

SMIRR AND SNPV CONSISTENCY

Another plausibility test includes the use of a sequential modified internal rate of return (SMIRR) method and a sequential net present value (SNPV) method. If all goes well in the forecast of free cash flow and the discounted cash flow analysis holds up, then the MIRR[1] and NPV of the cash flow stream should theoretically be smooth. That is, the entire stream of cash flow should have MIRR and NPV similar to that of the cash flow stream less the first year's free cash flow, eliminating the first year's free cash flow as a reduction of the original net present value and setting the first year's cash flows to zeros. This method is repeated for all subsequent years. The reinvestment rate and the discount rate could be set at different levels for the computation of the MIRR and NPV. This interest-rate-jackknifing approach looks at the consistency and smoothness of the predicted cash flows over time. However, this approach is cumbersome and is seldom used.

MINIMAX APPROACH

If relevant probabilities are provided by the firm's management on specific outcomes of the cash flow over time, a *regret analysis* can be performed as a means of calculating the relevant value of the intangible. This regret analysis takes the form of a Minimax approach in Bayesian probability theory in the context of decision sciences. Essentially, it measures the relevant outcome of a forward-looking cash flow series given the appropriate probabilities, calculates the expected monetary value of the scenario, and identifies the scenario at which one minimizes the maximum amount of regret—hence the name Minimax. However, even if relevant probabilities are provided, they should not be used because these forecasted values add an additional element of uncertainty and because management can hardly be expected to provide a solid, dependable, and reliable set of economic forecasts, let alone the respective probabilities associated with each forecast's outcome. The analysis can be coupled within a Game Theory framework, where the best strategic outcome under the Nash equilibrium will always be observed. The specifics of Game Theory are beyond the scope of this book.

IMPLIED VOLATILITY TEST

Using the developed real options model and approach, we could set the volatility measure as the dependent variable to calculate. This implied volatility can then be measured against the historical volatility of the firm's cash flow situation or benchmarked against the volatility of cash flows of corresponding comparable companies under similar risks, functions, and products. The implied volatility can then be tested using a parametric t-test or a nonparametric Wilcoxon sign-rank test[2] to see if it is statistically identical to the mean and median of the set of comparable firms' volatilities.

An alternative is to use the Newton-Raphson search criteria for implied volatility measures through a series of guesses.

$$\sigma_1^* = \sqrt{\left| \ln\left[\frac{S}{X}\right] + rT \right| \left(\frac{2}{T}\right)}$$

$$\sigma_2^* = \sigma_1^* - \frac{[C(\sigma_1^*) - C(\sigma)]e^{\frac{d_1^2}{2}} 2\sqrt{\pi}}{S\sqrt{T}}$$

where C is the call value

$$\sigma_3^* = \sigma_2^* - \frac{[C(\sigma_2^*) - C(\sigma)]e^{\frac{d_1^2}{2}} 2\sqrt{\pi}}{S\sqrt{T}}$$

$$\sigma_{i+1}^* = \sigma_i^* - \frac{[C(\sigma_i^*) - C(\sigma)]e^{\frac{d_1^2}{2}} 2\sqrt{\pi}}{S\sqrt{T}}.$$

Applying Monte Carlo Simulation to Solve Real Options

Monte Carlo simulation can be easily adapted for use in a real options paradigm. There are multiple uses of Monte Carlo simulation, including the ability to obtain a volatility estimate as input into the real options models, obtaining a range of possible outcomes in the discounted cash flow analysis, and simulating input parameters that are highly uncertain. Here, the discussion focuses on two distinct applications of Monte Carlo simulation: solving a real options problem versus obtaining a range of real options values. Although these two approaches are discussed separately, they can be used together in an analysis.

APPLYING MONTE CARLO SIMULATION TO OBTAIN A REAL OPTIONS RESULT

Monte Carlo simulation can be applied to solve a real options problem, that is, to obtain an option result. Recall that the mainstream approaches in solving real options problems are the binomial approach, closed-form equations, partial-differential equations, and simulation. In the simulation approach, a series of forecast asset values are created using the Geometric Brownian Motion, and the maximization calculation is applied to the end point of the series, and discounted back to time zero, at the risk-free rate. That is, starting with an initial seed value of the underlying asset, simulate out multiple future pathways using a Geometric Brownian Motion, where $\delta S_t = S_{t-1}(rf(\delta t) + \sigma \varepsilon \sqrt{\delta t})$. That is, the change in asset value δS_t at time t is the value of the asset in the previous period S_{t-1} multiplied by the Brownian Motion $(rf(\delta t) + \sigma \varepsilon \sqrt{\delta t})$. Recall that rf is the risk-free rate, δt is the time-steps, σ is the volatility, and ε is the simulated value from a standard-normal distribution with mean of zero and a variance of one.

Figure 7G.1 illustrates an example of a simulated pathway used to solve a European option. Note that simulation can be easily used to solve European-type options, but it is fairly difficult to apply simulation to solve American-type options.[1] In this example, the one-year maturity European option is divided into five time-steps in the binomial lattice approach, which yields $20.75, as compared to $19.91 using the continuous Black-Scholes equation, and $19.99 using 1,000 Monte Carlo simulations on 10 steps. In theory, when the number of time-steps in the binomial lattices is large enough, the results approach the closed-form Black-Scholes results. Similarly, if the number of simulation trials are adequately increased, coupled with an increase in the simulation steps, the results stemming from Monte Carlo simulation also approach the Black-Scholes value. The example Excel worksheet is located in the Real Options Analysis Toolkit software menu under the *Examples* folder. *See* Figure 7G.1

The first step in Monte Carlo simulation is to decide on the number of steps to simulate. In the example, 10 steps were chosen for simplicity. Starting with the initial asset value of $100 ($S_0$), the change in value from this initial value to the first period is seen as $\delta S_1 = S_0(rf(\delta t) + \sigma\varepsilon\sqrt{\delta t})$. Hence, the value of the asset at the first time-step is equivalent to $S_1 = S_0 + \delta S_1 = S_0 + S_0(rf(\delta t) + \sigma\varepsilon\sqrt{\delta t})$. The value of the asset at the second time-step is hence $S_2 = S_1 + \delta S_2 = S_1 + S_1(rf(\delta t) + \sigma\varepsilon\sqrt{\delta t})$, and so forth, all the way until the terminal 10th time-step. Notice that because ε changes on each simulation trial, each simulation trial will produce an entirely different asset evolution pathway. At the end of the 10th time-step, the maximization process is then applied. That is, for a simple European option with a $100 implementation cost, the function is simply $C_{10,i} = Max[S_{10,i} - X, 0]$. This is the call value $C_{10,i}$ at time 10 for the *ith* simulation trial. This value is then discounted at the risk-free rate to obtain the call value at time zero, that is, $C_{0,i} = C_{10,i}e^{-rf(T)}$. This is a single-value estimate for a single simulated pathway.

Applying Monte Carlo simulation for 1,000 trials and obtaining the mean value of C_0 yields $19.99. This is termed the path-dependent simulation approach. There is a less precise shortcut to this simulation. That is, collapse all the 10 time-steps into a single time-step, using $S_T = S_0 + \delta S_T = S_0 + S_0(rf(T) + \sigma\varepsilon\sqrt{T})$, where the time T in this case is the one-year maturity. Then the call option value can be estimated using $C_{0,i} = Max[(S_{T,i} - X)e^{-rf(T)}, 0]$. Simulating the results 1,000 times yields the estimated option value of $18.29. Obviously, the higher the number of simulations and the higher the number of steps in the simulation, the more accurate the results.

Figure 7G.2 illustrates the results generated by performing 1,000 simulation trials. The enclosed Real Options Analysis Toolkit software has an example spreadsheet that estimates the European option value using Monte Carlo simulation.[2] Notice the lognormal distribution of the payoff functions.

Input Parameters

Expiration in Years	1.00
Volatility	45.00%
PV Asset Value	$100
Risk-free Rate	5.00%
Dividend rate	0.00%
Strike Cost	$100

Simulation Calculation

Simulate Value	0.00
Payoff Function	4.76

Intermediate Calculations

Number of Time Steps	5
Time Step Size (dt)	0.2000
Up Jump Size (u)	1.2229
Down Jump Size (d)	0.8177
Risk-Neutral Probability (p)	47.47%

Results

Binomial Approach	**$20.7492**
Black-Scholes Model	**$19.9118**
Path Dependent Simulated	**$19.9929**
Path Independent Simulated	**$18.2891**

Step 0	Step 1	Step 2	Step 3	Step 4	Step 5
100.00	122.29	149.55	182.89	223.67	273.53
	81.77	100.00	122.29	149.55	182.89
		66.87	81.77	100.00	122.29
			54.68	66.87	81.77
				44.71	54.68
					36.56

20.75	34.35	55.07	84.87	124.66	173.53
	8.86	16.28	29.20	50.55	82.89
		2.31	4.92	10.48	22.29
			0.00	0.00	0.00
				0.00	0.00
					0.00

Time	Simulate	Steps	Value
0			100.00
1	0.0	0.50	100.50
2	0.0	0.50	101.00
3	0.0	0.50	101.50
4	0.0	0.50	102.00
5	0.0	0.50	102.50
6	0.0	0.50	103.00
7	0.0	0.50	103.50
8	0.0	0.50	104.00
9	0.0	0.50	104.50
10	0.0	0.50	105.00

4.76

This is the Monte Carlo simulation approach to solving real options models. The model is based on the examples in Chapter 7's appendixes on solving real options using simulation. The assumptions and forecasts have been predefined in this worksheet. You will need to have Crystal Ball installed to run the analysis. Simply hit the RUN icon in Crystal Ball to obtain the simulated results ($0.0000) cells, which will be replaced with the results.

continue	continue	continue	continue	Execute
	continue	continue	continue	Execute
	continue	continue	continue	Execute
				End
				End
				End

FIGURE 76.1 Path-Dependent Simulation Approach to Solving Real Options

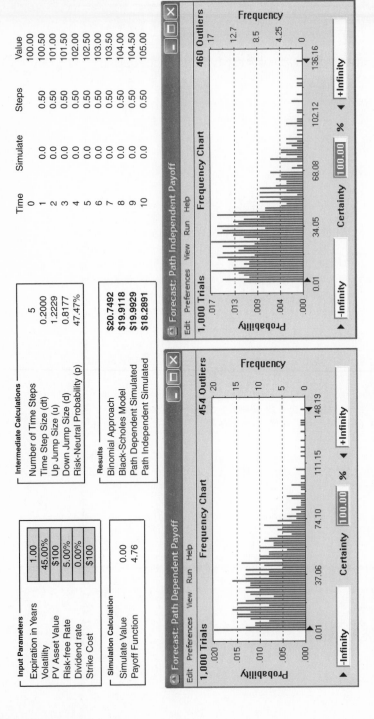

FIGURE 76.2 Path-Dependent Simulation Forecasting Results

APPLYING MONTE CARLO SIMULATION TO OBTAIN A RANGE OF REAL OPTIONS VALUES

Alternatively, Monte Carlo simulation can be applied to obtain a range of real options values. That is, as seen in Figure 7G.3, risk-free rate and volatility are the two example variables chosen for simulation. Distributional assumptions are assigned to these two variables, and the resulting options values using the Black-Scholes and binomial lattices are selected as forecast cells.

The results of the simulation are essentially a distribution of the real options values as seen in Figure 7G.4.[3] Notice that the ranges of real options values are consistent for both the binomial lattice and the Black-Scholes model. Keep in mind that the simulation application here is used to vary the inputs to a real options model to obtain a range of results, not to model and calculate the real options itself. However, simulation can be applied to both simulate the inputs to obtain the range of real options results and also solve the real options model through path-dependent modeling. However, a word of caution is in order. Recall that volatility is an input in a real options analysis, which captures the variability in asset value over time, and a binomial lattice is a discrete simulation technique, while a closed-form solution is obtained using continuous simulation models. Simulating real options inputs may end up double-counting a real option's true variability. *See* Figure 7G.4.

Note that the distribution of the terminal values is lognormal in nature, as all values are non-negative. Another word of caution is important here. Attempting to simulate just the terminal values without using the Brownian Motion approach will most certainly yield incorrect answers in general. The answers may be similar but will never be robust. Thus, simply simulating the terminal value outcomes and valuing them that way is completely flawed.

Input Parameters

Expiration in Years	1.00
Volatility	45.00%
PV Asset Value	$100
Risk-free Rate	5.00%
Dividend rate	0.00%
Strike Cost	$100

Intermediate Calculations

Number of Time Steps	5
Time Step Size (dt)	0.2000
Up Jump Size (u)	1.2229
Down Jump Size (d)	0.8177
Risk-Neutral Probability (p)	47.47%

Results

Binomial Approach	$20.7492
Black-Scholes Model	$19.9918

This is applying Monte Carlo simulation on existing real options models. The model is based on the example in Chapter7's appendixes on solving real options using simulation. The assumptions and forecasts have been predefined in this worksheet. You will need to have Crystal Ball installed to run the analysis. Simply hit the RUN icon in Crystal Ball to obtain the simulated forecast results.

Step 0	Step 1	Step 2	Step 3	Step 4	Step 5
100.00	122.29	149.55	182.89	223.67	273.53
	81.77	100.00	122.29	149.55	182.89
		66.87	81.77	100.00	122.29
			54.68	66.87	81.77
				44.71	54.68
					36.56

Step 0	Step 1	Step 2	Step 3	Step 4	Step 5
20.75	34.35	55.07	84.87	124.66	173.53
	8.86	16.28	29.20	50.55	82.89
		2.31	4.92	10.48	22.29
			0.00	0.00	0.00
				0.00	0.00
					0.00

continue	continue	continue	continue	continue	Execute
	continue	continue	continue	continue	Execute
		continue	continue	continue	Execute
			continue	continue	End
				continue	End
					End

FIGURE 76.3 Simulating Options Ranges

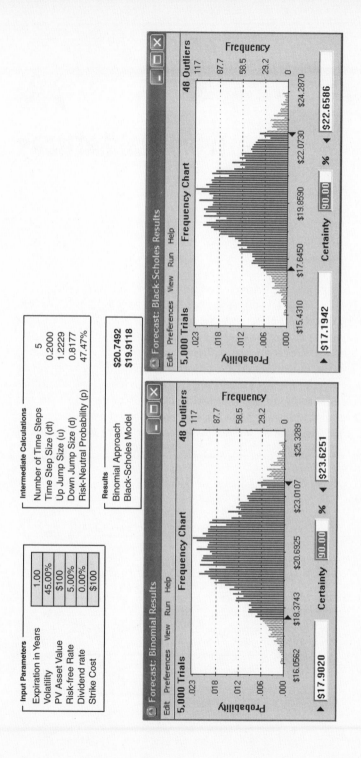

FIGURE 7G.4 Simulating Options Ranges Forecast Results

Trinomial Lattices

For the sake of completeness, below is an illustration of a trinomial tree (*see* Figure 7H.1). Building and solving a trinomial tree is similar to building and solving a binomial tree, complete with the up/down jumps and risk-neutral probabilities. However, the recombining trinomial tree below is more complicated to build. The results stemming from a trinomial tree are the same as those from a binomial tree at the limit, but the tree-building complexity is much higher for trinomials or multinomial trees. Hence, the examples thus far have been focusing on the binomial lattice, due to its simplicity and applicability. It is difficult enough to create a three-time-step trinomial tree as shown in Figure 7H.1. Imagine having to keep track of the number of

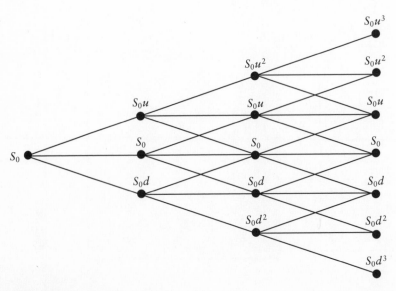

FIGURE 7H.1 Trinomial Tree

nodes, bifurcations, and which branch recombines with which, in a very large tree!

$$u = e^{\sigma\sqrt{3\delta t}} \text{ and } d = e^{-\sigma\sqrt{3\delta t}}$$

$$p_L = \frac{1}{6} - \sqrt{\frac{\delta t}{12\sigma^2}}\left[r - q - \frac{\sigma^2}{2}\right]$$

$$p_M = \frac{2}{3}$$

$$p_H = \frac{1}{6} + \sqrt{\frac{\delta t}{12\sigma^2}}\left[r - q - \frac{\sigma^2}{2}\right]$$

Non-Recombining Lattices

Figure 7I.1 illustrates a five-step non-recombining lattice for solving an American call option. Each node branches into two pathways that do not meet with other branches along the way (i.e., they do not recombine). The lattice shown here is the first lattice of the underlying asset.

Assumptions:

Asset = $100
Cost = $80
Maturity = 5 Years
Risk-free = 5%
Volatility = 40%

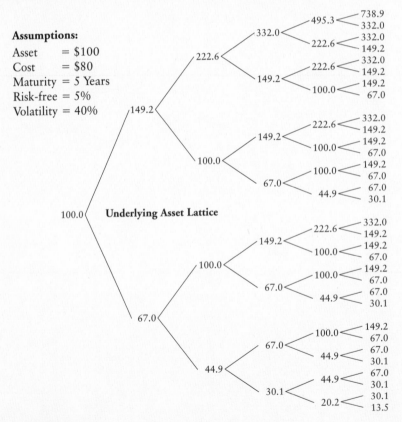

FIGURE 7I.1 Non-Recombining Underlying Asset Lattice

The lattice shown in Figure 71.2 is the valuation lattice of the American call option, obtained using the backward-induction approach and applying a risk-neutral probability analysis.

The problem can also be solved using a recombining lattice as shown in Figures 71.3 and 71.4. Notice the similar values along the non-recombining and recombining lattices. In the recombining lattice, the amount of computation work is significantly reduced because identical values for a particular time period are collapsed and summarized as unique nodes.

Notice the similar results obtained using the recombining and non-recombining lattices approach.

However, there is a caveat in comparing the recombining and non-recombining lattices. For instance, the six terminal nodes on a recombining tree are unique occurrences and a summary of the 32 terminal nodes on the non-recombining tree. Therefore, it is incorrect to assume that there is a $\frac{1}{6}$ probability of occurrence for the values 738, 332, 149, 67, 30, and 13. *See* Figure 71.5.

Intermediate Calculations:

Up Jump Size = 1.4918
Down Jump Size = 0.6703
Risk-Neutral
   Probability = 0.4637

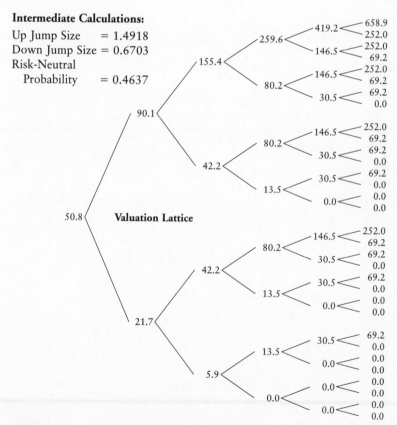

FIGURE 71.2 Non-Recombining Valuation Lattice

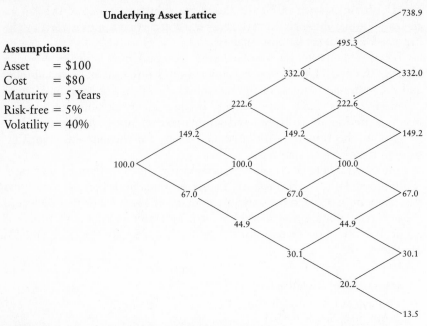

FIGURE 71.3   Recombining Underlying Asset Lattice

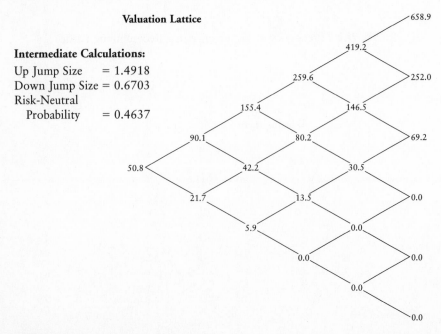

FIGURE 71.4   Recombining Valuation Lattice

In reality, the distribution of the terminal nodes looks somewhat normal, with different outcome probabilities as seen in Figure 7I.6. Depending on the input parameters, the distribution of the terminal nodes may change slightly (higher volatility means a higher frequency of occurrence in the extreme values).

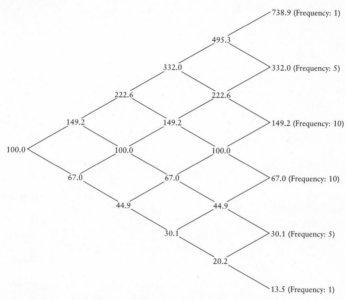

FIGURE 7I.5 Frequency of Occurrence in a Recombining Lattice

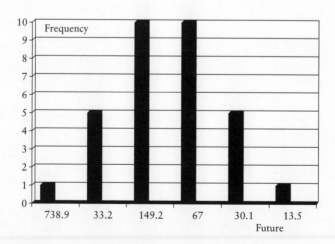

FIGURE 7I.6 Probability Distribution of the End Nodes on a Recombining Lattice

Although recombining lattices are easier to calculate and arrive at identical answers to the non-recombining lattices, there are conditions when non-recombining lattices are required for the analysis. These conditions include when there are multiple sources of uncertainty or when volatility changes over time, as in Figure 71.7.

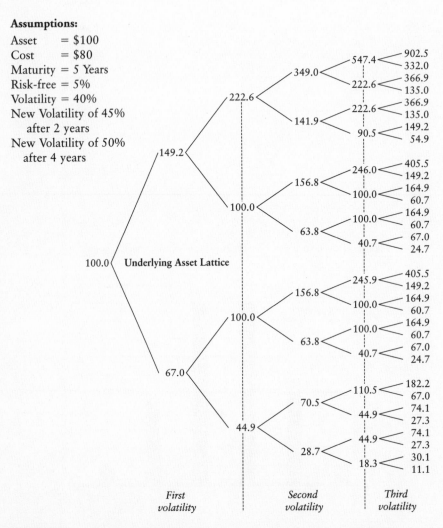

Assumptions:

Asset   = $100
Cost   = $80
Maturity = 5 Years
Risk-free = 5%
Volatility = 40%
New Volatility of 45%
    after 2 years
New Volatility of 50%
    after 4 years

First volatility   *Second volatility*   *Third volatility*

FIGURE 71.7   Non-Recombining Underlying Asset Lattice for a Changing
Volatility Option

Figure 7I.8 shows the valuation lattice on an American call option with changing volatilities using the risk-neutral probability approach.

Although non-recombining lattices are better suited for solving options with changing volatilities, recombining lattices can also be modified to handle this condition, thereby cutting down on analytical time and effort. The results

Calculations:

up (1)　　= 1.4918
down (1) = 0.6703
prob (1) = 0.4637

up (2)　　= 1.5683
down (2) = 0.6376
prob (2) = 0.4445

up (3)　　= 1.6487
down (3) = 0.6065
prob (3) = 0.4267

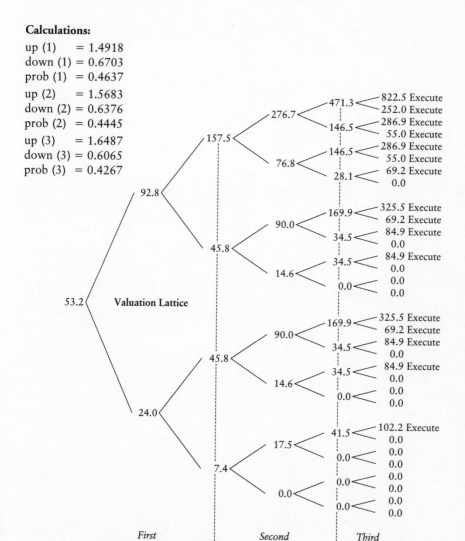

FIGURE 7I.8　Non-Recombining Valuation Lattice for a Changing Volatility Option

obtained are identical no matter which approach is used. The modified recombining lattice below makes use of the fact that although volatility changes three times within the five-year maturity period, volatility remains constant within particular time periods. For instance, the 40 percent volatility applies from time 0 to time 2, and the 45 percent volatility holds for time 2 to time 4. Within these time periods, volatility remains constant; hence, the lattice bifurcations are recombining. The entire lattice analysis in Figure 71.9 can be segregated into three stages of recombining lattices. At the end of a constant volatility period, each resulting node becomes the starting point of a new recombining lattice.

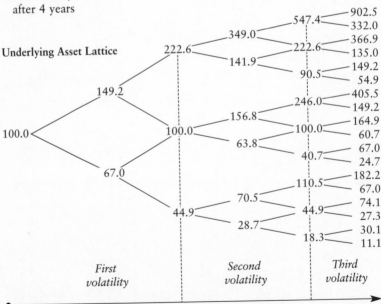

Assumptions:
Asset   = $100
Cost   = $80
Maturity = 5 Years
Risk-free = 5%
Volatility = 40%
New Volatility of 45%
    after 2 years
New Volatility of 50%
    after 4 years

FIGURE 71.9   Solving the Underlying Asset Lattice Using Multiple
                 Recombining Lattices

Figure 7I.10 is the modified recombining valuation lattice approach for the changing volatility option analysis. Notice that the resulting option value of $53.2 is identical to the result obtained using the non-recombining lattice.

Calculations:

up (1)   = 1.4918
down (1) = 0.6703
prob (1) = 0.4637

up (2)   = 1.5683
down (2) = 0.6376
prob (2) = 0.4445

up (3)   = 1.6487
down (3) = 0.6065
prob (3) = 0.4267

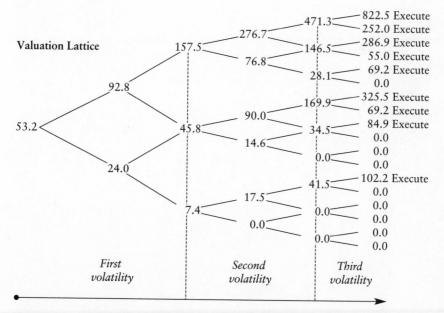

FIGURE 7I.10 Solving the Valuation Lattice Using Multiple Recombining Lattices

CHAPTER **8**

Advanced Options Problems

INTRODUCTION

This chapter deals with more advanced topics in real options. These include the optimal timing of projects, stochastic optimization of options, barrier-type exit and abandonment options, switching options, and multiple compound options. The problems of applying decision trees to real options analysis are also discussed, explaining why decision trees by themselves are problematic when trying to apply and solve real options. The technical appendixes at the end of the chapter detail the different approaches to stochastic optimization as well as present details of multiple exotic-options formulae.

THE ADVANCED PROBLEMS

One of the key uses of real options analysis is project ranking and selection, as shown in Figure 8.1. For example, using a traditional net present value metric, management would prioritize the initiatives A-D-B-C, from the most preferred to least. However, considering the strategic management flexibility inherent in each of the initiatives and quantified through the real options analysis, the initiative prioritization would now become A-D-C-B. If real options value is not included, the selection criteria may lead to the wrong initiative selection and conclusions.

For instance, suppose that Initiative B is to develop a certain automobile model, while Initiative C is to develop the similar model but with an option for converting it into a gas-electric hybrid. Obviously, the latter costs more than the former. Hence, the NPV for Initiative C is less than that for Initiative B. Therefore, choosing the project that has a higher NPV today is short-sighted. If the option value is included, Initiative C is chosen, the optimal decision, because given today's uncertain technological environment, hybrid cars may become extremely valuable in the future.

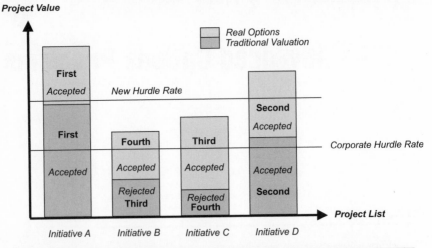

Real Options: A New Way to Look at Project Rankings

Captures option value and changes project priorities (from A-D-B-C to A-D-C-B), which avoids choosing the wrong projects. Provides optimal trigger values and timing for when execution is optimal translated back to market price or market share. Borderline negative NPV projects have in reality significant intrinsic option value. Simulation provides an added layer of confidence in the results.

FIGURE 8.1   Project Selection and Prioritization

DECISION TREES

Figure 8.2 shows an example of a decision tree. One major misunderstanding that analysts tend to have about real options is that they can be solved using decision trees alone. This is untrue. Instead, decision trees are a great way of depicting strategic pathways that a firm can take, showing graphically a decision road map of management's strategic initiatives and opportunities over time. However, to solve a real options problem, it is better to combine decision tree analytics with real option analytics, and not to replace it completely with decision trees.

Models used to solve decision tree problems range from a simple expected value to more sophisticated Bayesian probability updating approaches. Neither of these approaches is applicable when trying to solve a real options problem. A decision tree is not the optimal stand-alone methodology when trying to solve real options problems because subjective probabilities are required, as are different discount rates at each node. The difficulties and errors in forecasting the relevant discount rates and probabilities of occurrence are compounded over time, and the resulting calculated values are oftentimes in error. In addition, as shown in Chapter 7, binomial lattices are a much better way

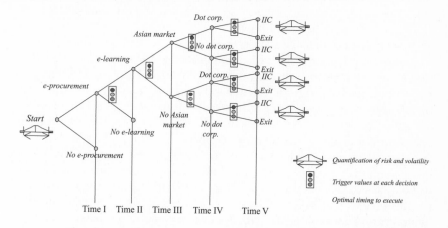

Binomial Decision Tree: Strategic Decision Road Map

Steps: Identify strategic downstream opportunities, collect historical data and management assumptions, generate a path-dependent strategic road map, create revenue and cost estimates for each path, value all strategies along different paths, obtain the optimal pathway and provide recommendations.

Notice that at each node, we can calculate the optimal trigger values, acting like traffic lights, indicating under which certain conditions execution waiting is optimal. The optimal timing can also be calculated at each time period. Finally, the uncertainty in cash flows and strategic option can also be quantified at certain branches through simulation

FIGURE 8.2   Decision Tree Analysis

to solve real options problems, and because these lattices can also ultimately be converted into decision trees, they are far superior to using decision trees as a stand-alone application for real options. Nonetheless, there is a common ground between decision trees and real options analytics.

Figure 8.2 shows a decision tree but without any valuation performed on it. On each node of the tree, certain projects or initiatives can be attached. The values of these nodes can be determined separately using binomial lattices, closed-form solutions, or any of the other number of ways used to solve real options problems.

Figure 8.2's hypothetical e-business strategy starts with e-procurement through globalization of an International Internet Coalition (IIC). The decision tree simply shows that there are multiple paths that can lead to this IIC end state. However, at each intermediate state, there is path-dependence. For instance, the firm cannot enter the Asian market without first having the correct infrastructure for setting up e-learning and e-procurement capabilities. The success of the former depends on the success of the latter, which is nothing but a compound sequential option. At each intermediate decision node, there are also abandonment options. In addition, simulation analysis, critical trigger values, and optimal timing can be applied and quantified along each decision node in a real options framework but cannot be done using a simple decision tree analysis. However, presenting strategies in a decision tree provides key insights to management as to what projects are available for execution, and under what conditions.

One of the fatal errors analysts tend to run into includes creating a decision tree and calculating the expected value using risk-neutral probabilities, akin to the risk-neutral probability used in Chapter 7. This is incorrect because risk-neutral probabilities are calculated based on a constant volatility. The risk structures of nodes on a decision tree (for instance, e-learning versus a dot.corp strategy have very different risks and volatilities). In addition, for risk-neutral probabilities, a Martingale process is required. That is, in a binomial lattice, each node has two bifurcations, an up and a down. The up and down jump sizes are identical in magnitude for a recombining tree. This has to hold before risk-neutral probabilities are valid. Clearly the return magnitudes of different events along the decision tree are different, and risk-neutralization does not work here. Because risk-neutral probabilities cannot be used, the risk-free rate therefore cannot be used here for discounting the cash flows. Also, because risks are different at each strategy node, the market risk-adjusted discount rate, such as a WACC, should also be different at every node. A correct single discount rate is difficult enough to calculate, let alone multiple discount rates on a complex tree, and the errors tend to compound over time, by the time the net present value of the strategy is calculated.

In addition, chance nodes are usually added in decision tree analysis, indicating that a certain event may occur given a specific probability. For instance, chance nodes may indicate a 30 percent chance of a great economy, a 45 percent chance of a nominal one, and a 25 percent chance of a downturn. Then events and payoffs are associated with these chances. Back-calculating these nodes using risk-neutral probabilities will be incorrect because these are chance nodes, not strategic options. Because these three events are complementary— that is, their respective probabilities add up to 100 percent—one of these events *must* occur, and given enough trials, all of these events must occur at one time or another. Real options analysis stipulates that one does not know what will occur, but only what the strategic alternatives are if a certain event occurs. If chance nodes are required in an analysis, the discounted cash flow model can accommodate them to calculate an expected value, which could then be simulated based on the probability and distributional assumptions. These simulated values can then be run in a real options modeling environment. The results can be shown on an event tree looking similar to a decision tree as depicted in the previous chapter. However, strategic decision pathways should be shown in the decision tree environment, and each strategy node or combinations of strategy nodes can be evaluated in the context of real options analysis as described throughout this book. Then the results can be displayed in the decision tree.

In summary, both decision tree analysis and real options analysis are incomplete as a stand-alone analysis in complex situations. Both methodologies approach the same problem from different perspectives. However, a common ground could be reached. Taking the advantages of both approaches and melding them into an overall valuation strategy, decision trees should be used to frame the problem, real options analytics should be used to solve any existing strategic optionalities (either by pruning the decision tree into sub-trees or solving the entire strategy tree at once), and the results should be presented back on a decision tree.

EXIT AND ABANDONMENT OPTIONS

Exit options are abundant in the real business world where projects can be scrapped and salvaged resources can then be redeployed elsewhere. However, certain projects may not be that easily abandoned at certain times because of "project stickiness" and business psychology, or the fact that management can be stubborn and reluctant to kill a project due to personal reasons.

Figure 8.3 shows a down and out barrier abandonment option. This type of option means that a project will not be terminated immediately once it falls out of profitability. Instead, management sets a critical barrier assumption, and should the project's profitability level fall below this barrier, the project will be abandoned. The barrier may be set after accounting for project stickiness and any other operational issues. The analysis can be solved using the Real Options Analysis Toolkit software on the enclosed CD-ROM. In addition, basic barrier options can be solved in a binomial tree by adding in *IF/AND/OR* statements nested with the regular *MAX* functions in Excel.

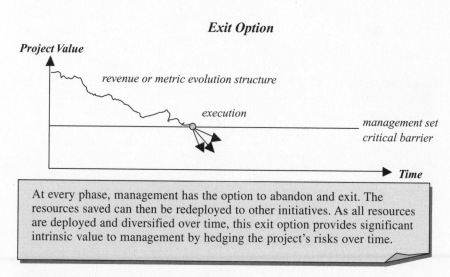

FIGURE 8.3   Exit Option with a Barrier

That is, the value of an option at a particular node comes into-the-money *if* the underlying asset value broaches a barrier.

COMPOUND OPTIONS

In some cases, there exist complex compound options, where the execution of one project provides downstream opportunities. For instance, in Figure 8.4, we see that the infrastructure in place provides a compound option comprising a series of three future phases. Notice that Phase III cannot proceed without the completion and execution of Phase II, which itself cannot proceed without the completion of Phase I. In some cases, these phases in the future can be a combination of different types of options. For example, Phase II options are simply an expansion of Phase I projects, while Phase III projects are only executed if some preset barriers in Phase II are achieved. The Real Options Analysis Toolkit software in the enclosed CD-ROM provides examples of a 10-phase sequential compound option as well as a multiple-phase option with different costs, expansion, contraction, and abandonment options at each phase.

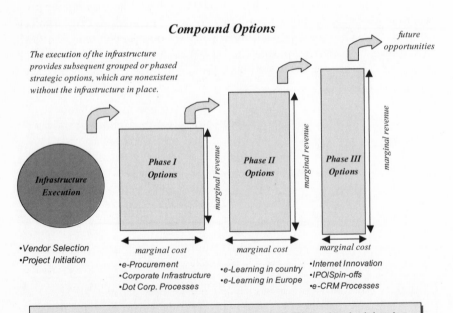

FIGURE 8.4 Multiple Complex Compound Option

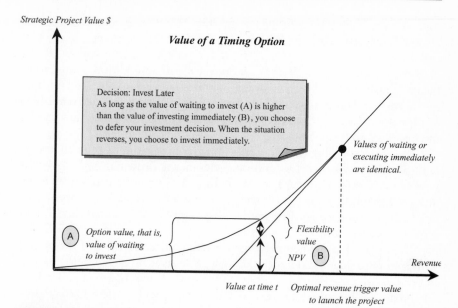

FIGURE 8.5 Timing Option

TIMING OPTIONS

Figure 8.5 shows the payoff profile on an option. The static line indicates the strategic options value of a project with respect to changes in the underlying variable, the revenues generated by the project assuming no volatility in the cash flows. This is in essence the NPV of the project at termination. The curved line above the static payoff line is the strategic options value, assuming there are risks and cash flows may be volatile. Hence, with uncertainty, cash flows can be higher than expected, and with time before expiration, the project is actually worth more than its NPV suggests.

Briefly, a timing option provides the holder the option to defer making an investment decision until a later time without much restriction. That is, competitive or market effects (market share erosion, first to market, strategic positioning, and the like) have negligible effect on the value of the project. Assuming that this holds true, then shifting a project for execution in the future only depends on two factors: the rate of growth of the asset over time and the discount rate or rate of erosion of the time value of money.

SOLVING TIMING OPTIONS CALCULATED USING STOCHASTIC OPTIMIZATION

Optimally timing an option execution is a tricky thing. This is because if there are highly risky projects with significant amounts of uncertainty, waiting is sometimes preferred to executing immediately. However, certain projects have an indefinite economic life and during this infinite economic life, certain real options exist. Hence, for an infinite life real option with high volatility, does this mean you wait forever and never do it? In addition, many other factors come into play with analyzing an optimal trigger value and optimal timing on a real option as shown in Figure 8.6. In certain cases, a Game Theory framework incorporating dynamic games competitors may play can be incorporated into the analysis.

To solve the timing option, start by assuming that the value of an underlying asset's process $X = (X_t)$ follows a Geometric Brownian Motion—that is, $dX_t = \alpha X_t dt + \sigma X_t dZ_t$. Then we define the value of a call option to be $\Phi(X) = E\max[(X_T - I)e^{-\rho T}, 0]$, where I is the initial capital investment outlay, X_T is the time value of the underlying asset at the terminal time T, and ρ is the discount rate.

The optimal investment strategy is to maximize the value of the option with respect to time T given the underlying stochastic investment process X—in other words, we want to find $\Phi^*(X) = \max_T E\max[(X_T - I)e^{-\rho T}, 0]$.

First, consider the near-zero volatility case, where there is negligible uncertainty. Next, we require a drift rate, usually measured as the growth rate in the asset value, and defined as α. We will further assume that $\rho > \alpha$, that is, the drift or growth rate of the underlying asset value does not exceed

Stochastic Optimization: Waiting versus Executing

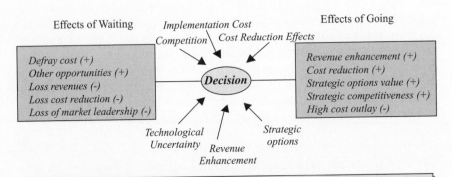

An optimal tool to use when we have two competing forces for waiting versus not waiting and we need to optimize the time to implementation, to calculate the optimal trigger value for implementation and to model different uncertainties. The analysis will provide the optimal trigger values (financial and non-financial metrics) and optimal timing for each decision node, to determine when and under what optimal conditions management should execute a strategic option.

FIGURE 8.6 Stochastic Optimization

the discount rate. Otherwise, the process keeps increasing at a much higher rate than can be discounted, the terminal value of the asset becomes infinite, and it is never optimal to exercise the option. Because we have defined α as the growth rate on the underlying investment process, it becomes the growth rate in the deterministic case. Now the problem above simplifies to the condition where $\Phi^*(X) = \max_T \max[(X_0 e^{\alpha T} - I)e^{-\rho T}, 0]$ That is, the underlying asset X_0 at time zero grows at this growth rate α such that at time T, the value of the continuously compounded asset value becomes $X_0 e^{\alpha T}$. In addition, due to the time value of money, the net present value is discounted at a continuous rate of $e^{-\rho T}$. Here we see that delaying the execution of an option creates the marginal benefit of the compounding growth of the asset value over time, while the marginal cost is the time value of money. The optimal timing can then be derived to obtain the equilibrium execution time where the net present value is maximized.

The optimal value of the option can be simply derived through the differential equation of the net present value with respect to time. Starting with $\Phi(X) = \max_T \max[(X_0 e^{\alpha T} - I)e^{-\rho T}, 0]$, we obtain:

$$\frac{d\Phi(X)}{dT} = (\alpha - \rho)X_0 e^{(\alpha - \rho)T} + \rho I e^{-\rho T} = 0$$

for the maximization process, yielding:

$$(\rho - \alpha)X_0 e^{(\alpha - \rho)T} = \rho I e^{-\rho T}$$

$$(\rho - \alpha)X_0 \frac{e^{\alpha T}}{e^{\rho T}} = \frac{\rho I}{e^{\rho T}}$$

$$\alpha T \ln(\rho - \alpha)X_0 = \ln(\rho I)$$

The *optimal time to execution* is therefore

$$T = \frac{1}{\alpha}\ln\left[\frac{\rho I}{(\rho - \alpha)X_0}\right]$$

Table 8.1 illustrates this example, where if the asset value at time zero is equivalent to the implementation cost \$100, while the discount rate is assumed to be 25 percent and the corresponding risk-free rate is 5.5 percent, the calculated optimal time to execution is 4.52 years, using

$$T = \frac{1}{0.55}\ln\left[\frac{(.25)(\$100)}{(.25 - .055)(\$100)}\right] = 4.52 \text{ years.}$$

Notice that the period 4.52 years provides the maximum NPV. Hence, this maximum NPV of \$9.12 is the option value of waiting, as compared to \$100 − \$100 = \$0 NPV if the project is executed immediately.

TABLE 8.1   The Optimal Value of the Option

Assumptions:	
Asset Value at Time 0 (X_0)	$100
Fixed Implementation Cost I	$100
Discount Rate	25%
Growth Rate of Underlying Asset	5.5%
Calculated Optimal Time to Execution	4.52

Time	NPV	
1.00	$4.40	
2.00	$7.05	
3.00	$8.47	
4.00	$9.05	
4.52	**$9.12**	This is the maximum NPV value
5.00	$9.07	
6.00	$8.72	
7.00	$8.16	
8.00	$7.48	

Finally, to avoid any negative or undefined values of the optimal timing, we can simply redefine the optimal timing to equal

$$T^* = Max\left[\frac{1}{\alpha}\ln\left(\frac{\rho I}{(\rho - \alpha)X_0}\right); 0\right].$$

Using this optimal timing value of

$$T = \frac{1}{\alpha}\ln\left[\frac{\rho I}{(\rho - \alpha)X_0}\right],$$

a very interesting result can be obtained. Specifically, rearranging this equation yields

$$e^{\alpha t} = \frac{\rho I}{(\rho - \alpha)X_0},$$

and we obtain the following:

$$\frac{X_0 e^{\alpha t}}{I} = \frac{\rho}{(\rho - \alpha)},$$

which is the *optimal trigger value* of the project. The left-hand-side equation is termed the profitability index, that is, the future value of the underlying asset divided by the implementation cost. If the profitability index exceeds 1.0, this implies that the NPV is positive, because the value of the asset exceeds the implementation cost. An index less than 1.0 implies that the NPV is negative. *See* Table 8.2. Hence, using this profitability index is akin to making decisions using the NPV analysis.

Table 8.3 shows the optimal timing to execute an option given the respective growth and discount rates. Notice that as discount rates increase, holding the growth rate constant, it is more optimal to execute the option earlier. This is because the time value of money and opportunity cost losses in revenues surpass the growth rate in asset value over longer periods of time. In contrast, holding the discount rate constant and increasing the growth rate, it is clear that waiting is more optimal than immediate execution. This is because the growth rate in asset value appreciation far surpasses the discount rate's opportunity cost of lost revenues. For example, assuming a 10 percent discount rate and a 1 percent growth rate, if a project's asset value exceeds the implementation cost by a ratio of 1.111, or if the net profit exceeds the implementation cost by 11.1 percent, it is optimal to execute the project immediately; otherwise, it is more optimal to wait.

TABLE 8.2 Profitability Indexes for Different Growth and Discount Rates

		Growth Rates				
		1.00%	2.00%	3.00%	4.00%	5.00%
Discount Rates	10%	1.111	1.250	1.429	1.667	2.000
	15%	1.071	1.154	1.250	1.364	1.500
	20%	1.053	1.111	1.176	1.250	1.333
	25%	1.042	1.087	1.136	1.190	1.250
	30%	1.034	1.071	1.111	1.154	1.200
	35%	1.029	1.061	1.094	1.129	1.167
	40%	1.026	1.053	1.081	1.111	1.143

TABLE 8.3 Optimal Timing for Different Growth and Discount Rates

		Growth Rates				
		1.00%	2.00%	3.00%	4.00%	5.00%
Discount Rates	10%	10.54	11.16	11.89	12.77	13.86
	15%	6.90	7.16	7.44	7.75	8.11
	20%	5.13	5.27	5.42	5.58	5.75
	25%	4.08	4.17	4.26	4.36	4.46
	30%	3.39	3.45	3.51	3.58	3.65
	35%	2.90	2.94	2.99	3.03	3.08
	40%	2.53	2.56	2.60	2.63	2.67
	Investment Cost	$100				
	Asset Value	$100				

Tables 8.2 and 8.3 above assume negligible uncertainty evolving through time. However, in the uncertain or stochastic case when the growth rate of the underlying asset value is uncertain—that is, α fluctuates at the rate of σ (volatility)—optimal timing can no longer be ascertained. Simulation is

preferred in this case. However, the optimal trigger value can still be determined.[1] The optimal trigger value measured in terms of a profitability index value is now as follows:

$$\frac{X_0 e^{\alpha t}}{I} = \frac{\left[\dfrac{2\rho}{\sigma^2} + \left(\dfrac{\alpha}{\sigma^2} - 0.5\right)^2\right]^{0.5} + 0.5 - \dfrac{\alpha}{\sigma^2}}{\left[\dfrac{2\rho}{\sigma^2} + \left(\dfrac{\alpha}{\sigma^2} - 0.5\right)^2\right]^{0.5} - 0.5 - \dfrac{\alpha}{\sigma^2}}$$

Table 8.4 illustrates the optimal trigger values with a stochastic 10 percent volatility on growth rates. Notice that the corresponding trigger values measured in terms of profitability indexes are higher for stochastic growth rates than for the deterministic growth rates. This is highly intuitive because the higher the level of uncertainty in the potential future of the underlying asset, the better off it is to wait before executing.

TABLE 8.4 Profitability Indexes for Different Growth versus Discount Rates

		Growth Rates				
		1.00%	2.00%	3.00%	4.00%	5.00%
Discount Rates	10%	1.333	1.451	1.616	1.848	2.184
	15%	1.250	1.315	1.397	1.500	1.629
	20%	1.206	1.250	1.303	1.367	1.442
	25%	1.179	1.211	1.250	1.295	1.347
	30%	1.160	1.186	1.216	1.250	1.289
	35%	1.145	1.167	1.191	1.219	1.250
	40%	1.134	1.152	1.173	1.196	1.222
	Volatility	10%				

SWITCHING OPTIONS

In the ability to switch from technology 1 to technology 2, the option value is

$$S_2 \Phi\left[\frac{\ln\left(\dfrac{S_2}{(1+X)S_1}\right) + \dfrac{T\sigma^2}{2}}{\sigma\sqrt{T}}\right] - S_1 \Phi\left[\frac{\ln\left(\dfrac{S_2}{(1+X)S_1}\right) - \dfrac{T\sigma^2}{2}}{\sigma\sqrt{T}}\right]$$

$$- S_1 X \Phi\left[\frac{\ln\left(\dfrac{S_2}{(1+X)S_1}\right) - \dfrac{T\sigma^2}{2}}{\sigma\sqrt{T}}\right]$$

where X is the proportional cost with respect to the current technology 1's asset value S_1. Hence, the optimal behavior is such that if the new technology's asset value S_2 exceeds the value of the current technology S_1 plus any associated switching costs $S_1 X$, then it is optimal to switch.

Obviously, if multiple switching options are available, the problem becomes more complicated. Recall from the chooser option example in Chapter 7 that the value of the chooser option is not a simple sum of the individual options to expand, contract, and abandon. This is due to the mutually exclusive and path-dependent nature of these options, where the firm cannot both expand and abandon its business on the same node at the same time, or both expand and contract on the same node at the same time, etc. Valuing these options individually and then adding them together implies that each option is performed independent of one another and that two option executions may occupy the same space. Hence, to obtain the correct results, any crossovers where two options interact in the same space have to be accounted for. The same rule applies here. Thus, when an option exists that allows the switching from technology 1 to technology 2 or 3, the total value of the option is not simply the option to go from 1 to 2 plus the option to go from 1 to 3.

Tables 8.5 through 8.9 illustrate the relationships between the value of a switching option from an old technology to a new technology, and its corresponding input parameters. For example, in Table 8.5, where the present value of both technologies is currently on par with each other and the volatility is very close to 0 percent, with this negligible uncertainty, the value of the option is close to $0, similar to the static net present value of $0 because there is no point in being able to switch technology if the value of both technologies is identical. In contrast, when volatility increases slightly in the second technology, the value of being able to switch to this second technology increases. The rest of the examples are fairly self-explanatory.

TABLE 8.5 The Higher the Volatility of the New Technology, the Greater the Value of the Ability to Switch Technology

PV First Asset	100.00	100.00	100.00	100.00	100.00	100.00
PV Second Asset	100.00	100.00	100.00	100.00	100.00	100.00
First Asset Volatility	0%	1%	1%	1%	1%	1%
Second Asset Volatility	**0%**	**1%**	**2%**	**3%**	**4%**	**5%**
Correlation between Assets	0.00	0.00	0.00	0.00	0.00	0.00
Cost Multiplier	0.00	0.00	0.00	0.00	0.00	0.00
Time to Expiration	1.00	1.00	1.00	1.00	1.00	1.00
Risk-Free Rate	0%	0%	0%	0%	0%	0%
Portfolio Volatility	0.00	0.01	0.02	0.03	0.04	0.05
Switching Option Value	**0.01**	**0.56**	**0.89**	**1.26**	**1.64**	**2.03**
Static NPV	**0.00**	**0.00**	**0.00**	**0.00**	**0.00**	**0.00**

TABLE 8.6 The Higher the Value of the Original Technology, the Lower the Value of the Ability to Switch Technology

PV First Asset	100.00	110.00	120.00	130.00	140.00	150.00
PV Second Asset	100.00	100.00	100.00	100.00	100.00	100.00
First Asset Volatility	10%	10%	10%	10%	10%	10%
Second Asset Volatility	10%	10%	10%	10%	10%	10%
Correlation between Assets	0.00	0.00	0.00	0.00	0.00	0.00
Cost Multiplier	0.00	0.00	0.00	0.00	0.00	0.00
Time to Expiration	1.00	1.00	1.00	1.00	1.00	1.00
Risk-Free Rate	0%	0%	0%	0%	0%	0%
Portfolio Volatility	0.14	0.14	0.14	0.14	0.14	0.14
Switching Option Value	5.64	2.21	0.72	0.20	0.05	0.01
Static NPV	0.00	−10.00	−20.00	−30.00	−40.00	−50.00

TABLE 8.7 The Higher the Value of the New Technology, the Higher the Value of the Ability to Switch Technology

PV First Asset	100.00	100.00	100.00	100.00	100.00	100.00
PV Second Asset	100.00	110.00	120.00	130.00	140.00	150.00
First Asset Volatility	10%	10%	10%	10%	10%	10%
Second Asset Volatility	10%	10%	10%	10%	10%	10%
Correlation between Assets	0.00	0.00	0.00	0.00	0.00	0.00
Cost Multiplier	0.00	0.00	0.00	0.00	0.00	0.00
Time to Expiration	1.00	1.00	1.00	1.00	1.00	1.00
Risk-Free Rate	0%	0%	0%	0%	0%	0%
Portfolio Volatility	0.14	0.14	0.14	0.14	0.14	0.14
Switching Option Value	5.64	12.21	20.72	30.20	40.05	50.01
Static NPV	0.00	10.00	20.00	30.00	40.00	50.00

TABLE 8.8 The Higher the Switching Cost, the Lower the Value of the Ability to Switch Technology

PV First Asset	100.00	100.00	100.00	100.00	100.00	100.00
PV Second Asset	100.00	100.00	100.00	100.00	100.00	100.00
First Asset Volatility	10%	10%	10%	10%	10%	10%
Second Asset Volatility	10%	10%	10%	10%	10%	10%
Correlation between Assets	0.00	0.00	0.00	0.00	0.00	0.00
Cost Multiplier	**0.00**	**0.10**	**0.20**	**0.30**	**0.40**	**0.50**
Time to Expiration	1.00	1.00	1.00	1.00	1.00	1.00
Risk-Free Rate	0%	0%	0%	0%	0%	0%
Portfolio Volatility	0.14	0.14	0.14	0.14	0.14	0.14
Switching Option Value	**5.64**	**2.21**	**0.72**	**0.20**	**0.05**	**0.01**
Static NPV	**0.00**	**−10.00**	**−20.00**	**−30.00**	**−40.00**	**−50.00**

TABLE 8.9 The Longer the Ability to Switch, the Higher the Value of the Ability to Switch Technology

PV First Asset	100.00	100.00	100.00	100.00	100.00	100.00
PV Second Asset	100.00	100.00	100.00	100.00	100.00	100.00
First Asset Volatility	10%	10%	10%	10%	10%	10%
Second Asset Volatility	10%	10%	10%	10%	10%	10%
Correlation between Assets	0.00	0.00	0.00	0.00	0.00	0.00
Cost Multiplier	0.00	0.00	0.00	0.00	0.00	0.00
Time to Expiration	**1.00**	**2.00**	**3.00**	**4.00**	**5.00**	**6.00**
Risk-Free Rate	0%	0%	0%	0%	0%	0%
Portfolio Volatility	0.14	0.14	0.14	0.14	0.14	0.14
Switching Option Value	**5.64**	**7.97**	**9.75**	**11.25**	**12.56**	**13.75**
Static NPV	**0.00**	**0.00**	**0.00**	**0.00**	**0.00**	**0.00**

SUMMARY

Multiple other real options problems requiring more advanced techniques are required in certain circumstances. These models include the applications of stochastic optimization as well as other exotic types of options. In addition, as discussed, decision trees are insufficient when trying to solve real options problems because subjective probabilities are required as well as different discount rates at each node. The difficulties in forecasting the relevant discount rates and probabilities of occurrence are compounded over time, and the resulting values are oftentimes in error. However, decision trees by themselves are great as a depiction of management's strategic initiatives and opportunities over time. Decision trees should be used in conjunction with real options analytics in more complex cases.

CHAPTER 8 QUESTIONS

1. Decision trees are considered inappropriate when used to solve real options problems. Why is this so?
2. What are some of the assumptions required for risk-neutral probabilities to work?
3. What is stochastic optimization?
4. Assuming a 25 percent discount rate, 5.5 percent growth rate, and $100 in both present value of underlying assets and investment cost, change each of these variables at one-unit steps. That is, holding all inputs constant, change discount rate from 25 percent to 26 percent and so forth, and explain what happens to the optimal time to execution. Repeat the steps for growth rate, investment cost, and underlying asset value. Explain your results.

Stochastic Processes

Throughout the book the author talks about using stochastic processes for establishing simulation structures, risk-neutralizing revenue and cost, and obtaining an evolution of pricing structures. A stochastic process is nothing but a mathematically defined equation that can create a series of outcomes over time, outcomes that are not deterministic in nature. That is, an equation or process that does not follow any simple discernible rule such as price will increase X percent every year or revenues will increase by this factor of X plus Y percent. A stochastic process is by definition non-deterministic, and one can plug numbers into a stochastic process equation and obtain different results every time. For instance, the path of a stock price is stochastic in nature, and one cannot reliably predict the stock price path with any certainty. However, the price evolution over time is enveloped in a process that generates these prices. The process is fixed and predetermined, but the outcomes are not. Hence, by stochastic simulation, we create multiple pathways of prices, obtain a statistical sampling of these simulations, and make inferences on the potential pathways that the actual price may undertake given the nature and parameters of the stochastic process used to generate the time-series.

Four basic stochastic processes are discussed, including the Geometric Brownian Motion, which is the most common and prevalently used process due to its simplicity and wide-ranging applications. The mean-reversion process, barrier long-run process, and jump-diffusion process are also briefly discussed.

SUMMARY MATHEMATICAL CHARACTERISTICS OF GEOMETRIC BROWNIAN MOTIONS

Assume a process X, where $X = [X_t : t \geq 0]$ if and only if X_t is continuous, where the starting point is $X_0 = 0$, where X is normally distributed with mean zero and variance one or $X \in N(0, 1)$, and where each increment in time is independent of each other previous increment and is itself normally distributed with mean zero and variance t, such that $X_{t+a} - X_t \in N(0, t)$. Then, the process $dX = \alpha X dt + \sigma X dZ$ follows a Geometric Brownian Motion, where α is a drift parameter, σ the volatility measure, $dZ = \varepsilon_t \sqrt{\Delta dt}$ such that

$$\ln\left[\frac{dX}{X}\right] \in N(\mu, \sigma)$$

or X and dX are lognormally distributed. If at time zero, $X(0) = 0$ then the expected value of the process X at any time t is such that $E[X(t)] = X_0 e^{\alpha t}$ and the variance of the process X at time t is $V[X(t)] = X_0^2 e^{2\alpha t}(e^{\sigma^2 t} - 1)$. In the continuous case where there is a drift parameter α, the expected value then becomes

$$E\left[\int_0^\infty X(t)e^{-rt}dt\right] = \int_0^\infty X_0 e^{-(r-\alpha)t}dt = \frac{X_0}{(r - \alpha)}.$$

SUMMARY MATHEMATICAL CHARACTERISTICS OF MEAN-REVERSION PROCESSES

If a stochastic process has a long-run attractor such as a long-run production cost or long-run steady state inflationary price level, then a mean-reversion process is more likely. The process reverts to a long-run average such that the expected value is $E[X_t] = \overline{X} + (X_0 - \overline{X})e^{-\eta t}$ and the variance is

$$V[X_t - \overline{X}] = \frac{\sigma^2}{2\eta(1 - e^{-2\eta t})}.$$

The special circumstance that becomes useful is that in the limiting case when the time change becomes instantaneous or when $dt \to 0$, we have the condition where $X_t - X_{t-1} = \overline{X}(1 - e^{-\eta}) + X_{t-1}(e^{-\eta} - 1) + \varepsilon_t$, which is the first order autoregressive process, and η can be tested econometrically in a unit root context.

SUMMARY MATHEMATICAL CHARACTERISTICS OF BARRIER LONG-RUN PROCESSES

This process is used when there are natural barriers to prices—for example, floors or caps—or when there are physical constraints like the maximum capacity of a manufacturing plant. If barriers exist in the process, where we define $\overline{X}$ as the upper barrier and $\underline{X}$ as the lower barrier, we have a process where

$$X(t) = \frac{2\alpha}{\sigma^2} \frac{e^{\frac{2\alpha X}{\sigma^2}}}{e^{\frac{2\alpha \overline{X}}{\sigma^2}} - e^{\frac{2\alpha \underline{X}}{\sigma^2}}}.$$

SUMMARY MATHEMATICAL CHARACTERISTICS OF JUMP-DIFFUSION PROCESSES

Start-up ventures and research and development initiatives usually follow a jump-diffusion process. Business operations may be status quo for a few months or years, and then a product or initiative becomes highly successful and takes off. An initial public offering of equities is a textbook example of this. Assuming that the probability of the jumps follows a Poisson distribution, we have a process $dX = f(X, t)dt + g(X, t)dq$, where the functions f and g are known and where the probability process is

$$dq = \begin{cases} 0 \; with \; P(X) = 1 - \lambda dt \\ \mu \; with \; P(X) = Xdt \end{cases}.$$

Differential Equations
for a Deterministic Case

One of the many approaches to solving a real options problem is the use of stochastic optimization. This optimization process can be done through a series of simulations or partial-differential equations to obtain a unique closed-form solution. Below is a very simplistic discussion and example of an optimization problem with constraints. Then a partial-differential equation framework is presented. Appendix 9C illustrates a more complex optimization technique known as stochastic optimization, used in portfolio optimization and capital resource allocation where the input variables are stochastic and solvable only using Monte Carlo simulation.

OPTIMIZATION

A simple optimization process is shown in Figure 8B.1, where we can set up simple optimization problems in an Excel spreadsheet environment. In addition, we can solve optimization problems mathematically, as seen in the simple steps below:

- Create an objective function $f(x, y) = 3xy$
- Set the constraint $c(x, y) = 200 - 5x - 15y$
- Set the LaGrange Multiplier $\ell(x, y, \lambda) = f(x, y) + \lambda c(x, y) = 3xy + \lambda(200 - 5x - 15y)$
- Optimize using partial-differentials:

  □ $\dfrac{\partial \ell}{\partial \lambda} = 200 - 5x - 15y$

  □ $\dfrac{\partial \ell}{\partial x} = 3y - 5\lambda$

Linear Programming - Graphical Method

Say there are two products X and Y being manufactured. Product X provides a $20 profit and product Y a $15 profit. Product X takes 3 hours to manufacture and product Y takes 2 hours to produce. In any given week, the manufacturing equipment can make both products but has a maximum capacity of 300 hours. In addition, based on market demand, management has determined that they cannot sell more than 80 units of X and 100 units of Y in a given week and prefers not to have any inventory on hand. Therefore, management has set these demand levels as the maximum output for products X and Y, respectively. The issue now becomes what is the optimal production levels of both X and Y such that profits would be maximized in any given week?

Based on the situation above, we can formulate a linear optimization routine where we have:

The Objective Function:	Max 20X + 15Y
subject to Constraints:	$3X + 2Y \leq 300$
	$X \leq 80$
	$Y \leq 100$

We can more easily visualize the constraints by plotting them out one at a time as follows:

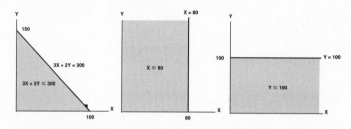

The graph below shows the combination of all three constraints. The shaded area shows the feasible area, where all constraints are simultaneously satisfied. Hence, the optimal should fall within this shaded region.

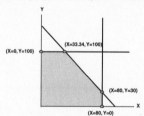

We can easily calculate the intersection points of the constraints. For example, the intersection between Y = 100 and 3X + 2Y = 300 is obtained by solving the equations simultaneously. Substituting, we get 3X + 2(100) = 300. Solving yields X = 33.24 and Y = 100.

Similarly, the intersection between X = 80 and 3X + 2Y = 300 can be obtained by solving the equations simultaneously. Substituting yields 3(80) + 2Y = 300. Solving yields Y = 30 and X = 80.

The other two edges are simply intersections between the axes. Hence, when X = 80, Y = 0 for the X = 80 line and Y = 100 and X = 0 for the Y = 100 line.

From linear programming theory, one of these four intersection edges or extreme values is the optimal solution. One method is simply to substitute each of the end points into the objective function and see which solution set provides the highest profit level.

Using the objective function where Profit = 20X + 15Y and substituting each of the extreme value sets:

When X = 0 and Y = 100:	Profit = $20 (0) + $15 (100) = $1,500
When X = 33.34 and Y = 100:	Profit = $20 (33.34) + $15 (100) = $2,167
When X = 80 and Y = 30:	Profit = $20 (80) + $15 (30) = $2,050
When X = 80 and Y = 0:	Profit = $20 (80) + $15 (0) = $1,600

Here, we see that when X = 33.34 and Y = 100, the profit function is maximized. We can also further verify this by using any combinations of X and Y within the feasible (shaded) area above. For instance, X =10 and Y =10 is a combination that is feasible, but their profit outcome is only $20 (10) + $15 (10) = $350. We can calculate infinite combinations of X and Y sets, but the optimal combination is always going to be at extreme value edges.

We can easily verify which extreme value will be the optimal solution set by drawing the objective function line. If we set the objective function to be:

20X + 15Y = 0	we get X = 20, Y = 15
20X + 15Y = 1000	we get X = 60, Y = 80

If we keep shifting the profit function upward to the right, we will keep intersecting with the extreme value edges. The edge that provides the highest profit function is the optimal solution set.

In our example, point B is the optimal solution, which was verified by our calculations above, where X = 33.34 and Y = 100.

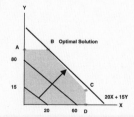

FIGURE 8B.1   Linear Programming

- $\dfrac{\partial \ell}{\partial y} = 3x - 15\lambda$

- Solving yields $x = 20$, $y = 6.67$, $\lambda = 4$ and

- Optimal output $f^*(x, y) = 3(20)(6.67) = 400$

- λ is the constraint relaxation ratio, where an increase of a budget unit increases the optimal output by $\lambda = 4$

- Using these optimization methods, we can then set up a more complex optimization process.

Exotic Options Formulae

BLACK AND SCHOLES OPTION MODEL—EUROPEAN VERSION

This is the famous Nobel Prize–winning Black-Scholes model without any dividend payments. It is the European version, where an option can only be executed at expiration and not before. Although it is simple enough to use, care should be taken in estimating its input variable assumptions, especially that of volatility, which is usually difficult to estimate. However, the Black-Scholes model is useful in generating ballpark estimates of the true real options value, especially for more generic-type calls and puts. For more complex real options analysis, different types of exotic options are required.

Definitions of Variables

S present value of future cash flows ($)
X implementation cost ($)
r risk-free rate (%)
T time to expiration (years)
σ volatility (%)
Φ cumulative standard-normal distribution

Computation

$$Call = S\Phi\left(\frac{\ln(S/X) + (r + \sigma^2/2)T}{\sigma\sqrt{T}} \right) - Xe^{-rT}\Phi\left(\frac{\ln(S/X) + (r - \sigma^2/2)T}{\sigma\sqrt{T}} \right)$$

$$Put = Xe^{-rT}\Phi\left(-\left[\frac{\ln(S/X) + (r - \sigma^2/2)T}{\sigma\sqrt{T}} \right] \right) - S\Phi\left(-\left[\frac{\ln(S/X) + (r + \sigma^2/2)T}{\sigma\sqrt{T}} \right] \right)$$

BLACK AND SCHOLES WITH DRIFT (DIVIDEND) — EUROPEAN VERSION

This is a modification of the Black-Scholes model and assumes a fixed dividend payment rate of q in percent. This can be construed as the opportunity cost of holding the option rather than holding the underlying asset.

Definitions of Variables

S present value of future cash flows ($)
X implementation cost ($)
r risk-free rate (%)
T time to expiration (years)
σ volatility (%)
Φ cumulative standard-normal distribution
q continuous dividend payout or opportunity cost (%)

Computation

$$Call = Se^{-qT}\Phi\left(\frac{\ln(S/X) + (r - q + \sigma^2/2)T}{\sigma\sqrt{T}} \right)$$

$$- Xe^{-rT}\Phi\left(\frac{\ln(S/X) + (r - q - \sigma^2/2)T}{\sigma\sqrt{T}} \right)$$

$$Put = Xe^{-rT}\Phi\left(-\left[\frac{\ln(S/X) + (r - q - \sigma^2/2)T}{\sigma\sqrt{T}} \right] \right)$$

$$- Se^{-qT}\Phi\left(-\left[\frac{\ln(S/X) + (r - q + \sigma^2/2)T}{\sigma\sqrt{T}} \right] \right)$$

BLACK AND SCHOLES WITH FUTURE PAYMENTS — EUROPEAN VERSION

Here, cash flow streams may be uneven over time, and we should allow for different discount rates (risk-free rate should be used) for all future times, perhaps allowing for the flexibility of the forward risk-free yield curve.

Definitions of Variables

S present value of future cash flows ($)
X implementation cost ($)
r risk-free rate (%)

T time to expiration (years)

σ volatility (%)

Φ cumulative standard-normal distribution

q continuous dividend payout or opportunity cost (%)

CF_i cash flow at time i

Computation

$$S^* = S - CF_1 e^{-rt_1} - CF_2 e^{-rt_2} - \ldots - CF_n e^{-rt_n} = S - \sum_{i=1}^{n} CF_i e^{-rt_i}$$

$$Call = S^* e^{-qT} \Phi\left(\frac{\ln(S^*/X) + (r - q + \sigma^2/2)T}{\sigma\sqrt{T}} \right)$$

$$- Xe^{-rT} \Phi\left(\frac{\ln(S^*/X) + (r - q - \sigma^2/2)T}{\sigma\sqrt{T}} \right)$$

$$Put = Xe^{-rT} \Phi\left(-\left[\frac{\ln(S^*/X) + (r - q - \sigma^2/2)T}{\sigma\sqrt{T}} \right] \right)$$

$$- S^* e^{-qT} \Phi\left(-\left[\frac{\ln(S^*/X) + (r - q + \sigma^2/2)T}{\sigma\sqrt{T}} \right] \right)$$

CHOOSER OPTIONS (BASIC CHOOSER)

This is the payoff for a simple chooser option when $t_1 < T_2$, or it doesn't work! In addition, it is assumed that the holder has the right to choose either a call or a put with the same strike price at time t_1 and with the same expiration date T_2. For different values of strike prices at different times, we need a complex variable chooser.

Definitions of Variables

S present value of future cash flows ($)

X implementation cost ($)

r risk-free rate (%)

t_1 time to choose between a call or put (years)

T_2 time to expiration (years)

σ volatility (%)

Φ cumulative standard-normal distribution

q continuous dividend payments (%)

Computation

$$OptionValue = Se^{-qT_2}\Phi\left[\frac{\ln(S/X) + (r - q + \sigma^2/2)T_2}{\sigma\sqrt{T_2}}\right]$$

$$- Se^{-qT_2}\Phi\left[\frac{-\ln(S/X) + (q - r)T_2 - t_1\sigma^2/2}{\sigma\sqrt{t_1}}\right]$$

$$- Xe^{-rT_2}\Phi\left[\frac{\ln(S/X) + (r - q + \sigma^2/2)T_2}{\sigma\sqrt{T_2}} - \sigma\sqrt{T_2}\right]$$

$$+ Xe^{-rT_2}\Phi\left[\frac{-\ln(S/X) + (q - r)T_2 - t_1\sigma^2/2}{\sigma\sqrt{t_1}} + \sigma\sqrt{t_1}\right]$$

COMPLEX CHOOSER

The holder of the option has the right to choose between a call and a put at different times (T_C and T_P) with different strike levels (X_C and X_P) of calls and puts. Note that some of these equations cannot be readily solved using Excel spreadsheets. Instead, due to the recursive methods used to solve certain bivariate distributions and critical values, the use of programming scripts is required.

Definitions of Variables

S present value of future cash flows ($)
X implementation cost ($)
r risk-free rate (%)
T time to expiration (years) for call (T_C) and put (T_P)
σ volatility (%)
Φ cumulative standard-normal distribution
Ω cumulative bivariate-normal distribution
q continuous dividend payout (%)
I critical value solved recursively
Z intermediate variables (Z_1 and Z_2)

Computation

First, solve recursively for the critical I value as below

$$0 = Ie^{-q(T_C-t)}\Phi\left[\frac{\ln(I/X_C) + (r - q + \sigma^2/2)(T_C - t)}{\sigma\sqrt{T_C - t}}\right]$$

$$- X_Ce^{-r(T_C-t)}\Phi\left[\frac{\ln(I/X_C) + (r - q + \sigma^2/2)(T_C - t)}{\sigma\sqrt{T_C - t}} - \sigma\sqrt{T_C - t}\right]$$

$$+ Ie^{-q(T_P-t)}\Phi\left[\frac{-\ln(I/X_P) + (q - r - \sigma^2/2)(T_P - t)}{\sigma\sqrt{T_P - t}}\right]$$

$$- X_P e^{-r(T_P-t)}\Phi\left[\frac{-\ln(I/X_P) + (q - r - \sigma^2/2)(T_P - t)}{\sigma\sqrt{T_P - t}} + \sigma\sqrt{T_P - t}\right]$$

Then using the I value, calculate

$$d_1 = \frac{\ln(S/I) + (r - q + \sigma^2/2)t}{\sigma\sqrt{t}} \quad \text{and } d_2 = d_1 - \sigma\sqrt{t}$$

$$y_1 = \frac{\ln(S/X_C) + (r - q + \sigma^2/2)T_C}{\sigma\sqrt{T_C}} \quad \text{and}$$

$$y_2 = \frac{\ln(S/X_P) + (r - q + \sigma^2/2)T_P}{\sigma\sqrt{T_P}}$$

$$\rho_1 = \sqrt{t/T_C} \text{ and } \rho_2 = \sqrt{t/T_P}$$

$$Option\ Value = Se^{-qT_C}\Omega(d_1; y_1; \rho_1) - X_C e^{-rT_C}\Omega(d_2; y_1 - \sigma\sqrt{T_C}; \rho_1)$$

$$- Se^{-qT_P}\Omega(-d_1; -y_2; \rho_2) + X_P e^{-rT_P}\Omega(-d_2; -y_2 + \sigma\sqrt{T_P}; \rho_2)$$

COMPOUND OPTIONS ON OPTIONS

The value of a compound option is based on the value of another option. That is, the underlying variable for the compound option is another option. Again, solving this model requires programming capabilities.

Definitions of Variables

S	present value of future cash flows (\$)
r	risk-free rate (%)
σ	volatility (%)
Φ	cumulative standard-normal distribution
q	continuous dividend payout (%)
I	critical value solved recursively
Ω	cumulative bivariate-normal distribution
X_1	strike for the underlying (\$)
X_2	strike for the option on the option (\$)
t_1	expiration date for the option on the option (years)
T_2	expiration for the underlying option (years)

Computation

First, solve for the critical value of I using

$$X_2 = Ie^{-q(T_2-t_1)}\Phi\left(\frac{\ln(I/X_1) + (r - q + \sigma^2/2)(T_2 - t_1)}{\sigma\sqrt{(T_2 - t_1)}}\right)$$

$$- X_1e^{-r(T_2-t_1)}\Phi\left(\frac{\ln(I/X_1) + (r - q - \sigma^2/2)(T_2 - t_1)}{\sigma\sqrt{(T_2 - t_1)}}\right)$$

Solve recursively for the value I above and then input it into

$$Call\ on\ call = Se^{-qT_2}\Omega\left[\begin{array}{c}\dfrac{\ln(S/X_1) + (r - q + \sigma^2/2)T_2}{\sigma\sqrt{T_2}}; \\[2ex] \dfrac{\ln(S/I) + (r - q + \sigma^2/2)t_1}{\sigma\sqrt{t_1}}; \sqrt{t_1/T_2}\end{array}\right]$$

$$- X_1e^{-rT_2}\Omega\left[\begin{array}{c}\dfrac{\ln(S/X_1) + (r - q + \sigma^2/2)T_2}{\sigma\sqrt{T_2}} - \sigma\sqrt{T_2}; \\[2ex] \dfrac{\ln(S/I) + (r - q + \sigma^2/2)t_1}{\sigma\sqrt{t_1}} - \sigma\sqrt{t_1}; \sqrt{t_1/T_2}\end{array}\right]$$

$$- X_2e^{-rt_1}\Phi\left[\frac{\ln(S/I) + (r - q + \sigma^2/2)t_1}{\sigma\sqrt{t_1}} - \sigma\sqrt{t_1}\right]$$

EXCHANGE ASSET FOR ASSET OPTION

The exchange asset for an asset option is a good application in a mergers and acquisition situation when a firm exchanges one stock for another firm's stock as a means of payment.

Definitions of Variables

S present value of future cash flows (\$) for Asset 1 (S_1) and Asset 2 (S_2)

X implementation cost (\$)

Q quantity of Asset 1 to be exchanged for quantity of Asset 2

r risk-free rate (%)

T time to expiration (years) for call (T_C) and put (T_P)

σ volatility (%) of Asset 1 (σ_1) and Asset 2 (σ_2)

σ^* portfolio volatility after accounting for the assets' correlation ρ

Φ cumulative standard-normal distribution

q_1 continuous dividend payout (%) for Asset 1
q_2 continuous dividend payout (%) for Asset 2

Computation

Option =

$$Q_1 S_1 e^{-q_1 T} \Phi \left[\frac{\ln(Q_1 S_1 / Q_2 S_2) + (q_2 - q_1 + (\sigma_1^2 + \sigma_2^2 - 2\rho\sigma_1\sigma_2)/2)T}{\sqrt{T(\sigma_1^2 + \sigma_2^2 - 2\rho\sigma_1\sigma_2)}} \right]$$

$$- Q_2 S_2 e^{-q_2 T} \Phi \left[\frac{\ln(Q_1 S_1 / Q_2 S_2) + (q_2 - q_1 + (\sigma_1^2 + \sigma_2^2 - 2\rho\sigma_1\sigma_2)/2)T}{\sqrt{T(\sigma_1^2 + \sigma_2^2 - 2\rho\sigma_1\sigma_2)}} - \sqrt{T(\sigma_1^2 + \sigma_2^2 - 2\rho\sigma_1\sigma_2)} \right]$$

FIXED STRIKE LOOK-BACK OPTION

The strike price is fixed in advance, and at expiration, the call option pays out the maximum of the difference between the highest observed price in the option's lifetime and the strike X, and 0, that is, *Call* = *Max*[$S_{MAX} - X$, 0]. A put at expiration pays out the maximum of the difference between the fixed strike X and the minimum price, and 0, that is, *Put* = *Max*[$X - S_{MIN}$, 0].

Definitions of Variables

S present value of future cash flows ($)
X implementation cost ($)
r risk-free rate (%)
T time to expiration (years)
σ volatility (%)
Φ cumulative standard-normal distribution
q continuous dividend payout (%)

Computation

Under the fixed strike look-back call option, when we have $X > S_{MAX}$, the call option is

$$Call = S e^{-qT} \Phi \left[\frac{\ln(S/X) + (r - q + \sigma^2/2)T}{\sigma\sqrt{T}} \right]$$

$$- X e^{-rT} \Phi \left[\frac{\ln(S/X) + (r - q + \sigma^2/2)T}{\sigma\sqrt{T}} - \sigma\sqrt{T} \right]$$

$$+ Se^{-rT} \frac{\sigma^2}{2(r-q)} \left[-\left(\frac{S}{X}\right)^{\frac{-2(r-q)}{\sigma^2}} \Phi \left(\frac{\ln(S/X) + (r - q + \sigma^2/2)T}{\sigma\sqrt{T}} - \frac{2(r-q)}{\sigma}\sqrt{T} \right) + e^{(r-q)T}\Phi \left[\frac{\ln(S/X) + (r - q + \sigma^2/2)T}{\sigma\sqrt{T}} \right] \right]$$

However, when $X \leq S_{MAX}$ the call option is

$$Call = e^{-rT}(S_{MAX} - X) + Se^{-qT}\Phi \left[\frac{\ln(S/S_{MAX}) + (r - q + \sigma^2/2)T}{\sigma\sqrt{T}} \right]$$

$$- S_{MAX}e^{-rT}\Phi \left[\frac{\ln(S/S_{MAX}) + (r - q + \sigma^2/2)T}{\sigma\sqrt{T}} - \sigma\sqrt{T} \right]$$

$$+ Se^{-rT} \frac{\sigma^2}{2(r-q)} \left[-\left(\frac{S}{S_{MAX}}\right)^{\frac{-2(r-q)}{\sigma^2}} \Phi \left(\frac{\ln(S/S_{MAX}) + (r - q + \sigma^2/2)T}{\sigma\sqrt{T}} - \frac{2(r-q)}{\sigma}\sqrt{T} \right) + e^{(r-q)T}\Phi \left[\frac{\ln(S/S_{MAX}) + (r - q + \sigma^2/2)T}{\sigma\sqrt{T}} \right] \right]$$

FLOATING STRIKE LOOK-BACK OPTIONS

Floating strike look-back options give the call holder the option to buy the underlying security at the lowest observable price and the put holder the option to sell at the highest observable price. That is, we have a *Call = Max* $(S - S_{MIN}, 0)$ and *Put = Max* $(S_{MAX} - S, 0)$.

Definitions of Variables

S present value of future cash flows ($)
X implementation cost ($)
r risk-free rate (%)
T time to expiration (years)
σ volatility (%)
Φ cumulative standard-normal distribution
q continuous dividend payout (%)

Computation

$$Call = Se^{-qT}\Phi\left[\frac{\ln(S/S_{MIN}) + (r - q + \sigma^2/2)T}{\sigma\sqrt{T}}\right]$$

$$- S_{MIN}e^{-rT}\Phi\left[\frac{\ln(S/S_{MIN}) + (r - q + \sigma^2/2)T}{\sigma\sqrt{T}} - \sigma\sqrt{T}\right]$$

$$+ Se^{-rT}\frac{\sigma^2}{2(r - q)}\left[\left(\frac{S}{S_{MIN}}\right)^{\frac{-2(r-q)}{\sigma^2}}\Phi\left(\begin{array}{c}\frac{-\ln(S/S_{MIN}) - (r - q + \sigma^2/2)T}{\sigma\sqrt{T}} \\ + \frac{2(r - q)}{\sigma}\sqrt{T}\end{array}\right) - e^{(r-q)T}\Phi\left[\frac{-\ln(S/S_{MIN}) - (r - q + \sigma^2/2)T}{\sigma\sqrt{T}}\right]\right]$$

$$Put = S_{MAX}e^{-rT}\Phi\left[\frac{-\ln(S/S_{MAX}) - (r - q + \sigma^2/2)T}{\sigma\sqrt{T}} + \sigma\sqrt{T}\right]$$

$$- Se^{-qT}\Phi\left[\frac{-\ln(S/S_{MAX}) - (r - q + \sigma^2/2)T}{\sigma\sqrt{T}}\right]$$

$$+ Se^{-rT}\frac{\sigma^2}{2(r - q)}\left[-\left(\frac{S}{S_{MAX}}\right)^{\frac{-2(r-q)}{\sigma^2}}\Phi\left(\begin{array}{c}\frac{\ln(S/S_{MAX}) + (r - q + \sigma^2/2)T}{\sigma\sqrt{T}} \\ - \frac{2(r - q)}{\sigma}\sqrt{T}\end{array}\right) + e^{(r-q)T}\Phi\left[\frac{\ln(S/S_{MAX}) + (r - q + \sigma^2/2)T}{\sigma\sqrt{T}}\right]\right]$$

FORWARD START OPTIONS

Definitions of Variables

S present value of future cash flows ($)

X implementation cost ($)

r risk-free rate (%)

t_1 time when the forward start option begins (years)

T_2 time to expiration of the forward start option (years)

σ volatility (%)

Φ cumulative standard-normal distribution

q continuous dividend payout (%)

Computation

$$Call = Se^{-qt_1}e^{-q(T_2-t_1)}\Phi\left[\frac{\ln(1/\alpha) + (r - q + \sigma^2/2)(T_2 - t_1)}{\sigma\sqrt{T_2 - t_1}}\right]$$

$$- Se^{-qt_1}\alpha e^{(-r)(T_2-t_1)}\Phi\left[\frac{\ln(1/\alpha) + (r - q + \sigma^2/2)(T_2 - t_1)}{\sigma\sqrt{T_2 - t_1}} - \sigma\sqrt{T_2 - t_1}\right]$$

$$Put = Se^{-qt_1}\alpha e^{(-r)(T_2-t_1)}\Phi\left[\frac{-\ln(1/\alpha) - (r - q + \sigma^2/2)(T_2 - t_1)}{\sigma\sqrt{T_2 - t_1}} + \sigma\sqrt{T_2 - t_1}\right]$$

$$- Se^{-qt_1}e^{-q(T_2-t_1)}\Phi\left[\frac{-\ln(1/\alpha) - (r - q + \sigma^2/2)(T_2 - t_1)}{\sigma\sqrt{T_2 - t_1}}\right]$$

where α is the multiplier constant.

Note: If the option starts at X percent out-of-the-money, α will be $(1 + X)$. If it starts at-the-money, α will be 1.0, and $(1 - X)$ if in-the-money.

GENERALIZED BLACK-SCHOLES MODEL

Definitions of Variables

S present value of future cash flows ($)
X implementation cost ($)
r risk-free rate (%)
T time to expiration (years)
σ volatility (%)
Φ cumulative standard-normal distribution
b carrying cost (%)
q continuous dividend payout (%)

Computation

$$Call = Se^{(b-r)T}\Phi\left(\frac{\ln(S/X) + (b + \sigma^2/2)T}{\sigma\sqrt{T}}\right)$$

$$-Xe^{-rT}\Phi\left(\frac{\ln(S/X) + (b - \sigma^2/2)T}{\sigma\sqrt{T}}\right)$$

$$Put = Xe^{-rT}\Phi\left(-\left[\frac{\ln(S/X) + (b - \sigma^2/2)T}{\sigma\sqrt{T}}\right]\right)$$

$$- Se^{(b-r)T}\Phi\left(-\left[\frac{\ln(S/X) + (b + \sigma^2/2)T}{\sigma\sqrt{T}}\right]\right)$$

Notes:

$b = 0$ Futures options model

$b = r - q$ Black-Scholes with dividend payment

$b = r$ Simple Black-Scholes formula

$b = r - r^*$ Foreign currency options model

OPTIONS ON FUTURES

The underlying security is a forward or futures contract with initial price F. Here, the value of F is the forward or futures contract's initial price, replacing S with F as well as calculating its present value.

Definitions of Variables

X implementation cost ($)

F futures single-point cash flows ($)

r risk-free rate (%)

T time to expiration (years)

σ volatility (%)

Φ cumulative standard-normal distribution

q continuous dividend payout (%)

Computation

$$Call = Fe^{-rT}\Phi\left(\frac{\ln(F/X) + (\sigma^2/2)T}{\sigma\sqrt{T}}\right) - Xe^{-rT}\Phi\left(\frac{\ln(F/X) - (\sigma^2/2)T}{\sigma\sqrt{T}}\right)$$

$$Put = Xe^{-rT}\Phi\left(-\left[\frac{\ln(F/X) - (\sigma^2/2)T}{\sigma\sqrt{T}}\right]\right) - Fe^{-rT}\Phi\left(-\left[\frac{\ln(F/X) + (\sigma^2/2)T}{\sigma\sqrt{T}}\right]\right)$$

SPREAD OPTION

The payoff on a spread option depends on the spread between the two futures contracts less the implementation cost.

Definitions of Variables

X implementation cost ($)

r risk-free rate (%)

T time to expiration (years)

σ volatility (%)

Φ cumulative standard-normal distribution

F_1 price for futures contract 1

F_2 price for futures contract 2

ρ correlation between the two futures contracts

Computation

First, calculate the portfolio volatility:

$$\sigma = \sqrt{\sigma_1^2 + \left[\sigma_2 \frac{F_2}{F_2 + X}\right]^2 - 2\rho\sigma_1\sigma_2 \frac{F_2}{F_2 + X}}$$

Then, obtain the call and put option values:

$$Call = (F_2 + X)\,e^{-rT}\left[\left\{\frac{F_1}{F_2 + X}\Phi\left[\frac{\ln\left[\dfrac{F_1}{F_2 + X}\right] + (\sigma^2/2)T}{\sigma\sqrt{T}}\right]\right.\right.$$
$$\left.\left. - \Phi\left[\frac{\ln\left[\dfrac{F_1}{F_2 + X}\right] + (\sigma^2/2)T}{\sigma\sqrt{T}} - \sigma\sqrt{T}\right]\right\}\right]$$

$$Put = (F_2 + X)\,e^{-rT}\left[\left\{\Phi\left[\frac{-\ln\left[\dfrac{F_1}{F_2 + X}\right] - (\sigma^2/2)T}{\sigma\sqrt{T}} + \sigma\sqrt{T}\right]\right.\right.$$
$$\left.\left. - \frac{F_1}{F_2 + X}\Phi\left[\frac{-\ln\left[\dfrac{F_1}{F_2 + X}\right] - (\sigma^2/2)T}{\sigma\sqrt{T}}\right]\right\}\right]$$

DISCRETE TIME SWITCH OPTIONS

The discrete time switch option holder will receive an amount equivalent to $A\Delta t$ at maturity T for each time interval of Δt where the corresponding asset price $S_{i\Delta t}$ has exceeded strike price X. The put option provides a similar payoff every time $S_{i\Delta t}$ is below the strike price.

Definitions of Variables

S present value of future cash flows ($)

X implementation cost ($)

r risk-free rate (%)

T time to expiration (years)

σ volatility (%)

Φ cumulative standard-normal distribution

    b   carrying cost (%), usually the risk-free rate less any continuous dividend payout rate

Computation

$$Call = Ae^{-rT}\sum_{i=1}^{n}\Phi\left(\frac{\ln(S/X) + (b - \sigma^2/2)i\Delta t}{\sigma\sqrt{i\Delta t}}\right)\Delta t$$

$$Put = Ae^{-rT}\sum_{i=1}^{n}\Phi\left(\frac{-\ln(S/X) - (b - \sigma^2/2)i\Delta t}{\sigma\sqrt{i\Delta t}}\right)\Delta t$$

TWO-CORRELATED-ASSETS OPTION

The payoff on an option depends on whether the other correlated option is in-the-money. This is the continuous counterpart to a correlated quadranomial model.

Definitions of Variables

S	present value of future cash flows ($)
X	implementation cost ($)
r	risk-free rate (%)
T	time to expiration (years)
σ	volatility (%)
Ω	cumulative bivariate-normal distribution function
ρ	correlation (%) between the two assets
q_1	continuous dividend payout for the first asset (%)
q_2	continuous dividend payout for the second asset (%)

Computation

$$Call = S_2e^{-q_2T}\Omega\left[\begin{array}{l}\dfrac{\ln(S_2/X_2) + (r - q_2 - \sigma_2^2/2)T}{\sigma_2\sqrt{T}} + \sigma_2\sqrt{T}; \\[3ex] \dfrac{\ln(S_1/X_1) + (r - q_1 - \sigma_1^2/2)T}{\sigma_1\sqrt{T}} + \rho\sigma_2\sqrt{T}; \rho\end{array}\right]$$

$$- X_2e^{-rT}\Omega\left[\begin{array}{l}\dfrac{\ln(S_2/X_2) + (r - q_2 - \sigma_2^2/2)T}{\sigma_2\sqrt{T}}; \\[3ex] \dfrac{\ln(S_1/X_1) + (r - q_1 - \sigma_1^2/2)T}{\sigma_1\sqrt{T}}; \rho\end{array}\right]$$

$$Put = X_2 e^{-rT} \Omega \left[\begin{array}{c} \dfrac{-\ln(S_2/X_2) - (r - q_2 - \sigma_2^2/2)T}{\sigma_2\sqrt{T}} \; ; \\[2em] \dfrac{-\ln(S_1/X_1) - (r - q_1 - \sigma_1^2/2)T}{\sigma_1\sqrt{T}} \; ; \rho \end{array} \right]$$

$$- S_2 e^{-q_2 T} \Omega \left[\begin{array}{c} \dfrac{-\ln(S_2/X_2) - (r - q_2 - \sigma_2^2/2)T}{\sigma_2\sqrt{T}} - \sigma_2\sqrt{T}; \\[2em] \dfrac{-\ln(S_1/X_1) - (r - q_1 - \sigma_1^2/2)T}{\sigma_1\sqrt{T}} - \rho\sigma_2\sqrt{T}; \rho \end{array} \right]$$

Real Options Analysis Toolkit Software (CD-ROM)

INTRODUCTION

Now that you are confident with the applicability of real options analysis and its intricate mathematical constructs, it is time to move on and use the real options modeling software on the enclosed CD-ROM. As shown in the previous two chapters, applying real options is not an easy task. The use of software-based models will allow the analyst to apply a consistent, well-tested, and replicable set of models. It reduces computational errors and allows the user to focus more on the process and problem at hand rather than on building potentially complex and mathematically intractable models. A complete list of the 69 Excel-based model functions that come with the Real Options Analysis Toolkit software CD-ROM is included in Appendix 9A.

INTRODUCTION TO THE REAL OPTIONS ANALYSIS TOOLKIT SOFTWARE CD-ROM

The enclosed CD-ROM has several demo software programs, including the Real Options Analysis Toolkit software, Crystal Ball's® Monte Carlo Simulation software, as well as example student problems and solutions. Appendix 9A lists the Excel-based functions available on the Real Options Analysis Toolkit software, while Appendix 9B provides a quick-start overview of using Crystal Ball's® Monte Carlo simulation package. The remainder of this chapter is devoted to providing examples of short real options problems and their solution using the enclosed Real Options Analysis Toolkit software. To install the software, browse the content of the CD-ROM and open the relevant Real Options Analysis Toolkit folder and run the setup.exe file.

After successfully installing the Real Options Analysis Toolkit software, run the software by clicking on *Start,* selecting *Crystal Ball* and *Real Options*

Analysis Toolkit. Then select *Toolkit (Demo).* Make sure you select *Enable Macros* when prompted. Leave the registration number field empty for a trial version of the software and select *OK* to continue. You will see a screen similar to Figure 9.1, which lists the different real options models available for use in the software. The models are aggregated into three distinct categories: *Binomial Lattices with Closed-Form Models, Closed-Form Partial-Differential Models,* and *Stochastic Differential Models.* The first category of models uses the binomial approach discussed in Chapters 6 and 7, in concert with closed-form models discussed in Appendix 8C. These two approaches are used together to confirm the analytical results. The second category of models consists purely of closed-form models or binomial lattice models performed in isolation. The last category of models focuses on stochastic modeling techniques. The demo version only has some models activated. The models with a yellow dot on the welcome screen have been deactivated. Click on *Purchase Full Version* or e-mail *JohnathanMun@cs.com* for further details on obtaining the fully functional version.

A simple example is now in order. Click on the *Abandonment* option button from the Real Options Analysis Toolkit Main screen. The American Abandonment Option will now appear, as seen in Figure 9.2. This modeling screen is similar for most of the models in the software. That is, there is a title bar, input parameters box, intermediate calculations box, results box, Index and Help buttons, options payoff graphics, pricing and valuation lattices, and a decision lattice. Take a moment to familiarize yourself with the modeling environment in Figure 9.2. Notice that there is a Help button that will provide the user more detailed information on the models currently in use.

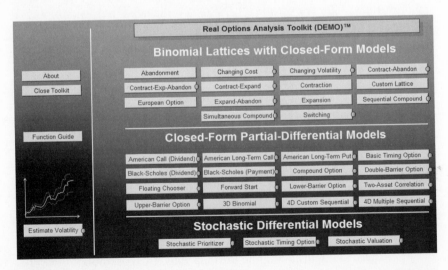

FIGURE 9.1 Real Options Analysis Toolkit

Let us revisit the Abandonment Option first introduced in Chapter 7's Figures 7.1 and 7.2. Recall that the example was a simple abandonment option with a five-year life, a cash flow volatility of 30 percent, $150 million in present value of future cash flows, 5 percent risk-free rate, no dividend outflows, and a $100 million salvage value. Figure 9.2 shows the *Input Parameters* in the colored input boxes. The *Intermediate Calculations* box shows the relevant calculations in the binomial context, representing the time-step size (δt), up jump size (u), down jump size (d), and risk-neutral probability (p) calculations. Compare these results with Figure 7.1.

The analysis also provides a view into two lattices. The first is a pricing lattice, where $150 can either have an up step jump or a down step jump, proportional to u and d. The second lattice shows the option valuation lattice. The value of the real option (NPV and options value) is calculated as $156.64 million, similar to that calculated in Figure 7.2. The decision lattice shows the individual decision nodes of the valuation lattice. That is, the decision lattice shows when the project should be abandoned and when the abandonment option should be kept open. Keeping an option open is sometimes more valuable than immediate execution as there is still time and hence a chance that executing the option at a later stage is more beneficial. Notice that there are two results in the *Results* box. The first comes from the simple five-step *Binomial Lattice* analysis. The second comes from the *Super Lattice* analysis, that is, the exact result that would be obtained if the five-step binomial lattice were extended to 1,000 steps. The user can define the number of steps (ranging from 5 to 5,000) using the drop-down box beside the Super Lattice result. Notice that if five steps were chosen, the result would

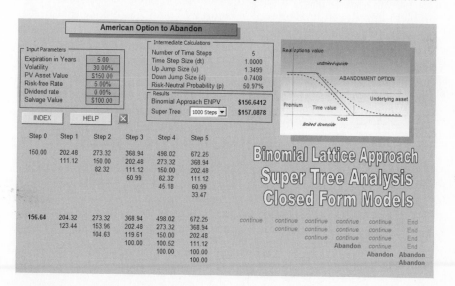

FIGURE 9.2 Abandonment Option

be identical to the binomial lattice approach. As seen in Chapter 6, the higher the number of steps, the greater the granularity in the binomial lattice and the more accurate the results. The user can perform a quick test by selecting progressively greater steps and notice the results converging to a single number. Notice that if the full-version software is installed, the user can also obtain the same results in his or her personal spreadsheet through the use of functions in Excel. For instance, a user can input the following formula in Excel:[1]

=ROBinomialAmericanAbandon
(Salvage, Asset, Years, Riskfree, Volatility, Dividend, Steps)

Replace the labels in the function with the relevant input assumptions. That is, if the following formula is entered into an Excel spreadsheet:

=ROBinomialAmericanAbandon(100,150,5,0.05,0.30,0,5)

the result will yield \$156.6412. Conversely, if the following is entered:

=ROBinomialAmericanAbandon(100,150,5,0.05,0.30,0,1000)

the result will yield \$157.0878, similar to the results shown using the 1,000-step Super Lattice analysis. To close out of the Abandonment Option, click on *Main* to return to the index of models. At the main index, click on *Contract-Exp-Abandon* to launch the American Chooser Option, that is, the option to contract, expand, or abandon at every time period up to and including the maturity date.

Figure 9.3 illustrates a simple chooser option calculation, similar to the problem introduced in Chapter 7's Figures 7.7 and 7.8. Notice that in this example, five steps were chosen for the Super Lattice analysis, which yields a result identical to that obtained with the binomial approach. In this example, two additional calculations are made as comparison benchmarks: the closed-form approximation of an American Option and a Black-Scholes model. Because there are no exact closed-form equations that exist for a chooser option as illustrated here, these two models are used only as a benchmark for the ballpark results, useful as a sanity check of the results. Similarly, the results can be obtained through a function in Excel:

=ROBinomialAmericanConExpAban(Salvage Value, Contraction Factor,
Contraction Savings, Expansion Factor, Asset Value, Expansion Cost,
Maturity in Years, Riskfree Rate, Volatility, Dividends, Number of Steps)

Replacing the labels with the relevant input parameter values such as

=ROBinomialAmericanConExpAban
(100, 0.90, 25, 1.30, 100, 20, 5, 0.05, 0.15, 0, 5)

will yield \$119.0291.

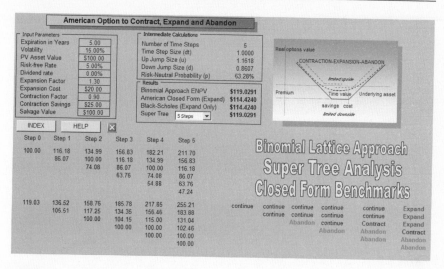

FIGURE 9.3   Chooser Option

CREATING AND SOLVING A CUSTOMIZED OPTION USING THE SOFTWARE

From the main index, select *Custom Lattice* to launch the customized options analysis. Click on *Step I: Reset Sheet* to reset the spreadsheet before creating a customized option model. This is important because any prior input parameters will be cleared from memory. Then, click on *Step II: Enter Starting Asset Value,* and you will see the dialog box shown in Figure 9.4.

Click on *OK,* and enter a starting value for the pricing lattice, which is essentially the present value of future cash flows. Type *100,* and hit enter, as seen in Figure 9.5.

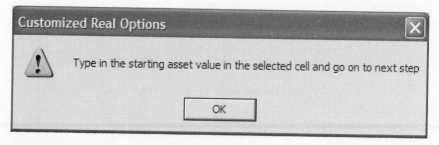

FIGURE 9.4   Customized Real Options Dialog Box with Simple Statement

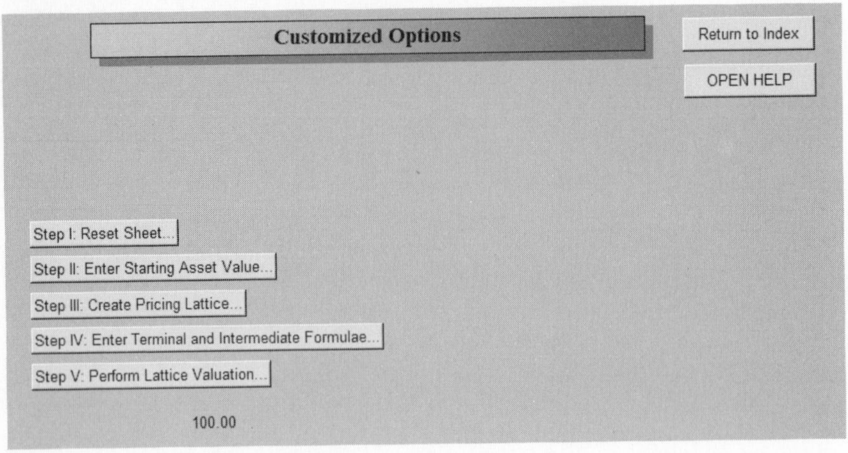

FIGURE 9.5 Customized Options

Then, click on *Step III: Create Pricing Lattice,* and you will be prompted for more information as seen in the dialog box in Figure 9.6.

Enter the cell reference (e.g., D22) that contains the *100* value previously entered. Enter the additional parameters requested, such as volatility in percent, maturity in years, risk-free rate in percent, dividends in percent, and the number of steps. The demo version will support up to 20 steps only, while the fully functional version will support up to 250 steps. Click on *Create,* and the pricing lattice is created, together with a summary of the input parameters, as seen in Figure 9.7.

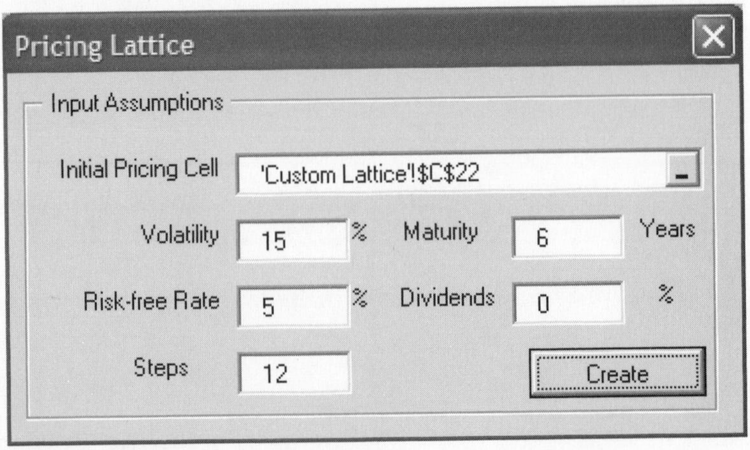

FIGURE 9.6 Pricing Lattice Dialog Box

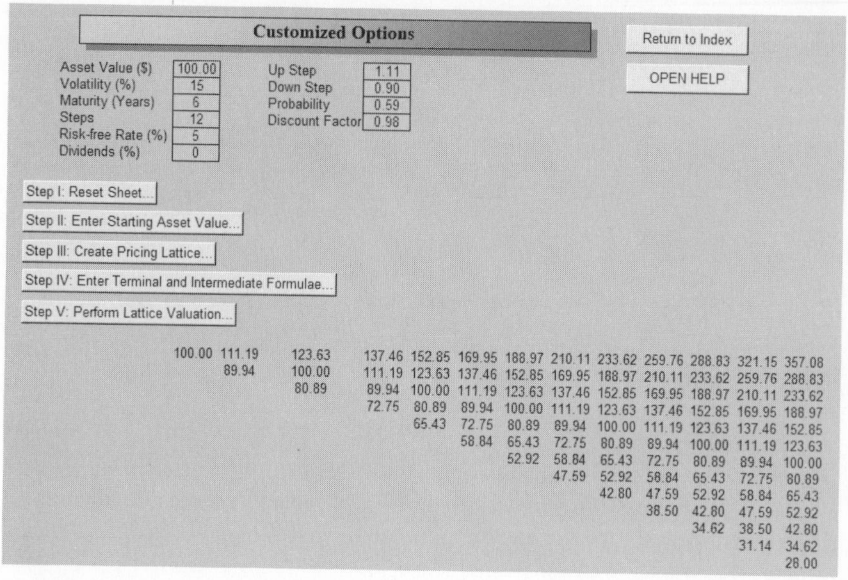

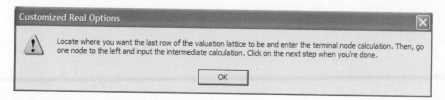

FIGURE 9.7 Pricing Lattice

Then click on *Step IV: Enter Terminal and Intermediate Formulae* to continue. A dialog box will provide further information. *See* Figure 9.8. The next step is to enter the customized valuation lattice equations, first for the terminal nodes and then for the intermediate nodes.

Figure 9.9 shows the next step. In cell P36, type in the terminal period formula; for example, type in the following equation:

$$=MAX(P22 - 100,0)$$

where P22 refers to the corresponding node on the pricing lattice and 100 is the cost to execute this option. Then, in cell O36, enter in the intermediate formula; for example, type in the following equation:

$$=MAX((Prob*P36 + (1 - Prob)*P37)*Discount, O22 - 100)$$

Customized Real Options ☒

⚠ Locate where you want the last row of the valuation lattice to be and enter the terminal node calculation. Then, go one node to the left and input the intermediate calculation. Click on the next step when you're done.

OK

FIGURE 9.8 Customized Real Options Dialog Box with Complex Statement

	C	D	E	F	G	H	I	J	K	L	M	N	O	P
21														
22		100.00	111.19	123.63	137.46	152.85	169.95	188.97	210.11	233.62	259.76	288.83	321.15	357.08
23			89.94	100.00	111.19	123.63	137.46	152.85	169.95	188.97	210.11	233.62	259.76	288.83
24				80.89	89.94	100.00	111.19	123.63	137.46	152.85	169.95	188.97	210.11	233.62
25					72.75	80.89	89.94	100.00	111.19	123.63	137.46	152.85	169.95	188.97
26						65.43	72.75	80.89	89.94	100.00	111.19	123.63	137.46	152.85
27							58.84	65.43	72.75	80.89	89.94	100.00	111.19	123.63
28								52.92	58.84	65.43	72.75	80.89	89.94	100.00
29									47.59	52.92	58.84	65.43	72.75	80.89
30										42.80	47.59	52.92	58.84	65.43
31											38.50	42.80	47.59	52.92
32												34.62	38.50	42.80
33													31.14	34.62
34														28.00
35														
36													221.15	257.08

FIGURE 9.9 Valuation Equations

where *Prob* is the risk-neutral probability based on the previous inputs and *Discount* is the discount factor, or the $e^{-rf(\delta t)}$ value. Replace the '*Prob*' and '*Discount*' with the relevant risk-neutral probability and discount factor values.

Then click on *Step V: Perform Lattice Valuation,* and you will be prompted with the dialog box shown in Figure 9.10.

Enter the number of steps corresponding to the number of steps entered previously when generating the pricing lattice. Enter or select the cell with the terminal equation (e.g., P36), and enter or select the cell with the intermediate equation (e.g., O36), and click on *Value!* to create the valuation lattice, as seen in Figure 9.11. The value of this simple option is $29.27.

Using the same approach, the user can create multiple and complex custom option types easily and effectively, by merely entering the correct terminal and intermediate equations for each successive valuation lattice.

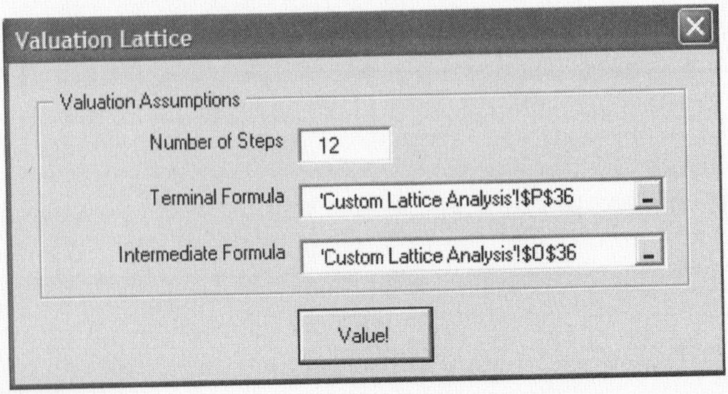

Valuation Lattice ☒

Valuation Assumptions

Number of Steps   12

Terminal Formula   'Custom Lattice Analysis'!$P$36   ▬

Intermediate Formula   'Custom Lattice Analysis'!$O$36   ▬

Value!

FIGURE 9.10 Valuation Lattice Dialog Box

	C	D	E	F	G	H	I	J	K	L	M	N	O	P
21														
22		100.00	111.19	123.63	137.46	152.85	169.95	188.97	210.11	233.62	259.76	288.83	321.15	357.08
23			89.94	100.00	111.19	123.63	137.46	152.85	169.95	188.97	210.11	233.62	259.76	288.83
24				80.89	89.94	100.00	111.19	123.63	137.46	152.85	169.95	188.97	210.11	233.62
25					72.75	80.89	89.94	100.00	111.19	123.63	137.46	152.85	169.95	188.97
26						65.43	72.75	80.89	89.94	100.00	111.19	123.63	137.46	152.85
27							58.84	65.43	72.75	80.89	89.94	100.00	111.19	123.63
28								52.92	58.84	65.43	72.75	80.89	89.94	100.00
29									47.59	52.92	58.84	65.43	72.75	80.89
30										42.80	47.59	52.92	58.84	65.43
31											38.50	42.80	47.59	52.92
32												34.62	38.50	42.80
33													31.14	34.62
34														28.00
35														
36		29.27	37.27	46.84	58.10	71.13	86.03	102.90	121.86	143.14	166.99	193.70	223.62	257.08
37			19.45	25.66	33.37	42.74	53.88	66.85	81.70	98.48	117.34	138.50	162.23	188.83
38				11.61	16.04	21.82	29.20	38.35	49.40	62.36	77.17	93.84	112.58	133.62
39					5.89	8.62	12.45	17.69	24.66	33.62	44.69	57.72	72.42	88.97
40						2.28	3.59	5.60	8.65	13.15	19.61	28.51	39.93	52.85
41							0.51	0.88	1.52	2.64	4.56	7.89	13.66	23.63
42								0.00	0.00	0.00	0.00	0.00	0.00	0.00
43									0.00	0.00	0.00	0.00	0.00	0.00
44										0.00	0.00	0.00	0.00	0.00
45											0.00	0.00	0.00	0.00
46												0.00	0.00	0.00
47													0.00	0.00
48														0.00

FIGURE 9.11 Valuation Lattice

ADVANCED REAL OPTIONS MODELS IN THE SOFTWARE

The sample screen shots on the following pages illustrate some of the more advanced models available on the CD-ROM, installed in the Real Options Analysis Toolkit software. Figure 9.12 shows the module used in estimating volatility using the logarithmic cash flow returns approach, as described in Appendix 9A.

Figure 9.13 shows the American closed-form approximation model for a long-term call option with multiple dividends, paid at a single percent continuous dividend payout rate. This is the closed-form counterpart of using binomial or Super Lattices in estimating the value of American options, which are exercisable at any time up to the time of maturity. The model also comes with a set of upside and downside sensitivities. That is, holding all the variables constant and changing each variable by the percentage sensitivity level, the difference in the option value is shown.

Figure 9.14 shows the double barrier European option, which provides four different models: Up and In & Down and In Call (when the asset level rises above the upper barrier or drops below the lower barrier, the call option kicks in and comes into-the-money); Up and In & Down and In Put (when the asset level rises above the upper barrier or drops below the lower barrier, the put option kicks in and comes into-the-money); Up and Out & Down and

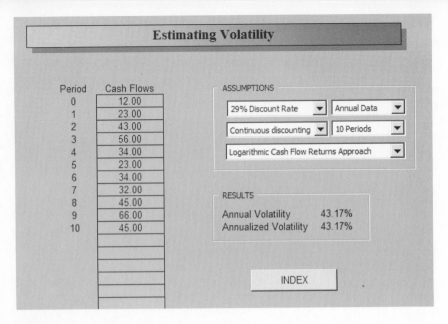

FIGURE 9.12   Volatility Estimation Model

American Long-Term Call Approximation

		upside	downside
Asset Value	100.00	3.0278	-2.7820
Implementation Cost	90.00	-1.8502	2.0966
Time to Maturity	3.0000	0.1474	-0.1572
Risk-free Rate	5.00%	0.1211	-0.1199
Dividend Rate	12.00%	-0.3927	0.4117
Volatility	35.00%	0.8692	-0.8650
Closed Form Approx.	18.7523		
Binomial Approach 5 Steps ▼	18.7088		

Reset to Zero

Reset to Original

SENSITIVITY

▲
▼   +/- 5%   ☒

INDEX

HELP

FIGURE 9.13   American Call Approximation

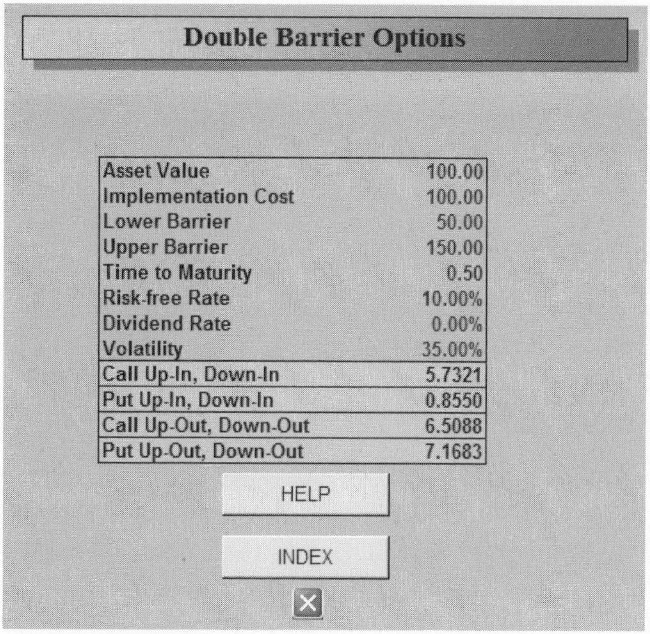

Double Barrier Options

Asset Value	100.00
Implementation Cost	100.00
Lower Barrier	50.00
Upper Barrier	150.00
Time to Maturity	0.50
Risk-free Rate	10.00%
Dividend Rate	0.00%
Volatility	35.00%
Call Up-In, Down-In	5.7321
Put Up-In, Down-In	0.8550
Call Up-Out, Down-Out	6.5088
Put Up-Out, Down-Out	7.1683

FIGURE 9.14 Barrier Options

Out Call (when the asset level rises above the upper barrier or drops below the lower barrier, the call option comes out-of-the-money and is worthless); Up and Out & Down and Out Put (when the asset level rises above the upper barrier or drops below the lower barrier, the put option comes out-of-the-money and is worthless).

Figure 9.15 shows a stochastic calculator, which uses marginal revenues, marginal operating costs, and marginal capital expenditures to calculate if and when an investment should be optimally executed. It takes into account the projected time when the project can be reasonably implemented and the potential value of implementing it at a later time. With later implementation, the marginal implementation capital expenditures can be defrayed, and by virtue of time value of money, a delay in implementation promulgates itself as a reduction in cost, making the project more profitable. However, by delaying implementation, the firm also loses out on the potential marginal revenues and growth in asset value that can be generated if the project were implemented on schedule. This balancing procedure is calculated here, resulting in a recommended time to execution and optimal trigger values whereby if the investment cash flow stream exceeds this trigger value, the investment becomes optimal and should begin immediately.

The stochastic prioritizer in Figure 9.16 allows the user to input five different alternative investment opportunities, calculates the resulting strategic

Stochastic Timing Real Options

Strategy	A	B	C
Project's Total Marginal Revenues ($ million)	$111	$212	$190
Project's Total Marginal Operating Costs ($ million)	$100	$10	$90
Project's Total Marginal Capital Implementation Costs ($ million)	$5	$2	$10
Projected Time to Implementation (Years)	1.0	1.0	1.0
Opportunity Cost (%)	5.00%	5.00%	5.00%
Hurdle Rate (%)	15.00%	18.00%	20.00%
Strategic Option Value ($ million)	$6.28	$525.96	$101.79
Synopsis	Has Option Value	Has Option Value	Has Option Value
Optimal Trigger Value	$15	$7	$40
Optimal Time to Execution	Optimal to Wait	Execute Now	Execute Now
Net Present Value (traditional)	$6	$200	$90
Present Value Free Cash Flow	$11	$202	$100

INDEX

HELP

FIGURE 9.15 Optimal Timing

Real Options Stochastic Prioritizer

INDEX

HELP

Strategy	A	B	C	D	E
Underlying Asset Value ($ million)	$100.00	$110.00	$120.00	$107.90	$100.00
Capital Expenditures ($ million)	$80.00	$113	$100	$140.00	$103.00
Timing (years)	3.000	1.000	3.000	1.000	1.000
Standard deviation (annualized)	35.00%	40.00%	35.00%	30.00%	40.00%
Risk free rate (annualized)	5.74%	5.74%	5.74%	5.74%	5.74%
Strategic Option Value ($ million)	$40.16	$18.88	$46.10	$5.29	$17.04
Strategic Decision	Second Choice	Third Choice	First Choice	Fifth Choice	Fourth Choice
Returns Index	1.478	1.029	1.419	0.815	1.027
Volatility Index	0.606	0.400	0.606	0.300	0.400
Net Present Value (traditional)	$32	$3	$35	($24)	$3
	$5.14	$2.41	$5.89	$0.54	$1.75

FIGURE 9.16 Stochastic Prioritization

optionality value, and prioritizes the alternatives from the most attractive to the least attractive. A net present value analysis is also included, as are the *returns index* and *volatility index*. First, enter the assumptions in the highlighted boxed region. The *underlying asset value* is the net present value of a time series of free cash flows. These free cash flows are the projected revenues less projected direct and indirect costs (cost of goods sold, operating expenses, depreciation, and taxes) with an add-back in depreciation expenses, capital expenditures, changes in net working capital, and so forth, after taxes. The *capital expenditures* input is simply the total capital expenditures needed to implement this strategy. *Timing* is simply when you intend to start this project in the future. *Standard deviation* is the volatility of the underlying. The *risk-free rate* is the rate of return on a risk-free asset for the time horizon of the investment.

The *strategic option value* provides the intrinsic value above what is normally tabulated under a net present value regime. Even when the project on the outset seems cashless and has a negative net present value, there may still be some intrinsic strategic value to implementing the project. This strategic intrinsic value comes from the ability to delay the project's start date, thereby waiting for new information and allowing uncertainties to be uncovered as well as being able to defray the initial investment cost. By virtue of time valuation of money, this equates to a cost reduction, making the project more profitable. However, by delaying, you are forgoing potential revenues until the project is undertaken.

The *returns index* is simply the ratio of projected free cash flows discounted at the hurdle rate, to the capital expenditures discounted at a risk-free rate over time. The *volatility index* is a time-adjusted volatility measure, and the *net present value* is the traditional application of a discounted cash flow analysis with two separate discount rates over time. The *returns index* should be used in tandem with the volatility index. A *returns index* greater than one implies a profitable project. A *returns index* of less than one implies an unprofitable project. However, even a static unprofitable project with a ratio less than one can still become optimal if the volatility index is sufficiently high. Given time, due to the higher volatility and with fixed capital expenditures, the uncertain flow of revenues could be high enough to make the project justifiable and acceptable due to the occurrence of some uncertain series of events.

The stochastic valuation model shown in Figure 9.17 assumes an option with an infinite life starting at a future time *t*. The model uses a partial-differential model in estimating the optimal trigger value of an option and the optimal execution time of an option given the relevant parameters.

The American 4-D multiple-sequential-compound option model shown in Figure 9.18 is exercisable any time up to its expiration as measured in years. The option value depends on the successful execution of another option in sequence. That is, the second option is interacting sequentially when the first option depends on the underlying asset, and the second option's values depend on the value of the first option as its underlying, and so forth, up to as many as 10 optional phases. Notice that the length of time of the second option is shorter than that of the first option, that of the third will be shorter than that of the second, and so forth. Otherwise this model would become a simultaneous compound option. *Volatility* is calculated based on the base case's underlying cash flow series (the natural logarithm of cash flow returns).

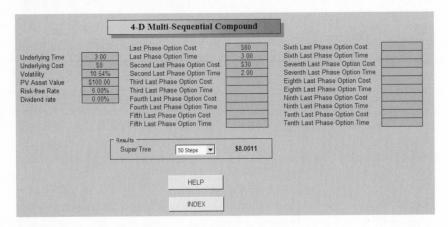

Stochastic Valuation Model

Strategic Options	Period Starting (t)	Annualized Discount Rates	Discounted Value of Future Cash Flows	Discounted Value of the Costs to Invest	DCF Value	Interest Rate (monthly basis)	Opportunity Cost
Option A	12	12%	11,271,993	5,983,913	5,288,079	0.949%	0.86%
Option B	13	12%	6,011,556	4,707,131	1,304,425	0.949%	0.86%
Option C	19	12%	4,519,909	5,687,783	-1,167,874	0.949%	0.86%
Option D	19	12%	4,399,742	4,118,739	891,003	0.949%	0.86%

Strategic Options	Standard Deviation (Actualized Cash Flows)	Optimal Exercise Value of the "Discounted Value of the Costs to Invest"	Option Value at t	Option Value at t = 0	Annualized Standard Deviation of Cash Flows	Flexibility Parameter	Decision To Invest
Option A	2.50%	7,489,764	10,807,506	9649559	34.5%	1.273	Execute Investment
Option B	2.50%	5,991,811	1,304,545	1153824	34.5%	1.273	Execute Investment
Option C	2.50%	7,232,825	171,040	142952	34.5%	1.272	Wait to Invest
Option D	2.50%	5,237,563	900,080	752240	34.5%	1.272	Wait to Invest

Total Option Value at t=0		11,698,574

INDEX

Marginal impact of changing each unit:

HELP

	Periods	Annualized Discount Rate	Discounted Future CF	Discounted Cost	Opportunity Cost	Standard Deviation
Option A	$445,064	$3,499,335	$4,694,694	$4,220,400	$9,720,052	$3,183,521
Option B	$53,218	$32,813	$1,211,149	$584,185	$74,469	$44,927
Option C	$6,593	$113,089	$221,414	$64,202	$70,587	$105,905
Option D	$34,695	$61,478	$1,013,985	$414,296	$11,648	$73,071
Total Portfolio	$539,570	$5,291,954	$7,141,242	$5,283,083	$9,712,286	$2,959,619

Magnitude of change: 5 ▼ | 2% ▼ | $1,000,000 ▼ | $1,000,000 ▼ | 0.10% ▼ | 20% ▼

FIGURE 9.17 Stochastic Valuation

4-D Multi-Sequential Compound

Underlying Time: 3.00
Underlying Cost: $0
Volatility: 10.54%
PV Asset Value: $100.00
Risk-free Rate: 5.00%
Dividend rate: 0.00%

Last Phase Option Cost: $80
Last Phase Option Time: 3.00
Second Last Phase Option Cost: $30
Second Last Phase Option Time: 2.00
Third Last Phase Option Cost:
Third Last Phase Option Time:
Fourth Last Phase Option Cost:
Fourth Last Phase Option Time:
Fifth Last Phase Option Cost:
Fifth Last Phase Option Time:

Sixth Last Phase Option Cost:
Sixth Last Phase Option Time:
Seventh Last Phase Option Cost:
Seventh Last Phase Option Time:
Eighth Last Phase Option Cost:
Eighth Last Phase Option Time:
Ninth Last Phase Option Cost:
Ninth Last Phase Option Time:
Tenth Last Phase Option Cost:
Tenth Last Phase Option Time:

Results
Super Tree: 50 Steps ▼ $8.0011

HELP

INDEX

FIGURE 9.18 Multiple Sequential Compound

PV of asset value is the present value of future net cash flows of the base case, not including the implementation costs of the option. *Risk-free rate* is the rate of return on a risk-free asset with maturity similar to that of the underlying option. *Dividend rate* is the single continuous percent cash opportunity outflow of holding on to the option and not executing. *First cost* is the implementation cost of the first option, and *Second cost* is the implementation of the second option, and so forth, until the 10th phase. The Real Options Analysis Toolkit software was created by the author based on the materials of this book and his upcoming book, which focuses purely on real options business problems and their step-by-step resolution. In this follow-up book, the problems are solved both analytically and using the accompanying real options software. The methodologies employed include stochastic forecasting, discounted cash flow analysis, Monte Carlo simulation, stochastic optimization, and real options analysis (using binomial lattices, risk-neutral probability, market-replicating approach, state-pricing, trinomials, and closed-form models).

SUMMARY

Having modeling software that performs real options is invaluable to a firm when evaluating projects and strategies. It frees analysts from having to create sophisticated models or keep a complex array of linked spreadsheets, and allows them instead to focus on framing the problem. This is most certainly true in complex problems that require complicated options mathematics that cannot be easily created in a spreadsheet environment. A software package with built-in modeling flexibility can allow a user to replicate results with ease through a repeatable, consistent, and reliable process.

CHAPTER 9 EXERCISES

1. Open the Real Options Analysis Toolkit software and rerun the expansion option example in Chapter 7.

2. Open the Real Options Analysis Toolkit software and rerun the abandonment option example in Chapter 7.

3. Open the Real Options Analysis Toolkit software and rerun the contraction option example in Chapter 7.

4. Open the Real Options Analysis Toolkit software and rerun the chooser option example in Chapter 7.

5. Re-create the expansion option example using the Custom Lattice module in the Real Options Analysis Toolkit software.

Real Options Analysis Toolkit's Function Description for Excel

These functions are available for use in the full version of the Real Options Analysis Toolkit software. Once the full version is installed, simply click on *Start,* select *Programs,* then *Crystal Ball* and *Real Options Analysis Toolkit.* Next, select *Functions.* The software will be loaded into Excel, and the following models are directly accessible through Excel by typing them directly in a spreadsheet or by clicking on the Equation Wizard and selecting the Financial/All categories. Scroll down to the RO section for a listing of all the models.

1. **American 3D Binomial Two Asset Call Option with Dual Strike Prices**

   This is a European option exercisable at termination, where the value of the option depends on two correlated assets with different implementation strike costs, calculated using a combination of multiple binomial lattices.

   Function: RO3DBinomialAmericanCallDualStrike(1st Asset, 2nd Asset, 1st Quantity, 2nd Quantity, 1st Cost, 2nd Cost, Maturity Time, Riskfree, 1st Carrying Cost, 2nd Carrying Cost, 1st Volatility, 2nd Volatility, Correlation, Steps)

2. **American 3D Binomial Two Asset Call Option on the Maximum**

   This is a European option exercisable at termination, where the value of the option depends on the maximum of two correlated underlying assets' values, calculated using a combination of multiple binomial lattices.

   Function: RO3DBinomialAmericanCallMax(1st Asset, 2nd Asset, 1st Quantity, 2nd Quantity, 1st Cost, 2nd Cost, Maturity Time, Riskfree, 1st Carrying Cost, 2nd Carrying Cost, 1st Volatility, 2nd Volatility, Correlation, Steps)

3. American 3D Binomial Two Asset Call Option on the Minimum

This is a European option exercisable at termination, where the value of the option depends on the minimum of two correlated underlying assets' values, calculated using a combination of multiple binomial lattices.

Function: RO3DBinomialAmericanCallMin(1st Asset, 2nd Asset, 1st Quantity, 2nd Quantity, 1st Cost, 2nd Cost, Maturity Time, Riskfree, 1st Carrying Cost, 2nd Carrying Cost, 1st Volatility, 2nd Volatility, Correlation, Steps)

4. American 3D Binomial Two Asset Portfolio Call Option

This is a European option exercisable at termination, where the value of the option depends on the portfolio effect of two correlated underlying assets' values, calculated using a combination of multiple binomial lattices.

Function: RO3DBinomialAmericanCallPortfolio(1st Asset, 2nd Asset, 1st Quantity, 2nd Quantity, 1st Cost, 2nd Cost, Maturity Time, Riskfree, 1st Carrying Cost, 2nd Carrying Cost, 1st Volatility, 2nd Volatility, Correlation, Steps)

5. American Call Option Approximation with a Single Dividend Payment

This American call option is based on a closed-form approximation of a call that can be exercised at any time up to and including its expiration date, and has a single lump sum dividend payment in the future prior to expiration.

Function: ROAmericanDividendCall(Asset, Cost, Dividend Time, Expiration Time, Riskfree, Volatility, Dividend)

6. American Long-Term Call Option Approximation with a Dividend Stream

This American call option is based on a closed-form approximation of a call, with a constant percent dividend stream and can be exercised at any time up to and including its expiration date.

Function: ROAmericanLongTermCall(Asset, Cost, Time, Riskfree, Carry, Volatility)

7. American Long-Term Put Option Approximation with a Dividend Stream

This American put option is based on a closed-form approximation of a put, with a constant percent dividend stream and can be exercised at any time up to and including its expiration date.

Function: ROAmericanLongTermPut(Asset, Cost, Time, Riskfree, Carry, Volatility)

8. Single Barrier Option: Down and In Call

This European single lower barrier call option is exercisable only at expiration. This call option becomes activated only when the asset value breaches a lower barrier.

Function: ROBarrierCallDownIn(Asset, Cost, Barrier, Cash Rebate, Time, Riskfree, Carrying Cost, Volatility)

9. Single Barrier Option: Down and Out Call

This European single lower barrier call option is exercisable only at expiration. This call option becomes activated only when the asset value does not breach a lower barrier.

Function: ROBarrierCallDownOut(Asset, Cost, Barrier, Cash Rebate, Time, Riskfree, Carrying Cost, Volatility)

10. Single Barrier Option: Up and In Call

This European single upper barrier call option is exercisable only at expiration. This call option becomes activated only when the asset value breaches an upper barrier.

Function: ROBarrierCallUpIn(Asset, Cost, Barrier, Cash Rebate, Time, Riskfree, Carrying Cost, Volatility)

11. Single Barrier Option: Up and Out Call

This European single upper barrier call option is exercisable only at expiration. This call option becomes activated only when the asset value does not breach an upper barrier.

Function: ROBarrierCallUpOut(Asset, Cost, Barrier, Cash Rebate, Time, Riskfree, Carrying Cost, Volatility)

12. Single Barrier Option: Down and In Put

This European single lower barrier put option is exercisable only at expiration. This put option becomes activated only when the asset value breaches a lower barrier.

Function: ROBarrierPutDownIn(Asset, Cost, Barrier, Cash Rebate, Time, Riskfree, Carrying Cost, Volatility)

13. Single Barrier Option: Down and Out Put

This European single lower barrier put option is exercisable only at expiration. This put option becomes activated only when the asset value does not breach a lower barrier.

Function: ROBarrierPutDownOut(Asset, Cost, Barrier, Cash Rebate, Time, Riskfree, Carrying Cost, Volatility)

14. Single Barrier Option: Up and In Put

This European single upper barrier put option is exercisable only at expiration. The value of this put option comes in-the-money only when the asset value breaches an upper barrier.

Function: ROBarrierPutUpIn(Asset, Cost, Barrier, Cash Rebate, Time, Riskfree, Carrying Cost, Volatility)

15. Single Barrier Option: Up and Out Put

This European single upper barrier put option is exercisable only at expiration. This put option becomes activated only when the asset value does not breach an upper barrier.

Function: ROBarrierPutUpOut(Asset, Cost, Barrier, Cash Rebate, Time, Riskfree, Carrying Cost, Volatility)

16. Basic Chooser Option

This option gives the holder the right to choose between a call or put. Both calls and puts are constrained by the same expiration date and strike price. Either option may be exercised prior to the expiration date.

Function: ROBasicChooser(Asset, Cost, Chooser Time 1, Maturity Time 2, Riskfree, Carrying Cost, Volatility)

17. American Call Option Using the Binomial (Super Lattice) Approach

This American option gives the holder the right to execute its existing operations, at any time within a particular period.

Function: ROBinomialAmerican(Asset, Cost, Time, Riskfree, Volatility, Dividend, Steps)

18. American Abandonment Option Using the Binomial (Super Lattice) Approach

This American option gives the holder the right to abandon existing operations at any time within a particular period and receive the salvage value.

Function: ROBinomialAmericanAbandon(Salvage, Asset, Time, Riskfree, Volatility, Dividend, Steps)

19. American Call Option Using the Binomial (Super Lattice) Approach

This American call option gives the holder the right to execute a project at any time within a particular period at a set implementation cost, calculated using the Binomial approach with consideration for dividend payments.

Function: ROBinomialAmericanCall(Asset, Cost, Time, Riskfree, Volatility, Dividend, Steps)

20. American Contraction and Abandonment Option Using the Binomial Approach

This American option gives the holder the right to either contract its existing operations by a contraction factor in order to create some savings, or abandon entirely its existing operations at any time within a particular period and receive the salvage value.

Function: ROBinomialAmericanConAban(Salvage, Contraction, Savings, Asset, Time, Riskfree, Volatility, Dividend, Steps)

21. American Contraction and Expansion Option Using the Binomial (Super Lattice) Approach

This American option gives the holder the right to either contract its existing operations by a contraction factor in order to create some savings in a market downturn, or expand its existing operations at an expansion factor at any time within a particular period by spending an appropriate implementation cost in a market upturn.

Function: ROBinomialAmericanConExp(Contraction, Savings, Expansion, Asset, Cost, Time, Riskfree, Volatility, Dividend, Steps)

22. American Contraction, Expansion, and Abandonment Option Using the Binomial (Super Lattice) Approach

This American option gives the holder the right to choose among contracting its existing operations by a contraction factor in order to create some savings, or expanding its existing operations at an expansion factor by spending an appropriate implementation cost, or abandoning its operations entirely and receiving a salvage value, at any time within a particular period.

Function: ROBinomialAmericanConExpAban(Salvage, Contraction, Savings, Expansion, Asset, Cost, Time, Riskfree, Volatility, Dividend, Steps)

23. American Contraction Option Using the Binomial (Super Lattice) Approach

This American option gives the holder the right to contract its existing operations by a contraction factor in order to create some savings, at any time within a particular period.

Function: ROBinomialAmericanContract(Contraction, Asset, Savings, Time, Riskfree, Volatility, Dividend, Steps)

24. American Expansion and Abandonment Option Using the Binomial (Super Lattice) Approach

This American option gives the holder the right to choose between expanding its existing operations at an expansion factor by spending an appropriate implementation cost, or abandoning its operations entirely and receiving a salvage value, at any time within a particular period.

Function: ROBinomialAmericanExpAban(Salvage, Expansion, Asset, Cost, Time, Riskfree, Volatility, Dividend, Steps)

25. American Expansion Option Using the Binomial (Super Lattice) Approach

This American option gives the holder the right to expand its existing operations at an expansion factor by spending an appropriate implementation cost, at any time within a particular period.

Function: ROBinomialAmericanExpansion(Expansion, Asset, Cost, Time, Riskfree, Volatility, Dividend, Steps)

26. **American Put Option Using the Binomial (Super Lattice) Approach**

This American put option approximation with dividends is exercisable at any time within a particular period, calculated using the Binomial approach, with consideration for dividend payments.

Function: ROBinomialAmericanPut(Asset, Cost, Time, Riskfree, Volatility, Dividend, Steps)

27. **American Sequential Compound Option Using the Binomial (Super Lattice) Approach**

This American option is the value of two option phases occurring in sequence, and is exercisable at any time within a particular period, where the execution of the second option depends on the successful implementation of the first option.

Function: ROBinomialAmericanSeqCompound(Asset, Underlying 1st Cost, Option 2nd Cost, Underlying 1st Time, Option 2nd Time, Riskfree, Volatility, Dividend, Steps)

28. **American Simultaneous Compound Option Using the Binomial (Super Lattice) Approach**

This American option is the value of two option phases occurring simultaneously, and is exercisable at any time within a particular period, where the execution of the second option depends on the successful implementation of the first option.

Function: ROBinomialAmericanSimCompound(Asset, Underlying Cost1, Option Cost2, Maturity Time, Riskfree, Volatility, Dividend, Steps)

29. **Changing Cost Option Using the Binomial (Super Lattice) Approach**

This is the value of an American option with different implementation costs at different times, where the option is executable at any time up to maturity.

Function: ROBinomialCost(Asset, Cost1, Cost2, Cost3, Cost4, Cost5, Time1, Time2, Time3, Time4, Time5, Volatility, Riskfree, Dividend, Steps)

30. **Binomial Lattice Down Jump-Step Size**

This is the calculation used in obtaining the down jump-step size on a binomial lattice.

Function: ROBinomialDown(Volatility, Time, Steps)

31. **European Call Option Using the Binomial (Super Lattice) Approach**

This is the European call calculation performed using a binomial approach, and is exercisable only at termination.

Function: ROBinomialEuropeanCall(Asset, Cost, Time, Riskfree, Volatility, Dividend, Steps)

32. European Put Option Using the Binomial (Super Lattice) Approach

This is the European put calculation performed using a binomial approach, and is exercisable only at termination.

Function: ROBinomialEuropeanPut(Asset, Cost, Time, Riskfree, Volatility, Dividend, Steps)

33. Binomial Lattice Risk-Neutral Probability

This is the calculation used in obtaining the risk-neutral probability on a binomial lattice.

Function: ROBinomialProb(Volatility, Time, Steps, Riskfree, Dividend)

34. Binomial Lattice Up Jump-Step Size

This is the calculation used in obtaining the up jump-step size on a binomial lattice.

Function: ROBinomialUp(Volatility, Time, Steps)

35. Black-Scholes Call Option with No Dividends

This is the European call calculated using the Black-Scholes model, with no dividend payments, and is exercisable only at expiration.

Function: ROBlackScholesCall(Asset, Cost, Time, Riskfree, Volatility)

36. Black-Scholes Call Option with a Carrying Cost

This is the European call calculated using the Generalized Black-Scholes model, with a carrying cost adjustment, and is exercisable only at expiration. The carrying cost adjustment is simply the difference between the risk-free rate and the dividend payments, both in percent.

Function: ROBlackScholesCarryingCall(Asset, Cost, Time, Riskfree, Volatility, Carrycost)

37. Black-Scholes Put Option with a Carrying Cost

This is the European put calculated using the Generalized Black-Scholes model, with a carrying cost adjustment, and is exercisable only at expiration. The carrying cost adjustment is simply the difference between the risk-free rate and the dividend payments, both in percent.

Function: ROBlackScholesCarryingPut(Asset, Cost, Time, Riskfree, Volatility, Carrycost)

38. Black-Scholes Call Option with Dividends

This is the European call calculated using the Generalized Black-Scholes model, with a dividend stream in percent, and is exercisable only at expiration.

Function: ROBlackScholesDividendCall(Asset, Cost, Time, Riskfree, Volatility, Dividend)

39. Black-Scholes Put Option with Dividends

This is the European put calculated using the Generalized Black-Scholes model, with a dividend stream in percent, and exercisable only at expiration.

Function: ROBlackScholesDividendPut(Asset, Cost, Time, Riskfree, Volatility, Dividend)

40. Black-Scholes Put Option with No Dividends

This is the European put calculated using the Black-Scholes model, with no dividend payments, and is exercisable only at expiration.

Function: ROBlackScholesPut(Asset, Cost, Time, Riskfree, Volatility)

41. Complex Chooser Option

This is the European complex chooser option exercisable only at expiration. This option gives the option holder the right to choose between a call or put at different times with different strike prices. The same expiration date applies to both puts and calls.

Function: ROComplexChooser(Asset, Call Cost, Put Cost, Chooser Time, Call End Time, Put End Time, Riskfree, Carrying Cost, Volatility)

42. Compound Call-on-Call Option

This is the European Compound option exercisable only at expiration, where the value of the option depends on another underlying option. This is the continuous counterpart of the Binomial Sequential Compound Option.

Function: ROCompoundCallonCall(Asset, Underlying Cost 1, Option Cost 2, Option Time 1, Underlying Time 2, Riskfree, Carry, Volatility)

43. Compound Put-on-Call Option

This is the European Compound option exercisable only at expiration, where the value of the option depends on another underlying option. This is the continuous counterpart of the Binomial Sequential Compound Option.

Function: ROCompoundPutonCall(Asset, Underlying Cost 1, Option Cost 2, Option Time 1, Underlying Time 2, Riskfree, Carry, Volatility)

44. Simple Sequential Compound Option Using the Binomial (Super Lattice) Approach

This is the American Compound option exercisable at any time up to expiration, where the value of the option depends on a series of up to 10 other options, occurring in sequence. Each option phase has its own implementation cost occurring at different times.

Function: ROCorrSeqCompound(Asset, Cost1...Cost11, Time1... Time11, Riskfree, Volatility, Dividends, Steps)

45. Customized Complex Sequential Compound Option Using the Binomial (Super Lattice) Approach

This is the Customized American sequential phased compound option exercisable at any time up to expiration, where the value of the option depends on a series of up to four other phases, occurring in sequence. Each option phase has its own asset value, volatility, implementation cost, and different implementation times. In addition, at any phase, there is an option to execute the expanded phase, abandon, or contract. Please note that this function is not available in the Equation Wizard due to limitations in Excel but is available by directly entering into Excel the function and its associated values.

Function: ROCustomLattice(Asset, Cost1...Cost4, Time1... Time4, Riskfree, Volatility, Dividends, Steps, ExpansionPhase1, ExpansionPhase2, ExpansionPhase3, ExpansionPhase4, AbandonvaluePhase1, AbandonvaluePhase2, AbandonvaluePhase3, AbandonvaluePhase4, ContractionPhase1, ContractionPhase2, ContractionPhase3, ContractionPhase4, SavingsPhase1, SavingsPhase2, SavingsPhase3, SavingsPhase4)

46. Double Barrier Option: Up-and-In, Down-and-In Call Option

This is the European double barrier call option that becomes activated and in-the-money when the asset value crosses above the upper barrier or below the lower barrier, and is exercisable only at expiration.

Function: RODoubleBarrierUIDICall(Asset, Cost, Lower Barrier, Upper Barrier, Time, Riskfree, Carrying Cost, Volatility)

47. Double Barrier Option: Up-and-In, Down-and-In Put Option

This is the European double barrier put option that becomes activated and in-the-money when the asset value crosses above the upper barrier or below the lower barrier, and is exercisable only at expiration.

Function: RODoubleBarrierUIDIPut(Asset, Cost, Lower Barrier, Upper Barrier, Time, Riskfree, Carrying Cost, Volatility)

48. Double Barrier Option: Up-and-Out, Down-and-Out Call Option

This is the European double barrier call option that becomes in-the-money and activated when the asset value does not breach the upper barrier or cross below the lower barrier, and is exercisable only at expiration.

Function: RODoubleBarrierUODOCall(Asset, Cost, Lower Barrier, Upper Barrier, Time, Riskfree, Carrying Cost, Volatility)

49. Double Barrier Option: Up-and-Out, Down-and-Out Put Option

This is the European double barrier put option that becomes in-the-money and activated when the asset value does not breach the upper barrier or cross below the lower barrier, and is exercisable only at expiration.

Function: RODoubleBarrierUODOPut(Asset, Cost, Lower Barrier, Upper Barrier, Time, Riskfree, Carrying Cost, Volatility)

50. Forward Start Call Option

This is the European call option that starts only sometime in the future, and is exercisable only at expiration.

Function: ROForwardStartCall(Asset, Alpha, T1, Time, Riskfree, Carrying Cost, Volatility)

51. Forward Start Put Option

This is the European put option that starts only sometime in the future, and is exercisable only at expiration.

Function: ROForwardStartPut(Asset, Alpha, T1, Time, Riskfree, Carrying Cost, Volatility)

52. Futures Call Option

This is the European call option that depends on an underlying asset that resembles a futures contract, and is exercisable only at expiration.

Function: ROFuturesCall(Futures, Cost, Time, Riskfree, Volatility)

53. Futures Put Option

This is the European put option that depends on an underlying asset that resembles a futures contract, and is exercisable only at expiration.

Function: ROFuturesPut(Futures, Cost, Time, Riskfree, Volatility)

54. Standard-Normal Cumulative Distribution

This is the standard-normal cumulative distribution of a Z-value, based on a normal distribution with a mean of zero and variance of one.

Function: ROPhiDist(Z)

55. Multiple Volatility Option Analysis

This is the American option applying different volatilities at different times.

Function: ROMultiVolatility = oRo.ROMultiVolatility(Asset, Cost, Time, Riskfree, Volatility, Dividends, Steps, Volatility2, TimeStep2, Volatility3, TimeStep3, Volatility4, TimeStep4, Volatility5, TimeStep5)

56. Standard Bivariate-Normal Cumulative Distribution

This is the standard Bivariate-Normal cumulative distribution of two correlated variables.

Function: ROOmegaDist(Variable 1, Variable 2, Correlation)

57. Stochastic Option Flexibility Parameter

This is the Flexibility Parameter calculated using stochastic methodologies, where the optimal exercise price is obtained by multiplying this parameter by the option's implementation cost.

Function: ROStochasticFlexibility(InterestRate, OpportunityCost, Volatility)

58. Stochastic Option Value

This is the stochastic valuation of an option based on its asset value, implementation cost, volatility, interest rate, and opportunity cost.

Function: ROStochasticOptionValue (InterestRate, OpportunityCost, Volatility, ImplementationCost, AssetValue)

59. Switching Option

This is the European switching option valuing two exchangeable assets, each with its own risk structure or volatility, but that at the same time may be correlated to each other. There is a cost associated with switching, which is the cost multipler multiplied by the value of the first asset.

Function: ROSwitching(Asset1, Asset2, Volatility1, Volatility2, Correlation, CostMultiplier, Time, Riskfree)

60. Stochastic Timing Option—Option Value

This is the value of the timing option assuming the execution of the option falls exactly on the optimal time to execute.

Function: ROTimingOption(Revenue, OperatingExpenses, ImplementationCost, Time, GrowthRate, DiscountRate)

61. Stochastic Timing Option—Optimal Timing

This model provides the optimal time to executing an option given a growth rate in the asset value and a discount rate.

Function: ROTimingTime(Revenue, OperatingExpenses, ImplementationCost, GrowthRate, DiscountRate)

62. Stochastic Timing Option—Trigger Value

This is the optimal trigger value on a timing option, where if the net value of the asset exceeds this trigger, it is optimal to exercise the option immediately.

Function: ROTimingTrigger(ImplementationCost, GrowthRate, DiscountRate)

63. Two Asset Correlation Call Option

This is the European call option exercisable only at expiration, where the value of the option depends on two correlated underlying assets.

Function: ROTwoAssetCorrelationCall(Asset1, Asset2, Cost1, Cost2, Time, Dividend1, Dividend2, Riskfree, Vol1, Vol2, Correlation)

64. Two Asset Correlation Put Option

This is the European put option exercisable only at expiration, where the value of the option depends on two correlated underlying assets.

Function: ROTwoAssetCorrelationPut(Asset1, Asset2, Cost1, Cost2, Time, Dividend1, Dividend2, Riskfree, Vol1, Vol2, Correlation)

65. Call Sensitivity on Asset

This is the instantaneous sensitivity on asset value—that is, the change in option value given a unit change in asset value.

Function: ROSensitivityAsset(Asset, Cost, Time, Riskfree, Dividend, Volatility)

66. Call Sensitivity on Cost

This is the instantaneous sensitivity on cost—that is, the change in option value given a unit change in cost.

Function: ROSensitivityCost(Asset, Cost, Time, Riskfree, Dividend, Volatility)

67. Call Sensitivity on Risk-Free

This is the instantaneous sensitivity on risk-free rate—that is, the change in option value given a unit change in risk-free rate.

Function: ROSensitivityRiskfree(Asset, Cost, Time, Riskfree, Dividend, Volatility)

68. Call Sensitivity on Time

This is the instantaneous sensitivity on time—that is, the change in option value given a unit change in time.

Function: ROSensitivityTime(Asset, Cost, Time, Riskfree, Dividend, Volatility)

69. Call Sensitivity on Volatility

This is the instantaneous sensitivity on volatility—that is, the change in option value given a unit change in volatility.

Function: ROSensitivityVolatility(Asset, Cost, Time, Riskfree, Dividend, Volatility)

Getting Started with Crystal Ball® Monte Carlo Simulation

This appendix serves as a guide to getting started with Crystal Ball's® Monte Carlo simulation software provided in the enclosed CD-ROM. To begin using your sample simulation software, run the *setup.exe* file in the Crystal Ball® simulation folder in the CD-ROM. Follow the online instructions. Once installation is complete, restart the computer and open Excel. The Crystal Ball® splash screen should appear momentarily, and the icon bar in Figure 9B.1 should appear in Microsoft Excel®.

To get started and to run a simple simulation, we are only concerned with three functions: *Assign Assumption, Assign Forecast,* and *Run Simulation.* Every Monte Carlo simulation analysis requires a minimum of these three sets of commands. If the toolbar does not appear, click on *Tools* and select *Add-Ins.* Then make sure the check-box beside *Crystal Ball®* is selected, and hit *OK.* Assigning an assumption means selecting a cell in Excel populated with a simple numerical entry and assigning a relevant distribution to it. Assigning a forecast means to select a cell with a numerical equation and requesting Crystal Ball® to capture its output results. Running a simulation means the program initiates a Monte Carlo simulation of several thousand trials, randomly selecting numbers from the assigned distribution and inputting these random numbers into the selected assumption cell. The resulting calculations in the forecast cell are then captured in the software.

Assign Forecast

Assign Assumption   *Run Simulation*

FIGURE 9B.1   Icon Bar on Crystal Ball®

A simple example is in order here. Open the file *Simulation* from the *Examples* folder in the *Real Options Analysis Toolkit* menu item in the *Crystal Ball* folder from the *Start* taskbar. The Excel file looks like Figure 9B.2.

The Excel file opened is a simple discounted cash flow model that provides a single-point estimate of net present value. Suppose that the user wishes to simulate the discount rate on cash flow and each of the revenue estimates, as they have been previously determined to be stochastic and uncertain. In order to simulate the model, select cell D9 for the discount rate. Click on the *Assign Assumption* icon, and the assumption dialog appears, as shown in Figure 9B.3.

A set of different distributions appears in the *Distribution Gallery*. For help in choosing the correct distribution, click on Help, visit the online Tutorial included in the software, or revisit Appendix 5B for a detailed listing of different distributional assumptions. For illustration, choose the *Normal Distribution*. The dialog box in Figure 9B.4 appears.

Here, the user can input the appropriate distributional parameters—in this case, the mean and standard deviation of the normal distribution. Suppose the user does not know the relevant distributional parameters. If that is the case, a distributional fitting function can be executed. This *Fit* function is located on the distribution gallery shown in Figure 9B.3. Otherwise, enter 15 percent as the mean and 5.17 percent as the standard deviation. In addition, the user can click on the *Parms* button to obtain the *alternate parameters* input box. *See* Figure 9B.5. Select *5%, 95% - tile.*

Sample Simulation for Discounted Cash Flow

	A	C	D	E	F	G	H
Key Inputs							
9		Discount Rate (Cash Flow)	15.00%		Present Value (Cash Flow)		$328.24
10		Discount Rate (Impl. Cost)	5.00%		Present Value (Impl. Cost)		$189.58
11		Tax Rate	10.00%		Net Present Value		$138.67

		2002	2003	2004	2005	2006
18	Revenue	$100	$200	$300	$400	$500
22	Cost of Revenue	$40	$80	$120	$160	$200
26	Gross Profit	$60	$120	$180	$240	$300
27	Operating Expenses	$22	$44	$66	$88	$110
31	Depreciation Expense	$5	$5	$5	$5	$5
35	Interest Expense	$3	$3	$3	$3	$3
39	Income Before Taxes	$30	$68	$106	$144	$182
40	Taxes	$3	$7	$11	$14	$18
41	Income After Taxes	$27	$61	$95	$130	$164
42	Non-Cash Expenses	$12	$12	$12	$12	$12
46	Cash Flow	$39	$73	$107	$142	$176
48	Implementation Cost	$25	$25	$50	$50	$75

FIGURE 9B.2   Sample Simulation DCF without Colors

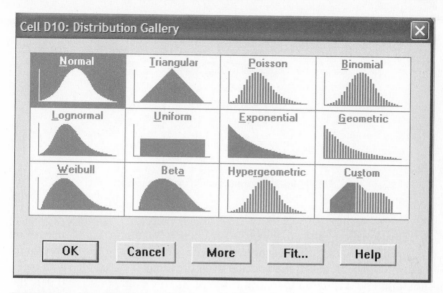

FIGURE 9B.3   Distribution Gallery

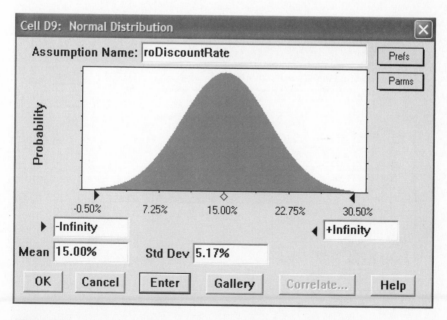

FIGURE 9B.4   Discount Rate Using Mean and Standard Deviation

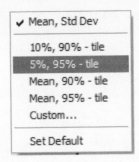

FIGURE 9B.5   Parameter Drop-Down Box

This function calls up alternate parameters for input. *See* Figure 9B.6.

In this case, the 5th percentile and the 95th percentile are the required inputs. Management can then decide what the range of actual discount rates should fall between 90 percent of the time. In our example, the 90 percent confidence interval is between 6.5% and 23.5%. Hit *OK* to continue.

Next, select cell D18 for year 2002's revenue value and click on the *Assign Distribution* icon. This time, select *Uniform Distribution* in the *Distribution Gallery*. Enter 90 for the minimum and 110 for the maximum, and click on *OK* to continue. This implies that the revenue in year 2002 can

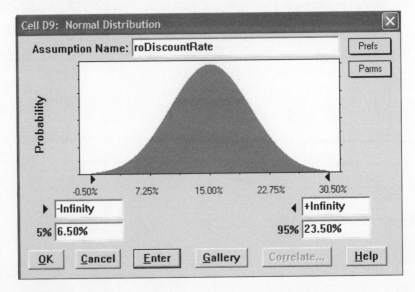

FIGURE 9B.6   Discount Rate Using 5 Percent and 95 Percent

fluctuate randomly between $90 and $110 with equal probability. Continue this procedure with these revenue figures:

Year 2003	Min = 180	Max = 220
Year 2004	Min = 270	Max = 330
Year 2005	Min = 360	Max = 440
Year 2006	Min = 450	Max = 550

Now that the assumptions have been defined, select cell H11 for the net present value. Notice that the cell has an equation for net present value associated with it, a requirement for assigning a forecast. Then click on the *Assign Forecast* icon and click on *OK* to continue. The Excel sheet should now look like Figure 9B.7.

Notice that on-screen the assumption cells have been colored green and the forecast cell has been colored blue, for easy recognition. The simulation is now ready to be run. Crystal Ball® automatically sets the number of trials at 1,000. The number of trials can be changed by clicking on the *Run* menu, selecting *Run Preferences,* and changing the number of trials. For now, keep the 1,000 trials for this exercise. Click the *Run* icon on the toolbar to start the Monte Carlo simulation routine. The Excel sheet now comes to life, and numbers will change on the screen.

Sample Simulation for Discounted Cash Flow					

Key Inputs

		Summary	
Discount Rate (Cash Flow)	15.00%	Present Value (Cash Flow)	$328.24
Discount Rate (Impl. Cost)	5.00%	Present Value (Impl. Cost)	$189.58
Tax Rate	10.00%	Net Present Value	$138.67

	2002	2003	2004	2005	2006
Revenue	$100	$200	$300	$400	$500
Cost of Revenue	$40	$80	$120	$160	$200
Gross Profit	$60	$120	$180	$240	$300
Operating Expenses	$22	$44	$66	$88	$110
Depreciation Expense	$5	$5	$5	$5	$5
Interest Expense	$3	$3	$3	$3	$3
Income Before Taxes	$30	$68	$106	$144	$182
Taxes	$3	$7	$11	$14	$18
Income After Taxes	$27	$61	$95	$130	$164
Non-Cash Expenses	$12	$12	$12	$12	$12
Cash Flow	$39	$73	$107	$142	$176
Implementation Cost	$25	$25	$50	$50	$75

FIGURE 9B.7 Sample Simulation DCF

At the conclusion of the simulation run, the forecast screen shown in Figure 9B.8 appears. This is the resulting net present value based on simulating the model 1,000 times. The net present value's 90 percent confidence interval is between $70.85 and $234.70. That is, based on all the input assumptions, 90 percent of the time, the actual net present value will fall between these values. In addition, the 5 percent worst-case scenario can be interpreted as $70.85. The user can type in a certainty value, press enter, and obtain another confidence interval. In addition, the black triangles straddling the X-axis can also be dragged around, to obtain the corresponding probabilities of occurrence based on the net present value selected.

Another view that may be of interest is the forecast statistics screen. Press the space bar once on the keyboard to access the forecast statistics screen. This view provides the user with the basic statistics of the forecast net present value, as seen in Figure 9B.9.

This is only a simple getting started guide for using Crystal Ball's® Monte Carlo simulation software. For more information and example files on running Monte Carlo simulation, click on the *Start* button in Microsoft Windows®, select *Programs,* and select *Crystal Ball®.* Here, help files and example Excel simulation models are available for use. Remember that the simulation software is a 30-day trial version. It will not run if you have a previous version of Crystal Ball®. Visit the Crystal Ball® Web site at *www.decisioneering.com* for additional technical information.

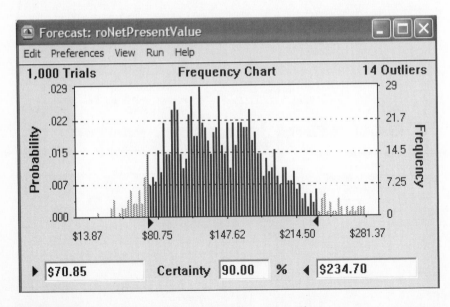

FIGURE 9B.8 Forecast Net Present Value Frequency Chart

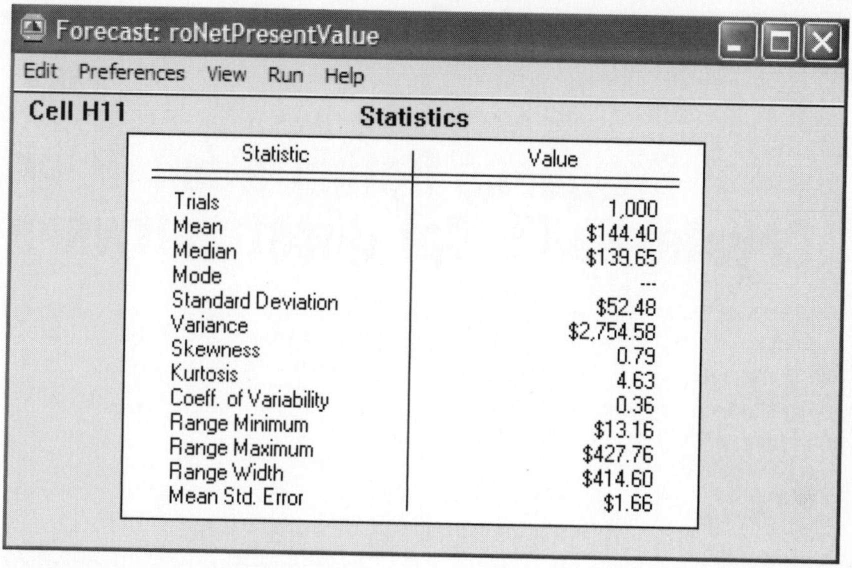

Cell H11	Statistics

Statistic	Value
Trials	1,000
Mean	$144.40
Median	$139.65
Mode	...
Standard Deviation	$52.48
Variance	$2,754.58
Skewness	0.79
Kurtosis	4.63
Coeff. of Variability	0.36
Range Minimum	$13.16
Range Maximum	$427.76
Range Width	$414.60
Mean Std. Error	$1.66

FIGURE 9B.9 Forecast Net Present Value

Resource Optimization Using Crystal Ball's® Opt-Quest Software

Figure 9C.1 illustrates a sample model on resource portfolio optimization on four projects. For each project, a set of forecast cash flows is obtained and simulated. The highlighted cells (first-year revenues and revenue growth rates) indicate where Monte Carlo simulation is performed. The analysis results include a set of financial metrics, including the net present value (NPV), internal rate of return (IRR), and so forth.

Each project has these sets of identical metrics. In addition, the portfolio assumptions are seen at the bottom of the figure. The total portfolio NPV of $286 is calculated using a weighted average of returns on the portfolio: $R_P = \omega_A R_A + \omega_B R_B + \omega_C R_C + \omega_D R_D$, where R_P is the return on the portfolio, $R_{A,B,C,D}$ are the individual returns on the projects, and $\omega_{A,B,C,D}$ are the respective weights or capital allocation across each project. In addition, the value 938 is the portfolio level risk coefficient (σ_P), where we define the portfolio risk coefficient as

$$\sigma_P = \sqrt{\sum_{i=1}^{i} \omega_i^2 \sigma_i^2 + \sum_{i=1}^{n} \sum_{j=1}^{m} 2\omega_i \omega_j \rho_{i,j} \sigma_i \sigma_j}.$$

Here, $\rho_{A,B,C,D}$ are the respective cross-correlations. Hence, if the cross-correlations are negative, there are risk diversification effects, and the portfolio risk decreases.

Before optimization can be performed, simulation assumptions, decision variables, and forecast variables first have to be assigned. Assign the simulation assumptions and forecast variables the same way as discussed in Appendix 9B. A predefined spreadsheet is available in the CD-ROM for your use and to follow along with this example.[1] To access this example, click on *Start*, then select *Crystal Ball, Real Options Analysis Toolkit, Examples*, and *Resource Optimization*.

Project A

		2001	2002	2003	2004	2005		
Revenues		$1,200	$1,320	$1,465	$1,644	$1,869	NPV	$585
Opex/Revenue Multiple		0.10	0.15	0.20	0.22	0.25	IRR	48.04%
Operating Expenses		$120	$198	$293	$362	$467	Risk Adjusted Discount Rate	12.00%
EBITDA		$1,080	$1,122	$1,172	$1,282	$1,402	Growth Rate	3.00%
FCF/EBITDA Multiple		0.19	0.20	0.23	0.25	0.30	Terminal Value	$4,814
Free Cash Flows	($450)	$205	$224	$270	$321	$421	Terminal Risk Adjustment	30.00%
Initial Investment	($450)						Discounted Terminal Value	$1,296
							Terminal to NPV Ratio	2.21
Revenue Growth Rates		10.00%	11.00%	12.21%	13.70%	15.58%	Payback Period	2.08

Project B

		2001	2002	2003	2004	2005		
Revenues		$1,200	$1,350	$1,700	$1,900	$2,050	NPV	$502
Opex/Revenue Multiple		0.10	0.15	0.20	0.22	0.25	IRR	59.16%
Operating Expenses		$120	$203	$340	$418	$513	Risk Adjusted Discount Rate	19.00%
EBITDA		$1,080	$1,148	$1,360	$1,482	$1,538	Growth Rate	3.75%
FCF/EBITDA Multiple		0.19	0.20	0.23	0.25	0.30	Terminal Value	$3,138
Free Cash Flows	($400)	$205	$230	$313	$371	$461	Terminal Risk Adjustment	30.00%
Initial Investment	($400)						Discounted Terminal Value	$845
							Terminal to NPV Ratio	1.68
Revenue Growth Rates		17.00%	19.89%	23.85%	29.53%	38.25%	Payback Period	1.85

Project C

		2001	2002	2003	2004	2005		
Revenues		$1,200	$1,350	$1,700	$1,900	$2,050	NPV	$260
Opex/Revenue Multiple		0.10	0.15	0.20	0.22	0.25	IRR	26.34%
Operating Expenses		$120	$203	$340	$418	$513	Risk Adjusted Discount Rate	15.00%
EBITDA		$1,080	$1,148	$1,360	$1,482	$1,538	Growth Rate	5.50%
FCF/EBITDA Multiple		0.19	0.20	0.23	0.25	0.30	Terminal Value	$5,122
Free Cash Flows	($750)	$205	$230	$313	$371	$461	Terminal Risk Adjustment	30.00%
Initial Investment	($750)						Discounted Terminal Value	$1,380
							Terminal to NPV Ratio	5.31
Revenue Growth Rates		12.50%	14.06%	16.04%	18.61%	22.08%	Payback Period	3.01

Project D

		2001	2002	2003	2004	2005		
Revenues		$1,200	$1,350	$1,700	$1,900	$2,050	NPV	$25
Opex/Revenue Multiple		0.10	0.15	0.20	0.22	0.25	IRR	21.17%
Operating Expenses		$120	$203	$340	$418	$513	Risk Adjusted Discount Rate	20.00%
EBITDA		$1,080	$1,148	$1,360	$1,482	$1,538	Growth Rate	1.50%
FCF/EBITDA Multiple		0.19	0.20	0.23	0.25	0.30	Terminal Value	$2,531
Free Cash Flows	($850)	$205	$230	$313	$371	$461	Terminal Risk Adjustment	30.00%
Initial Investment	($850)						Discounted Terminal Value	$682
							Terminal to NPV Ratio	26.80
Revenue Growth Rates		10.67%	11.80%	13.20%	14.94%	17.17%	Payback Period	3.28

	Implementation Cost	Net Present Value	Weight	Project Cost	Project NPV	Risk
Project A	$450	$488	25.00%	$300	$122	65.4227%
Project B	$400	$419	25.00%	$0	$105	11.6459%
Project C	$750	$216	25.00%	$30	$54	38.1816%
Project D	$850	$21	25.00%	$270	$5	123.7306%
Total	$2,450	$1,144	100.00%	$600	$286	30.4866%
						938.14361

Correlation Matrix	B	C	D
A	0.2	0.4	-0.4
B		0.56	0.12
C			-0.2

FIGURE 9C.1   Optimization Example

The weights assigned to each project are the decision variables. That is, select the project weights and click on the assign decision variable icon in Crystal Ball®. The assign decision variable icon is between the assign assumption and assign forecast icons. The dialog box in Figure 9C.2 appears. Input the relevant name for the decision and any minimum or maximum constraints on this particular weight (for instance, no individual project may exceed 50 percent of the total portfolio budget).

Notice that this optimization process assumes a continuous allocation, which means that given the budget constraint, the proportion of budget can be allocated as a percentage of the whole budget. In contrast, the project analysis can be assumed to be discrete, which means that each project is either a "go" or "no-go." *See* Figure 9C.3. That is, the optimal portfolio project selection that maximizes returns and minimizes risks subject to the constraints can be A only; B only; C only; D only; A and B; A and C; A and D; B and

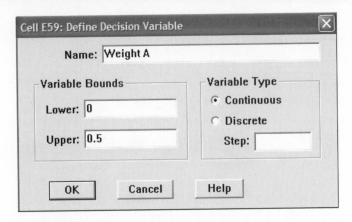

FIGURE 9C.2 Defining Decision Variables Using Continuous Optimization Steps

FIGURE 9C.3 Defining Decision Variables Using Discrete Optimization Steps

C; A, B, and C only; and so forth. For now, assume a continuous allocation example.

Then, in Microsoft Excel, click on *CB Tools,* and select *OptQuest,* and click on the new project icon. The screen in Figure 9C.4 comes up.

The upper and lower bounds may now be changed if necessary. Click on *Next* to continue. On the next screen, shown in Figure 9C.5, click on *Sum All Variables,* and set it equal to one before continuing. This forces the budget weight allocations to sum to 100 percent.

In the following step, select *Maximize Objective* with respect to the *Final Value,* for the Sharpe Ratio. *See* Figure 9C.6. The Sharpe Ratio is simply the

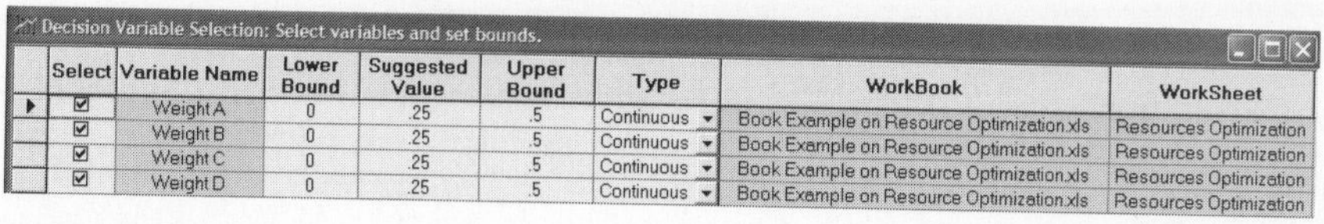

	Select	Variable Name	Lower Bound	Suggested Value	Upper Bound	Type	WorkBook	WorkSheet
▶	☑	Weight A	0	.25	.5	Continuous ▾	Book Example on Resource Optimization.xls	Resources Optimization
	☑	Weight B	0	.25	.5	Continuous ▾	Book Example on Resource Optimization.xls	Resources Optimization
	☑	Weight C	0	.25	.5	Continuous ▾	Book Example on Resource Optimization.xls	Resources Optimization
	☑	Weight D	0	.25	.5	Continuous ▾	Book Example on Resource Optimization.xls	Resources Optimization

FIGURE 9C.4   Decision Variables in Optimization

Weight A + Weight B + Weight C + Weight D = 1

Variables
Sum All Variables
Weight A

FIGURE 9C.5   Sum-of-Weights-Equals-One Constraint

ratio of portfolio NPV to portfolio risk. Because projects should not be chosen on the basis of maximum return or minimum risk alone, the Sharpe Ratio is often used for portfolio optimization to obtain the efficient frontier of project portfolio allocation, where the maximum return is obtained with the combination of the minimum risk, subject to any constraints. In addition, the portfolio level returns and risks are used. The portfolio risk also accounts for any diversification effects among individual projects selected. The individual project risks used to calculate the portfolio risk come from the standard deviation of the simulated NPV results of each project.

Obviously, other criteria may be appropriate here. For instance, a budget constraint can be included. This is done in the objective screen, where instead of simply maximizing the Sharpe Ratio, an additional requirement can be added, the *Total Cost* variable. Here, the mean of the total cost after simulation can never exceed $3,250, the budget constraint. Then, click on *Next,* and begin the optimization process.

After the optimization process is complete, the results look like Figure 9C.7.

The best result based on running thousands of simulations is such that based on the optimization assumptions, the total budget should be allocated

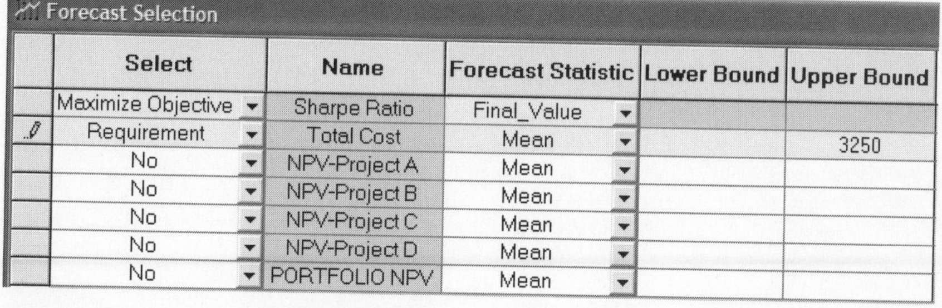

	Select	Name	Forecast Statistic	Lower Bound	Upper Bound
	Maximize Objective ▾	Sharpe Ratio	Final_Value ▾		
𝒥	Requirement ▾	Total Cost	Mean ▾		3250
	No ▾	NPV-Project A	Mean ▾		
	No ▾	NPV-Project B	Mean ▾		
	No ▾	NPV-Project C	Mean ▾		
	No ▾	NPV-Project D	Mean ▾		
	No ▾	PORTFOLIO NPV	Mean ▾		

FIGURE 9C.6   Objective Maximization

Simulation	Maximize Objective Sharpe Ratio Final_Value	Weight A	Weight B	Weight C	Weight D
2	1293.35	0.266074	0.228905	0.281255	0.223766
6	1720.72	0.274505	0.231336	0.445483	4.8676E-02
7	1737.17	0.279747	0.410679	9.4881E-02	0.214693
12	2063.04	0.239522	0.429436	0.312146	1.8896E-02
29	2428.90	5.0990E-02	0.500000	0.411360	3.7650E-02
52	2516.86	7.7840E-02	0.485352	0.404863	3.1944E-02
Best: 76	2610.81	2.7735E-02	0.500000	0.423604	4.8660E-02

FIGURE 9C.7   Results on Optimization

2.8 percent to Project A, 50 percent to Project B, 42.4 percent to Project C, and 4.8 percent to Project D. This capital allocation ensures that the maximum return is obtained, with minimum amount of risk, subject to satisfying the budget constraint.

Results Interpretation and Presentation

INTRODUCTION

Now that you've done some fancy real options analytics, the difficult part comes next: explaining the results to management. It would seem that getting the right results was half the battle. Explaining the results in such a convincing way that management will buy into your recommendations is another story altogether. This chapter introduces some novel approaches to presenting your real options results in a clear and convincing manner, converting black box analytics into nothing more than a series of transparent steps of a logical analytical process. The chapter is arranged in a series of key points that analysts should contemplate when attempting to interpret, present, and defend their results. Each key point is discussed in detail, and examples of how to broach a particular point are also provided. These include high-powered graphics, charts, tables, and explanatory notes. The major key issues and questions that management may ask that are discussed are as follows:

1. How does real options analysis compare with traditional analysis? What are some of the key characteristics? What one-liner can you use to convince management that real options are nothing different from traditional analysis but provide increased insights and greater accuracy while taking into consideration the uncertainty of outcomes and risks of projects?

2. What are some of the steps taken in a real options analysis? What is the process flow? Does it make logical sense? Have you discarded the traditional approach and replaced it with real options? Where do the traditional analyses end and the new analytics begin?

3. At the executive summary level, can an analyst differentiate traditional results from the new analytics results? What is the relationship, and how do they compare against one another?

4. How do multiple projects compare against one another? How do you compare larger initiatives with smaller ones? What about project-specific risks?

5. Have you looked at both risk and return profiles of the projects? Which projects have the best bang-for-the-buck?

6. What is the impact to the company's bottom line?

7. What are the major critical-success-factors driving the decision?

8. What are the risks underlying the results? How confident are you of the analysis results?

9. When will the project pay for itself? What is the break-even point? How long before payback occurs?

10. How did you get the relevant discount rate for the projects? What were some of the assumptions?

11. What were some of the assumptions underlying your real options analysis? Where did the assumptions come from?

12. How was your real options analysis performed? What are some of the key insights obtained through the analysis?

13. How confident are you of the real options analysis results?

This chapter discusses each of these questions in turn, with a series of examples on how to appropriately discuss and broach the issues with management.

COMPARING REAL OPTIONS ANALYSIS WITH TRADITIONAL FINANCIAL ANALYSIS

We begin by discussing the comparison between the real options process and traditional financial analysis. Senior management is always skeptical about using new, fancy analytics when old methods have served them so well in the past. It would seem that the main approach to alleviate management's concerns is to show that the real options methodology is not that far off— in principle, at least—from the conventions of traditional financial analysis. As a matter of fact, traditional discounted cash flow analysis can be seen as a special case of real options analysis when there is negligible uncertainty. That is, when the underlying asset's volatility approaches zero, the real options value approaches zero, and the value of the project is exactly as defined in a discounted cash flow model. It is only when uncertainty exists, and management has the flexibility to defer making mid-course corrections until uncertainty becomes resolved through time, that a project has option value.

Change-management specialists have found that there are several criteria to be met before a paradigm shift in thinking is found to be acceptable in a corporation. For example, in order for senior management to accept a new and novel set of analytical approaches, the models and processes themselves must have applicability to the problem at hand, and not be merely an academic exercise. As we have seen previously, the former is certainly true in that large multinationals have embraced the concept of real options with significant fervor, and that real options is here to stay. It is not simply an academic exercise, nor is it the latest financial analysis fad that is here today and gone tomorrow. In addition, the process and methodology has to be consistent, accurate, and replicable. That is, it passes the scientific process. Given similar assumptions, historical data, and assertions, one can replicate the results with ease and predictability. This is especially so with the use of software programs like the ones included in the CD-ROM.

Next, the new method must provide a compelling value-added proposition. Otherwise, it is nothing but a fruitless and time-consuming exercise. The time, resources, and effort expended must be met and even surpassed by the method's value-add. This is certainly the case in larger capital investment initiatives, where a firm's future or the future of a business unit may be at stake. Other major criteria include the ability to provide the user a comparative advantage over competitors, which is certainly the case when the additional valuable insights generated through real options analysis will help management identify options, value, prioritize, and select strategic alternatives that may otherwise be overlooked.

Finally, in order to accept a change in mindset, the new methodology, process, or model must be easy to explain and understand. In addition, there has to be a link to previously acceptable methods, whether it is an extension of the old or a replacement of the old due to some clear superior attributes. These last two points are the most difficult to tackle for an analyst. The sets of criteria prior to this are direct and easy to define. However, how does one explain to senior management the complexities of real options and that the approach is the next best thing since sliced bread? How do real options extend the old paradigm of discounted cash flow models with which management has been brought up? An effective method that the author has found useful with clients has been to boil it down to its simplest parts. Figure 10.1 shows a simple example.

In a traditional financial analysis, the analyst usually calculates the net present value (NPV), which simply defined is benefits less cost (first equation), where benefits equal the present value of future net cash flows after taxes, discounted at some market risk-adjusted cost of capital, and cost equals the present value of investment costs discounted at the risk-free rate. Management is usually knowledgeable of NPV and the way it is calculated. Conventional wisdom is such that if benefits outweigh costs, that is, when NPV is positive, one would be inclined to accept a particular project. This is simple and intuitive enough. However, when we turn to options theory, the call option is also nothing but benefits less cost (second equation) with a slight

$$NPV = Benefits - Cost$$
$$Option = Benefits\ \Phi(d_1) - Cost\ \Phi(d_2)$$
$$eNPV = NPV + Options\ Value$$

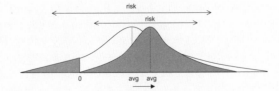

FIGURE 10.1   Enhanced Return with Risk Reduction

modification. The difference is the introduction of a *Φ(d)* multiplier behind benefits and costs. Obviously, the multipliers are nothing but the respective probabilities of occurrence.

Hence, in real options theory, one can very simply define the value of an option as nothing but benefits less costs, taking into account the risk or probabilities of occurrence for each variable. It is easy to understand that option value in this case is far superior to the NPV analysis because it provides an added element of stochastic variability around benefits and costs. It is hubris to say that we know for certain (on a deterministic level) what future benefits and costs will be, when in reality, business conditions change daily. In addition, we can say that the expanded net present value (eNPV), shown as equation three in Figure 10.1, is the sum of the deterministic base-case NPV and the strategic flexibility option value. The option value takes into account the value of flexibility, that is, the option to execute on a strategic option but not the obligation to do so. The eNPV accounts for both base-case analysis plus the added value of managerial flexibility. If there is negligible uncertainty, volatility approaches zero, which means that the probability multiplier approaches one (outcomes are certain). The options equation reverts back to the NPV equation, indicating that the NPV analysis is a special case of an options analysis when there is no uncertainty.

Finally, the two graphs in Figure 10.1 tell a compelling story of why real options provide an important insight into decision analysis. The first graph in the background shows the distribution of the base-case NPV analysis. That is, the first moment or the mean, median, and mode of the graph show the central tendency location of the most likely occurrence of a project's value. Some analysts will call this the expected value of the project. The second moments or the standard deviation, width, variance, and range of the distribution tell of the risk of the project. That is, a wider distribution implies a higher risk because there is a wider range of outcomes the project value may fall between. Clearly, the graph in the foreground shows a much smaller risk structure but a higher average return, which is attributable to real options analysis. We know from many previous illustrations that employing a real options strategy—for example, the passive and active options to wait—will create a higher value because we are hedging project risks by not betting the entire investment outlay now but instead waiting until we get a better idea of the uncertainty that exists over time. Once uncertainty becomes resolved, we can act accordingly. This delaying action helps hedge our losses and thus truncates the distribution in terms of width and moves it to the right because management will never execute a bad strategy assuming they know what will happen if they do. This moves the entire distribution to the right and at the same time reduces the risk, as seen through a reduction in width. Thus, real options, just like its cousins the financial options, help the holder of the option to hedge project risk (lower second moment) while increasing its financial returns leverage (higher first moment).

THE EVALUATION PROCESS

The next issue an analyst should discuss with management pertaining to real options analysis is the steps taken to obtain the results—in other words, what the process flow looks like, how it makes logical sense, and where the traditional analysis ends and the new analytics take over. A thorough understanding of the process flow will make management more comfortable in accepting the results of the analysis. A career-limiting or a high-potential career-ending move is to show management a series of complicated stochastic differential Ito calculus equations, crunch out a number, and then ask the CEO to bet the company's future on it. How can management buy in on an analysis if the analyst can't even explain the process flow properly? Figure 10.2 shows a visual representation of the process flow for a robust real options analysis process.

In the first step, the analyst starts off with a list of qualified projects, that is, projects that have been through qualitative screening by management. Having met preset criteria, whether they be strategic visions or goals of the company, these are the projects that need to be analyzed. They may of course be different courses of actions, initiatives, or strategies. For each of these strategies or projects, the base-case NPV analysis is performed, as indicated in step two. This could be done in terms of the market, income, or cost approach, using something akin to a discounted cash flow model, as seen in the third step. In certain circumstances, the analyst may elect to perform some intermediate calculation like time-series forecasting and simulation to predict future revenue and cost streams. Depending on the availability of historical data, some fancy econometric, forecasting, regression, time-series, cross-sectional, or stochastic model may be constructed for this

1. List of projects and strategies

A
B
C
D
E

We start with a list of projects or strategies to be evaluated...

2. Base Case NPV Analysis for each project

Time Series Forecasting

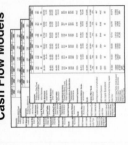

...with the assistance of time series forecasting...

3. Static Discounted Cash Flow Models

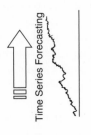

...the user generates a traditional series of static discounted cash flow models for each project...

4. DCF Outputs as Real Options Inputs

Volatility and Correlations are imputed

Simulation
Lognormal

...Monte Carlo simulation is added to the analysis and the DCF outputs become inputs into the real options analysis...

5. The type of option(s) analytics is chosen

Real Options Selection

...the next step is to frame the problem in terms of a real options structure, and to choose the relevant options for analysis

6. Options analytics, simulation and optimization

Simulation   Binomial Lattices

Closed Form Models

$$\frac{1}{2}\delta t^2 + \varepsilon\sigma\sqrt{\delta t}$$

...options results are calculated through binomial lattices and closed form partial differential models with simulation... in some circumstances, portfolio resource optimization and allocation are performed...

7. Reports presentation

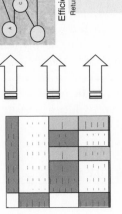

Project Selection   Critical Success Drivers

Return

Risk

Efficient Portfolio Allocation

Return

CE AB

AE D

Risk

...then, the analyst compiles the results and generates analysis reports...

...powerful reports and graphics that get to the point are generated... and the analysis is updated over time...

FIGURE 10.2   Real Options Process Summary

purpose. These three steps encapsulate the traditional approach. Using the revenues and cost structures coupled with conventional accounting procedures, the analyst would calculate the net present value of the projects or strategies. Occasionally, other financial metrics may be used, such as an internal rate of return (IRR) or some form of return on investment (ROI) measure. In most cases, a decision will be made based on these deterministic results.

In more advanced financial analysis, specifically, a recommended step for the real options approach is the application of Monte Carlo simulation. Based on some sensitivity analysis, the analyst decides which input variables to the discounted cash flow model previously constructed are most vulnerable to risks and sudden exogenous and systemic shocks. Using historical data, the analyst can take the time-series or cross-sectional data and fit them to a multitude of different distributions. The analyst may also opt to use management assumptions, hunches, experience, or economic behaviors of variables to make the distributional determination. The discounted cash flow model is then simulated. The result is a distribution of the variable of interest, for example, the net present value. Instead of obtaining single-point estimates, the analyst now has a probability distribution of outcomes, indicating with what probabilities certain outcomes will most likely occur. Based on this Monte Carlo simulation, certain intrinsic variables key to the real options analysis are calculated and imported into the real options analysis. These key variables that flow out of the simulation procedures include the volatility of the underlying variable, typically the lognormal returns on the future free cash flows; the implied cross-correlation pairs between the underlying projects; and the expected present value of cash flows.

The fifth and sixth steps involve framing the problem in terms of a real options paradigm. That is, having identified the optionality of the project or strategy, the analyst then chooses the relevant sets of options to analyze. Based on the types of models chosen, the calculation may then proceed automatically in different ways, whether through the use of binomial lattices, closed-form solutions, or path-dependent simulation.

The results are then presented in the seventh and last step of the analysis. The reports may include charts on sensitivity, tables of the financials, including the impact to bottom line, graphs of different risk and returns, and combinations of projects in portfolios. Here, an optional step depending on the type of analysis is the application of portfolio optimization for efficient resource allocation. Portfolio optimization incorporates the interrelationships between projects or strategies as they evolve in a portfolio. Firms usually do not have stand-alone projects; rather, firms usually have multiple projects interacting with each other. Therefore, management is usually more interested in seeing how these projects interact with each other on a rolled-up basis, that is, on a portfolio of options, projects, and strategies. In addition, management usually wants to see what the optimal mix of projects should look like, given budgetary, resource, or timing constraints. The result is usually an optimal portfolio mix plotted on an efficient frontier, where every point along this efficient frontier is an optimal mix of project combinations, depending on management's risk and return appetite. Having shown management the process and steps taken to perform the analysis as well as receiving their buy-in into viability and importance of a real options analysis, we can now proceed with the results presentation.

SUMMARY OF THE RESULTS

Figure 10.3 shows a quick and easy-to-understand executive summary of each project or strategy, allowing management to differentiate between traditional results and the new real options analytics results. It also shows the relationships among projects and how they compare with each other in terms of risk, return, and time horizon. On the right, we see the traditional analysis valuation results (NPV Phases I and II) coupled with the real options results, where together they form the expanded net present value (eNPV) pie chart. On the left, we see a set of summary projects or strategies as delineated by risk on the vertical axis, time on the horizontal axis, and returns (eNPV) as the size of the spheres. Management can very easily view all projects at a glance, with respect to their relevant risk, return, and timing.

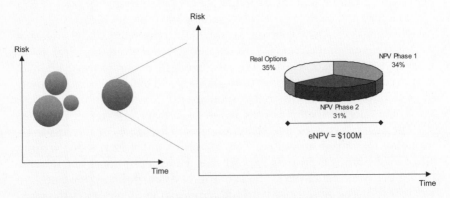

Description
This report displays the relative size of each of the project returns. The chart on the left indicates the relative positioning of the projects or strategies with respect to their risk (measured in volatility of free cash flows) and time horizon of their strategic options. The size of the circles indicates the relative dollar amount of their expanded NPV. On the right chart, the diameter of the pie chart indicates the magnitude of the expanded NPV (eNPV), which comprises the projects that make up the strategy as well as their real options strategic value. The pie chart is located on a two-dimensional axis of risk and timing.

FIGURE 10.3   Project Comparison (Risk and Return)

COMPARING ACROSS DIFFERENT-SIZED PROJECTS

Another issue to be discussed is how these multiple projects compare against one another when their relative sizes are dramatically different. That is, how do you compare a $10 million investment that provides a $20 million return to a larger $1 billion investment that returns $100 million? Should the project with the 200 percent return be chosen over the 10 percent return? Should the project returning a higher $100 million face value be chosen? What about the risks inherent in each project?

Can we create a replicating portfolio where we can spend the $1 billion investment on 100 identical $10 million projects and yield $2 billion in return as compared to only $100 million? Obviously, the answer is not a simple one. It strictly depends on whether the firm has the $1 billion budget to begin with. Not to mention that there would need to be 100 projects you can invest in, different projects with similar functions, markets, risks, and so forth. What about diversification effects across different projects? Regardless, we have shown previously in Figure 10.3 that we can depict the absolute revenue, risk, and time horizons across multiple projects. In Figure 10.4, we show the relative comparisons. That is, using some common-size ratios, we can compare across multiple different projects and strategies.

Categories		Project A	Project B	Project C
Growth	Net Revenue	15%	10%	25%
	Net Income	30%	25%	17%
	Total Assets	15%	15%	15%
Profitability	Gross Margin	75%	80%	91%
	EBITDA Margin	70%	69%	82%
	EBIT Margin	65%	60%	80%
	EBT Margin	65%	58%	73%
	Net Income	10%	15%	17%
	Effective Tax Rate	40%	40%	40%
DuPont	Net Income/Pretax Profit	40%	39%	52%
	Pretax Profit/EBIT	43%	50%	55%
	EBIT/Sales	45%	55%	50%
	Sales/Assets	3%	3%	4%
	Assets/Equity	2%	2%	2%
	ROE	12%	15%	
Liquidity	Working Capital	22%	15%	23%

Description

This report details the common size ratios for each of your projects. You can quickly view how your projects stack up against each other on a common basis. Common sized ratios provide a way to analyze and compare different financial statements.

The categories displayed include growth, DuPont, profitability, and liquidity ratios.

FIGURE 10.4 Project Comparison (Common Sizing)

COMPARING RISK AND RETURN OF MULTIPLE PROJECTS

Not only should we common-size the projects with respect to growth rates, profitability ratios, and other accounting ratios, we should also compare each project's return to its risk, that is, the proverbial bang-for-the-buck, as seen in Figure 10.5.

This return-to-risk ratio is important; otherwise, bad projects may be selected depending on management's strategic goals and risk tolerance. For example, using the same analogy presented previously, where Project X costs $10 million but provides $20 million in return and Project Y costs $1 billion but returns $100 million. Suppose Project X has a standard deviation of $10 million (we use standard deviation here as a measure of risk) while Project Y has a standard deviation of $100 million. Budget-constrained managers may choose Project X because they may have no choice. Returns-driven managers may, on the other hand, choose Project Y because it is more lucrative, assuming these managers are not resource-constrained. A risk-adverse manager may simply choose Project X due to the lower risk levels. Add a few more projects with different risk and return characteristics, and you have a conundrum on your hands.

Obviously, the best way is to calculate a standardized ratio such as the return-to-risk ratio.[1] That is, the return to risk ratio of Project X is 2.0, while Project Y has a ratio of 1.0. Clearly, Project X has the higher bang-for-the-

		Project A	Project B	Project C
Categories				
Return	Present Value of Cash Flows	$125M	$137M	$250
	Net Present Value	$75M	$73M	$100
	Expanded NPV	$200M	$210M	$350
	Internal Rate of Return	70%	80%	103%
Risk	Cash Flow Volatility	20%	34%	44%
	Simulated Value at Risk (5%)	$12M	$14M	$34M
	Simulated Value at Risk (1%)	$2M	$2M	$10M
Return to Risk	NPV/Volatility	60%	42%	61%
	ENPV/Volatility	76%	52%	77%
	VaR/ENPV	34%	23%	34%

Description

This report displays a risk and return profile for each project. The risk is measured as cash flow volatility and simulated VaR. Returns are measured as NPV, options value, ENPV (expanded NPV), IRR, and ROI. VaR, or Value at Risk, is defined as worst-case scenario losses 5% of the time. ENPV, or expanded NPV, is defined as a project s NPV and option value.

FIGURE 10.5 Project Comparison (Risk-Return Profiling)

buck. That is, for each unit of risk, Project *X* provides two units of return, but Project *Y* only provides one unit of return. Conversely, for each unit of return, Project *X* only requires half a unit of risk, while Project *Y* requires a full unit of risk. The smart manager may simply create a replicating portfolio to maximize profit and minimize risk, by spending $50 million on five identical Project *X*s returning $100 million while only being exposed to $50 million in risk. Compare that to spending $1 billion on a single Project *Y* and receiving $100 million in return while being exposed to $100 million in risk! This shows similar returns can cost less and have less risk when we take risk and return into consideration. Imagine the disastrous decision made by the first returns-driven manager who would only consider Project *Y* due to its whopping absolute return levels.

IMPACT TO BOTTOM LINE

One of the key questions that will come up is what impact a specific project will make to the company's bottom line. This can be clearly presented through the use of revenue and cost projections in a discounted cash flow model. Depending on whether management wants to see operating income before taxes or net income after taxes or free cash flows after taxes, the discounted cash flow model will do a fairly decent job. Figure 10.6 illustrates a sample discounted cash flow model summary. However, one thing that must

Discounted Cash Flow								
Line Items	2000	2001	2002	2003	2004	2005	2006	2007
Revenue	300	310	360	380	432	500	550	650
Cost of Revenue	150	150	150	130	160	150	150	60
Gross Profit	150	160	210	250	272	350	400	590
Operating Expenses	200	160	155	129	137	90	100	160
Depreciation Expense	60	60	40	60	30	40	30	60
Interest Expense	5	7	10	5	8	5	5	5
Income Before Taxes	-115	-67	5	56	97	215	265	365
Taxes	-40.25	-23.45	1.75	19.6	33.95	75.25	92.75	127.75
Income After Taxes	-74.75	-43.55	3.25	36.4	63.05	139.75	172.25	237.25
Non-Cash Expenses	10	11	12	13	14	15	16	17
Cash Flow	-84.75	-54.55	-8.75	23.4	49.05	124.75	156.25	220.25

Description

This report displays your discounted cash flow (DCF) model. The DCF shows a summary of all key income statement line items used in generating free cash flows for the specified forecast years.

Key Assumptions

The key assumptions used to generate free cash flows include:

Discount rate	=	20%
Tax rate	=	35%
Depreciation profile	=	Straight Line

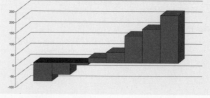

Results Summary

Sum of present value cash flows = $145M (no implementation cost)

Net present value (NPV)=$100M (with implementation cost)
Internal rate of return (IRR)=75.50% (with implementation cost)

FIGURE 10.6 Impact to Bottom Line

be made clear to management is that there is a difference between strategic option value and explicit value.

A discounted cash flow will show the explicit value of a project, assuming that the forecasted revenues and cost structures are correct, and the impact to bottom line will be the cash flow stream calculated in the model. However, strategic optionality value may or may not exist, depending on whether the option is executed. Assuming that a strategic option is left to expire without execution, there is actually zero value derived from the strategic flexibility inherent in an option.

CRITICAL SUCCESS FACTORS AND SENSITIVITY ANALYSIS

A sensitivity analysis akin to the one seen in Figure 10.7 is vital for management to understand what drives their business decisions. That is, what are some of the key critical success drivers of the projects? The sensitivity analysis could be done in several ways. The most prevalent method is simply choosing the resulting variable of interest, for example, net present value, and identifying all its precedent variables. Precedent variables include revenues, costs, taxes, and so forth, which are required to derive the final net present value result. While holding all precedent variables *ceteris paribus* or constant and unchanging, select one precedent variable, change its value by some predefined range, and gauge what happens to the net present value.

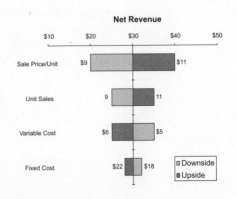

Description

This report contains a sensitivity analysis of your discounted cash flow model. The tornado chart displays each variable and the range between the variables' minimum and maximum forecast values, with the variable with the greatest range at the top.

Tornado charts are useful for measuring the sensitivity of variables that determine the free cash flows and allow you to do a quick pre-screening of the variables which drive the analysis. This analysis provides added insights into the critical success drivers in the project or strategy. In addition, it provides a list of candidates for performing Monte Carlo simulation.

Results

Based on the 10% change of the variables that drive the DCF model, the most sensitive line items in decreasing order for determining free cash flows are:

	NPV			Input		
Variable	Downside	Upside	Range	Downside	Upside	Base Case
Revenues	183.00	334.78	151.78	1.80	2.20	2.00
Tax Rate	183.29	334.46	151.17	37.80	46.20	42.00
Operating Expenses	183.29	334.46	151.17	1,350.00	1,650.00	1,500.00
Discount Factor	227.25	292.93	65.67	11.00	9.00	10.00
Depreciation	225.53	288.03	62.50	9.00	11.00	10.00

FIGURE 10.7   Critical Success Factors

The results can be tabulated and plotted into a Tornado diagram as seen in Figure 10.7, starting from the highest and most sensitive precedent variable and going to the lowest and least sensitive variable. This is a key analysis for identifying the variables upon which to perform a Monte Carlo simulation. Armed with the knowledge of which variables are the most sensitive, an analyst can decide which ones have the most variability or risk, which are then selected as prime candidates for Monte Carlo simulation.

RISK ANALYSIS AND SIMULATION ON NPV

Having performed a barrage of analyses, how confident are you of your results, and how sure are you the assumptions and data entered were correct? Because most business cases involve risks and uncertainty, there is no doubt that a margin of error exists. As we have shown in previous chapters the errors of using point estimates, as illustrated in the Flaw of Averages example, it is essential that when reporting results to management, to also present a picture of the risks involved. Typically, risk-analysis results will take the form of a Monte Carlo simulation forecast output, as shown in Figure 10.8. The graphical output is from Crystal Ball's® simulation package.

Description

This report shows the levels of risk in your discounted cash flow analysis. The probability distribution shows each value as a fraction of the total.

Results

The chart shows all possible outcomes based on Monte Carlo simulation of the input variables in the DCF. The frequency chart shows the probability at the 90% confidence level occurring between $250 and $6850.

Percentiles (description):

10% = $20	20% = $50	30% = $250	40% = $650
50% = $2300	60% = $2950	70% = $4200	80% = $5820
90% = $6520	100% = $7000		

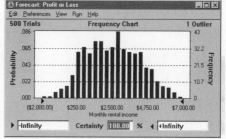

FIGURE 10.8 Project-Based Risk Analysis

BREAK-EVEN ANALYSIS AND PAYBACK PERIODS

One of the most infamous questions relating to project evaluation is the concept of payback period or break-even analysis. That is, when will the project pay for itself? As any good financial analyst knows, payback period analysis is fraught with problems. It does not account for different time horizons of projects, and the payback periods are usually based on an undiscounted cash flow basis, usually leading to wrong decisions. For example, suppose we have two projects, A and B, each costing $100. Project A will yield cash flows of $50 for only two years. Project B will yield cash flows of $49 for 10 years. Clearly Project A has a payback period of two years, while Project B has a payback period of 2.04 years. Strictly speaking, Project A should be undertaken; but although Project B yields a slightly lower cash flow, its economic life is 10 years. Net present value would have picked this up, but not a simple break-even payback analysis. Even with this said and done, management still wants to know what the payback period of a particular project is, even if it is used as a gross approximation of the value of a project.

There are ways to improve upon a break-even analysis, as shown in Figure 10.9. Instead of relying on single-point estimates—for example, instead of saying that a particular project will take 4.0 years to pay back its costs— we can add slightly more sophistication. Using discounted cash flow streams in present value terms, we can say that a project has a 5 percent probability of breaking even the first year, a 15 percent probability of breaking even the second year, a 45 percent probability of breaking even the third year, a 92 percent probability of breaking even the fourth year, and a 99 percent probability of breaking even all subsequent years. So, we are stating not only when the break-even point will occur but also how likely it will occur on a present value basis.

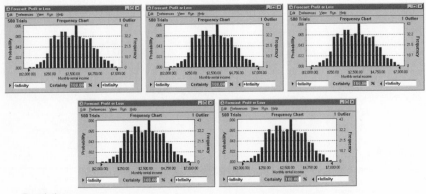

Description

This report details the probability of the project breaking even at different time periods. This analysis uses the assumption of $45M in implementation cost in present value dollars, discounted at 5.5%. The free cash flows used to calculate the payback probabilities are derived from the NPV models and discounted using 20.0%

For year 1, there is a 5.0% probability of breaking even.
For year 2, there is a 15.5% probability of breaking even.
For year 3, there is a 45.5% probability of breaking even.
For year 4, there is a 92.5% probability of breaking even.
For year 5, there is a 99.5% probability of breaking even.

FIGURE 10.9   Simulated Discounted Payback Analysis

DISCOUNT RATE ANALYSIS

One of the key assumptions in discounted cash flow analysis, which forms the basis for real options analysis, is the calculation of the discount rate. *See* Figure 10.10.

Due to the significance of the discount rate in the overall analysis, management should feel comfortable with the assumptions used. The methods of calculating discount rates abound; therefore, they should be used with due care and diligence. Even using and explaining the most widely used discount rate analysis, such as the CAPM (capital asset-pricing model) or WACC (weighted average cost of capital), it still requires significant care and caution in that the estimates are truly based on the underlying variable, which in real options are usually nontradable assets. One should not use tradable and highly liquid firm-level financial asset prices as a proxy for risk-adjustment at the project or strategy level. For instance, the beta of traded stocks for a particular firm may not be the best proxy for the beta-risk used in calculating the project-level specific risk. Rather, comparables should be used if there are insufficient historical data of the underlying variables' behavior. That is, stripped-down firms with similar functions, markets, and risks should be selected with care, and their financials should be sanitized to avoid including any anomalous nonrecurring events or any financial window-dressing

Description

This report shows the discount rate used in the analysis and its corresponding assumptions and results. The discount rate method used is **weighted average cost of capital**. This calculated rate is used for discounting future cash flows into today's present value.

Assumptions

Risk free rate = 8%

Return on the market = 6%

Equity risk premium = 7%

Beta = 1.1

Size premium = 5%

Minority premium = 10%

Corporate tax rate = 35%

Outstanding debt = 10

Return on debt = 8%

Shares outstanding = 1,458,990

Current stock price = $4.68

Results

CAPM = 14.6%

Percent debt = 30%

Percent equity = 15%

Equity capitalization = 14%

Total capitalization = 12%

WACC = 11.8%

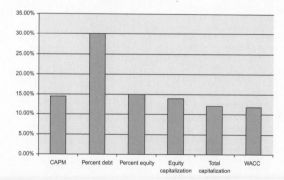

FIGURE 10.10 Discount Rate Analysis

phenomenon. If historical data abound, the analyst can then determine the firm's risk structure and calculate the risk-adjusted discount rate appropriately.

Appendix 2B's discussion on discount rates should suffice as a guide on how this is done. Nevertheless, management should be convinced of and comfortable with the results of such discount rate analyses. In most cases, the problem of finding the correct single discount rate for each project is a gruesome task, but given the capability of performing Monte Carlo simulation, the analyst can simulate the discount rate with certain management assumptions, and, with a 90 percent confidence that the proper discount rate is between two particular numbers, the resulting forecast will be more palatable to management.

REAL OPTIONS ANALYSIS ASSUMPTIONS

The next topic is real options analysis. What are the assumptions, and where do they come from? These issues should be discussed clearly and concisely. One approach is to show management something akin to Figure 10.11. It doesn't really matter if the approach you used to solve the real options was a closed-form model or stochastic differential equation. You should be able to present your results but at the same time be expositionally concise and precise. That is, you know that using a binomial lattice with many time-steps at the limit, where the time between nodes approaches zero, the value calculated approaches the value of the closed-form equations. However, it is

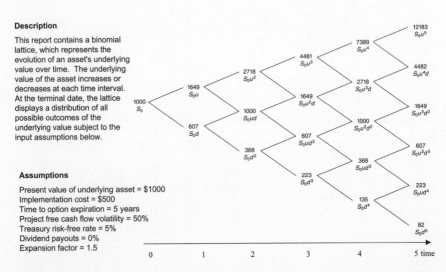

Description

This report contains a binomial lattice, which represents the evolution of an asset's underlying value over time. The underlying value of the asset increases or decreases at each time interval. At the terminal date, the lattice displays a distribution of all possible outcomes of the underlying value subject to the input assumptions below.

Assumptions

Present value of underlying asset = $1000
Implementation cost = $500
Time to option expiration = 5 years
Project free cash flow volatility = 50%
Treasury risk-free rate = 5%
Dividend payouts = 0%
Expansion factor = 1.5

FIGURE 10.11   Real Options Assumptions

most certainly easier to explain and show management a simple binomial lattice than it is to explain the intricacies of a stochastic partial-differential equation. At least for presentation purposes, the binomial lattice is highly favored. The analyst can caveat the results of the lattice—say, of five steps—that it is only an approximation value, that the higher the number of time-steps, the more accurate the results become. It is then that you present the results from the closed-form equations.

A good explanation of the assumptions surrounding the real options analysis should include where these assumptions come from—for example, the fact that the present value of the underlying variable comes from the present value of free cash flows in the discounted cash flow model, or that the volatility estimates come from the volatility of the simulated free cash flow's lognormal returns.

REAL OPTIONS ANALYSIS

This is the crux of the analysis and is worthy of detailed explanation, including how the valuation process works as well as the decisions that can be derived from the real options analytics. One method the author has found highly successful in disseminating results of a real options analysis is through the use of collaborating methods. For example, Figure 10.12 shows the valuation lattice for an expansion option. The value calculated is $638 million through the lattice and should be collaborated with that of a closed-form solution, if one exists. If we can show that both figures are in the ballpark, the

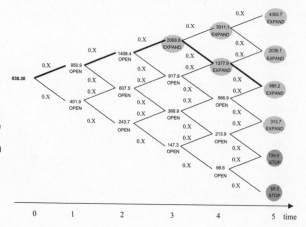

Description

This report displays the valuation of the option. The approach used is the risk-neutral probability applied backward from the terminal period to the initial period.

Results

The value of the option is calculated as $638. The option lattice has been converted into a decision tree.

Open = keeping the option open and not executing the option is the optimal decision at a particular node

Expand = exercising the option at this node is the optimal decision

Stop = the option should be left to expire without exercising it.

The bold path demarcates optimal option execution versus keeping the option open.

FIGURE 10.12 Real Options Analysis

analysis tends to hold more water. Although the analyst should understand that at the limit the binomial lattice approach is identical to the closed-form solution for generic types of options, the approaches tend to be different when you have different real options interacting with each other or when you are creating customized options analysis. However, a good sanity check of the binomial models using closed-form approximations is always warranted in such circumstances. No matter which models are used, the binomial lattice is a more powerful graphical representation of decisions than an otherwise complex mathematical model. The binomial lattice can then be converted into a series of decision nodes. These nodes correspond to optimal decisions that should be made under specific timing and underlying variable conditions. For example, in the expansion option, the decisions include when to expand, when to keep the option open for future use, or when to let the option expire without exercising it. For instance, in Figure 10.12, expanding the project prior to time period 3 is suboptimal, and it is wise to consider executing this option starting from time period 3.

REAL OPTIONS RISK ANALYSIS

Similar to the risk analysis for discounted cash flow, we can perform a risk analysis on real options. Because some of the input variables into the real options models come directly from the discounted cash flow, and if Monte Carlo simulation is performed in the discounted cash flow analysis, the simulated events flow through to the real options models. In addition, any of the other input variables that do not flow through from the discounted cash flow models can be simulated in the real options analysis. Figure 10.13 shows the distribution of results from the eNPV analysis.

Description

This report shows the levels of risk in your option value analysis. The probability distribution shows each value as a fraction of the total.

Results

The chart shows all possible outcomes based on Monte Carlo simulation of the input variables in the real options models. The frequency chart shows the probability at the 90% confidence level occurring between $230 and $6850.

Percentiles (description):

10% = $250   20% = $350   30% = $750   40% = $1050

50% = $2550   60% = $3150   70% = $4900   80% = $6220

90% = $6520   100% = $7000

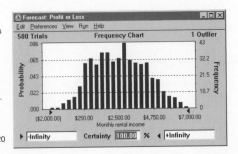

Summary

FIGURE 10.13   Real Options Risk Analysis

SUMMARY

Presenting and explaining the results of a real options analysis are vital. This is because real options have always been viewed at a distance with reverence, and its methodologies are assumed to be black box. To do a good job in explaining the results, the analyst has to make this black box transparent. A good approach is to start by comparing real options and traditional analysis, understanding that real options are built on the precepts of discounted cash flow models, where the value of an option can be seen as benefits less costs. This is similar to a discounted cash flow model, with the exception that a real options analysis assumes stochastic or unknown levels of benefits and costs. In addition, the real options process has to be transparent, indicating a step-by-step process acknowledging when the traditional analysis ends and where the new analytics begin, complete with assumptions, input data, and their results. Risk analysis results should also be presented, because single-point estimates are highly unreliable. This is especially true when it comes to real options analysis where management is skeptical of the inputs and results; hence, providing a probability range of outcomes will make the analysis more robust and results more trustworthy.

CHAPTER 10 QUESTIONS

1. Instituting a cultural change in a company is fairly difficult. However, real options analysis has a very good chance of being adopted at major corporations. What are some of the fundamental characteristics required in a new paradigm shift in the way decisions are made before real options analysis is accepted in a corporate setting?

2. Why is explaining to management the relevant process and steps taken in a real options analysis crucial?

3. What does critical success factor mean?

4. Why is risk analysis a recommended step in a real options analysis?

5. Why is the use of payback period flawed?

Summary of Articles

This section lists a summary of articles published both in academic journals and popular press. The article summary has been carefully screened, and only selected articles deemed relevant to the topics discussed are summarized. The article listings are sorted by date of publication, starting from the most current. This listing is by no means complete and exhaustive.

1. Gregory Taggart. November 2001. "Wait and Seek." Taggart talks about the value of waiting and says that "real options provide a powerful way of thinking and I can't think of any analytical framework that has been of more use to me in the past 15 years that I've been in this business."

2. Gunnar Kallberg and Peter Laurin. November 2001. "Real Options in R&D Capital Budgeting—A Case Study at Pharmacy & Upjohn." Their model shows that a user-friendly spreadsheet including an options approach could be a valuable and descriptive tool to add to a traditional NPV technique. The conclusion of the thesis is that Pharmacia & Upjohn should consider implementing the real options approach in order to value the flexibility and opportunities inherent in their future projects.

3. Jerry Flatto. November 2001. "Using Real Options in Project Evaluation." This article discusses the concept of real options, which can be used to expand your existing analysis methods. It also discusses why many of the existing analysis techniques underestimate the value of a project and how real options can capture some of the benefits that slip through the cracks under existing analysis methods.

4. John M. Charnes, David Kellogg, and Riza Demirer. October 2001. "Valuation of a Biotechnology Firm: An Application of Real Options Methodologies." This paper computes the value of a biotechnology firm, Agouron Pharmaceuticals, Inc., as the sum of the values of its current projects. Each project's value is found using the decision tree and binomial-lattice methods.

5. Robert Barker. *Business Week Online*. October 2001. "A new book on investing is being endorsed by a veritable murderer's row of finance sluggers, from strategist Peter Bernstein and TIAA-CREF's resident rocket scientist, Martin Leibowitz, to that DiMaggio of money managers, Legg Mason's Bill Miller. The book promotes real options as a great way to gauge hard-to-value stocks."

6. Peter Buxbaum. *BudgetLink*. October 2001. "There is a movement afoot to incorporate into business strategic thinking analytic intelligence techniques that take into account the fast moving and uncertain world in which we live. These methodologies are increasingly being incorporated into systems that help managers plan pricing and revenue strategies, as well as supply-chain requirements. One of these emerging techniques is called real options, a concept developed in the halls of academe as an analogy to the financial option."

7. Timothy A. Luehrman, PricewaterhouseCoopers LLP. Society of Petroleum Engineers. October 2001. "Investments in oil and gas are subjected to increasingly advance financial analyses. Real option valuation is prominent among the new financial analytical tools being applied prospectively to projects in the industry. This paper begins with the observation that many real option analyses are formally, technically correct and yet clearly lack substantial influence on decisions and ongoing project management."

8. Steven R. Rutherford, SPE, Anadarko Petroleum Corporation. Society of Petroleum Engineers. October 2001. This paper describes a Real Options evaluation of a real-world farm-out opportunity in case-history format.

9. S.H. Begg and R.B. Bratvold, Landmark Graphics Corporation; and J.M. Campbell, International Risk Management. Society of Petroleum Engineers. October 2001. "This paper addresses the need for a holistic, integrated approach to assessing the impacts of uncertainty on oil and gas investment decision-making. Further applications are to the optimization of development plans, real options and the generation of consistent, risked cash flows for input to portfolio analysis."

10. A. Galli, SPE, ENSMP; T. Jung, Gaz de France; M. Armstrong, ENSMP; and O. Lhote, Gaz de France. Society of Petroleum Engineers. October 2001. "This case study is on a satellite platform close to a large gas and condensate oil field in the North Sea."

11. H.T. Hooper III and S.R. Rutherford, SPE, Anadarko Petroleum Corporation. Society of Petroleum Engineers. October 2001. "Three approaches to economic evaluations that have been widely discussed in the literature are decision trees, Monte Carlo simulation, and real options. Authors have shown that the incorporation of decision tree logic into Monte Carlo simulation offers an added degree of insight into the evaluation, and generally provides a more realistic valuation of an asset by incorporating

some degree of management decision-making. While probabilistic economics (either decision trees or Monte Carlo simulations) and real options differ significantly in the type and amount of input data, as well as the format and applicability of output, they both have capability to capture some value of active decision-making by management. This paper attempts to bridge the gap between the two approaches, at least conceptually, for the practicing engineer."

12. Soussan Faiz, SPE, Texaco Inc. Society of Petroleum Engineers. October 2001. "Various business technologies will distinguish future industry winners. The real options paradigm is emerging as the state-of-the-art method for asset valuation. The concept of an 'efficient frontier' is making headway for portfolio optimization within the energy sector."

13. Lynn B. Davidson. Society of Petroleum Engineers. September 2001. "This paper examines practical barriers to effectively using risk-based decision tools and provides guidelines to overcome the barriers. The second section explores real options: their appeal, problems, and best use. The third section of the paper focuses on challenges related to portfolio optimization. The paper ends with a summary of recommendations to improve decision quality."

14. Deloitte Consulting. Yahoo. September 2001. "Utilities and other energy companies need better methods of deciding how heavily to bet on particular services and facilities, methods that foster flexibility in the face of an uncertain business environment. It also includes interviews with Doug Lattner, global director of the Deloitte Consulting energy practice."

15. Christopher L. Culp. *The RMA Journal.* September 2001. "This article explores common types of real options in the context of banking. Knowing the various types of options can help managers identify often-hidden opportunities and risks."

16. Kevin Sullivan, William Griswold, Yuanfang Cai, and Ben Hallen. ACM SIGSOFT Symposium and Joint International Conference on Software Engineering. September 2001. "We evaluate the potential of a new theory—developed to account for the influence of modularity on the evolution of the computer industry—to inform software design. The theory uses design structure matrices to model designs and real options techniques to value them."

17. David Newton. *Financial Times.* June 2001. Newton gives the reader a clear understanding of how real options are applicable to decisions in the R&D industry and recognizes that knowledge has a value offset by the time it takes to acquire.

18. Ash Vesudevan. *CommerceNet.* March 2001. "The greatest rewards go to those companies that can create new business models in the context of changing technological and demographic trends. Often times [sic], risk

reduction becomes a competitive imperative in response to uncertainty. An options approach, on the other hand, invokes a new perspective—profiting from uncertainty. It gives you a chance to be at the edge of the future. Doing that requires the right combination of breadth and depth. Innovation today is a competitive imperative."

19. Zeke Ashton and Bill Man. Motleyfool.com. February 2001. "Looking at some real-world companies that use Real Options."

20. Zeke Ashton. Motleyfool.com. February 2001. "Investors can use the concept of real options to explain part of the difference in market value and the intrinsic value as calculated using traditional methods. Real options represent what is possible beyond the current business operations. Investors can ignore real options, try to find real option value for free, or consciously seek out companies that have abundant real option value."

21. Shi-Jie Deng, UC Berkeley; Blake Johnson, Stanford; and Aram Sogomonian, Pacificorp. *Decision Support Systems*. January 2001. "Valuing electricity derivatives using replicating portfolios. These valuation results are used to construct real options-based valuation formulae for generation and transmission assets."

22. Hemantha S.B. Herath, University of Northern British Columbia; and Chan S. Park, Auburn University. *The Engineering Economist*. January 2001. Herath and Park show that the option value is equivalent to the Expected Value of Perfect Information (EVPI). Models include environmental preservation that involves a decision to develop a track of land; and manufacturing of a new toy.

23. Chana R. Schoenberger. *Forbes Global*. December 2000. Schoenberger writes about using real options theory to value entertainment and cable stocks.

24. Rita Gunther McGrath and Ian MacMillan. *Business and Management Practices*. July 2000. McGrath and MacMillan present a methodology called STAR (strategic technology assessment review) for assessing uncertain projects that approximates option value through scoring a series of statements.

25. Diana Angelis, Naval Postgraduate School. *Business and Management Practices*. July 2000. Angelis uses Black-Scholes to capture the value of a research and development project. Her model is based on determining volatility from the underlying distributions of costs and revenue rather than net cash flows. She uses an example from Merck Pharmaceutical.

26. *European Journal of Operational Research*. July 2000. Real options are used to determine the optimal time of a phased rollout as well as the optimal rollout area—that is, the article views a phased rollout of new

products as an option on a worldwide launch. The article illustrates the model with the rollout of a CD-I at Philips Electronics.

27. Peter Boer, CEO of Tiger Scientific; and John Lee, Yale University. *Business and Management Practices*. July 2000. The article describes the separation of unique risk (amount of oil in proposed well, and the like) and market risk (price of oil), using the Black-Scholes solution.

28. Michel Beneroch and Robert Kauffman. Information Access Company (Thomson). July 2000. Beneroch and Kauffman present a case study involving the deployment of point-of-sale debit services by the Yankee 24 shared electronic banking network of New England. The study used an adjusted Black-Scholes model to evaluate a timing option.

29. John Rutledge. *Forbes.* May 2000. "Real options are the secret that allows an investor to both pay a fair price for a business and earn extraordinary returns."

30. Michael Stroud. *Business 2.0.* April 2000. "Creating a standardized way of valuing intellectual property and patents, and then allow them to be bought and sold over the Web. Black-Scholes equation is used. The principles, they decided, could be brought to bear on intellectual property— replacing a call option's variables with the price and volatility of its underlying technology, the development costs and time remaining, and baseline capital costs."

31. Mohamed Ahnani and Mondher Bellalah. *www.business.com.* January 2000. Ahnani and Bellalah undertake a comparative analysis of the real options method of pricing projects and the more traditional net present value method.

32. Brian F. Lavoie and Ian M. Sheldon. *AgBioForum.* January 2000. Sources of heterogeneity within the process of research and development investment, such as international differences in the maximum per-period rate of investment and regulatory uncertainty, offer a plausible explanation that can be incorporated into a real options approach to investment.

33. CFO Staff. *CFO Magazine.* January 2000. "Experts have touted the merits of real options for at least a decade, but the sophisticated mathematics required to explain them has penned up those merits in ivory towers. That's changing, as proponents tout the virtues of real options as a mindset for decision-making."

34. J.M. Campbell and Robert A. Campbell, CPS, Inc.; and Stewart Brown, Florida State University. Society of Petroleum Engineers. October 1999. "This paper summarizes the recent criticisms of traditional methods, especially the gap between individual project valuation methods and the strategic objectives of the organization. After reviewing the limitations of traditional discounted cash flow (DCF) analysis, including NPV, IRR, etc., we seek to outline a more comprehensive understanding of DCF that

corrects the inherent contradictions at work in most organizations, especially with the tendency to emphasize short-run objectives at the expense of longer-term, strategic investments."

35. Goldense Group Press Release. *Business Wire.* July 1999. "Fewer than 40% of companies surveyed measure new product development in relation to its contribution to the bottom line."

36. Martha Amram, Nalin Kulatilaka, and John C. Henderson. *CIO Magazine.* July 1999. "Real options theory evaluates technology investments by linking them to the financial market. [This article discusses] how to use options thinking to measure the value of IT projects and why real options build flexibility into technology investments, and the importance of linking technology decisions to market conditions."

37. Peter Coy. *Business Week Online.* June 1999. "Although conceived more than 20 years ago, real options analysis is just now coming into wide use. Rapid change has exposed the weaknesses of less flexible valuation tools. Experts have developed rules of thumb that simplify the formidable math behind options valuation, while making real options applicable in a broader range of situations. And consulting firms have latched on to the technique as the Next Big Thing to sell to clients. 'Real options valuation has the potential to be a major business breakthrough,' says Adam Borison of Applied Decision Analysis Inc., a real options expert whose Menlo Park (California) firm was snapped up last year by PricewaterhouseCoopers."

38. Thor Valdmanis. *USA Today.* May 1999. "An introductory piece for the general public. Gives the reader a perspective of the breadth of application and some of the industries using real options today."

39. Wayne Winson, Kelley School of Business, Indiana University. April 1999. "Introducing new techniques for valuing financial derivatives and real options using risk-neutral technique to develop the new technique."

40. A. Galli, SPE; M. Armstrong, Ecole des Mines de Paris; and B. Jehl, Elf Exploration Production. Society of Petroleum Engineers. March 1999. "Option pricing, decision trees and Monte Carlo simulations are three methods used for evaluating projects. In this paper their similarities and differences are compared from three points of view—how they handle uncertainty in the values of key parameters such as the reserves, the oil price and costs; how they incorporate the time value of money and whether they allow for managerial flexibility."

41. Michael H. Zack. *California Management Review.* March 1999. "A framework for describing and evaluating an organization's knowledge strategy."

42. Justin Claeys and Gardner Walkup Jr., Applied Decision Analysis. March 1999. Society of Petroleum Engineers. "Techniques from the burgeoning

area of real options are helping petroleum companies to better value and manage their important assets."

43. Martha Amram and Nalin Kulatilaka. *Harvard Business Review.* January 1999. Amram and Kulatilaka have done an excellent job taking the complexity of the subject and delivering its merits through a series of case studies.

44. Timothy A. Luehrman. *Harvard Business Review.* September 1998. "This article builds on the previous examples to provide a method for comparing a portfolio of projects using real options analysis. An excellent extension of the real options framework to strategic issues illustrating the compelling rationale for utilizing this valuable tool."

45. Timothy A. Luehrman. *Harvard Business Review.* July 1998. This article offers a step-by-step approach to a real options analysis. The example was kept simple in order to be accessible, so the solution is only applicable to the simpler single-stage decisions; nevertheless, it is an excellent introduction to the mathematics of real options.

46. Chris F. Kemerer. *Information Week.* April 1998. "The bottom line is that many IT investments are likely to provide their organizations with significant potential opportunities in addition to their estimated direct benefits. Real options modeling provides a way to quantify these opportunities and may help justify projects in circumstances where vague claims of intangible benefits may not."

47. Ian Runge. *Capital Strategy Letter.* March 1998. "Many projects have imbedded options that cost you nothing. Most new investments offer scope for expansion, and the expansion, though not profitable today, frequently becomes a very profitable investment in the future. In effect, today's investment includes an imbedded option to expand. Many assessments overlook the value of these imbedded options."

48. M.J. Brennan and L. Trigeorgis. London, *Oxford University Press.* March 1998. "Real option considerations can be a significant component of value, and firms which appropriately take them into account should outperform firms which do not. This paper asks whether the use of seemingly arbitrary investment criteria, such as hurdle rates and profitability indexes, can proxy for the use of more sophisticated real options calculation. We find that for a variety of parameters, particular hurdle rate and profitability index rules can provide close-to-optimal investment decisions. This suggests that firms using seemingly arbitrary 'rules of thumb' may be trying to approximate optimal decisions."

49. Karen Kroll. *Industry Week.* February 1998. "Options theory applied to business decisions—known as real options theory recognizes the value in companies being able to make a limited initial investment that allows them to take action in the future and hopefully, realize a gain. One brief page notes the growing interest in real options. Focused primarily on experiences in the U.K., the author suggests that the topic may be too difficult for corporate analysts to undertake."

50. M.A.G. Dias, Petrobras S.A. Society of Petroleum Engineers. September 1997. "This paper analyzes the problem faced by an oil company with investment rights over the tracks subject to relinquishment requirements, which limit the time the company can hold the tract before developing it. Some concepts of the modern real options theory are described briefly, with focus on the timing aspects: economic uncertainty and irreversibility incentive the learning by waiting, and delay the investment; technical uncertainty incentives the learning by doing, and generally speeds investment up."

51. Timothy A. Luehrman. *Harvard Business Review*. May 1997. "Three complementary tools will out-perform WACC-based DCF that most companies now use as their workhorse valuation methodology; Valuing Operations (Adjusted Present Value), Valuing Opportunities (Option Pricing), Valuing Ownership Claims (Equity Cash Flows)."

52. Avinash Dixit and Robert Pindyck. *Harvard Business Review*. May 1995. The article provides foundation concepts from which to begin a study of real options and is an introductory piece to the textbook by Dixit and Pindyck on investment under uncertainty.

53. Nancy Nichols. *Harvard Business Review*. May 1993. Although this article contains limited detail about the concept of real options, it reveals some of the pharmaceutical industry applications where it has been applied successfully.

54. J.T. Markland, British Gas E and P. Society of Petroleum Engineers. April 1992. "This paper outlines the basis of option pricing theory for assessing the market value of a project. It also attempts to assess the future role of this type of approach in practical petroleum exploration and engineering economics."

55. Anthony Fisher, Department of Economics, UC Berkeley; and W. Michael Hanemann, Department of Agriculture and Resource Economics, UC Berkeley. *Journal of Environmental Economics and Management*. January 1987. "Quasi-options are always positive, but are often confused with the net benefit of preservation (of a natural environment subject to development) which can be negative."

56. Stewart Myers. *Journal of Financial Economics* Vol. 5. January 1977. "Critical insight into the first introduction of the concept of real options."

case studies and problems in real options

The following case studies require the use of Real Options Analysis Toolkit software.*

CASE STUDY: OPTION TO ABANDON

Suppose a pharmaceutical company is developing a particular drug. However, due to the uncertain nature of the drug's development progress, market demand, success in human and animal testing, and FDA approval, management has decided that it will create a strategic abandonment option. That is, at any time period within the next five years of development, management can review the progress of the research and development effort and decide whether to terminate the drug development program. After five years, the firm would have either succeeded or completely failed in its drug development initiative, and there exists no option value after that time period. If the program is terminated, the firm can potentially sell off its intellectual property rights of the drug in question to another pharmaceutical firm with which it has a contractual agreement. This contract with the other firm is exercisable at any time within this time period, at the whim of the firm owning the patents.

Using a traditional discounted cash flow model, you find the present value of the expected future cash flows discounted at an appropriate market risk-adjusted discount rate to be $150 million. Using Monte Carlo simulation, you find the implied volatility of the logarithmic returns on future cash flows to be 30 percent. The risk-free rate on a riskless asset for the same time frame is 5 percent, and you understand from the intellectual property officer of the firm that the value of the drug's patent is $100 million contractually, if sold within the next five years. For simplicity, you assume that this $100 million salvage value is fixed for the next five years. You attempt to calculate how much this abandonment option is worth and how much this drug development effort on the whole is worth to the firm. By virtue of having this

---

*A full version of the software is required. Answers to the cases are available via Wiley Higher Education for downloading by registered faculty members. Wiley Higher Education may be accessed through the John Wiley & Sons, Inc., Web site (*www.Wiley.com*).

safety net of being able to abandon drug development, the value of the project is worth more than its net present value. You decide to use a closed-form approximation of an American put option because the option to abandon drug development can be exercised at any time up to the expiration date. You also decide to confirm the value of the closed-form analysis with a binomial lattice calculation. With these assumptions, do the following exercises, answering the questions that are posed:

1. Solve the abandonment option problem analytically and confirm the results using the software.

2. Select the right choice for each of the following:

   a. Increases in maturity (increase/decrease) an abandonment option value.

   b. Increases in volatility (increase/decrease) an abandonment option value.

   c. Increases in asset value (increase/decrease) an abandonment option value.

   d. Increases in risk-free rate (increase/decrease) an abandonment option value.

   e. Increases in dividend (increase/decrease) an abandonment option value.

   f. Increases in salvage value (increase/decrease) an abandonment option value.

3. Verify the results using the software's closed-form *American Put Option Approximation*.

4. Using the *Custom Lattice*, build and solve the abandonment option.

5. Use the *Black-Scholes* model to benchmark the results.

6. Apply 1,000 steps using the software's binomial lattice.

   a. How different are the results as compared to the 5-step lattice?

   b. How close are the closed-form results compared to the 1,000-step lattice?

7. Apply a 3 percent continuous dividend yield to the 1,000-step lattice.

   a. What happens to the results?

   b. Does a dividend yield increase or decrease the value of an abandonment option?

8. Assume that the salvage value increases at a 10 percent annual rate. Show how this can be modeled using the software's *Custom Lattice* function.

CASE STUDY: OPTION TO EXPAND

Suppose a growth firm has a static valuation of future profitability using a discounted cash flow model (in other words, the present value of the expected future cash flows discounted at an appropriate market risk-adjusted discount rate) is found to be $400 million. Using Monte Carlo simulation, you calculate the implied volatility of the logarithmic returns on the projected future cash flows to be 35 percent. The risk-free rate on a riskless asset for the next five years is found to be yielding 7 percent. Suppose that the firm has the option to expand and double its operations by acquiring its competitor for a sum of $250 million at any time over the next five years. What is the total value of this firm assuming you account for this expansion option?

You decide to use a closed-form approximation of an American call option because the option to expand the firm's operations can be exercised at any time up to the expiration date. You also decide to confirm the value of the closed-form analysis with a binomial lattice calculation. Do the following exercises, answering the questions that are posed:

1. Solve the expansion option problem analytically, using the software.

2. Rerun the expansion option problem using the software for 100 steps, 300 steps, and 1,000 steps. What are your observations?

3. Show how you would use the *American Call Approximation* to estimate and benchmark the results from an expansion option. How comparable are the results?

4. Show the different levels of expansion factors but still yielding the same expanded asset value of $800. Explain your observations in terms of why the expansion value changes, and why the *Black-Scholes* and *American Option Approximation* models are insufficient to capture the fluctuation in value.

   a. Use an expansion factor of 2.00 and an asset value of $400.00 (yielding an expanded asset value of $800).

   b. Use an expansion factor of 1.25 and an asset value of $640.00 (yielding an expanded asset value of $800).

   c. Use an expansion factor of 1.50 and an asset value of $533.34 (yielding an expanded asset value of $800).

   d. Use an expansion factor of 1.75 and an asset value of $457.14 (yielding an expanded asset value of $800).

5. Add a dividend yield, and see what happens. Explain your findings.

   a. What happens when the dividend yield equals or exceeds the risk-free rate?

   b. What happens to the accuracy of closed-form solutions like the *Black-Scholes* and *American Call Approximation* models?

6. What happens to the decision to expand if a dividend yield exists?

CASE STUDY: OPTION TO CONTRACT

You work for a large aeronautical manufacturing firm that is unsure of the technological efficacy and market demand of its new fleet of long-range supersonic jets. The firm decides to hedge itself through the use of strategic options, specifically an option to contract 50 percent of its manufacturing facilities at any time within the next five years.

Suppose the firm has a current operating structure whose static valuation of future profitability using a discounted cash flow model (in other words, the present value of the expected future cash flows discounted at an appropriate market risk-adjusted discount rate) is found to be $1 billion. Using Monte Carlo simulation, you calculate the implied volatility of the logarithmic returns on the projected future cash flows to be 50 percent. The risk-free rate on a riskless asset for the next five years is found to be yielding 5 percent. Suppose the firm has the option to contract 50 percent of its current operations at any time over the next five years, thereby creating an additional $400 million in savings after this contraction. This is done through a legal contractual agreement with one of its vendors, who has agreed to take up the excess capacity and space of the firm, and at the same time, the firm can scale back its existing workforce to obtain this level of savings.

A closed-form approximation of an American option can be used, because the option to contract the firm's operations can be exercised at any time up to the expiration date and can be confirmed with a binomial lattice calculation. Do the following exercises, answering the questions that are posed:

1. Solve the contraction option problem analytically, using the software.

2. Modify the continuous dividend payout rate until the option breaks even. What observations can you make at this break-even point?

3. Use the *American Long-Term Put Approximation* to benchmark the contraction option. What are the input parameters?

4. How can you use the *American Option to Abandon* model as a benchmark to estimate the contraction option? If it is used, are the resulting option values comparable?

5. Change the contraction factor to 0.7, and answer Question 4. Why are the answers different?

CASE STUDY: OPTION TO CHOOSE

Suppose a large manufacturing firm decides to hedge itself through the use of strategic options. Specifically, it has the option to choose among three strategies: expanding its current manufacturing operations, contracting its manufacturing operations, or completely abandoning its business unit at any time within the next five years. Suppose the firm has a current operating structure whose static valuation of future profitability using a discounted cash flow model (in other words, the present value of the future cash flows discounted at an appropriate market risk-adjusted discount rate) is found to be $100 million.

Using Monte Carlo simulation, you calculate the implied volatility of the logarithmic returns on the projected future cash flows to be 15 percent. The risk-free rate on a riskless asset for the next five years is found to be yielding 5 percent annualized returns. Suppose the firm has the option to contract 10 percent of its current operations at any time over the next five years, thereby creating an additional $25 million in savings after this contraction. The expansion option will increase the firm's operations by 30 percent, with a $20 million implementation cost. Finally, by abandoning its operations, the firm can sell its intellectual property for $100 million. Do the following exercises, answering the questions posed:

1. Solve the chooser option problem analytically, using the software.
2. Recalculate the option value accounting only for an expansion option.
3. Recalculate the option value accounting only for a contraction option.
4. Recalculate the option value accounting only for an abandonment option.
5. Compare the results of the sum of these three individual options in Questions 2 to 4 with the results obtained in Question 1 using the chooser option.
   a. Why are the results different?
   b. Which value is correct?
6. Prove that if there are many interacting options, if there is a single dominant strategy, the value of the project's option value approaches this dominant strategy's value. That is, perform the following steps, then compare and explain the results.
   a. Reduce the expansion cost to $1.
   b. Increase the contraction savings to $100.
   c. Increase the salvage value to $150.
   d. What inferences can you make based on these results?

CASE STUDY: COMPOUND OPTIONS

In a compound option analysis, the value of the option depends on the value of another option. For instance, a pharmaceutical company currently going through a particular FDA drug approval process has to go through human trials. The success of the FDA approval depends heavily on the success of human testing, both occurring at the same time. Suppose that the former costs

$900 million and the latter $500 million. Further suppose that both phases occur simultaneously and take five years to complete. Using Monte Carlo simulation, you calculate the implied volatility of the logarithmic returns on the projected future cash flows to be 25 percent. The risk-free rate on a riskless asset for the next five years is found to be yielding 7.7 percent. The drug development effort's static valuation of future profitability using a discounted cash flow model (in other words, the present value of the future cash flows discounted at an appropriate market risk-adjusted discount rate) is found to be $1 billion. Do the following exercises, answering the questions that are posed:

1. Solve the simultaneous compound option analytically, using the software. Use 5 and 100 steps for comparison.

2. Swap the implementation costs such that the first cost is $500 and the second cost is $900. Is the resulting option value similar or different? Why?

3. What happens when part of the cost of the first option is allocated to the second option? For example, make the first cost $450 and the second cost $950. Does the result change? Explain.

4. Show how an *American Long-Term Call Option Approximation* can be used to benchmark the results from a simultaneous compound option.

5. Show how a *Sequential Compound Option* can also be used to calculate or at least approximate the simultaneous compound option result. Use the software's *4D Multi-Sequential Compound Option* module.

CASE STUDY: CLOSED-FORM COMPOUND OPTIONS

Compound options can also be analyzed using closed-form models rather than binomial lattices. In theory, the results obtained from binomial lattices have to approach closed-form models. As additional practice, do the following exercises, answering the questions pertaining to compound options:

1. Using the *American Simultaneous Compound Option* module in the software, obtain the option value of an asset worth $1,000, 50 percent volatility, five years to maturity, and an assumed 5 percent risk-free rate. Further, assume that the costs of the first and second options are both $500. Show the value obtained using a 5-step lattice and a 100-step super lattice analysis.

2. Compare the answers above by using the *Compound Options on Options* closed-form model. Note that to approximate and benchmark a simultaneous compound option, you must set the time to maturity for the option on option as 4.9999 years and set the time to maturity of the underlying as 5.0000 years. This is because the *Compound Options on Options*

module only directly calculates sequential compound options, not simultaneous compound options.

3. Compare the answers using the *4D Multi-Sequential Compound Option* with 1,000 steps.

4. Now, suppose the compound option occurs in sequence and not simultaneously. That is, assume that the underlying time is now four years and the option time is two years. All other input parameters are identical.

   a. Use the *American Sequential Compound Option* to calculate the new option value (use 5 steps and 1,000 steps in the binomial lattice).

   b. Confirm your results using the *Compound Options on Options* module.

   c. Confirm your results again using the *4D Multi-Sequential Compound Option*.

CASE STUDY: SEQUENTIAL COMPOUND OPTION

A sequential compound option exists when a project has multiple phases and latter phases depend on the success of previous phases. Suppose a project has two phases, the first of which has a one-year expiration that costs $500 million. The second phase's expiration is three years and costs $700 million. Using Monte Carlo simulation, the implied volatility of the logarithmic returns on the projected future cash flows is calculated to be 20 percent. The risk-free rate on a riskless asset for the next three years is found to be yielding 7.7 percent. The static valuation of future profitability using a discounted cash flow model—in other words, the present value of the future cash flows discounted at an appropriate market risk-adjusted discount rate—is found to be $1,000 million. Do the following exercises, answering the questions posed:

1. Solve the sequential compound option analytically, using the software.

2. Change the sequence of the costs. That is, set the first phase's cost to $700 and the second phase's cost to $500. Compare your results. Explain what happens.

CASE STUDY: CHANGING STRIKES

A modification to the option types we have thus far been discussing is the idea of changing strikes—implementation costs for projects may change over time. Putting off a project for a particular period may mean a higher cost. Keep in mind that changing strikes can be applied to any previous option types as well; in other words, one can mix and match different option types. Suppose implementation of a project in the first year costs $80 million but increases to $90 million in the second year due to expected increases in the cost of raw materials and input costs. Using Monte Carlo simulation, you calculate the implied volatility of the logarithmic returns on the projected future cash flows to be 50 percent. The risk-free rate on a riskless asset for the next two years is found to be yielding 7.0 percent. The static valuation of future profitability using a discounted cash flow model (in other words, the present value of the future cash flows discounted at an appropriate market risk-adjusted discount rate) is found to be $100 million. Do the following exercises, answering the questions posed:

1. Solve the changing strikes option analytically, using the software. However, change the maturity to five years instead for the software. Use the binomial lattice of five steps.

2. Rerun the analysis after changing the first year's costs to $90 million and the second year's costs to $80 million. Explain the results. Are they intuitive?

CASE STUDY: CHANGING VOLATILITY

Instead of changing strike costs over time, in certain cases volatility on cash flow returns may differ over time. Assume a two-year option in which volatility is 20 percent in the first year and 30 percent in the second year. In this circumstance, the up and down factors are different over the two time periods. Thus, the binomial lattice will no longer be recombining. Assume an asset value of $100, implementation costs of $110, and a risk-free rate of 10 percent. (Note that changing volatility options can also be solved analytically using non-recombining trees—see the section on non-recombining lattices).

1. Solve the problem analytically, using the software.

2. Change the first volatility to 30 percent and the second to 20 percent. What happens?

CASE STUDY: OPTION TO CONTRACT AND ABANDON

1. Solve the following Contraction and Abandonment option: Asset value of $100, five-year economic life, 5 percent annualized risk-free rate of return, 25 percent annualized volatility, 25 percent contraction with a $25 savings, and a $70 abandonment salvage value.

2. Show and explain what happens when the salvage value of abandonment far exceeds any chances of a contraction. For example, set the salvage value at $200.

3. In contrast, set the salvage value back to $70, and increase the contraction savings to $100. What happens to the value of the project?

4. Solve just the contraction option in isolation. That is, set the contraction savings to $25 and explain what happens. Change the savings to $100 and explain the change in results. What can you infer from dominant option strategies?

5. Solve just the abandonment option in isolation. That is, set the salvage value to $70, and explain what happens. Change the salvage value to $200, and explain the change in results. What can you infer from dominant option strategies?

CASE STUDY: BASIC BLACK-SCHOLES WITH DIVIDENDS

The Black-Scholes equation is applicable for analyzing European-type options—that is, options that can be executed only at maturity and not before. The original Black-Scholes model cannot solve an option problem when there are dividend payments. However, extensions of the Black-Scholes model, termed the Generalized Black-Scholes model, can accommodate a continuous dividend payout for a European Option.

Do the following exercises and answer the questions posed, assuming that a European call option's asset value and strike cost are $100, subject to 25 percent volatility. The maturity on this option is five years, and the corresponding risk-free rate on a similar asset maturity is 5 percent.

1. Using the software, calculate the European call option.

2. Compare your results using 5, 10, 50, 100, 300, 500, 1,000, and 5,000 steps in the super lattice routine. Explain what happens when the number of steps gets higher.

3. Now assume that a continuous dividend payout yielding 3 percent exists. What happens to the value of the option?

4. Show that the value of an American option is identical to the European option when no dividends are paid. That is, it is never optimal to execute an American call option early when no dividend payouts exist.

5. Show that as a 3 percent dividend yield exists, the value of the American call option exceeds the value of a European option. Why is this so?

CASE STUDY: BARRIER OPTIONS

Barrier options are combinations of call and put options such that they become in-the-money or out-of-the-money when the asset value breaches an artificial barrier.

Standard single upper barrier options can be call-up-and-in, call-up-and-out, put-up-and-in, and put-up-and-out. Standard single lower barrier options can be call-down-and-in, call-down-and-out, put-down-and-in, and put-down-and-out. Double barrier options are combinations of standard single upper and lower barriers.

1. Using the double barrier option, change each input parameter, and explain the effects on the up-and-in and down-and-in call option, up-and-in and down-and-in put option, up-and-out and down-and-out call option, and up-and-out and down-and-out put option. Explain your observations when the barrier levels change or when volatility increases.

2. Replicate the analysis using a standard lower barrier option.

3. Replicate the analysis using a standard upper barrier option.

CASE STUDY: SWITCHING OPTION

A switching option looks at the flexibility of being able to switch resources, assets, or technology. This ability to switch use provides added value to a project as a risk-hedging mechanism, in case the value of another technology or project becomes more profitable in the future, subject to a switching cost.

1. Calculate the value of switching technologies assuming that the first technology is worth $100, but the second is worth only $90. Assume a five-year maturity, 10 percent switching costs, and a negligible 0.001 percent risk-free rate. The first asset has a volatility of 20 percent, while the second has 35 percent volatility. Further, assume a cross-correlation coefficient of −0.2. How does the switching option compare with a static NPV?

2. Change the correlation coefficient to +0.2. What happens to the value of the switching option? Explain.

3. Run a series of switching option calculations. Change the following input parameters and explain what happens to the value of the switching option:

   a. Second asset's volatility.

   b. Present value of the first asset.

   c. Present value of the second asset.

   d. Cost multiplier.

   e. Time to expiration.

answers to chapter questions

CHAPTER 1

1. What are some of the characteristics of a project or a firm that is best suited for a real options analysis? *The project has to be faced with uncertainty, management must have flexibility to make mid-course corrections when uncertainty becomes resolved over time, and management must be credible enough to execute the profit-maximizing behavior at the appropriate time.*

2. Define the following:

   a. Compound option. *The value of an option depends on the value of another option executed either concurrently or in sequence.*

   b. Barrier option. *The value of an option depends on the asset's breaching an artificial barrier.*

   c. Expansion option. *The value of an option where a project has the strategic ability but not the obligation to expand its existing operations.*

3. If management is not credible in acting appropriately through profit-maximizing behavior, are strategic real options still worth anything? *No. All the strategic options in the world are worthless if they will all be left to expire without execution because management does not act appropriately.*

CHAPTER 2

1. What are the three traditional approaches to valuation? *The market approach, the income approach, and the cost approach.*

2. Why should benefits and costs be discounted at two separate discount rates? *Benefits and costs have different sets of risks. Benefits are usually driven by a project's or firm's revenues, which are subject to market risks and uncertainty; hence, benefits should be discounted at the market risk-adjusted rate of return. In retrospect, costs are usually faced with private risk, which means that the market will not compensate the project for this risk; hence, costs should be discounted at the risk-free rate.*

3. Is the following statement true? Why or why not? "The value of a firm is simply the sum of all its individual projects." *False. The value of a firm is greater than the sum of its parts. This is due to network effects, diversification, synergy, and the ability to leverage on existing projects to provide growth options for the future.*

4. What are some of the assumptions required in order for the CAPM to work? *Investors are risk-averse individuals who maximize their expected utility of their end-of-period wealth; investors are price-takers and have homogeneous beliefs and expectations about asset returns; there exists a risk-free asset and investors may borrow or lend unlimited amounts at the risk-free rate; the quantities of assets are fixed and all assets are marketable and perfectly divisible; asset markets are frictionless and information is costless and available to all investors; and there are no market imperfections like taxes, regulations, or restrictions on short sales.*

5. The answer is available for downloading by registered faculty members on the John Wiley & Sons, Inc., Web site (*www.Wiley.com*).

CHAPTER 3

1. Can an option take on a negative value? *No, the value of an option is always positive or zero, by definition. However, the value of an option may be surpassed by the premium required to create the strategic option to begin with. Hence, the net value may be negative, but the option itself is never negative.*

2. Why are real options sometimes viewed as strategic maps of convoluted pathways? *In traditional analyses, the discounted cash flow assumes that all decisions are made at the outset, with no recourse for mid-course corrections. In retrospect, real options analysis assumes that future outcomes are uncertain and that management has the strategic flexibility to make mid-course corrections whenever it deems appropriate, when some of these uncertainties become known. That is, management sees projects as having different potential outcomes, akin to a strategic roadmap, which it can navigate.*

3. Why are real options seen as risk reduction and revenue enhancement strategies? *Because real options imply that certain projects should not be executed if conditions are poor, or that instituting certain strategic options increases the value of the project. Thus, real options mitigate downside risks. This is the risk reduction effect, while the revenue enhancement effect comes from the ability of real options to leverage certain exogenous business conditions, such as expanding when conditions are appropriate, to capture the upside potential of a project.*

4. Why are the real options names usually self-explanatory and not based on names of mathematical models? *Using basic names is important—when*

it comes to explaining the process and results to management, it makes it easier for management to understand, and therefore increases the chances of acceptance of the methodology and results. The use of mathematical or formulaic names is irrelevant and serves no special purpose here.

5. What is a Tornado diagram as presented in Figure 3.5's example? *A tornado diagram is named for its shape—it lists the variables that drive an analysis, where the most sensitive variables are listed first, in descending order of magnitude. For example, in a net present value analysis, a tornado diagram will list the inputs that the net present value is most sensitive to. Armed with this information, the analyst can then decide which key variables are highly uncertain in the future and which are deterministic. The uncertain key variables that drive the net present value and hence the decision are called critical success drivers. These critical success drivers are prime candidates for Monte Carlo simulation.*

CHAPTER 4

1. What is Monte Carlo simulation? *Monte Carlo simulation is a generic type of parametric simulation, that is, a simulation where the particular variable to be simulated is assumed to follow certain distributional parameters, hence the term parametric. The variable under simulation is replaced with randomly generated numbers from the specified distribution and its associated parameters thousands of times. This is akin to creating thousands of scenario analyses. The result of a simulation is usually a distribution of forecasts of the variable of interest, complete with probabilities of outcomes.*

2. What is portfolio optimization? *Portfolio optimization considers the interconnected behavior and diversification effects of multiple projects grouped into a portfolio. The goal of portfolio optimization is usually to maximize a certain variable (returns, profits, profit-to-risk index) or to minimize a certain variable (cost, risks, and so forth) in the context of a rolled-up portfolio, while considering the project's interrelationships. These goals are achieved subject to certain requirements or constraints (budget, timing resources, and so forth). The results are usually a set of criteria on how resources should be optimally allocated across multiple projects to meet these goals.*

3. Why is update analysis required in a real options analysis framework? *Because real options analysis is a dynamic decision analysis, where there is value in uncertainty, updates are required because when uncertainty becomes resolved through the passage of time, decisions need to be made. Update analysis reflects the decisions made and what future actions may be appropriate going forward.*

4. What is problem-framing? *Problem-framing is viewing the project under analysis within a real options paradigm—in other words, identifying where strategic flexibility value exists and how management can exert its flexibility in decision-making and create value.*

5. Why are reports important? *Reports are important because they provide a concise and coherent view of the analytical process as well as the results obtained through this process.*

CHAPTER 5

1. What do you believe are the three most important differences between financial options and real options? *The length of maturity in real options far surpasses that of a financial option. The underlying assets in financial options are highly liquid and tradable, and historical data are available. In real options, assets are usually nontradable and illiquid. The value of a financial option is relatively small compared to significant values in real options.*

2. In the Flaw of Averages example, a nonparametric simulation approach is used. What does nonparametric simulation mean? *Nonparametric means no parameters. That is, nonparametric simulation does not make any distributional and parameter assumptions. Instead, the simulation uses historical data.*

3. In simulating a sample stock price path, a stochastic process called Geometric Brownian Motion is used. What does a stochastic process mean? *A stochastic process is the opposite of a deterministic process. That is, the outcome of a stochastic process cannot be predicted in advance; instead, it has an uncertainty variable that changes at every simulation trial. A stochastic process can be easily valued through Monte Carlo simulation.*

4. What are some of the restrictive assumptions used in the Black-Scholes equation? *The stocks underlying the call or put options provide no dividends during the life of the option; there are no transaction costs involved with the sale or purchase of either the stock or the option; the short-term risk-free interest rate is known and is constant during the life of the option; the security buyers may borrow any fraction of the purchase price at the short-term risk-free rate; short-term selling is permitted without penalty, and sellers immediately receive the full cash proceeds at today's price for securities sold short; call or put options can be exercised only on their expiration date; security trading takes place in continuous time, and stock prices move in continuous time.*

5. The answer is available for downloading by registered faculty members on the John Wiley & Sons, Inc., Web site (*www.Wiley.com*).

CHAPTER 6

1. Why does solving a real options problem using the binomial lattices approach the results generated through closed-form models? *The underlying mathematical structures of both approaches are identical. That is, closed-form models are derived through stochastic differential calculus to obtain the results of a continuous simulation process. In retrospect, the binomial lattices approximate this continuous process through the creation of a discrete simulation. Hence, when the number of steps in a binomial lattice approaches infinity, such that the time between steps in a lattice approaches zero, the discrete lattice simulation becomes a continuous simulation; thus, the results are identical.*

2. Is real options analysis a special case of discounted cash flow analysis, or is discounted cash flow analysis a special case of real options analysis? *Discounted cash flow analysis is a special case of real options analysis. This is because when all uncertainty is resolved (volatility equals zero), or at the point of expiration with no time left for the option, the value of the project is exactly the discounted cash flow result, because the real options value is zero at that point.*

3. Explain what a risk-neutral probability means. *Risk-neutralization means taking the risk away from something. Risk-neutral probability means to risk-adjust the asset values at each node by taking away the risk through an adjustment of the probabilities that lead to these asset values in the first place. It is used in valuing options with binomial lattices.*

4. What is the difference between a recombining lattice and a non-recombining lattice? *In recombining lattices—a binomial lattice, for example—the middle branches of the lattice converge to the same result; in a non-recombining lattice, they do not. Sometimes non-recombining trees are required, especially when there are two or more stochastic underlying variables, or when volatility of the single underlying variable changes over time.*

5. The answer is available for downloading by registered faculty members on the John Wiley & Sons, Inc., Web site (*www.Wiley.com*).

CHAPTER 7

Answers are available for downloading by registered faculty members on the John Wiley & Sons, Inc., Web site (*www.Wiley.com*).

CHAPTER 8

1. Decision trees are considered inappropriate when used to solve real options problems. Why is this so? *Decision trees are great for setting*

up a real options problem as well as presenting the results. However, stand-alone decision trees are inadequate in solving real options problems. This is because subjective probabilities have to be assigned to each branch on a decision tree, and in a complex tree, incorrect probabilities will be compounded over different periods and the errors will grow the further out in time. In addition, because decision trees have different strategies attached to each decision node, the values assigned to each node have to be discounted using a different market risk-adjusted discount rate. Establishing the correct risk-based discount rate at each node is fairly difficult to do, and errors tend to compound over time.

2. What are some of the assumptions required for risk-neutral probabilities to work? *Risk-neutral probabilities can be applied to binomial lattices and not to decision trees because of some of their underlying assumptions. Recall that in order for a risk-neutral probability to work, the underlying asset evolution lattice needs to be created using discrete Brownian Motion simulations. For example, a binomial lattice node has two bifurcations, one above and one below its current level, a property called the Martingale process. This spreads out to multiple time periods. However, in a decision tree analysis, the values on each strategy node in the future do not necessarily have to be above as well as below the origin node or have the same magnitude. Thus, using risk-neutralized probabilities in discounting a decision tree back to its origination point will yield grossly incorrect results.*

3. What is stochastic optimization? *Stochastic optimization is similar to a simple optimization analysis with the exception that its inputs are stochastic and changing. For instance, in Modern Portfolio Theory, the optimal portfolio allocation of resources is obtained through the maximization of returns and the minimization of risks, resulting in an efficient frontier, which can be solved mathematically. However, in a stochastic optimization problem, the inputs that drive returns and risks are stochastic and changing at every instance. Hence, stochastic optimization that utilizes Monte Carlo simulation is required to obtain the optimal values, rather than being solved mathematically.*

4. The answer is available for downloading by registered faculty members on the John Wiley & Sons, Inc., Web site (*www.Wiley.com*).

CHAPTER 9

Answers are available for downloading by registered faculty members on the John Wiley & Sons, Inc., Web site (*www.Wiley.com*).

CHAPTER 10

1. Instituting a cultural change in a company is fairly difficult. However, real options analysis has a very good chance of being adopted at major corporations. What are some of the fundamental characteristics required in a new paradigm shift in the way decisions are made before real options analysis is accepted in a corporate setting? *The new shift in paradigm must be applicable to solving particular problems, flexible enough to be applicable across multiple types of problems, compatible with the old approach, and able to provide significant value-added insights and competitive advantage.*

2. Why is explaining to management the relevant process and steps taken in a real options analysis crucial? *Management may find it difficult to accept the results stemming from a series of black-box analyses. Instead, if a series of logical and transparent steps are instituted and explained, management buy-in may be simpler.*

3. What does critical success factor mean? *Critical success factors are the key variables that are highly uncertain and variable, and that also drive the value of the project, such that the success or failure of the project, measured financially, is subject to these factors.*

4. Why is risk analysis a recommended step in a real options analysis? *Risk analysis using Monte Carlo simulation provides a probability range of outcomes that will make the analysis more robust and results more trustworthy. Simulation also accounts for the uncertainty in the input variables that affect the analysis results.*

5. Why is the use of payback period flawed? *Payback period or break-even analysis ignores the time value of money and ignores the highly valuable stream of future cash flows beyond the break-even point. Making capital investment decisions based solely on payback period will yield incorrect and oftentimes disastrous decisions.*

endnotes

CHAPTER 1. A NEW PARADIGM?

1. For a more detailed listing of articles, *see* Appendix 10A.

APPENDIX 1B. SCHLUMBERGER ON REAL OPTIONS IN OIL AND GAS

1. Unlike sandstones—which are made from mineral grains—carbonate rocks (like chalk) are made up of much finer particles (the calcified remains of plankton and other tiny sea creatures). As such, they have a much smaller porosity but may still contain quantities of extractable hydrocarbons that are found in fractures (from microns to meters in length) that are common to such rocks.

2. R.C. Selley, *Elements of Petroleum Geology—Second Edition,* Academic Press, 1998.

3. Pressure is needed to produce from the fluids from deep down in the ground. Sometimes the reservoir has enough pressure of its own to allow us to produce without any assistance. Other times we need to assist the reservoir in some way (most commonly by injecting water). Once we start producing oil (and/or gas), reservoir pressure goes down—as with a toy water pistol, which when fully primed can produce a high-pressure stream of water; but once the pressure is lower, the water jet becomes weak and eventually dies out. The same occurs in a reservoir, so it is important to maintain the pressure necessary to maintain flow.

4. Often (especially in the latter stages of the life of a reservoir) oil flows in conjunction with water and sometimes solid particles (like sand and possibly scale deposits). These flows need to be treated in a separator before being sent off along a pipeline (or vessel) to be refined.

5. FPSO: Floating Production and Storage Operation. These can have several forms—storage can be made on the rig and then offloaded by a buoy to a dedicated tanker that commutes back and forth from the refinery.

6. Oil (and gas) is considered to "sweep" through a reservoir. We may observe areas of a field which, for some reason, have not been swept thereby residual deposits remain to be exploited.

7. J. Paddock, D. Siegel, and J. Smith, "Option Valuation of Claims on Physical Assets: The Case of Offshore Petroleum Leases," *Quarterly Journal of Economics* 103, no. 3 (1988), 479–508.

8. T.A. Luehrman, "Extending the Influence of Real Options: Problems and Opportunities," paper SPE 71407, presented at the 2001 Annual Technical Conference and Exhibition, New Orleans, Louisiana, September 30 to October 3, 2001.

APPENDIX 1C. INTELLECTUAL PROPERTY ECONOMICS ON REAL OPTIONS IN PATENT AND INTANGIBLE VALUATION

1. Source: Brookings Institute.

2. *See* Business Week Online, "Royalties: A Royal Pain for Net Radio," by Stephen Wildstrom, McGraw-Hill Publishing, Mar. 29, 2002.

APPENDIX 1E. SPRINT ON REAL OPTIONS IN TELECOMMUNICATIONS

1. Federal Communications Commission, Trends in Telephone Service, Aug. 2001, pg. 16-3.

2. Federal Communications Commission, Trends in Telephone Service, Aug. 2001, pg. 12-3.

3. AT&T 10-K.

CHAPTER 2. TRADITIONAL VALUATION APPROACHES

1. The NPV is simply the sum of the present values of future cash flows less the implementation cost. The IRR is the implicit discount rate that forces the NPV to be zero. Both calculations can be easily performed in Excel using its "NPV(. . .)" and "IRR(. . .)" functions.

2. *See* Appendix 2B for a more detailed discussion on discount rate models.

3. A multiple regression or principal component analysis can be performed but probably with only limited success for physical assets as opposed to financial assets because there are usually very little historical data available for such analyses.

4. Chapter 5 and its corresponding appendixes detail the steps and requirements for a Monte Carlo simulation.

5. Appendix 2A provides details on calculating free cash flows from financial statements.

APPENDIX 2B. DISCOUNT RATE VERSUS RISK-FREE RATE

1. Use the after-tax cost of debt because interest paid on debt is tax deductible. We need to include this tax shield. Therefore, *Cost of Debt* = *Interest Paid* − *Taxes Saved*. Similarly, we have *Cost of Debt* = $K_d - TK_d = K_d(1 - T)$.

2. The cost of preferred stock is $K_{ps} = D_{ps} \div P_{net}$, *where D* is the dividend paid (assumed to be a perpetuity) and *P* is the net or clean price paid on the preferred stock after taking into account any accrued interest and carrying costs.

3. There are generally three accepted methods to calculating the cost of equity: (a) The CAPM Approach uses $K_s = K_{rf} + \beta_i(K_m - K_{rf})$, *where* β is the beta-risk coefficient of the company's equity, K_m is the equity market portfolio rate of return, and K_{rf} is the corresponding maturity's risk-free Treasury rate. (b) The Discounted Cash Flow (Gordon Growth Model) assumes $K_s = [D_1 \div P_0(1 - F)] + g$, *where g* = Retention Rate × Return on Equity and *F* is the floatation cost. (c) The Risk Premium over Bond Yield approach assumes that K_s = *Bond Yield* + *Risk Premium*, corresponding to the appropriate risk structure.

4. Suppose you have an asset that costs $100 and increases to $110 in the first period but reverts to $100 the second period. The return in period one is 10%, and the return in period two is −9.09%. Hence, the arithmetic average of both periods' returns is 0.455%, but it is illogical because you ended up with what you started off with. The geometric average is calculated as

$$\sqrt[2]{\frac{110}{100} \times \frac{100}{110}} - 1 = 0\%,$$

which seems more logical.

5. Book value is generally used because it captures the value of the security when it was issued. However, critics have argued that the market value more closely reflects the current situation the firm faces when operating in its current condition. Furthermore, market values tend to be forward-looking, and book values tend to be backward-looking. Because the valuation analysis looks at forecast values, we can argue for the use of market value weightings. The problem with that logic is magnified when there is significant volatility in the equity and debt market due to speculation.

6. The assumptions for the CAPM include the following: investors are risk-averse individuals who maximize their expected utility of their end-of-period wealth; investors are price-takers and have homogeneous beliefs and expectations about asset returns; there exists a risk-free asset, and investors may borrow or lend unlimited amounts at the risk-free rate;

the quantities of assets are fixed and all assets are marketable and perfectly divisible; asset markets are frictionless, and information is costless and available to all investors; and there are no market imperfections like taxes, regulations, or restrictions on short sales.

7. The CAPM requires that in equilibrium the market portfolio be efficient. It must lie on the upper half of the minimum variance opportunity set where the marginal rate of substitution equals the marginal rate of transformation (*MRS = MRT*). The efficiency can be established based on homogeneous expectation assumptions. Given this, they will all perceive the same minimum variance opportunity set. The market portfolio must hence be efficient because the market is simply the sum of all holdings and all individual holdings are efficient. Given market efficiency, the market portfolio *M* where all assets are held according to their market value weights by simple algebraic manipulation, that is, equating the slope of the capital market line with the slope of the opportunity set, we can derive the following expression: $E(R_i) = R_f + [E(R_m) - R_f] (\sigma_{i,m}/\sigma^2_m)$. This CAPM model can also be derived using the *MRT = MRS* convention, where a linear programming method is used to solve for minimum variance opportunity set and the maximum expected return efficiency set.

8. For instance, multicollinearity, autocorrelation, random walk (nonstationarity), seasonality, and heteroskedasticity pose a problem in macroeconomic time-series. The model should be developed carefully.

CHAPTER 3. REAL OPTIONS ANALYSIS

1. These figures are for illustrative purposes. We will work through similar problems as well as more complicated real option models in later chapters.

2. This is obtained using the Gordon constant growth model for collapsing all future cash flows into a single figure. *See* Appendix 2A on financial statements analysis for details.

CHAPTER 4. THE REAL OPTIONS PROCESS

1. Chapter 2 provides a good in-depth overview of using discounted cash flow analysis, while Appendix 5C provides an overview of forecasting approaches.

2. *See* Appendix 5B on Monte Carlo simulation for the technical details on how specific distributions are chosen and what some of the simulation conditions are.

3. Chapter 7 provides the technical step-by-step approach to applying real options analysis for multiple types of options. Chapter 8 previews more of the mathematical intricacies in options modeling.

4. Appendix 5D explains the approach to portfolio optimization.

5. Chapter 10 shows a step-by-step series of reports and how to present them to senior management, providing a novel way to explain and break down a difficult series of black-box analysis into clear, concise, and transparent procedures.

CHAPTER 5. REAL OPTIONS, FINANCIAL OPTIONS, MONTE CARLO SIMULATION, AND OPTIMIZATION

1. In an abandonment option, there is usually a maximum to the salvage value; thus, the payoff function may actually look like a put but with a limit cap on the upside.

2. In this example, the median is a better measure of central tendency.

3. *See* Appendix 8A for details on Geometric Brownian Motion.

APPENDIX 5C. FORECASTING

1. The following texts provide detailed explanations of time-series forecasting and regression analysis, arranged from more advanced to more basic applications:

> *Time Series Analysis,* by James D. Hamilton, Princeton University Press, 1994.

> *Forecasting with Dynamic Regression Models,* by Alan Pankratz, Wiley Series in Probability and Mathematical Statistics, 1991.

> *Econometrics,* edited by John Eatwell, Peter Newman, and Murray Milgate, W.W. Norton, 1990.

> *Handbook of Financial Analysis, Forecasting and Modeling,* by Jae Shim and Joel Siegel, PrenticeHall, 1988.

CHAPTER 6. BEHIND THE SCENES

1. Appendix 7B shows the derivation of the Black-Scholes model, while Appendix 8C shows some of the closed-form solutions of the Generalized Black-Scholes model and other exotic options.

2. This is simply an illustration of the size and computational requirements for an exact binomial approximation where data from all the simulated trials are saved.

3. The simulated actual values are based on a Geometric Brownian Motion with a volatility of 20 percent calculated as the standard deviation of the simulated natural logarithms of historical returns.

4. *See* Appendix 8A for details on Brownian Motions.

5. In certain rare cases, these equations need to be modified, cases when multinomial trees are used or when there are complex stochastic processes that need to be incorporated, including jump-diffusions or mean reversion.

6. In reality, this drift rate in a Martingale process is the risk-free rate, which is also used in discounting the binomial lattice values back in time.

7. This assumes a continuous discounting approach. The continuous compounding approach ($e^{-rf(\delta t)}$) is used throughout the book rather than a discrete discounting approach ($(1 + rf)^{-\delta t}$) because both approaches will provide identical results when a high number of time steps is used (usually above 10 steps). In addition, because the enclosed software allows the user to calculate a high number of time steps quickly, using the continuous compounding approach will facilitate the convergence of the results at a higher rate.

CHAPTER 7. REAL OPTIONS MODEL

1. A similar approach is to use the Roll-Geske-Whaley (RGW) approximation. Note that these approximation models cannot be readily or easily solved within an Excel environment but instead require some programming scripts or the use of software. The Real Options Analysis Toolkit software CD-ROM has these American approximation models as well as the ability to solve up to 5,000 time-steps in the binomial approach.

2. Note that these approximation models cannot be readily or easily solved within an Excel environment but instead require some programming scripts or the use of software. Be aware that closed-form American option approximation models can only provide benchmark values for an expansion option.

3. There is an end-of-chapter problem analyzing the expansion option when the competition grows at a different rate and faces different risk structures. The problem can be easily tackled using binomial lattices.

4. The model is shown in Appendix 8C. Note that these approximation models cannot be readily or easily solved within an Excel environment but instead require some programming scripts or the use of software.

APPENDIX 7A. VOLATILITY ESTIMATES

1. *See* Tom Copeland and Vladimir Antikarov's *"Real Options,"* by Texere Publishing.

APPENDIX 7F. REALITY CHECKS

1. The modified internal rate of return (MIRR) takes the sum of the future values of all cash flows and discounts it to equal the present value of implementation costs. The discount rate that equates these two values is the MIRR.

2. The Wilcoxon *signed-rank* statistic calculation is represented by

$$W(X, \theta) = \sum_{i=1}^{n} S(X_i - \theta)\psi(|X_i - \theta|),$$

where S is the sign function and ψ is the rank function. From here, the *p*-value is calculated using

$$P\left(\left|\frac{W(\theta) - E(\theta)}{\sqrt{\dfrac{n(n+1)(2n+1)}{6}}}\right| < b^*\right) \cong 1 - \alpha.$$

APPENDIX 7G. APPLYING MONTE CARLO SIMULATION TO SOLVE REAL OPTIONS

1. This is due to the mathematical properties of American options, which require the knowledge of what the optimal stopping times and optimal execution barriers are. Using simulation to obtain American-type options is fairly difficult and is beyond the scope of this book.

2. The Excel spreadsheet is located in the *Examples* folder under the name *Simulated Options Model*. Note that the example spreadsheet requires that Crystal Ball's simulation software be installed to run properly. To obtain similar results shown above, simply open the spreadsheet and hit the *RUN* icon. Finally, note that because Monte Carlo simulation is by definition a random selection of values from predefined distributions, the results may not match exactly those seen in the examples. Finally, to obtain similar results in the charts, the range of results shown is set from 0.01 to infinity in Crystal Ball®.

3. The Excel spreadsheet is located in the *Examples* folder under the name *Simulating Options Analysis*. Note that the example spreadsheet requires that Crystal Ball's simulation software be installed to run properly. To obtain similar results shown above, simply open the spreadsheet and hit the *RUN* icon. Finally, note that because Monte Carlo simulation is by definition a random selection of values from predefined distributions, the results may not match exactly those seen in the examples.

CHAPTER 8. ADVANCED OPTIONS PROBLEMS

1. The derivation of this optimal value is beyond the scope of this book, because it applies stochastic calculus analytics. Dixit and Pindyck's *Investment under Uncertainty* (1994) provides a good guide to some of the analytics on stochastic derivations.

CHAPTER 9. REAL OPTIONS ANALYSIS TOOLKIT SOFTWARE (CD-ROM)

1. Appendix 9A lists all 69 models available in the software, as well as their corresponding Excel-based function calls.

APPENDIX 9C. RESOURCE OPTIMIZATION USING CRYSTAL BALL'S® OPT-QUEST SOFTWARE

1. The example is provided in the CD-ROM, under the Excel file name *Resource Optimization*. A preinstalled version of Crystal Ball Professional is required to run the portfolio optimization example.

CHAPTER 10. RESULTS INTERPRETATION AND PRESENTATION

1. This is also sometimes referred to as the inverse of the coefficient of variation, and its concept is related to the profitability index, Tobin's q-ratio, the Sharpe ratio, and Jensen's alpha measure.

index